THE CLASSICS
OF **WESTERN**
SPIRITUALITY

THE CLASSICS OF WESTERN SPIRITUALITY
A Library of the Great Spiritual Masters

President and Publisher
Mark-David Janus, CSP

EDITORIAL BOARD

Wycliffite Spirituality

EDITED AND TRANSLATED BY
J. PATRICK HORNBECK II, STEPHEN E. LAHEY, AND FIONA SOMERSET

PAULIST PRESS
NEW YORK • MAHWAH

Cover art: Figure from the Luther Memorial in Fulda (Germany) by Ernst Rietschel (German sculptor, 1804–1861). Original woodcut, published in 1877. Courtesy of iStockphoto.

Cover and caseside design by Cynthia Dunne, www.bluefarmdesign.com
Book design by Lynn Else

Library of Congress Cataloging-in-Publication Data
    Wycliffite spirituality / edited and translated by J. Patrick Hornbeck II, Stephen E. Lahey, Fiona Somerset.
        p. cm.
    Includes bibliographical references and index.
    ISBN 978-0-8091-0605-9 (alk. paper) — ISBN 978-0-8091-4765-6 (alk. paper) — ISBN 978-1-893757-84-4 1. Lollards. 2. Wycliffe, John, d. 1384. I. Hornbeck, J. Patrick, 1982– II. Lahey, Stephen E. III. Somerset, Fiona.
    BX4901.3.W93 2013
    284'.3—dc23

                                                                    2012028137

Published by Paulist Press
997 Macarthur Boulevard
Mahwah, New Jersey 07430

www.paulistpress.com

Printed and bound in the
United States of America

CONTENTS

CONTENTS

Contributors to This Volume

J. PATRICK HORNBECK II is associate professor of theology at Fordham University in New York. His studies focus on the interface between the shifting categories of "heresy" and "orthodoxy" in medieval and early modern Christianity, particularly regarding the Lollards or Wycliffites. Dr. Hornbeck earned his PhD in theology/ecclesiastical history from Oxford University.

STEPHEN E. LAHEY is assistant professor in the Department of Classics and Religious Studies at the University of Nebraska. He has published extensively in the field of medieval studies. A priest of the Episcopal Church of the United States of America, Dr. Lahey earned his PhD in medieval studies from the University of Connecticut.

FIONA SOMERSET is professor of English at the University of Connecticut and has published extensively about literature and movements in medieval England, especially about Chaucer and about Lollardy. A coeditor of *The Yearbook of Langland Studies*, Dr. Somerset earned her PhD from Cornell University.

ACKNOWLEDGMENTS

We would like to thank Bernard McGinn for having the idea for this book in the first place, for his closely engaged readings of everything we have produced, and for his and Nancy de Flon of Paulist Press's enthusiasm for the project as it has developed. We are all grateful to William Revere, Jennifer Illig, and Jack Bell for assistance with research and formatting and for closely attentive reading of the translations. Fiona thanks the students in her heresy class for the verve and insight with which they test drove a draft of the volume, and Patrick likewise thanks the students in his dissenters and heretics seminar for their generous feedback. We have depended upon the helpfulness and hospitality of several libraries; we thank the manuscript librarians, reference librarians, and staff of the British Library, the Bodleian Library in Oxford, Cambridge University Library, Duke University Library, and the National Humanities Center for their invaluable assistance. Fiona thanks the National Humanities Center and Duke University for research leave during her work on this book. Stephen thanks the University of Nebraska Layman Grant for funds used to assist in translating Wyclif's Latin works. All three editors thank the Theology Department of Fordham University for financial support that made it possible to publish the full volume in print form.

It would not even have been possible to conceive of a volume on Wycliffite spirituality without the sustained effort of generations of scholars who have labored to make the dissenting views and religious aspirations of Wyclif and his followers better known. Even where our motivations or conclusions may differ from theirs, we are very conscious of our debts to them. These extend from the early researches of scholars such as John Bale, William Crashaw, and James Ussher, through the massive editorial labors of the Wyclif Society, Thomas Arnold, Josiah Forshall, Frederick Madden, and

F. D. Matthew, to the work of literary, social, and intellectual historians, including H. B. Workman, K. B. McFarlane, J. A. F. Thomson, Howard Kaminsky, Henry Hargreaves, Anthony Kenny, J. A. Robson, Jeremy Catto, Margaret Aston, and Anne Hudson, to the producers of modern critical editions of Wyclif's and Wycliffite writings and of trial documents: Johann Loserth, Anne Hudson, Pamela Gradon, Christina Von Nolcken, Mary Dove, Shannon McSheffrey, Norman Tanner. There are of course many others.

Among scholars currently active, we are grateful for the collegiality of Jennifer Arch, John Arnold, Mishtooni Bose, Andrew Cole, Michael Cornett, the now late Mary Dove, Alan Fletcher, Ian Forrest, Kantik Ghosh, Vincent Gillespie, Ralph Hanna, Jill Havens, Anne Hudson, Judith Jefferson, Maureen Jurkowski, Henry Ansgar Kelly, Maryanne Kowaleski, Michael Kuczynski, Ian Levy, Anna Lewis, Rob Lutton, Shannon McSheffrey, Derrick Pitard, Helen Spencer, Robert Swanson, Norman Tanner, Christina Von Nolcken, and Nicholas Watson. Specific debts to some of them for kindly sharing findings and resources are recorded in the Notes, while many of them read and responded to drafts. Among so many generous interlocutors we have surely overlooked somebody, and we apologize in advance.

The editors also wish to thank one another. Working together on this volume has been a great pleasure. All three contributors participated in the planning of the volume's overall shape from the beginning, and all read and critiqued one another's work.

Finally, Steve thanks Julia and Thea, and Fiona thanks Tim, Declan, Eoin, and Teagan, for tolerating their absorption in (and even occasionally sharing their excitement over) the contents of this volume.

INTRODUCTION

For more than six centuries, John Wyclif and his followers have divided Christians. Wyclif himself, though never excommunicated, was declared heretical by Gregory XI in 1377. Those who were considered Wycliffites or lollards were often treated more harshly, in a long series of heresy investigations and trials beginning in Oxford in the early 1380s, and continuing intermittently across England and beyond up until the 1520s. Wyclif's thought catalyzed Bohemians and contributed to the revolution that followed the burning of Jan Hus at Constance in July 1415, when the term *Wycliffism* became formally associated with heresy. After the Reformation, Protestants embraced the memory of Wycliffism, which led to a renewed antipathy toward the movement by the Roman Catholic Church. Such was the state of opinions about Wyclif and the theological movement associated with his ideas until the middle decades of the twentieth century.

More recently, thoughtful readers have been questioning many aspects of the conventional account of Wyclif and his followers. In part, this is because *heresy* is not understood the way it once was. Early evangelicals condemned some types of theology as heretical, but they admired many of those the medieval church had condemned as heretics, viewing them, instead, as their own precursors, martyrs to the truth; this kind of glamor still hangs about the word.[1] More recently, *heresy* has become a neutral descriptive term, even while some have sought to reassert a more negative meaning and discourage ordinary Christians from any possible attraction it might hold.[2] Behind all these usages often lies the assumption that one decides to embrace a heresy, the way one might join a political party. In the high and later Middle Ages, though, heresy was a crime in both canon and secular law. Nobody wanted to be a heretic, and nobody chose to be affiliated with what he or she thought was a heresy.

1

People were labeled heretics not merely if they believed in a heresy—this is crucially important—but if when examined for heresy they stubbornly refused to submit to correction and renounce that belief, forever.[3]

Heresy, however, also had a somewhat looser sense, common in polemical or controversial writings and originating in the early church, where the Greek word *hairesis*, meaning "choice," was widely used to refer to a school of thought, at that point without any implied condemnation.[4] Any given heresy—for example, Arian, Pelagian, Waldensian, or Wycliffite—might designate a set of beliefs. But the same adjective also described the group of people who were said to hold them and their leader or founder. Those being examined for heresy might vehemently deny being heretics, all the while retaining a strong sense of identity with the group their examiners had singled out for attention. They might still feel very strongly that they, their associates, and others they admired were the most true and faithful followers of Christ. In encouraging his followers to abandon their previous lives and follow him instead, regardless of the persecution they might encounter, Christ set a radical precedent whose implications have never been fully absent from Christianity. Nobody "chose" to be a heretic, then—but it seems that a good number chose to follow Christ, as they interpreted that injunction, by following Wyclif. They did so even when they were well aware that their beliefs and practices placed them at risk of prosecution for heresy.

Whether to call these people Wycliffite or lollard has been a subject of much debate in recent years; in this volume we keep things simple for newcomers to the field by using *Wycliffite* and *lollard* more or less interchangeably throughout. More fundamentally, who were these Wycliffites? What did they think made them the true followers of Christ? All of the writings in this volume, many of them appearing in print for the first time, can aid readers in considering these questions anew.

Many standard accounts of Wyclif and his followers are based in the late-fourteenth-century *Chronicle* of the Augustinian canon Henry Knighton.[5] Knighton's *Chronicle* contains the closest thing to a first-hand narrative of the development of lollardy that we have, written in the form of a detailed account of current events by a well-informed observer with access to a wide range of written sources. Knighton describes Wyclif as having translated the Bible into English: a controversial act, since both the capacity of the English language to serve as an appropriate vehicle for scriptural teaching, and the consequences of making difficult texts broadly accessible to less-educated readers, were much debated.[6] Next, Knighton describes Wyclif and his followers as rejecting the sacraments of the Eucharist and of confession, as well as the mass. He describes them as thinking that no bishop or priest in mortal sin can perform the sacraments, refusing the authority of the pope and excommunication. Instead, Knighton says, they insisted on preaching, even without ecclesiastical license; they contended that no ecclesiastical institution should have temporal goods, and indeed that temporal lords should seize them. Yet, they also argued that not even secular authorities might hold office if in mortal sin, and that the people by their own judgment should correct temporal lords and refuse tithes to sinful priests. They rejected intercessory prayer, insisted that friars should engage in manual labor rather than begging, and asserted that the religious orders should be abolished as a hindrance to holy living.[7]

Knighton notes that despite Wyclif's death, his followers continued to travel far and wide spreading his false teachings, adding others of their own (for example, rejection of images, pilgrimages, crusades, the canonical hours, and worldly pleasures), but in remarkable unanimity. They had support in high places; knights, even dukes and earls, protected them and provided them with opportunities to preach. Some of them held meetings, even what could be called schools, through which their views were taught. This teaching program, the pretended piety and virtue of these preachers, and their fierce disparagement of the friars led to the dramatic increase in the numbers of lollards, or Wycliffites. More and more preachers were trained and recruited as the sect spread throughout the country. The Wycliffites were persecuted as heretics in an increasingly systematic way. According to later chroniclers, the heresy persisted in various places across the country right up until the Reformation, for which it may have prepared the ground.[8]

Just what about this story is so controversial? The account, appealing as it may be, is too simplistic in its connection of Wyclif to the movement that embraced him. What role Wyclif may have played in the Bible translation associated with his name, and who

3

else may have participated, is unknown; while some have sought to assert the involvement of one or more known writers, others have contended that such assertions must remain purely speculative.[9] Similarly, we remain unable to identify who produced the many vernacular writings associated with lollardy—adaptations of previous sources, translations from Wyclif's works, scholarly tools, commentaries, sermons, pastoralia, and so on. Most scholars recognize that the absence of definite evidence makes it impossible to assign anonymous works to one or another named individual, or for that matter to Wyclif.[10] Less agreement can be found on the issues of whether Wyclif's academic ideas match up closely with those of his followers, of how far and how rapidly Wycliffite ideas spread, of how doctrinally consistent they remained over time, of how successfully and how severely they were pursued and suppressed, and of what role they may have played, if any, in the early years of the Reformation. In general, positions have divided sharply between Protestants and Catholics, with Catholics arguing for the insignificance and inconsistency of Wycliffism, and Protestants for its importance, persistence, stability, and influence.[11]

Post-Reformation divides have influenced our understanding of other aspects of this account, too. The precise details of what Wyclif and his followers thought about the sacraments, the liturgy, papal authority, clerical disendowment, and the literal sense of scripture have not always been closely examined. Nor has the equation of the church with the predestined elect been analyzed with the care with which Wyclif described it. The list of condemnations made of Wyclif's theology by Gregory XI in 1377, by the archbishop of Canterbury in 1382, and by the assembled dignitaries at the Council of Constance in 1415 is dizzying. In each of these instances, the standard approach was to draw up a "list of errors." By 1411, the lists contained over two hundred distinct errors, and because in many cases his adherents had been creative in interpreting Wyclif's writings, the bishops and theologians condemned positions foreign to Wyclif. By 1415, the list of errors had grown to 305. How many of these articles accurately reflect Wyclif's own thought, the beliefs of the majority of Wycliffites, or the specters that their opponents feared might lurk unrecognized within Wycliffism has been a matter of great disagreement over the centuries.

4

Since John Wyclif has traditionally been viewed as the "Morning Star of the Reformation," his views and those of his followers have often been assumed to be identical with those of later Protestants rather than examined closely in their own setting.[12] For example, it has often been assumed that Wyclif must have asserted that Christ's body was not present in the Eucharist, that instead the bread and wine remain merely bread and wine, and the sacrament's purposes are commemorative. This does seem to have been the position of some later lollards, as the trial records included here show.[13] But it was not Wyclif's position, nor that of many of his earlier followers.[14] Similarly, it has been asserted that Wyclif and all his followers were strictly determinist predestinarians, firmly convinced that some are chosen for salvation while most are irrevocably damned, regardless of the choices they may make in this life. Yet Wyclif's writings do not support this claim, and neither do Wycliffite writings.[15] More positions need to be reconsidered. For example, Wyclif and his followers are thought to have rejected the sacrament of confession outright, despite plentiful evidence that they did not.[16] And while Wyclif's and Wycliffite reliance on church tradition has sometimes been viewed as inconsistent or hypocritical, we might instead reexamine the assertion that they rejected church tradition, for their writings do not sustain that claim. They may have derided some of Aquinas's conclusions, for example, but others they embraced.[17]

So while some version of many of these articles can indeed be found in Wyclif's or Wycliffite polemical writings, it does not necessarily follow that these articles form the core of lollard belief, let alone provide insight into lollard practices. An account of lollardy based exclusively on what it rejected and its most strenuously polemical arguments will be only very partial. It would be accurate to label such a version of lollardy "religiously [and] imaginatively...sterile," and it would be understandable to wonder what ever attracted anyone to it, espccially to the point of dying for it.[18] Yet, this would be to ignore the untold riches at our fingertips. We have the opportunity to ask the right people the right questions. In contrast to most heterodox medieval ideologies, where few original sources survive, we have many manuscripts including lollard writings, and a large number of Wyclif's works. Rather than relying on hostile accounts to set our agenda, we ought to begin from a different ground, as we do in this book. We can begin, in Parts I and II, with what Wyclif and what lollards themselves have to say about the grounds of their belief—what teaching is most central, how it should be taught, and to whom. While the trial evidence in Part III needs to be weighed carefully, it can then be reevaluated in light of what the study of Wyclif's and lollard writings on their own terms has conveyed. After careful study of all three kinds of sources, we will be in a position to reevaluate where they tell us the same things, and where they seem to diverge. We can also reconsider what those similarities and differences might mean for an account of Wycliffism's development over time, one that no longer reflexively attributes differences to inconsistency and decline, and similarities to stability and persistence. These are the invitations we offer to the readers of this volume.

It will be important to consider the limitations of each of the kinds of evidence presented here, as well as the opportunities they offer. Wyclif's writings in Part I, for example, can offer us little direct insight about the followers they inspired. They offer a full, systematic development of ideas often mentioned more allusively in later writings, yet in a kind of academic prose that few outside the university would have found it easy to understand. Despite their difficulty, close comparison of Wyclif's and Wycliffite writings reveals many influences. Some of these influences were sought out in heresy investigations or by early Protestant historians and have received a great deal of attention. Others have scarcely been noticed. Wycliffite writings in Part II, for their part, can tell us a great deal about how highly educated followers of Wyclif sought to shape a wider religious movement. We should be cautious, however, about assuming that the norms they articulate for the group they seek to address—how they wanted to be read, what they wanted their readers to believe, how they wanted them to act—will match up perfectly with what readers did. The records of heresy trials in Part III, on the other hand, can tell us more about the reception of Wyclif's and Wycliffite ideas among a wider audience. Admittedly, these records were produced not by anthropologists seeking to understand the culture of the individuals and groups they examine, but by inquisitors, in the course of their efforts to discover and extirpate heresy. Still, these records give us much valuable information about how individuals responded to lists of questions, sometimes volunteering explanations of their own that may also be recorded; what books people owned and how those volumes were loaned around and read; and other religious practices, whether those of individuals or groups, that attracted attention.[19] They also show us how defendants were related to one another—though we should remember that in a case where heresy has come to light, those relationships may have gone wrong somehow.

Our hope is that this volume will provide at once a useful introductory survey for readers with interests in many things and a starting point for readers who find that they want to study Wyclif and Wycliffism in more depth. In the rest of this Introduction we provide first a brief, synthetic account of some key aspects of Wycliffite spirituality, then a detailed introduction to each of the parts of the volume and each of the selections included.

WYCLIFFITE SPIRITUALITY

The following survey of Wycliffite spirituality's most central concerns and characteristics ranges through a series of topics that appear frequently in Wycliffite writings. It cites examples chiefly from the selections in this volume, but its observations draw as well on the larger canon of writings associated with Wycliffism, polemical, pastoral, and devotional. As will be discussed in more detail below, there has been considerable scholarly disagreement about which writings belong in the Wycliffite canon—disagreement even over some of the selections included here. Thus, a central criterion for the characteristics described here is that they should appear in the core writings of the movement whose canonical status is not disputed. These core writings include various translations and adaptations of Wyclif, the *Testimony of William Thorpe*, the *Letter of Richard Wyche*, the *Sermon of William Taylor*, the two very long sermons printed as the *Works of a Lollard Preacher*, the *Four Wycliffite Dialogues*, prologues and glosses to the *Wycliffite Bible*, and the poem *Piers the Ploughman's Creed*.[20] Books clearly produced by lollards should also be accounted among their core writings, though with some careful attention to their incorporation (and, often, modification) of pre-lollard sources. These books include the most obviously coherent of the early manuscript anthologies and early texts rapidly produced in multiple, high-quality copies in the movement's most organized phase, for example, the *English Wycliffite Sermons*, the alphabetical encyclopedia of sources called the *Floretum* and its shorter version the *Rosarium*, the *Glossed Gospels*, and the interpolated commentaries on Rolle's English psalter and the canticles.[21]

God's Law

In Wycliffite writings, "God's law" and "Christ's law" are frequently invoked. Most broadly, either of them refers to the moral instruction contained in the Bible. But more narrowly, all that is essential to this teaching may be found in the commandments: the decalogue of Exodus 20 and Deuteronomy 5:6–21, Christ's commandments that we should love God above all things and our neighbor as ourself in Matthew 22:37–39 (see also Mark 12:29–31; Luke 10:27), and Paul's exhortation to charity as the fulfillment of the law in Romans 13:10 (cf. Gal 5:14). This is not to suggest that either Wyclif or Wycliffites held the naive view that the words of the commandments alone, or even of the Bible as a whole, express all legitimate moral instruction in and of themselves, even if some scholars have attributed to them this sort of reliance on scripture alone (*scriptura sola*). Rather, while Wycliffites do dismiss some human laws and doctrinal positions on the grounds that they have no scriptural basis, their view is not so much that the scriptural words themselves must stand alone, as that some conclusions may legitimately be extrapolated from them through commentary, while others may not.

For Wycliffites, the words of the commandments, as expounded through commentary, embody all necessary truth about the moral life, that is, all that concerns our relationship with God, and all that concerns our relations with one another. Wycliffite emphasis on the commandments as the core of pastoral teaching contrasts with a far more common medieval emphasis on the seven deadly sins, often counterposed with the seven virtues that should counteract them. John Bossy has influentially suggested that it was only with Gerson and Luther that the commandments began to replace the sins as the central theme of popular moral instruction, a development that culminated after the Reformation.[22] Wycliffite preoccupation with the commandments, while their contemporaries among the Modern-Day Devout were centering their moral life around the seven sins and virtues, suggests that this chronology is in need of some revision.[23]

A scholar of late medieval England might object to Bossy that interest in the commandments was not at all unusual in the Wycliffites' fourteenth- and fifteenth-century milieu. Certainly there were plenty of mainstream vernacular commentaries on the commandments in medieval England and catechetical writings in which the commandments are among the items covered.[24] Still, even against this backdrop, the intensity and depth of Wycliffite attention to the commandments is striking. Not only are there several freestanding Wycliffite commentaries on the commandments, some of them related, some extraordinarily long. But nearly every Wycliffite text with the aim of pastoral instruction contains an exposition of the commandments; what is more, it is common, rather than a sign of especially bad planning, for this section to bulge out of proportion and distort the shape of the work as a whole, as in *The Lantern of Light* (excerpted in item 19), where the treatment of the commandments in chapter 12 spans more than one-third of the work's total length.[25] Repetitious emphasis on the commandments or on God's law where another pastoral treatise might choose to develop more varied themes can also be revealing. Consider, for example, the attention given to the commandments in *The Seven Works of Mercy* (item 15) in this volume, where the works of mercy are each in turn interpreted spiritually as advising all Christians to know the commandments, to keep them, and to teach others to do so through both their words and their actions. *A Form of Confession* (item 16) not only derives this same interpretation of the works of mercy from the *Seven Works*, but recasts the sins it encourages its reader to confess to God as a version of the Decalogue; each sin in turn breaks a commandment, and each commandment is interpreted spiritually as a violation of the sinner's proper love for God.

Creative reworking and novel spiritual interpretations are common more generally as Wycliffites engage the commandments. Another example appears in the sermon cycle in Sidney Sussex 74 (see below, item 22, for selections), where the commandments are discussed out of their biblical sequence to suit the author's thematic development.[26] Equally common is an emphasis on the integral unity

9

of the moral system the commandments propound, such that any of them can be interpreted spiritually in such a way that it refers globally to all sin, and breaking any one of them breaks them all (as in Jas 2:10). All misdirected love is a form of idolatry and thus a violation of the first commandment in *The Ten Commandments*, for example (item 12, see p. 209). Similarly, swearing is idolatry in *The City of Saints*, even as it is discussed under the second commandment (item 20, see p. 280). Swearing, in turn, is treated as a form of the idle speech that is tantamount to spiritual murder, a violation of the fifth commandment, in *A Dialogue between a Wise Man and a Fool* (item 17, see p. 248). Each commandment foregrounds a different aspect of sin, rather than a different kind. This blending and shifting of commandments might easily be overwhelming for less practiced readers. Perhaps it is for this reason that these commentaries often repeat biblical assurances that God's commandments are not difficult to keep (Matt 11:30; 1 Cor 10:13; 1 John 5:3). See *The Two Ways* (item 8, pp. 178–79) and *The Ten Commandments* (item 12, pp. 202, 203, 205).

Even among Wycliffite writings that are not as single-mindedly focused on the commandments throughout their length, the commandments are a leitmotif of Wycliffite moral instruction. There is a sense of vast system, of communal interpretations allusively cited.[27] When *The Ten Commandments* quotes "the Wise Man" to warn "*let all your telling, all your diversion, be the commandments of almighty God*" (item 12, p. 205),[28] the implicit opposition between proper tale-telling and vain diversion that the interpolated "all your diversion" introduces irresistibly recalls the conflict staged over the course of *A Dialogue between a Wise Man and a Fool* (item 17), where the Wise Man urges the Fool to believe and keep the commandments, while the Fool protests that he prefers a good tale. More distantly it echoes the concern for proper instruction of children in the commandments rather than in vain tales found in *Of Wedded Men and Wives* (item 10, pp. 194–95). Worries about idle tales as opposed to proper instruction are a commonplace, of course; what is unusual about these examples is their strong emphasis that all the proper instruction that should replace idle tales can be extrapolated from the commandments. The commandments are similarly fundamental in *The Our Father*; "our daily bread" is both food and the commandments:

10

"When we say, '*give us today our daily bread*,' we pray for the sustenance necessary for our body, and to understand and keep God's word, and especially God's commandments, which are spiritual sustenance for our soul" (item 11, p. 199). Interpretation of "daily bread" as God's word is not at all new, but "The Our Father" goes out of its way to emphasize that God's word is most especially the commandments. Word and commandments are similarly made equivalent in *The Ten Commandments*: "For Christ says in the gospel, '*He who does not love me does not keep my words*,' that is, his commandments" (item 12, p. 219). In *The City of Saints*, the primary obligation of the citizens as a group is to keep the commandments (item 20, p. 279). Conversion toward God, in the *Commentary on Psalm 87* as in *A Dialogue between a Wise Man and a Fool*, takes the form of keeping the commandments (item 14, p. 237). Wycliffite writings very frequently cite Christ's response to the rich man who asked him what he should do to attain everlasting life: "*If you will enter into life, keep the commandments*" (Matt 19:17).[29] It is important to them that this should be enough, that this reply stands alone. They do not go on to quote Christ's second response, the one that most inspired St. Francis: "*If you will be perfect, go sell what you have, and give to the poor*" (Matt 19:21). Indeed, they reject Franciscan poverty as a means to greater perfection (see further below, p. 14). In *A Dialogue between Jon and Richard*, Richard's claim that friars are more perfect than other Christians because they keep not only the commandments but more besides inspires Jon's most lyrical polemical flight (item 21, pp. 297–98).

Wyclif himself devoted extended attention to the commandments as he was developing his account of dominion (see below, p. 37). Wycliffite writings on the commandments draw extensively on Wyclif's own commentary upon them. Some of this influence has been recognized, for example, when a commentary on the seventh commandment in three manuscripts cites Wyclif's theory that nobody sinful can own anything.[30] Other elements of the influence of Wyclif's commentary are less well known. For example, Wyclif develops a carefully qualified account of how images used in churches may be beneficial in *On the Divine Commandments (Selections)* (item 4, pp. 108–13). *The Ten Commandments* follows suit, citing Wyclif and drawing on his examples and quotations at length in its commentary on the first commandment (item 12, pp. 214–18).[31] Certainly, strong opposition to images later became an important element of Wycliffism.[32] Still, this evidence of Wyclif's influence on Wycliffite writers offers some complications for scholars who might attempt to use iconoclastic views as a kind of litmus test for Wycliffism and encourages more and closer attention to how Wycliffites made use of Wyclif's writings.

Prayer without Ceasing

The necessity of keeping the commandments and living in love that Wycliffites so frequently enjoin can also be viewed through the lens of another necessary activity: prayer. As *On Holy Prayers* explains, in showing how we can follow Christ's and Paul's injunctions to *pray at all times* and *pray without ceasing* (Luke 18:1; 1 Thess 5:17), "As long as a man lives a just life, keeping God's commandments and charity, then he prays well, regardless of what he is doing; and whoever lives best, prays best" (item 9, p. 183). We *pray without ceasing* when we keep the commandments. But prayer is more than simply equivalent to living well by keeping the commandments. Talk about prayer allows a closer focus on how one should feel, how one should think, how one should turn one's will toward God—on how, that is, to cultivate the love that God commands. So it is that Wyclif wrote five commentaries on the Lord's Prayer in different forms (see p. 38 below), while Wycliffites reworked the vast cultural storehouse of both learned and catechetical materials on this prayer to produce at least five commentaries, three of them expository, two others polemical spinoffs.[33]

It should be no surprise that the tradition of commentary on the Lord's Prayer should inspire polemical commentary. Commentary on the Lord's Prayer is another means, alongside commentary on the commandments, for describing proper human conduct in the world (see p. 38 below). What is more, the biblical context within which the Lord's Prayer is introduced as the best possible prayer, and an epitome of all virtuous prayer, is itself polemical (see Matt 6:9–13, where the prayer is part of Christ's instructions on how to avoid hypocrisy in religious practice; cf. Luke 11:2–4). However, Wycliffites not only use commentary on prayer to instruct their readers about how they should and should not act, but also about how they should feel as they dispose their souls toward God in prayer.

The proper disposition of the soul for prayer involves a careful balancing, even sequencing, of feeling. Fear and love must work in tandem. Wyclif devotes chapter 10 of *On the Divine Commandments* to explaining this balance, then employs it through the rest of that work (item 4, pp. 89–145). Wycliffites share his interest in the topic and his tendency to devote more attention to fear than is perhaps the norm. The final verse of the *Commentary on Psalm 87* gives an unusually detailed explanation of how emotions should work together in prayer:

> Each effectual prayer has this condition and strength in it. First, it prays to be cleansed of all evil done before. And after that, to be defended from all evil to come. Then, it desires and yearns after God's will, to be his heir in the bliss of heaven. And so each effectual prayer to God has in it sorrow and dread, desire and hope. (item 14, p. 240)

The aim of this focused address toward God is to dispose the self, as *The Our Father* puts it, toward "holy desire and perseverance": a will conformed to God's will as far as human frailty will allow, and filled with hope that its efforts to persevere—and to renew its proper orientation when those efforts fail—will prevail (item 11, p. 197). The emphasis in that perseverance, once again, is upon action. In this present life we cannot know whether we, or our neighbors, will finally be saved or damned. Still, on the basis of a person's present actions we can make shrewd guesses about which path he or she is on right now. Wycliffite writings, following Wyclif, insist on these two points over and over again.[34] The prevailing emotion is hope. In the face of uncertainty about their own futures as well as those of others, hope is the bulwark of the sometimes wavering or agonized will. This is the hallmark of Wycliffite spirituality.[35]

Imitation of Christ

As we would rightly expect of a spirituality that places such strong emphasis on action, Wycliffites had a great deal to say about what right action is. The common late medieval model that would encourage readers to cultivate the virtues in place of the sins is not the primary focus of their ethics of action (though they do sometimes treat the virtues and sins cursorily, and very occasionally at length).[36] Nor, despite their polemical leanings and their interest in the negative injunctions of the decalogue, was all of what they had to say about action expressed in terms of what one should not do. Instead, they looked to Christ. They paid close attention to all the passages in the gospels where Christ teaches his would-be followers, and especially his instructions to the apostles. They also looked closely at the further advice on following Christ found in Paul's letters and the Catholic Epistles.

Of course, Wycliffites were very far from being the only medieval religious group to be gripped by the impulse to return to the original model of Christianity laid out in the gospel. They had plenty of competition, and they knew it. Perhaps the most compelling alternative open to them was that offered by Franciscanism. The late medieval controversies over poverty that Francis and his followers sparked seem strongly to have shaped Wyclif's and his followers' descriptions of how they hope to imitate Christ; some sort of careful description of what exactly it means to be poor in the right sort of way is never absent.[37] Poverty in spirit, rather than material poverty, is what Wycliffites admire; those who lack bodily necessities through no fault of their own, on the other hand, should be provided for from what others can spare.

Wycliffite imitation of Christ is also characterized by an especially strong interest in models of response to persecution. Again, an interest in what Christ has to say about persecution is far from unique to Wycliffites, but in Wycliffite writings it has a special sort of intensity, visible in the frequent quotation of Christ's comforts to his apostles in the face of tribulation and in a preoccupation with martyrdom. The *Five Questions on Love* (item 7) follows Wyclif in his *On Love* (item 3) by exhorting its readers to embrace at the very least metaphorical (and quite possibly actual) martyrdom as the best means of loving God, by means of a carefully interpolated exegesis of Psalm 116:16–17. *The Lantern of Light* explains four ways of being crucified in this world, concluding by exhorting its readers toward the best of them: "Let us join that cross of God to our bare flesh, so

14

that our place may be found among these holy saints that willingly forsake themselves and rejoice in tribulation" (item 19, p. 276). And *A Dialogue between a Wise Man and a Fool* revalues the insulting epithet "loller" that had often been applied to Wycliffites by giving the word a different etymology; rather than a noun derived from Dutch *lollaert* (mumbler) or from Latin *lolium* (darnel), this writer reads it as derived from the verb *to loll*, meaning "to hang."[38] While it is possible to *loll* in a negative sense, for example by persecuting others ("hanging them high") or committing suicide ("hanging oneself"), the author foregrounds the positive senses of "loller":

> As for where they call men lollers for speaking God's word, I read of two kinds of lollers in the law of grace. Some loll toward God, and some toward the fiend. I intend to talk about both these kinds. The most blessed loller that ever was or shall be was our Lord Jesus Christ, who lolled for our sins on the cross. Wearing his livery and belonging to his retinue were Peter and Andrew and others as well. These were blessed lollers, lolling on the right hand of Jesus with the repentant thief, trusting in God's mercy [Luke 23:40–43], to whom our Lord promised the bliss of paradise on that same day. But good friends, what was the reason why Christ and his followers were lolled in this way? Certainly, because of their faithful speaking out against the sins of the people. And especially because they spoke against the covetousness and sins of untrue bishops and of the false, feigned religious. (item 17, p. 249)

Christ is the ideal loller whom Christians should imitate, as did Peter and Andrew and others; Christ hangs on, even when he is hanged up for it, and he speaks out against sin regardless of the consequences.[39]

Communal Responsibility for Sin and Its Repair

But Wycliffism is not all about the cultivation of the self. Indeed, the Wycliffite predilection on the one hand toward architectural metaphors of the self as the church in which God dwells (or where Christians dwell in God), and on the other hand toward corporate models of society as a single human body made up of parts whose functions are incomplete on their own, means that self and community are always collapsing one into the other in their writings.[40] Even as Wycliffites place an extraordinary weight of moral responsibility upon the individual, their sense of mutual responsibility within the community is also unusually strong. This leads them to urge practical implementation of the seven works of mercy in both their material and metaphorical senses: the genuine poor must be provided for, those in need of pastoral instruction must be properly taught. It also leads them to align the mourning (or "pleyning," in Middle English) of the blessed who mourn in Matthew 5:4, whose sorrow will be turned to joy in John 16:20, with the "pleyning," or "complaining," of social complaint: blessed are those who speak out about inconvenient truths, who hunger and thirst for justice, and do not hesitate to complain about injustice when they see it. This impulse in Wycliffite thinking may stem, or gain impetus, from Wyclif's realist theory of sin, according to which any sin harms all created things. Certainly Wycliffites frequently justify their "sharp speech"—whose harshness would normally be considered a violation of the proper conditions of fraternal correction—by recourse to a theory of social consent that they draw directly from Wyclif, and that Wyclif himself links to his theory of sin.[41]

Wyclif's theory of social consent draws on a topic that had been much debated by twelfth- and thirteenth-century canonists and theologians: whether the innocent should be punished along with the guilty.[42] It was generally agreed that sons should not be punished for their fathers' sins unless they imitate them; this was a topic discussed by Gratian in his *Decretum* C.1 q.4, with reference to Ezekiel 18:20 and Exodus 20:5, and two of our selections reproduce these conclusions.[43] But how, then, can it be legitimate to disinherit the orthodox sons of heretical fathers? Or, even more harshly, since this punishment might bring about their eternal damnation as well as pain in this life, to impose a papal interdict, or mass excommunication, on a ruler and all his subjects? The solution was to develop an explanation of the various ways in which one person, or a whole community, might be responsible for the sins of another because it had consented to them; consent in and of itself was defined as a form of culpable

16

imitation. By Wyclif's time, these various kinds of consent had become a mnemonic verse that he quotes very frequently in his writings, and that Wycliffites commonly translate or refer to: "He consents who cooperates with the sinner, who defends him, who offers advice, / who authorizes his sin, who fails to help prevent it, or who fails to criticize him sharply."[44] Paul's comment on consent in Romans 1:32, that "they who do such things, are worthy of death: and not only they that do them, but they also that consent to them that do them," provided support for these theories.[45] Yet, canonists of the twelfth century were divided on the question of who could be culpable for failing to prevent or criticize a sin: Was it only those in authority who were culpable, by virtue of their office? Or were their subjects, their inferiors, equally responsible, being required to criticize sharply the sins of their rulers and preventing them if they could?[46]

These could remain safely academic questions when they were being discussed among canon lawyers and theologians, and largely with reference to the justifiability, and hoped-for effects, of papal interdicts. It was quite another matter for Wyclif to insist that any person's failure sharply to criticize, and to prevent if possible, the sin of any other person, is also a sin, and to develop the implications of this idea. And it was another matter again for Wycliffite writers to propound this theory in vernacular writings urging their practical moral implications upon their readers. Consider, for example, this example, from a commentary on the Ten Commandments in Bodley 789:

> As clerks say, there are six kinds of consent, and men should know them well. He consents to an evil who works with the person who does it, who defends him, who counsels him to do it, who authorizes it, who does not help to stop it, or who does not sharply criticize it, when he is able to do so, and should according to God's law. Among all the sins by which the fiend beguiles men, none is more subtle than this consent. Therefore, the prophets of the old law told men of their perils until they suffered death for it. And this is the cause for which the apostles of Christ were martyred, and so should we be, if we were true men. But cowardice and lack of love for God makes us start back from doing so, as traitors do.[47]

17

The rhetoric of this passage is compelling; it implicates readers, along with the writer, in a failure of the will, stemming from insufficient love for God, that leads them to this subtlest of sins. But now that they know their sin, now that they recognize that they are behaving as traitors do, they should overcome their fear and act. While there are other medieval English writers who mention the topic of consent to sin in their writings, only Wycliffites develop its social implications in this direction, and this far.

The Few Who Are Chosen and the Many Who Are Called

Wycliffite writings frequently exhibit some sort of ambivalence about the size of the community they hope to address, as well as that community's relationship to the larger society of which it is a part. *The City of Saints* is characteristic in this regard; at one moment the "little flock" of Christ's chosen is small simply (though to us repellently) because it does not include "heathens, Jews, [and] Saracens." At the next moment, slipped in at the end of the list, the greater flock of the rejected has expanded to include as well all "false Christian men" (item 20, p. 278). Only "true men" (a favorite self-descriptive term of Wycliffites') belong to the one true church of those that shall be saved (a frequent descriptive term for the community Wycliffites hope will be theirs).[48] What, then, of the greater society in which they lived, and its Christians false as well as true?

It seems doubtful that all Wycliffite writers, all reading groups that gathered to hear Wycliffite preachers or read Wycliffite writings, and all individuals involved with Wycliffite ideas in these and other ways, shared in exactly the same attitudes about what sort of group they were part of, what its relationship to the larger community was, whether their version of Christianity was different or better than that of their neighbors—indeed, whether their neighbors *were* their neighbors in the Christian sense and so ought to be a focus of proselytizing effort. We already have some evidence from historians that the degree to which Wycliffites were integrated in their communities and shared in mainstream practices varied from one locale to another.[49] The case of Margery Baxter in this volume, who seems to have annoyed a good number of other women through her claims to be holier than they were, suggests that personality could be a factor as well (item

24, pp. 329–35). And surely these relations also varied over time and depending on the religio-political climate; there may have been times, for example, where it was all too clear that Wycliffites would never persuade the lay nobility to disendow and reform the clergy, but at other times that hope may have been renewed. Nevertheless, with all these factors in mind, it is probably correct to assert that Wycliffite writers rarely if ever thought of their readers as a special group chosen by Christ for salvation and separate from a greater group for whom there was no hope.

This claim may seem unlikely to some readers, for if there is one thing many people think they know about Wyclif, it is that he thought he and his followers were God's chosen, a special church of the saved who were assured of their direct route to heaven in the next life. Wyclif and his followers believed, that is, in predestination. More than that, they believed they were predestined to salvation, while nearly all others were foreknown to be damned. Certainly there are plenty of passages in Wyclif's and Wycliffite writings that might be selectively quoted in support of this claim. Wyclif is fond of separating the "predestinate" from the "foreknown," and when Wycliffite writers talk of the "church that shall be saved," as they frequently do, many readers have thought they knew exactly what that meant.

In fact, as is often the case in historical study, it is more complicated than that. Any student of late medieval theologies of salvation needs to begin by understanding that there was more than one kind of predestination.[50] Virtually all medieval Christians believed in predestination in the very soft sense that they believed that since God knows everything, therefore he must know everything that will happen in the future, and therefore he knows in advance who will be saved and who will be damned. In this sense, of course there are people who are predestined and people who are foreknown, and of course there is a group that could be called the church of those that shall be saved (though in Middle English writings it is nearly always Wycliffites who call them that). Where things get more difficult, and more divisive, is in explaining who else can know who is predestined and who is foreknown, how and when this can be known, and in what sense human beings can retain any choice in the matter or any influence over their fates, if God knows them all in advance. Only an extreme determinist predestinarian believes that God's foreknowl-

19

edge somehow rules out human free will. On the other hand, those who find this conclusion absurd and repugnant must explain how it is that God can know a fact without God's knowledge unalterably determining that fact.

What did Wyclif think? And what did Wycliffites mean when they talked of the "church of those that shall be saved"? The intricate subtlety of medieval debates over salvation need not concern us further here, for these are not difficult questions to answer. The terms that Wyclif and Wycliffites used to describe those who will be saved and those who will be damned are misleading, and have misled many. *Predestined, foreknown,* and *church that shall be saved* make it sound as though those who used these labels believed that they could know who belonged in each category, that the categories were fixed and stable in the present as well as the future, and that human beings had no ability to influence them. Instead, Wyclif and Wycliffites insist over and over again that nobody but God can know who will be saved and who will be damned. The membership of the group on the way to salvation is imperiled and constantly shifting, as some fall away into sin (perhaps never to return, who knows?), while others turn from sin, ask God for mercy, and step away from the path of damnation. We can make shrewd guesses about who is on the right path and who is not on the basis of their actions. But it is not past actions that decide the salvation of Christians, but the disposition of their soul—their feelings, their choices, their conformity to Christ—at the point of death. Since death could come at any moment, there is no time to waste; but at every moment when death has not yet come, there is still time to turn from sin to Christ. Thus, even in emphasizing the littleness of the flock of the saved, Wycliffite writers always recall the radical uncertainty of its membership. And in articulating hopes for social reform, they never fail to urge that everyone should be properly taught.

Social Reform

Conservative, revolutionary, radical, reactionary, egalitarian. Many value-laden political labels of the present day have been attached to Wycliffites, usually without conveying much. In looking around them at their own society, Wycliffites saw much that needed fixing. While they were not so optimistic as to think that sin could simply be eliminated, they were often hopeful that conditions could be improved. That improvement, in their view, generally took the form of a return to the way things should be.

While Wycliffites are not naively invested in tradition, as we see when the Wise Man dismisses the Fool's contention that the old ways are best (item 17, pp. 244–45), they do typically give strong endorsement to traditional hierarchies, for example, when the *Commentary on Psalm 87* approvingly compares God with a shepherd, bailiff, husband, lord, lady, king, and father, each with his or her proper sphere of authority (item 14, p. 231). Fathers should rule their households just as kings should rule their countries, and social inferiors should obey their rulers. Yet these endorsements of traditional authority structures sometimes harbor surprising reservations, especially when Wycliffites consider the messiness of life in the world. As an example, let us consider Wycliffite treatments of the three estates.

Most of the time, when Wycliffites need to describe society as a whole, they resort to dividing it in the most traditional of medieval ways, that is, into the three estates of those who fight, those who pray, and those who work: the nobility and gentry, the clergy, and the commons. This is a very common medieval habit of thought, but there are some idiosyncrasies in how Wycliffites deploy it.[51] First, the three estates are very obviously a kind of hypostatization of an idealized relationship among social roles that was never so simple, yet in the later Middle Ages even more obviously so than earlier.[52] When later medieval writers talk about the estates in society, it is less common for them to stick with the traditional three categories, and more common for them to expand the list to include many other social groups that do not fit into any of these three categories. If they do squash these subdivided groups into the three categories, they do so with strain—strain that may well be overtly discussed.[53] Wycliffites never complicate the model in this way; they stick to three estates. Very few other later medieval English works deploy such a simplistic model, but two that do are a famous sermon delivered by Thomas Wimbledon in 1387 or 1388 and *Piers Plowman*. Wimbledon's sermon seems to have been very popular among Wycliffites; many of the extant copies appear in manuscripts that also contain Wycliffite writings, and its use of the three-estates model may help to explain why.[54] *Piers Plowman* was also popular among Wycliffites, but while this lengthy and complicated poem does sometimes use a three-estates model, it also uses a variety of far more complex models and raises problems both with the simplicity of the former and the complexity of the latter.[55]

What is more, when Wycliffites talk about the three estates, their categories exhibit a characteristic metonymy: lords, or sometimes knights, stand alone for the first estate; priests invariably represent the second; and the third is often represented by workers who produce food, or sometimes more generally by "commons." This way of thinking about society seems oddly reductive in ways that clearly would not reflect the everyday experience of readers. Curiously, among those this model seems to leave out are many of the kinds of people who seem to have been the most avid readers of Wycliffite writings: townspeople involved in buying and selling, artisans, participants in the book trade, minor gentry, clerks and clerics of various kinds, households and their servants.[56] Part of the answer to why this model is nevertheless so appealing is surely the polemical work it can do. Each of the estates can be exhorted to behave as it should, in sometimes very traditional ways. Their relative success in fulfilling their obligations can be compared in a way that reflects much more poorly on one group than on another. But at the same time the three-estate structure allows Wycliffites to insist, over and over, that the relationship *among* the estates ought to be otherwise than it is. Producers of food fulfill their obligation to provide bodily sustenance for all, even if what they produce may not always be fairly distributed. Priests, on the other hand, fail to provide spiritual sustenance for all, while the newer religious orders brought in to remedy their deficiencies only make things worse. Lords and knights, for their part, should fulfill their obligation to protect society by ensuring that priests fulfill their primary obligation to preach. What is more, they should remove the clergy's excess wealth and distribute it to the poor, so that everyone gets adequate sustenance of both kinds. If lords fail in this duty, then the commons should impel reform from below. Usually they are enjoined to do so through obedience that reforms superiors through sheer good example; more rarely they are exhorted toward resistive obedience that refuses the commands of a sinful lord.[57]

INTRODUCTION

Exegesis and Interpolation

Wycliffites took very seriously, and to its logical conclusions, Augustine's claim in *De Doctrina Christiana* that all of scripture contains the same truth, sometimes expressed openly, sometimes more obscurely. This is the basis of both the pervasive interpolative habits in their writing and the lurking sense of a larger system produced out of much close discussion that these convey. Quotation of scripture that uses interpolation as an expository tool for rapid assignment of the "spiritual" meaning is very common in Wycliffite texts, and it is always revealing. It shows where authors feel justified in specifying a significance that is of great importance to them—for example, that a command requires both words and actions or must be interpreted both bodily and spiritually—but that is not overtly expressed by the biblical text. (We have signaled these interpolations, in this volume, by placing biblical words in italics; see below, "Notes on the Translations," p. 52.) Some critics unfamiliar with the larger body of Wycliffite writings have tried to suggest, in attentive readings of individual texts, that their interpolative habit is uncharacteristic of Wycliffism more broadly.[58] In fact, it is entirely characteristic. It is true that some writings, and some books in which those writings are preserved, are more careful than others to distinguish biblical text from explanatory gloss, for example, through visual differentiation such as ink color or underlining. Some writers are also more careful about quoting passages they plan to discuss in full or providing full versions in both Latin and English. We suggest, though, that these are differences in production values, not in the habits of thought that lie behind them. That writers or book producers might diverge from an agreed-upon style, especially when pursuing their own individual projects, is something that any copyeditor knows only too well. The writers know exactly which words are biblical, even if they, or a scribe, may fail to make this clear to readers. What they have in common, even when they diverge from the kind of very meticulous differentiation of text and gloss that we see in some biblical manuscripts or in the *English Wycliffite Sermons*, is the density of their allusive interpolation, the chains of piled-up quotations that may even seem to lose the thread of any discussion.[59] These feats are perhaps impelled by Wycliffite writers' conviction that everything true can and should be grounded in the Bible, as well as the sort of creative interpretative synergy that this conviction inspires. They do not seem to us to be fraught with theoretical conflict, as some have suggested.[60] This tension may be in the eye of the beholder.

Wycliffite Spirituality in Heresy Trials: Personal Holiness and Spiritual Simplicity

Many of the characteristics of Wycliffite spirituality that we have been describing also appear in the records of suspected heretics' trials. Heresy defendants experienced themselves as members of a persecuted few; for instance, Margery Baxter, tried in Norwich in 1428, reportedly announced that "holy church is only in the place where those of her sect lived" and invited one of her acquaintances to join a secret reading group presided over by her husband.[61] She also disclosed which of her neighbors shared her beliefs, saying of one of them that she "is in the good way of salvation."[62] Other defendants emphasized fidelity to the law of Christ, rejecting what they saw as superfluous regulations instituted by the church in contradiction to the gospel and calling, implicitly or explicitly, for the reform of the clergy.

We have already begun to explore the interpretative challenges that accompany the use of trial records as evidence for heresy suspects' beliefs, yet despite these challenges, trial records remain an important source of information about the ways in which Wycliffite Christians envisioned and practiced their religion. In particular, the themes that emerge from trial records point toward Wycliffites' interest in the holiness of the human person and the cultivation of spiritual simplicity. This drive toward simplicity did not, however, keep Wycliffites from criticizing the institutional church, or from continuing to participate in the rituals of traditional religion. Nevertheless, for at least some Wycliffites the records of whose trials remain extant, criticism of institutionally sanctioned beliefs and practices flowed from spiritual ideals, not the other way around.

Testifying in the case of Margery Baxter, the domestic servant Joan Clifland told the Norwich court that Baxter asked her what she did every day in the church. And she [Clifland] responded, saying that first after entering the church, she was accustomed to genuflect before the crucifix, saying in honor of the crucifix five Our Fathers and the same number of Hail Marys in honor of the blessed Mary, the mother of Christ. And then the said Margery, rebuking her, said to this witness, "you do an evil thing by genuflecting and praying before images in churches, because God was never in any church, nor did God nor will God ever go out from heaven.... [And] if you desire to see the true cross of Christ, I will show it to you in your own house." And this witness asserted that she would gladly see the true cross of Christ. And the said Margery said, "see," and then she extended her arms to their full length, saying to this witness, "this is the true cross of Christ, and you should and can see and adore this cross every day in your own house, and to the same degree that you in vain labors go to churches to adore or pray to whatever images or dead crosses."[63]

Later in her testimony Clifland also reported that Baxter had said to her that no infant born of Christian parents needs to be baptized, because infants are baptized in their mothers' wombs; the sacrament of baptism, in contrast, is "idolatry" that priests commit in order to enrich themselves and their concubines with donations from the people.[64]

This last claim does carry with it the negative overtones traditionally associated with Wycliffite criticism of the institutional church, but the underlying logic of Baxter's spiritual world is far more interesting than the simple claim that baptism, like other sacraments and ceremonies, serves only as a vehicle for clerical greed. For her, the reason that Clifland does not need to go to church in order to pray before the crucifix and the reason a mother does not need to have her newborn baptized are the same: the same dignity, if not a greater dignity, that is in the wooden crucifix or the waters of the baptismal font is already present in the human person. A similar understanding animates the remark that Margery Jopson, tried in Winchester diocese in 1512, purportedly made to a "gentlewoman" who came to her house but refused to accept water until she had made an offering to the crucifix. According to the records of her trial, which do not identify the source of this claim, Jopson allegedly said, "Why will you drink so sparingly; why should you offer your money to the Rood? Give to a poor body, for priests have enough money!"[65] In both cases, Baxter and Jopson explicitly drew comparisons between the wooden body of Christ on the crucifix and the fleshly body of a person's neighbor; in both cases, they privileged attention to the living body over the inanimate one. It would seem, therefore, that they not only feared that churchmen would misuse their donations, but they were also making a theological point, that human persons made in the image of God deserve more care than the "stocks and stones," to borrow a phrase that commonly appears in Wycliffite texts and trial records, found in churches.

The focus of Baxter, Jopson, and other suspects on the holiness of the human person provided the groundwork for theological and polemical claims about the relationship between clergy and laity. Baxter's abjuration included the claim that "any good person is a priest, and... no person will finally come to heaven unless he or she is a priest," a belief that had earlier been voiced by defendants in Lincoln diocese in the 1380s. The same ideas also appear in the trial of Wyclif's so-called *secretarius*, John Purvey, who was said to have taught that every good Christian who is predestined for salvation is a true priest, ordained by God in order to offer up the body of Christ.[66] For these and other defendants, spirituality is centered on the relationship between God and the human person, not on the regulations and practices of the institutional church. It is the human person who is to be cared for, who is the best image of Christ, who transcends the superfluous regulations of the institutional church.

The simplicity that many Wycliffites aimed to cultivate can be discerned, among many other places, in their views on prayer. In 1428, John Kynget of Nelond appeared before Bishop Alnwick accused not only of heretical beliefs but also of associating with other known heretics, among them the infamous Wycliffite evangelist William White. Like other defendants, Kynget spoke out against the ways in which the church had bureaucratized the sacraments; he also demonstrated sympathy with Margery Baxter's emphasis on the goodness of the human person, being accused of believing that "no pilgrimage should be made, except to poor people." His abjuration also included two articles on prayer: first, that "prayer should be made only to God, and to no other saint," and second, that "no prayer should be said other than the Pater Noster."[67] Similar claims appear in the trial of a later defendant, Robert Clerke, who was tried in 1490 before Bishop John Blythe of Coventry and Lichfield. Though the records do not indicate the source of this charge, he was accused of having preached that "the Lord's Prayer and the angelic salutation were of no effect and that it is damnable to say the Our Father and the Hail Mary, for the whole effect of prayer is in the Creed." What precisely Clerke's inquisitors thought that he had meant is unclear; as a starting point, it should be obvious that a creed, if a prayer at all, is not the same sort of prayer as the Pater Noster or the Ave Maria. His accusers may have misunderstood Clerke's beliefs, or they may have been given bad information, as is confirmed in the next sentence of the record of his trial: "To this article the said Robert responded with this qualification, that the Lord's Prayer should not be said by anyone outside charity, because this would be more to his damnation than to his edification."[68]

Clerke was not so much putting the Our Father out of bounds for Christian prayer as he was setting a condition for its use. He was imagining an essentially moral criterion, that the person praying the Pater Noster should be in a state of charity. This concept, unparalleled in other trial records, seems to function not unlike the traditional theological category of a person's being in a state of grace. Indeed, the notion that a person should assess his or her moral fitness before saying the Our Father evokes Paul's admonition about receiving the Eucharist: "For he who eats and drinks unworthily, eats and drinks damnation to himself" (1 Cor 11:29). By means of this parallel, Clerke elevated the saying of the Lord's Prayer to a level of reverence that mainstream religion reserved only for the consecrated Eucharist, the very body and blood of Christ; this is all the more striking coming from the mouth of an individual who was accused of skepticism about the doctrine of transubstantiation. If many trial records depict Wycliffites as anti-sacramental—a judgment not wholly without merit—Clerke's case may serve as a helpful reminder that for some defendants, at least, simple, biblical prayer functioned not unlike the sacraments.

Both the ways in which Baxter and Jopson criticized the adoration of images yet presented the living human body as an alternative image, and the ways in which Kynget and Clerke criticized innovative forms of prayer yet elevated biblical prayer to the level of sacrament illustrate the complex interplay between Wycliffite and mainstream Christianity. As we have already observed with regard to the Wycliffites' own texts, it is often adaptation rather than wholesale rejection of traditional ideas that marks their spirituality. What is more, the trial records also indicate that many Wycliffites were willing to conform their spiritual practices to those of the mainstream communities of which they were part, not least in order to evade detection. Again, Joan Clifland's testimony against Margery Baxter presents a clear example:

> And the said Margery said to this witness that she often went falsely to confession to the dean of St. Mary in the Fields, so that the dean might think that she had a good life. And therefore he often gave Margery money. And then this witness said to her, surely she confessed all her sins to the priest? And Margery said to her that she never did wrong to any priest, and for that reason she never wished to confess to a priest nor submit herself to a priest, because no priest had the power of absolving anyone from sins, and priests sinned every day more gravely than other men. And indeed Margery said that every man and every woman who was of her opinion were good priests, and that holy church is only in the place where those of her sect lived.[69]

Not only did Margery participate in an ecclesiastically sponsored ritual, auricular confession, in order to persuade a local cleric that "she had a good life," but she also borrowed from the discourses of traditional religion many of the concepts with which she organized her thought-world: sin and confession, priesthood and church. Her challenge, then, was not so much a challenge to Christianity as it was to church structures, and her logic once again focused on the spiritual dignity of the rightly acting human person. Though she did not quail from taking part in a ritual that reinforced the notion of an

28

ontological divide between ordained priests and lay people, she did so in a way that reflected a different set of theological principles. Whether he was the dean of St. Mary's or her local parish priest, if Margery had done nothing wrong to her confessor, why should she confess her sins to him? The claim that auricular confession to priests is unnecessary, which we find echoed in the records of trials in Winchester diocese nearly a century later, harks back a broader theme. Margery devalued the sacramental powers of priests because they "sinned every day more gravely than other men"; she assigned value to her co-religionists and elevated them to the priesthood because of their spiritual wisdom. It is fidelity to God and, implicitly, to God's commandments that marks a person out as a member of the church, and faithful people are of inherent dignity.

These two themes from the records of late medieval English heresy trials—a focus on the human person rather than ecclesiastical ordinances and an emphasis on simple, biblically grounded prayer—are of a piece with the spiritual values to be found in John Wyclif's writings and those of his followers. They are also of a piece with the few Wycliffite practices of which the records of heresy trials make mention; the reading, circulation, and copying of scriptural and theological texts within a circle of likeminded believers, for instance, testifies to the value of the written and spoken word for many Wycliffites.

Partly because dissenters' practices were often uncontroversial in themselves—speaking, praying, reading—the inquisitorial process has occluded many details about their devotional and spiritual lives. Only when practices marked an individual out as a member of a dissenting community or else were illegal on their face, as in the case of the reading and copying of vernacular theological works in the wake of Archbishop Thomas Arundel's *Constitutions* of 1407–1409, do they stand out in the records. It is nevertheless possible to locate in these fascinating but frustrating documents ideas about spirituality and traces of the practices in which Wycliffites incarnated those ideas.

THE TEXTS IN CONTEXT

John Wyclif: Spiritual and Devotional Guide?

Wycliffism, the late medieval spiritual movement that served as the essence of lollardy in England and the Hussite revolution in what is now the Czech Republic, has its origins in the writings and teachings of John Wyclif (ca. 1331–84). Wyclif came from minor nobility in Yorkshire and became active in Oxford in the late 1350s.[70] This was the age of Edward III; England had endured the plague just ten years earlier and was engaged in ongoing war with France. The church was on the verge of serious internal conflict. It had been based in Avignon since 1309 and had been subject to an increased French royal influence, much to the consternation of the Holy Roman Emperor. By 1378, when Wyclif was becoming an important voice in English criticisms of the ecclesiastical status quo, the papacy had reached the breaking point. Gregory XI had attempted to return the papal see to Rome, and upon his death the cardinals elected Urban VI. In response to widespread dissatisfaction with Urban, another conclave elected Clement VII, who moved the see back to Avignon. Western Christianity was torn between two rivals claiming papal authority at a time when the traditional social system was breaking apart and increasing numbers of lay Christians were demanding moral leadership by example from the church. Before the mid-1370s, Wyclif had gained a reputation as a notable Oxford theologian, but he entered into royal service in 1374, when he decided to occupy himself as much with practical as with theoretical affairs. The theoretical framework for what would become Wycliffism was set by then. He had constructed a formal, theological structure upon which to base his practical theology and would complete a *postilla*, or book-by-book running commentary, of the entire Bible by 1376.[71]

Opinions about Wyclif's works in the last decade of his life continue to vary widely. Some interpret Wyclif as having foreseen the Protestant Reformation and since the sixteenth century have called him the Morning Star of the Reformation. Others perceive his disregard for many important elements in medieval theology and continue to endorse the Council of Constance's 1415 condemnation of him as a detestable heresiarch. It has only been within the past century that scholars have managed to set aside sectarian biases about Wyclif in favor of analysis grounded in an understanding of the fourteenth century.[72] Because of the uproar his writings caused during his lifetime, scholarship continues to focus on Wyclif the controversialist. The controversies he engendered were indeed veritable hornets' nests for the later medieval Christian mindset: he questioned papal authority, championing secular monarchy in its place; he doubted the validity of the doctrine of transubstantiation; and he relentlessly criticized clerical abuses of the ecclesiastical system. Further, he demanded that the laity have a vernacular version of the Bible available to them for their spiritual nourishment. While the church was not as opposed to this innovation as later critics would claim, it would be an exaggeration to say that the ecclesiastical hierarchy looked favorably upon the idea. Small wonder that Wyclif's reputation has been determined to such an extent by controversy; his eye seemed to fall upon every problem that afflicted the late medieval church.[73]

Wyclif's political and ecclesiological thought, accompanied by his rejection of excessive sacramentalism in general and transubstantiation in particular, has accurately been described as an "ideology of revolution."[74] Theorists had been exploring the nature of property ownership and its hindrance of the Christian ideal for more than a century before Wyclif was born. The best known arena for arguments about the justifiability of ownership for Christians had been the controversy between the Franciscans and John XXII, in which arguments about the connection of the exemplarity of Christ's life and the communalism of the early church led to a dangerous split within the Franciscan order. Most (the Conventuals) were willing to compromise on Francis's ideal of poverty to preserve the special place Franciscans enjoyed in the church as nonparochial preachers and priests, but some, the Minorites, rejected compromise and began a full-scale critical engagement with the very nature of the fourteenth-century church. While the Black Death brought an end to most of the players in the controversy, the Minorites' arguments remained searing indictments of the imperial church. Wyclif adopted many of the ideals of the Minorites: private property is the result of original sin, as is secular society and justice; the church is obliged to follow the apostolic communalist lead; and any case of clergy involvement in secular or political affairs is evidence of unacceptable compro-

31

mise. The Donation of Constantine, the ninth-century document supposedly showing the Emperor Constantine's having willed control of the Western Roman Empire to the church, introduced secular authority into the church, and by Wyclif's estimation, only the firm hand of a secular lord could hope to rid the church of this contamination. His solution was for the king, whom grace endowed with power over property and civil society, to divest the church of all its holdings and take all secular authority away from its ministers. These arguments earned Wyclif papal condemnation as early as 1377, and had he not been under the protection of the Duke of Lancaster, he would most certainly have been tried at Avignon.[75]

Wyclif's understanding of the church was a source of great disagreement. His demand that the body of Christ be understood to be the elect, those eternally foreknown to be saved by grace, was not a departure from traditional Augustinian theology; indeed, his famous predecessor Thomas Bradwardine, briefly Archbishop of Canterbury (d. 1349) had made very similar arguments. Wyclif's departure from Bradwardine involved philosophical attempts to explore God's eternally necessary knowledge that led him to think that he had improved upon Bradwardine's determinism. But Wyclif's criticisms of the clergy, especially his regular suggestions that priests and bishops whose primary interests centered on possessions and political power were not truly functioning as "evangelical lords," sounded to many like Donatism. When this was combined with a philosophically unsophisticated reading of his thought on the foreknown nature of the church, many were led to conclude that Wyclif advocated a dangerous combination of Donatism and determinism, deemphasizing the sacraments and putting emphasis instead on preaching. The body of Wyclif's writings was viewed as a potent brew of radical politics and heretical ideology that smacked of ecclesiastical anarchism, denied clerical authority, questioned the efficacy of sacraments, and cast doubt on the church's magisterial authority in interpreting scripture and determining the Christian life.

Wyclif himself was never excommunicated for this, despite regular condemnations by the archbishop of Canterbury and the pope, because throughout his writings he regularly indicated his willingness to be corrected by appropriate authority.[76] His followers were not so theologically adept, though, and Wycliffism became the cause

32

of great concern in England and Bohemia within two decades of his death. That his ideas were popular in England is readily comprehensible to anyone familiar with the spirit of vernacular English literature in the later Middle Ages; many of Wyclif's criticisms are echoed in Middle English prose and poetry. William Langland's *Piers Plowman* is an example of a text that reflects many Wyclif-like criticisms and concerns without actually entering into the dangerous territory of heterodox theology. It is very likely that Wyclif had an organized group of students and supporters while he was in exile at Lutterworth in the last years of his life, and there is some evidence that he envisioned a group of "poor preachers," traveling throughout the countryside and preaching the gospel in direct competition with the Franciscans, Dominicans, and other friars. The past hundred years have seen disagreement about this subject, with some scholars arguing that an absence of evidence of Wyclif having purposefully organized "poor preachers" reveals this as part of the "Wyclif myth." More recently, scholars have adopted the corollary that an absence of evidence does not indicate evidence of absence and, following Michael Wilks and Anne Hudson, have regarded the "poor preachers" movement as having been instigated by Wyclif.[77]

That Wyclif's writings became popular in Bohemia and Moravia is likely to be surprising. Why would an English theologian and preacher inspire the Czechs? This is, after all, what happened; the great revolution that had been set in motion by followers of Jan Hus after his murder at Constance in 1415 claimed Wyclif as the source of its theological ideology. The young king of England, Richard II, married Anne of Bohemia, the daughter of Holy Roman Emperor Charles IV. Charles had established a new university in Prague in 1347, and scholars there were interested in connections with other universities. Czech scholars were hostile to German universities and ideas, and when the royal marriage occurred, they eagerly embraced Oxford theology as a tonic against what they felt to be an imperialistic German stranglehold on intellectual life in Prague. A certain amount of popular dissatisfaction with the ecclesiastical status quo had been brewing in the Czech lands, exemplified in the preaching of Mattias of Janow (d. 1394). The first Bohemian scholars to return from Oxford in the 1390s brought with them copies of Wyclif's works, which served as the spark for a longstanding tradition of Czech reformist preaching, and by the first decade of the fifteenth century, Wycliffism had captured the attention of important minds in Prague, including Jerome of Prague, Jakoubek Stříbro, Peter Chelčicky, and most important, Jan Hus. After Hus and Jerome of Prague were burnt at Constance in 1415, Wycliffism became the ideology that would sustain the Czech revolution against imperial and papal authority for the next twenty years.[78]

What was it about Wycliffism that appealed to lollards and Hussites? It is not enough for an ideology to be defined by what it aims to overthrow, nor is a general feeling of the need for reform sufficient to articulate its structure. Scholars have usually pursued lollard and Hussite criticisms of the ecclesiastical and social status quo, but in general one is left wondering whether lollards and Hussites had any concrete, positive alternatives in mind. We have a good idea of what Wycliffism was against. After all, its opponents were careful to draw up lists of propositions they believed central to its heterodoxy, and much of the literature now available very effectively corresponds to these lists. What is missing from both sets of literature, both the condemnatory anti-Wycliffite material and the polemic Wycliffite material, is the underlying vision of the Christian life as envisioned by Wycliffism. It is not enough to say that it was a general kind of late medieval Christian spirituality; this series of volumes is testimony to the rich and varied nature of late medieval Christian spirituality.

The selections from Wyclif's works that follow are meant to serve as the beginning of an answer to this question. In fact, Wyclif had a distinct moral theology in mind when criticizing the friars and the papacy for errors and abuses. Further, he had developed a complex biblical hermeneutic, what he called the "logic of scripture," meant to illuminate the Bible's ideal for the Christian life, the *lex Christi* or law of Christ.[79] Wyclif's writings include the building blocks for a moral theology intended to support an active Christian spiritual life, and the surviving manuscripts attest to this. While some of his philosophical and polemical works exist in only a few manuscripts, the treatises described as pastoral tend to have many extant manuscripts.[80] Three works in particular provide the fullest picture of Wyclif's moral theology: *De Mandatis Divinis*, *Trialogus*, and *Opus Evangelicum*. Correspondingly, these three works are very well represented in the manuscript tradition, with seventeen and eight copies of the first two, and four complete copies of the third, which is twice the size of the first two treatises. *Trialogus* is a three-way dialogue structured similarly to Aquinas's *Summa Theologiae* and written in a simple Latin likely to be accessible to readers not trained in formal theology.[81] The *Opus Evangelicum* is Wyclif's sustained commentary on Matthew 5–7, the Sermon on the Mount; Matthew 23–25, the "little apocalypse"; and the "priestly sermon" of John 13–17. The last commentary is unfinished and likely occupied Wyclif's final weeks alive.

Readers already familiar with Wyclif's writing may wonder how such a volatile academic theologian could have inspired a spiritual movement. His philosophical and political works are abstract and repetitive, and his polemical works are anything but spiritually uplifting. What little of his work has been translated into English suggests a sour-tempered Oxford don with scant ability to speak to the daily needs of everyday Christian life.[82] Further, it is likely that the works described as critical to his moral theology were the product of the last four years of Wyclif's life. This is also the period of Wyclif's active anti-fraternal campaign, when he wrote most of the shorter polemics against sects in general and friars in particular. Before Wyclif's exile to Lutterworth in the summer of 1381, his fires did not burn with quite so much heat against the four orders of mendicant preachers. These two facts may be connected to one another.

The friars were like monks in that they lived according to a rule defining their daily life and work, but unlike monks, they espoused poverty and were active in the world, especially as preachers and pastors independent of the authority of the diocese in which they worked. This gave them a degree of power that other clergy did not have, and as readers of late medieval prose and poetry know well, the friars occasionally abused their authority. There were four orders of friars active in England: the Franciscans, the Order of Preachers (also known as the Dominicans), the Augustinians, and the Carmelites. Anti-mendicant sentiments arose as the friars became widespread. Formal theologians, like William of St. Amour and Archbishop Richard FitzRalph, as well as William Langland and Geoffrey Chaucer, voiced complaints indicating the prominent role the friars played in later medieval religion. Wyclif's antipathy toward the friars was part of his broader conviction that any human addition to the perfect morality of the law of Christ in scripture could only be founded in pride. It is perfectly sensible to distinguish between a Scotist and a Thomist species of Aristotelian moral thought, for both are learned men interpreting the ethics of another learned man, but to imagine that a Dominican or a Franciscan rule of living is a useful addition to the divine moral legislation of Christ is blasphemy. Any sect, whether of monks, nuns, friars, or lay men that follows the rule of a saintly patron makes this error, and Wyclif's criticisms of the possessioners, or the cloistered monastic houses, are equally caustic. The friars draw Wyclif's anger particularly because of their preaching. They purport to preach Christ's morality to the laity while following the rule of another man, something Paul or Peter never did.

The fact that Wyclif criticizes both the basis for the friars' existence and the many instances in which they abused their authority cloaks his demonstrable admiration for their moral theology. Two Dominicans in particular figure importantly in Wyclif's description of the Christian life: William Peraldus (d. 1271) and Thomas Aquinas (d. 1275). Peraldus was widely known by most later medieval and early modern preachers as the author of the *Summa de Virtutibus et Vitiis*, an extensive and exhaustive description of the virtues and vices designed to give the preacher grist for any sort of sermon on Christian behavior. Indeed, Peraldus's *Summa* appears to have been the stimulus for Aquinas's own *Summa Theologiae*, with its comprehensive theological account of the Christian moral life. Wyclif borrows liberally from Peraldus in his description of the virtues and vices in *Trialogus*, his sermons, and elsewhere, occasionally even referring to him by name.[83] Wyclif's admiration for Thomas is evident throughout his works, despite his frequent disagreement with the Angelic Doctor. Aquinas had borrowed Augustine's *Enchiridion* when he began compiling a work containing the basic elements of the faith at the request of his friend and secretary Raynald. The *Compendium Theologiae* is organized around the three theological virtues, with Aquinas's line-by-line analysis of the Creed accounting for faith, and a beginning of an analysis of the Lord's Prayer intended for hope. Had he lived to finish it, Aquinas would likely have engaged in an analysis of the decalogue for love.[84]

Wyclif's own works on moral theology can well be understood according to the same pattern. *Trialogus*, finished by 1382, fits as an overview of the faith; Wyclif devotes only one sermon to the Creed but provides a careful introduction to the basic issues of the catechism in *Trialogus*.[85] Wyclif composed five separate commentaries of the Lord's Prayer, each distinct, but comprehensible by their articulation of Wyclif's understanding of hope. Finally, Wyclif's treatise on love serves as an introduction to his study of the decalogue, as well as his study of the Sermon on the Mount in Matthew, and the priestly sermon in John in *Opus Evangelicum*. The three major works of moral theology already described, as well as his sermons, can be understood as Wyclif's attempt to describe the Christian life, as did Augustine and Aquinas, according to the three theological virtues.

De Mandatis Divinis, the source of the selections to follow, appears to have undergone extensive revision later in Wyclif's life. It began as a commentary on the Ten Commandments, giving evidence of being imitative of Robert Grosseteste's widely read commentary *De Decem Mandatis*.[86] Grosseteste (d. 1253) was almost a patron saint for secular English Scholastic thinkers, and Wyclif was an enthusiastic disciple of "Lincolniensis," the customary honorific for this thirteenth-century theologian, scientist, and bishop of Lincoln. Wyclif's decalogue commentary was then expanded to include material on the nature of *ius*, or "the right," and justice in general, perhaps as a means of connecting his exposition of the basic rules of monotheism to his political thought.[87] Further, Wyclif (or a redactor) then included several brief treatises within the decalogue commentary. On the logic that the Ten Commandments can be divided into rules defined by love of God and those defined by love of one's neighbor, a work entitled *The Treatise on Love* has been included to introduce the fundamentally Christian understanding of the logic of the decalogue.[88] Using the same editorial reasoning, another treatise on the theological essence of the Lord's Prayer, likely entitled *De Virtute Orandi*, is included between the analyses of the "God commandments" and the "neighbor commandments." Scholars are beginning to understand how several of Wyclif's works have been constructed from what appear to have been meant to be brief, stand-alone treatises, and the *De Mandatis Divinis* serves as a good example of this. We cannot know with certainty whether Wyclif himself did the final arranging of the treatise as we have it now, or whether this is the editorial work of one of his disciples, but its polished form suggests the former possibility as likely.

Wyclif composed five theologically distinct commentaries on the Lord's Prayer. The first, and likely earliest, is the *De Virtute Orandi* (On the Power of Praying), included here as chapters 19 and 20 of *De Mandatis*. The second is more in keeping with Wyclif's better-known critical voice. It is entitled *De Oratione Dominica* (On the Lord's Prayer) and is included here not only to show how Wyclif incorporated polemics into his theology, but also to give an example of the anti-fraternalism for which he remains famous. Wyclif devoted a sermon on John 16:23 to a further exposition of the logic of the Lord's Prayer.[89] Finally, the second book of *Opus Evangelicum* is a prolonged theological analysis of the Lord's Prayer, filled with selections from Augustine's commentary on the prayer as well as selections from the *Opus Imperfectum in Mattheum*. The tone and purpose of this longer commentary are similar to *De Virtute Orandi*.

It is fair to wonder how Wyclif sees himself as different from Francis, Benedict, or Dominic. After all, he is presuming to organize a band of poor preachers according to his own program of teaching and preaching the Christian life. How is he *not* creating a de facto sect? Wyclif would respond that Christ has provided the rule and scriptures the example for its preachers and ministers; his only role is in elucidating the "logic of scripture" for those without the necessary education, just as any master of the sacred page had done in centuries past. In the selections that follow, we perceive his conviction that the fundamental elements of the Christian spiritual life, the *lex Christi*, are contained within the logic of scripture. Wyclif's use of the Bible is typical for medieval theological literature; it is not uncommon to find medieval theologians interlarding their thought with frequent, if not continual, references to scriptural authority. Wyclif expects his readers, whether they are itinerant preachers, interested nobility, or disaffected clergy, to incorporate these references into an ongoing spiritual orientation to the Bible, seeking to find the connective elements uniting each part of scripture to every other part. This was the business of the master of the sacred page in medieval schools, but Wyclif conceived of this as possible, to some extent, for everyone capable of reading. Masters of the sacred page have their place, as Wyclif himself seems to have assumed was evident, but he was convinced that the Bible is so perfect an iteration of God's mind that its basic elements are evident to any faithful reader. Hence, Christ's teachings and the Law of Moses must themselves be understood as the fundamental rules for human life. The absence of a printing press or other means by which scripture could be made readily available to Christians meant that preaching scripture—the whole of scripture, and not simply selections—was the responsibility of the church's stewards, the priest class. The method of preaching then popular, replete with entertaining stories, "word pictures" meant to captivate as well as edify, and catchy rhymes, failed to convey the stern yet loving simplicity of the Bible.[90]

The word *love* figures importantly throughout these selections, as it does in all Wyclif's works. The terms *caritas* and *amor* refer to two overlapping senses, and Wyclif's use of these terms usually assumes synonymy between the English "charity" and "love." This is, in part, because of Paul's use of *caritas* in 1 Corinthians; in his well-known section on love in chapter 13, Paul's Greek *agápe* is translated to *caritas* in the Vulgate Latin that was the standard in the European Middle Ages. For the selections in this volume, this assumed synonymy is especially prevalent. Likewise, in Matthew 22:37–39, the Latin verb is *diligo, diligere* ("Love the Lord your God with all your heart....Love your neighbor as yourself.") for the Greek *agápe*. Wyclif did not read Greek but had sufficient sensitivity to the biblical sense of *agápe* to understand that Paul's noun translated as *caritas* and Matthew's verb translated *diligo* had the same referent. On the translation of these terms within this volume, see below, "Notes on the Translations," p. 54.

English Wycliffite Writings

All of the writings in Part II, the largest section of this volume, were composed in or translated into English. All have some relationship to Wyclif's writings, even though in some cases this relationship has been questioned, while in others it is newly demonstrated in this volume. Readers will notice a marked shift in idiom from the writings by Wyclif presented in Part I. Even though the authors of these writings in English are likely to have been well educated, they aim in these works to address a broader audience and do not assume the level of background knowledge that Wyclif seems always to have expected from his readers, even at times when he strives to broaden his scope of address. The contrast is especially marked in items 7 and 14, each of which is a translation and adaptation of one of Wyclif's writings presented in Part I (cf. items 3 and 1).

Why has the Wycliffism of many of these items been questioned? Readers whose introduction to Wycliffism was through condemnations or heresy trials, or all the more so through later Protestant accounts of those trials such as Foxe's *Actes and Monuments*, have not found the beliefs they expected to find. Here there is no rigidly deterministic account of predestination, no outright rejection of the sacrament of penance, no insistence that the Eucharist is simply commemorative (indeed, only rarely any mention of the Eucharist).[91] However, once we understand that these were not in fact common Wycliffite claims any more than they were Wyclif's, and discover on the other hand that Wyclif's and Wycliffite writings do make consistent assertions on these as well as other, unnoticed topics, we may begin to suspect that something has gone wrong.

Again, readers who first encountered Wycliffites in the most single-mindedly polemical of their writings, such as the *Twelve Conclusions*, for example, may expect to find the same tone and the same preoccupations on every page of their more pastoral and devotional productions. They may even deploy an extraordinarily narrow definition of what is Wycliffite, where they are willing to attach this label only to overtly polemical or heretical statements. Polemic is not entirely absent from the selections presented in Part II, any more than it was from Wyclif's writings in Part I. But polemic is not the only mode of Wycliffite discourse, particularly at the moments when writers want to instruct their readers or deepen their religious feeling. What is more, not every Wycliffite text needs to make all the same polemical assertions. It is possible, for example, for a text to be Wycliffite even if it does not make assertions about the importance of translating the Bible into English, and possible too for texts that are not Wycliffite to urge biblical translation into English. Every one of the twelve tracts in Cambridge University Library MS Ii 6 26 supports biblical translation, but some of the selections draw on sources earlier than Wyclif or Wycliffism, sometimes with little alteration; interest in biblical translation is not the sole essential criterion of each selection's Wycliffism, but rather the collection's unifying theme. There are other Wycliffite manuscripts, such as London, British Library Additional MS 24202, in which biblical translation is never mentioned. In this last example, the unifying theme is instead disapproval of secular pleasures, of a rather idiosyncratic kind that is not expressed anywhere else in exactly this form; for example, no other Wycliffite collection includes a tract against playing dice. Yet the Wycliffite writings in these two manuscripts frequently return to the core themes of Wycliffite spirituality explained here, even if the reforming interests of the compiler and writers of each manuscript are articulated in different ways.

Finally, readers who are well versed in mainstream medieval English religious writings may complain that much of the content of these selections is entirely conventional—even, as they might say, "orthodox." How, then, can they possibly be Wycliffite? This concern about how to pinpoint what, if anything, distinguishes these selections from more conventional mainstream religious writings is an entirely legitimate one. Behind it, though, may lurk an assumption that the study of religion has now left behind: that heresy and orthodoxy should be separate, rigidly demarcated, and entirely different in kind.[92] Since this is not the case, we all need to learn to be patient readers; to be on the lookout, not so much for the opposite of what we are used to, as a series of systematic yet sometimes subtle differences in style and emphasis that we will find these writings share. For even if manuscript anthologies or individual texts may have their own idiosyncrasies, just like the individual believers who may have written or compiled them, still there is a great deal that these writings have in common. The process of discovering these commonalities is inductive rather than presumptive, painstaking rather than immediate, self-correcting rather than infallible. It involves meticulous comparison of versions against one another, sources and quotations with their adaptations, newly discovered texts with the better-known core writings of the early lollard movement.[93] Yet it also involves serendipity and intuition. Any reader of this volume may develop a new insight that will become crucial to our understanding of Wyclif and Wycliffism.

This volume includes only a small selection of the large number of Wycliffite writings that a curious reader might go on to discover. In choosing texts and organizing them into four subsections, we have sought to present a range of themes that are sounded frequently in English Wycliffite writings, across a range of genres. Each subsection focuses on an area of emphasis common in these writings, and on at least one way in which Wycliffites sought to differentiate themselves from mainstream religion.

Forms of Living

Many later medieval writers whose audiences include members of the laity attempt to encourage or else respond to their readers' growing spiritual ambitions—their thirst to engage in some form of life in the world that might allow them to aspire to the sort of special holiness sought by members of religious orders. Quasi-religious rules or "forms of living" composed for devout individuals who had not taken a vow of religion attempt to provide their readers with means of attaining some of the same goals without abandoning the obligations of their daily lives. It has often been recognized that Wyclif and Wycliffites were critical of the religious orders. But fewer have noticed that they too wrote forms of living, often basing them on existing models or even responding to well-known mainstream examples in this genre. The selections gathered here may indulge in criticism of existing religious orders along the way, but this is not their principal aim; their focus is upon describing a mode of religious life that is available to all Christians rather than confined to a few, and that offers the hope of spiritual perfection to everyone. "Christ's religion," as Wycliffites like to call it, is something all Christians should practice, even if not a form of living in which everyone will succeed in persevering to the end.

Exegesis and Commentary

By means of these selections we hope to allow readers to see that Wycliffite writers are remarkably consistent in their exegetical methods, that their methodological comments mesh far more closely with their reading habits than has often been claimed, and that they are in some ways (though not all—there are some marked idiosyncrasies) far more typical of late medieval exegesis and far more immersed in mainstream tradition than many have assumed.

Wycliffite Devotion

Many of the manuscript anthologies in which polemical Wycliffite writings or parts of the Wycliffite Bible appear also contain mainstream devotional works. Scholars have sometimes found these conjunctions difficult to explain and have suggested that these apparently incongruous combinations are the product of scribes not understanding what they were copying and including Wycliffite texts in error, or else of deliberate camouflage by Wycliffites.[94] We would instead suggest that in many cases a simpler and more obvious explanation is probably correct, that is, that mainstream readers were reading Wycliffite writings in a textual milieu in which their Wycliffism was not always perceived as threatening or even especially significant, and that Wycliffite readers, and writers, were very much engaged with mainstream devotional writings.

The selections included here are designed to allow readers to test this hypothesis for themselves. Each of them encourages a reader's attentiveness to God, and each imitates, interpolates, or otherwise engages with well-known mainstream devotional writings or genres. Each includes some pastoral instruction as well as encouraging meditation or prayer; catechesis and devotion can rarely be separated in Middle English vernacular writings, and Wycliffite examples are no exception. But in other ways, their differences from what is typical in devotional writing (and especially in their models) are telling and significant. We aim to demonstrate that the ways in which the selections here modify existing examples of devotional writing are characteristically Wycliffite (even if not always unique to Wycliffites).

Ecclesial Spirituality

Wycliffites frequently refer to their Christian community as the "church that shall be saved"—yet if no person in this life can know its membership, as they frequently insist, then what kind of Christian community can be built on such an unstable basis? The selections gathered here aim to demonstrate how Wycliffites thought about Christian community, and also how they coped with its instability. The usual mainstream solution to uncertainty about salvation was to think of all Christians as a single community, as members of the church, sinful or not. Christ's parable of the tares in Matthew 13:24–30, with its insistence that all of the crop must grow together until the harvest, was helpful here. Wycliffites, in contrast, seem to have focused on the little flock of Luke 12:32 and the few who find the strait gate and narrow path of Matthew 7:14. Their sense of church membership was far more tightly focused. However, they found many ways to compensate for their uncertainty about that community's makeup; rather than fragile, their sense of community and of mutual obligation was (at least in aspiration) remarkably strong. They constructed manifold divisions of the parts of the larger community and their functions; they were partial to the three-estate model but also to metaphors of society as a body, or as a building, or to distinctions built on actions and dispositions such as the four kinds of crucified in *The Lantern of Light*. They insisted on the importance of loving enemies as well as friends, on mutual obligations between ranks in society. They asserted that true Christians are proven by persecution, something anyone should be ready to undergo, and on the obligation to speak truth, to correct those in the wrong (lovingly, and yet sharply, if necessary), regardless of the consequences. Those who do not attempt to prevent the sins of others when they see them and have the opportunity to speak out are as guilty of those sins through their silent consent as are their perpetrators (see above, pp. 16–18). In practice, these convictions may sometimes have made them uncomfortable neighbors—trial evidence supports this suspicion on occasion—but they did not usually cause them to separate themselves from the larger community and its religious observances. While most lollards seem to have gathered in smaller or larger groups to read and discuss their communal texts, these meetings seem to have been a supplement to rather than a substitute for mainstream observances. As far as we know, nearly all lollards attended church services and participated in the sacraments, while some even held positions of greater involvement, as churchwardens, for example.

INTRODUCTION

Records of Heresy Trials

Throughout this Introduction we have been calling into question the classic portrait of Wycliffites as spiritually bereft, carping critics of late medieval Christianity. This picture, of course, is painted most effectively in the records of suspected heretics' trials before diocesan bishops and other ecclesiastical officials. These texts, which as we have already noted rarely convey the fullness of Wycliffite belief and practice, portray the faith and spirituality of dissenters in overwhelmingly negative terms: one suspect denied this doctrine; another refused to take part in that religious practice. Limited and biased as they may be, however, the records of heresy trials sit alongside the texts written by Wyclif and his followers as important sources of evidence about what late medieval women and men believed, what they valued, and how they practiced their religion. By including in the present collection a number of these records, including some that have never before appeared in print, we hope to highlight both the opportunities and the pitfalls they offer to students of Wycliffite spirituality.

Before turning to the records themselves, though, an overview of the inquisitorial process seems to be in order.[95] In late medieval England, there existed two parallel sets of courts: civil courts, which handled offenses against the crown, secular criminal matters, and some civil disputes; and church courts, which dealt with a range of matters judged to be spiritual. The division of cases between civil and church courts reflects some of the differences between medieval and modern thinking on what we have become accustomed to calling the relationship between church and state. Defamation, for instance, was a spiritual crime, because it involved the bearing of false witness and thus the breaking of one of the commandments; petitions for divorce were also heard by ecclesiastical rather than civil courts, because marriage ranked among the seven sacraments of the church. Heresy (or, in technical terms, "heretical depravity") ranked among the gravest of spiritual crimes, and as a result, suspected heretics almost always appeared before ecclesiastical judges.[96] Since heresy was a high-profile matter, the venue for heresy cases was usually the court of the local diocesan bishop, who either presided himself or delegated his authority to a senior aide; less regularly, heresy trials were heard in the consistory court of the diocese or in the court of an archdeacon.

As in other medieval courts, heresy trials were divided between "instance" and "office" cases, the former involving accusations of heresy by individuals against one another and the latter involving charges emanating directly from church officials. Regardless of the source, a heresy investigation usually entailed four phases: detection, arrest, trial, and punishment. Responsibility for these phases often alternated between the church and the crown, with secular authorities arresting and punishing defendants who were identified and tried by the church.

Unlike in the modern world, where the term *detection* carries the sense of an investigation by a police force, in the Middle Ages the word signified a process of reporting and informing on a suspect. People were "detected to" church authorities, either by accusation (a formal process involving a written statement by a named accuser, supported by at least two witnesses), denunciation (a less formal process involving anonymous or unwritten reports), or inquisition. The inquisitorial process, which from the 1410s English churchmen envisioned as a regular feature of ecclesiastical life, involved the selection of six to eight "trustworthy men" from each parish who were expected to inform church authorities of any heterodox beliefs or suspicious practices on the part of their fellow parishioners. Over time, inquisition became the usual process for the identification of heresy defendants, though given the existence of stereotypes about the institutional inquisition of early modern Spain, it is helpful to stress that inquisition in our period was a *procedure* rather than an *organization*. As Ian Forrest has explained, heresy investigations in England were carried out by bishops and religious officials playing the role of inquisitors, not by an independent cadre of clergy standing outside the usual diocesan structures.[97]

The dominant role that bishops played in the inquisitorial process can go a long way toward explaining why the frequency and intensity of investigations varied so substantially by time and place. On the one hand, external events such as the convocation of the Fifth Lateran Council and the English government's desire to be seen as an active force in the fight against heresy, or on the other hand, the personal disposition of a particular bishop might serve as a spur to a series of heresy trials. Other events, such as the outbreak of the Wars of the Roses, might divert bishops' attention elsewhere. During the period from Wyclif's exile through the English Reformation, a number of bishops initiated large-scale heresy investigations. Others allowed years or decades to elapse between heresy trials, prosecuting cases only in response to external stimuli.

However brought to trial, the accused would be presented with a list of the charges against them, along with a crucial choice: should they admit that they had taught or done certain erroneous things; should they deny the charges; or should they admit that the charges were true yet maintain that they firmly believed in what they had said or done? As we have already noted, in theological terms the crime of heresy did not involve merely the existence of heterodox belief. Rather, to quote fourteenth-century Archbishop Robert Grosseteste, it entailed "an opinion chosen by human perception contrary to Holy Scripture, publicly avowed and obstinately defended."[98] The moment at which defendants are presented with the choice to abjure the erroneous teachings or practices in which they had been involved is also the moment at which, formally speaking, they can most clearly commit the crime of heresy.

For defendants who chose to abjure, the usual procedure was for them to list and forswear their erroneous teachings publicly, using a formula prepared for them (and sometimes even read aloud for them) by court officials. This formal abjuration was then entered into the record of the trial. The bishop or other presiding official would then restore the defendants to good standing (*bona fama*) with the church, oftentimes on condition that they complete some sort of penance.[99] Bishops had a variety of possible penances at their disposal, ranging from public acts of penitence in suspects' home parishes to restrictions on their liberty or temporary or permanent incarceration.[100] It was not uncommon for heretics who had admitted their crime to be required to carry some marker of the event either on their clothes or on their bodies; some bishops mandated that abjured heretics sew a badge depicting burning wood onto their clothes, while at least one other bishop ordered the abjured to be branded with the letter *H*.[101] These markers were especially significant for the future, since if an individual who had abjured heresy was later found to have again disseminated erroneous teachings, the penalty for relapse was death at the stake.

If, on the other hand, a defendant chose to contest the charges, he or she was normally required to produce a certain number of witnesses, called compurgators (literally, "fellow-purgers"). These witnesses were local residents of good character, ideally of high standing in the church and civil society, who would testify to the moral character of the defendant and put their own reputations behind the person's innocence. If a sufficient number of these witnesses came forward, the case against the defendant could be dismissed.

Most heresy trials in late medieval England ended with the abjuration of the defendant or the appearance of enough compurgators to restore the defendant's *bona fama*. Nevertheless, the stake cast its shadow across all heresy proceedings, even those that did not end in the condemnation of the suspect. Heresy defendants were sentenced to death for two reasons: relapse into heresy, in the case of those who had previously abjured but were found to have again propounded heterodox ideas; and obstinacy, in the case of those who on their first appearance refused to change their beliefs when confronted with the authoritative teachings of the church. In either case the presiding official would, in the language of the records, relinquish the defendant to the secular arm for execution. Canon law provided that no cleric should shed blood, so death sentences against relapsed or obstinate heretics were carried out by officials of the crown rather than the church.

Abjuration, compurgation, and execution were the three most common outcomes of late medieval heresy trials. But how have the records of these proceedings come down to us? In most ecclesiastical courts, a scribe or registrar would be present for each stage of the proceedings and would be responsible for entering into the court's records the facts of the case. The records available to historians today often include information on the charges against the defendant, the defendant's replies to those charges, the statements of witnesses, the verdict of the court, the names of the presiding official and his assistants, and the date and location of the trials. Many records include, in the first person, what purport to be verbatim abjurations by defendants and verbatim sentences by their judges.

Yet these records are not as transparent as at first they might seem. The critiques that historians and others have recently leveled at trial records are as numerous as they are diverse, ranging from the application of Michel Foucault's theories about confession and the unequal power dynamics between the accused and the accuser, to more traditional, textual arguments about the process by which the original records of heresy proceedings were compiled into official documents such as bishops' registers, perhaps being condensed, abbreviated, or made more scandalous along the way.[102] In England the situation is made more complicated by the fact that many records of heresy trials are no longer extant in their original forms, so their contents are available to scholars only through the work of Reformation-era propagandists like John Foxe, with his agenda to narrate English religious history as the scene of an ongoing conflict between Christ and antichrist. Foxe was not averse to removing from his history mention of the most outlandish beliefs that late medieval heresy suspects were accused of holding; to include these ideas would have made medieval dissenters look like something other than early evangelicals in the making.[103]

Thus, the proceedings of heresy trials, preserved primarily in bishops' registers but also in dedicated court-books and the records of consistory and archidiaconal courts, are to be approached with caution. Scholars have argued, first, that the procedures that governed the trial and sentencing of heresy defendants tended to oversimplify their views. As early as the 1420s, Archbishop Henry Chichele commissioned his theologians and canon lawyers to produce a questionnaire to be administered to heresy suspects; similar to the questionnaires employed against heresy defendants on the continent, this document listed dozens of beliefs that heretics were thought to hold and about which inquisitors should ask suspects. Other bishops, including Thomas Polton of Worcester, Thomas Bekynton of Bath and Wells, and William Aiscough of Salisbury, also employed questionnaires, as did many of their sixteenth-century counterparts.[104] The widespread use of questionnaires not only limited the range of topics that an inquisitor might explore with a defendant, but they also made it more likely that defendants who abjured heterodox ideas did so in consistent language. The repetition of many articles in surviving abjurations (including the abjurations from Winchester diocese printed in this volume) suggests that the preconceptions of inquisitors and the convenience of formulaic statements of faith shaped the manner in which defendants' beliefs were recorded for posterity.

Second, even if a trial included an unusually free-ranging dialogue between defendant and inquisitor, the records extant today are often at a remove of several degrees from the original event. The scribe recording a particular proceeding would often have transformed a defendant's English words into a series of formal Latin articles and then later would have used those articles to compose an abjuration in the vernacular for the defendant to sign. The linguistic difference alone, notwithstanding the defendant's and registrar's different levels of education and theological knowledge, was sure to have garbled some ideas. In addition, the bishops' registers and heresy court-books available to historians are not always the original records of the trials they document; a scribe's notes would often have been recopied into a more elegant form, possibly resulting in a summary rather than a verbatim transcript of the original material.[105]

Last, and perhaps most important for the history of spirituality as opposed to doctrine, there is no way for historians to go behind the adversarial nature of the inquisitorial process; no way to determine how a particular suspect would have articulated himself or herself if the person were preaching to co-religionists rather than facing a tribunal of ecclesiastical officials. Just as Rowan Williams has shown in his study of fourth- and fifth-century "Arian" beliefs, the frequency with which particular topics appear in the records of church authorities does not necessarily correlate with the importance those topics held for the individuals who spoke about them.[106] Especially when defendants' spiritual and devotional practices were not controversial in and of themselves, why would their explanation of them have been significant enough to appear in the distilled account of their trials preserved in a bishop's register?

This account of the records of late medieval heresy trials is a pessimistic one, and indeed, there are many reasons to wonder how it is possible to use heresy proceedings as evidence for the spirituality of religious dissenters. But the limitations of the records, while real, have often been exaggerated.[107]

In 1428, Bishop William Alnwick of Norwich tried the first of between eighty and 120 suspects to appear before him over the four-year period through 1431. The proceedings of these trials appear in a court-book now preserved in the archives of the Roman Catholic Archdiocese of Westminster, containing copies of the original minutes of the trials, which were likely taken down by Alnwick's registrar, John Exeter. In the trial of the defendant William Masse of Earsham, the reader discovers something of an anomaly—the scribe has crossed out one of the eight articles Masse was accused of believing.[108] It is not unfair to assume that the article, which accused Masse of denying the doctrine of transubstantiation, had been included in the original record mistakenly. Perhaps as a result of the stereotyping effects of inquisitorial questionnaires, at least thirty-four other defendants who appeared before Alnwick had been charged with the same heresy. It is harder, however, to explain why the scribe erased it. If medieval inquisitors were as keen to stereotype heresy defendants as some critics have suggested, then Exeter would have had no reason to regret, much less to correct, his error. There was little propaganda value in ensuring that the record of Masse's trial was accurate; the court-book was prepared only for the internal use of the bishop and his colleagues. And from a legal point of view, the specific heresies that Masse had abjured were irrelevant; if he had been tried again at some later date, then conviction of any heresy would have constituted relapse. The most likely explanation, therefore, is that Exeter was a conscientious scribe and was genuinely concerned for the accuracy of his record.

With a critical eye, readers can find in records like Exeter's fleeting glimpses into what was actually said in the ecclesiastical courtrooms of the Later Middle Ages. For instance, one of the curious features of the Norwich court-book is the way in which it breaks down the boundaries between Latin and vernacular discourse. In recording the trial of John Burell, Exeter notes that the defendant

> dicit…quod quidam sutor, famulus Thome Mone, docuit …quod nullus homo tenetur ieiunare diebus Quadragesimalibus nec sextis feriis nec vigiliis apostolorum, quia talia ieiunia nunquam erant instituta ex precepto divino sed tantum ex ordinacione presbiterorum, for every Fryday is fre day.[109]

said that a certain shoemaker, a servant of Thomas Mone, taught that no man is obligated to fast on the days of Lent, or on Fridays or the vigils of the apostles, for no fast was instituted by divine command, but rather by the commandment of the priests, for every Friday is a free day.

It should stand out that in the original record, Exeter slides without comment from the formal Latin of his notarial voice into vernacular speech, recording Burell's pun on the word Friday. We will never know why Exeter chose to use Middle English at this precise moment, but the evidentiary value of interjections such as this is significant. In other dioceses as well, many defendants' words are preserved not in their abjurations, which, as we have seen, ecclesiastical officials usually prepared for them, but instead in the surviving depositions of witnesses. Thus, the Coventry tailor Roger Landesdale's vernacular explication of the Eucharist as a memorial of Jesus' death appears in the testimony of his fellow suspect Thomas Abell. The dissenters' passwords ("May we all drink of a cup" and "God keep you and God bless you"), by which they identified themselves to one another, were disclosed in Landesdale's own testimony.[110] Taken together, considerations such as these suggest that while the lists of beliefs preserved in defendants' abjurations and witnesses' depositions are incomplete, they are nonetheless not usually fabricated.

NOTES ON THE TRANSLATIONS

In the Wycliffite writings in this volume, quotations from the Bible are presented in italics so that readers may easily distinguish explanations of the meaning interpolated into the quotation from the biblical text itself. Only when they are presented in the text as the words of a speaker are biblical and other quotations, together with any interpolations they contain, placed within double quotation marks. In most cases the Latin version of the bible used by our authors seems to have been close to that of the Vulgate, though on occasion there are important differences. In developing our biblical translations we have therefore consulted the Vulgate's early modern translation into English, the Douay-Rheims Bible as revised in the eighteenth century by Challoner. We modernize this version at our discretion, and modify its content to align it more closely with the biblical text quoted by our authors when necessary.

A number of words that readers normally see capitalized appear here in lowercase. The most noticeable may be *lollard* and *protestant*. With regard to *lollard*, there are multiple reasons for this, but the most important is that moving from *Lollard* as proper noun to *lollard* as adjective represents an important de-essentialization of lollardy as a religious movement. Capital-L *Lollardy* has suggested to many readers an organized, almost denominational alternative to mainstream Christianity in late medieval England. However, recent research on lollardy, to which we hope this volume will be a contribution, has emphasized the ways in which the notion of a single, consistent *Lollard* identity was constructed by church leaders as well as officials of the Crown, and perpetuated by later protestant historiographers. At the same time, *lollard* functioned, both in England and on the European continent in places like the modern-day Netherlands, as a generalized term of insult and disapprobation. But *lollard* also functioned as a highly flexible means of questioning the terms of that disapprobation when it was applied to those who were called Lollards, a technique used both by writings that share the characteristics we associate with Wycliffism and by mainstream writers worried by this increasing tendency. What is more, *lollard* was a term of self-definition employed in some Wycliffite writings. We feel that it is important to register this variable and contested usage by emphasizing the word's adjectival status.

Likewise, although the practice of writing *Protestant* with a capital P has been usual for many years, recent developments in the study of early modern religion, history, and literature have suggested that at least in the early to mid-sixteenth century, the term was not thought of as a discrete category (members of the Protestant churches, as we might say today) so much as it was a descriptor of certain ways of living, believing, and praying, in contrast to "traditional religion" (that is, what we would know today as Roman Catholicism). In this regard, *Protestant* has been treated very much in the same way as *Lollard* has—what was originally an adjective has been turned into a category, with all the potential for misunderstanding that comes with that transition. In addition to this, scholars of early modern

England have pointed to evidence that the word *p/Protestant* was not even commonly used to denote people we would think of as Protestants until well into the reign of Elizabeth I. Thus, during the periods we are discussing in this volume (say, the early sixteenth century), *Protestant* with all that the capital P implies is anachronistic. We therefore use *protestant* or, in some cases, *evangelical*, a word the earliest English "protestants" used for themselves.

Finally, a comment about gendered language is necessary. Every "man or woman" in our modernizations is there in the original. We have not imposed gender-neutral language, but where our texts do mention women, we have retained the mention, and we think it is very important to do so. Where the texts mention women, they typically then subsume them into a masculine pronoun. The resulting clash between subject and pronoun, even though it is not consonant with modern usage, is a manifestation of the texts' struggle with inclusiveness.

Part I: Wyclif

The selections from Wyclif's writings included in Part I have been newly translated from Wyclif's Latin. All translations of Wyclif's own sources are Lahey's, although consultation of other translations of these sources, where available, are acknowledged in the notes. Every effort has been made to simplify Wyclif's syntax and sentence structure, and the reader is encouraged to consult the ample explanatory notes. In translating Wyclif's references to the various biblical discussions of love, "love" will be used for the nouns *caritas, amor,* and the verbs *diligo, diligere* and *amo, amare*, except in cases where "charity" in the modern sense is a better fit. However, it is important to realize that for Wyclif and his contemporaries, "charity" in either Latin or English was a near-synonym for *amor* or "love." In addition we have followed the common practice, in modern translations of medieval theological writings, of leaving the Latin term *viator*, meaning "traveler," untranslated; it refers to any person living life in this world.

INTRODUCTION

Part II: English Wycliffite Writings

The selections from Wycliffite writings in Part II are modernized from Middle English; their sources are detailed in the Notes. Some of these items are well known, and of these about half have been available in print since the nineteenth century, though in many cases a number of additional manuscripts have been discovered since they were first printed. We have used the printed versions of these texts but have compared them with their manuscript witnesses, both those known and those unknown to their early editors. Only major textual issues are identified in the notes. More recently edited texts have similarly been checked against their manuscript witnesses. Nearly half of the items included here are unprinted and are presently known only to a handful of scholars. One of these appears in a thesis edition not yet published: we are grateful to Judith Jefferson for allowing us to consult and work from her dissertation. The others have been transcribed and edited from their original manuscripts, then subsequently modernized. Acknowledgments of scholars who have brought texts to our attention, and in some cases shared their transcriptions with us, appear in the Notes.

In some of the original versions of these texts, some or all quotations from the bible or from recognized authorities are quoted in Latin. Since our translation of them smooths away the language difference, all Latin quotations are pointed out in the notes. In most cases when Wycliffite works in English quote Latin, they also provide a full translation, or even a fuller translation where only the opening of the Latin quotation is provided. The translation is not always exact: its differences from the Latin previously quoted are often important. For this reason we always include both our translation of the Latin and our modernization of the Middle English author's translation, even where this entails some repetition.

Several of the selections here are written in highly crafted prose containing stylistically heightened passages that are heavily alliterative, rife with rhetorical devices, and highly metrical. We have made some effort to retain some of these stylistic features, where doing so does not impede clarity.

Part III: Heresy Trials

The translations from the Norwich court-book (Godesell, Baxter, Kynget) have been made from the published Latin editions of those texts. Where the text contains vernacular material as well as Latin, transitions from one language to the other are indicated in the text or the notes.

The proceedings of the Winchester trials have been transcribed from the manuscript records of those trials preserved in the register of Bishop Fox and translated; where the more formulaic parts of the records have been excerpted to avoid repetition, this is indicated in the text.

NOTE ON CONTRIBUTIONS

The contributors are listed in alphabetical order on the cover. The division of responsibility was as follows:

J. Patrick Hornbeck II: Introduction, Part 2, subsection "Wycliffite Spirituality in Heresy Trials"; and all of section 3, "Records of Heresy Trials." "Notes on the Translations" discussion of translating Part III, with contributions to the discussion of translating Part II. In Part II, "English Wycliffite Writings," headnotes, translation, and annotation of *The Two Ways, On Holy Prayers, Of Wedded Men and Wives*, and *The Sermon of Dead Men (Selections)*, along with translation and annotation of *The Our Father*. Part III: "Heresy Trials," all translation and annotation.

Stephen E. Lahey: Introduction, Part 3, section 1, "John Wyclif: Spiritual and Devotional Guide?" Part I: Wyclif, all headnotes excepting *On Love*; translation and annotation of all texts.

Fiona Somerset: Introduction, Part 1, Part 2 all subsections but the final one, Part 3 section 1, entry on *On Love*, Part 3 section 2, Wycliffite Writings, and entries on Notes on the Translations except for the discussion of translating part III. Part I: headnote on *On Love*. Part II: Wycliffite Writings, headnotes, modernization, and annotation of *A Short Rule of Life, Five Questions on Love, The Ten Commandments (Selections), Sermon 57, Commentary on Psalm 87, The Seven Works of Mercy, A Form of Confession, A*

INTRODUCTION

Dialogue between a Wise Man and A Fool, A Commendation of Holy Writ, The Lantern of Light (Selections), The City of Saints, A Dialogue between Jon and Richard (Selections), and *Sermons from Sidney Sussex 74 (Selections),* in addition to headnote on *The Our Father.*

Suggestions for Further Reading

For more comprehensive guidance, see the bibliographies for the study of Wyclif, Wycliffism, and lollardy available online at www.lollardsociety.org and in Ian Christopher Levy, ed., *A Companion to John Wyclif: Late Medieval Theologian* (Leiden: Brill, 2006), 463–70.

PRIMARY SOURCES

Arnold, Thomas. *Select English Works of John Wyclif*. Vol. 3. Oxford: Clarendon Press, 1871.

Cigman, Gloria, ed. *Lollard Sermons*. Early English Text Society 294. Oxford: Oxford University Press, 1989.

Dove, Mary, ed. *The Earliest Advocates of the English Bible: The Texts of the Medieval Debate*. Exeter: Exeter University Press, 2010.

Hudson, Anne, ed. *Selections from English Wycliffite Writings*. Cambridge: Cambridge University Press, 1978.

———. *Two Wycliffite Texts*. Early English Text Society 301. Oxford: Oxford University Press, 1993.

———. *The Works of a Lollard Preacher*, Early English Text Society 317. Oxford: Oxford University Press, 2001.

Hudson, Anne, and Pamela Gradon, eds. *English Wycliffite Sermons*. Oxford: Clarendon Press, 1983–98.

Matthew, F. D., ed. *The English Works of Wyclif Hitherto Unprinted*. Early English Text Society 74. 2nd ed. London: Trübner, 1880.

McSheffrey, Shannon, and Norman P. Tanner, eds. *Lollards of Coventry, 1486–1522*. Camden Society Fifth Series 23. Cambridge: Cambridge University Press, 2003.

Somerset, Fiona, ed. *Four Wycliffite Dialogues.* Early English Text Society 333. Oxford: Oxford University Press, 2010.

Tanner, Norman P., ed. *Heresy Trials in the Diocese of Norwich, 1428–31.* London: Royal Historical Society, 1978.

Von Nolcken, Christina, ed. *The Middle English Translation of the Rosarium Theologie.* Heidelberg: Carl Winter, 1979.

SECONDARY SOURCES

Aston, Margaret. *England's Iconoclasts.* Oxford: Clarendon Press, 1988.

———. *Lollards and Reformers.* London: The Hambledon Press, 1985.

Aston, Margaret, and Colin Richmond, eds. *Lollardy and the Gentry in the Later Middle Ages.* New York: St. Martin's Press, 1997.

Barr, Helen, and Ann M. Hutchison, eds. *Text and Controversy from Wyclif to Bale: Essays in Honor of Anne Hudson.* Turnhout: Brepols, 2005.

Bose, Mishtooni, and J. Patrick Hornbeck II, eds. *Wycliffite Controversies.* Turnhout: Brepols, 2011.

Cole, Andrew. *Literature and Heresy in the Age of Chaucer.* Cambridge: Cambridge University Press, 2008.

Dove, Mary. *The First English Bible: The Text and Context of the Wycliffite Versions.* Cambridge: Cambridge University Press, 2007.

Forrest, Ian. *The Detection of Heresy in Late Medieval England.* Oxford: Clarendon Press, 2005.

Ghosh, Kantik. *The Wycliffite Heresy: Authority and the Interpretation of Texts.* Cambridge: Cambridge University Press, 2002.

Hornbeck, J. Patrick, II. *What Is a Lollard? Dissent and Belief in Late Medieval England.* Oxford: Oxford University Press, 2010.

Hudson, Anne. *Lollards and Their Books.* London: Hambledon Press, 1985.

———. *The Premature Reformation: Wycliffite Texts and Lollard History.* Oxford: Clarendon Press, 1988.

Jurkowski, Maureen. "Lollardy and Social Status in East Anglia." *Speculum* 82 (2007): 120–52.

Lahey, Stephen E. *John Wyclif*. Oxford: Oxford University Press, 2009.

Lambert, Malcolm. *Medieval Heresy: Popular Movements from the Gregorian Reform to the Reformation*, 3rd ed. Oxford: Blackwell, 2002.

Levy, Ian Christopher. *John Wyclif: Scriptural Logic, Real Presence, and the Parameters of Orthodoxy*. Milwaukee: Marquette University Press, 2003.

———. "Grace and Freedom in the Soteriology of John Wyclif." *Traditio* 60 (2005): 279–33.

Lutton, Robert. *Lollardy and Orthodox Religion*. Rochester, NY: Boydell and Brewer, 2006.

McSheffrey, Shannon. *Gender and Heresy: Women and Men in Lollard Communities 1420–1530*. Philadelphia: University of Pennsylvania Press, 1995.

———. "Heresy, Orthodoxy, and English Vernacular Religion 1480–1525." *Past and Present* 186 (2005): 47–80.

Somerset, Fiona, Jill C. Havens, and Derrick G. Pitard, eds. *Lollards and Their Influence in Late Medieval England*. Rochester, NY: Boydell Press, 2003.

Thomson, J. A. F. *The Later Lollards, 1414–1520*. Oxford: Oxford University Press, 1965.

PART I

Wyclif

1. Sermon 29[1]

This sermon, for the feast day of an apostle, is from the large collection of Wyclif's Latin sermons compiled during his years in Lutterworth. This collection of 120 sermons on gospel readings and 58 on epistolary readings was edited and published in three of the four volumes of Wyclif's sermons by the Wyclif Society in 1887. Wyclif described his aim in formulating this collection of sermons for the people, "so that the things they might recognize in the right teaching of Christ be better known, and the things by which they might slide away from the truth be avoided." Two themes stand out in this sermon. First, Wyclif's habitual painstaking care with how terms in sentences refer, and his attention to philosophical distinctions regarding the subject, the object, and the species of love, are typical of his Latin sermons. His comment at the end regarding the need for preachers to adapt these ideas for their audiences shows that he is aware of the subtleties the sermon contains. Second, there are references to civil relationships of lordship and fealty and to property ownership that point to Wyclif's extensive analysis of human lordship and justice in his political works, such as *De Civili Dominio*. He assumes that his readers are to some extent familiar with his political thought in constructing analogies between human and divine lordship, analogies that may be understood as referring to his politically charged ideology.

John 15:12

"This is my commandment, that you love one another as I have loved you."

Because the purpose of this commandment is love, and Christians have taken both Christ and his apostles as exemplars for this love, this gospel teaches how the rule of love should be obeyed. The realization of this love is obedience to the whole of the decalogue. Thus Gregory says, "That just as a branch grows out of a trunk, so all the other virtues grow from love." So, in 1 Timothy 1[:5], "The purpose of this commandment is love." Because Christ wanted to lead the apostles to the satisfaction and consolation of the faith, he places great emphasis on love of one's neighbor, which involves the love of God, and that love by which Christ loved us is the perfect exemplar, from which we see that the highest love is giving one's soul for one's friends. So the evangelist says, "This is my commandment, that you love one another as I have loved you; greater love no one has than to give one's soul for one's friends" (John 15:12–13).

And there are three degrees of love: the first is that by which the Father loves the humanity of the Son. Since this love is eternal, it is fitting that one would have another, closer example coming from Christ's humanity, by which love Christ loved the apostles and those who were close to him. The third love is that by which the apostles and apostolic men rightly and justly love their sheep. The greatest love a creature can experience is that with which Christ gave his soul for his friends.

Because of this, some think that there are six degrees of things to be loved. God is the highest, the self is next, one's spirit is third, one's neighbors are fourth, one's body is fifth, and other bodies are sixth. These degrees are not indivisible, for inasmuch as a body is better, it is worthy of more love. But by understanding the soul as the animation of the body of which it is the life, it is clear that it is reasonable and just, albeit difficult, to give one's soul for one's friends. This is because a friend is equally good in nature as someone else, and is greater than one's own body, and so should be loved more than a soul or one's corporeal life. It is certainly just to put one's soul in the place of a friend, and since a friend and an enemy are said of varying people, it is clear that any other man is a friend. Even Christ asked Judas, "Friend, why have you come?" (Matt 26:50). Christ gave his soul for his friends and enemies, for every man, however much evil might benefit him by accident. For those who first were enemies and then were friends, he gave his soul that they be saved, and (as it pleases some) he gave his soul for all the damned, that their condemnation be milder.[2]

But there are many doubts that crop up. First, how can every man love God more than himself? The answer seems to be that he cannot, because man himself causes all human love, so he ought to hold it to himself rather than in God. This is borne out by the fact that nobody loves God unless it is good for him, and if God were not

64

good for him, there would be no love for God. The reason why a man loves God is because God is good for him, and since the purpose of all of this, in the end, is to be human, self-love is what motivates a man to love God. And since according to philosophers the principle by which anything is, is greater in itself, so it appears that because of the goodness of his act of loving God, man himself is more worthy of love. When the parent loves the nurse because of the child, the child is loved all the more.

God should be loved above all men, even above the self. The reasoning of this argument should be denied, because while man himself causes human love naturally, efficiently, and to an extent, finally, yet it is caused first and more efficiently by God, who is the final end of every creature. Thus, human love should principally be directed to God, since there would be no such thing as love unless it were an instrumental means and a partial end for a man's love of God. As proof of this, the assumption in the argument above is false. [The assumption was that] just as a man should acknowledge God because God is good, so he should love God for the same reason. And since the good exists prior to being good for something, he should first love himself, not only because he is good for himself, but because his being is good. So it is certain that the human love of God will not be used up before it had been absorbed by any love suitable for a creature, in the same way as the blessed love God in heaven, because he is good in himself, and not because he is good to them or to other creatures. Yet it is clear in this argument that no one ought to love God unless it were good for him. Otherwise, if God were not good for him, it would be a contradiction for him to be a man or some other creature. If something is good, it is the same as its being, and this good is either God or comes from God, since God is the first good. So for every creature, insofar as it exists, it is a good from God and thus God is its good. God has a prior reason of goodness by which he is simply good, and the good in himself. So the philosophers hold that God is, in himself, infinitely better than he is for me.

Second, one might doubt how a man loving his neighbor follows from his love for God, because any human love should take the love of the Lord as its exemplar. God loves things insofar as they are good, and since man is not best after God, it appears that he should not be loved after the primary love of God. Whoever warps his will away from the divine will in this way appears to sin as gravely as Lucifer did.

Again, it appears that the spirit of man is not third in the order of loving, since every man is a "wind that goes and does not return" (Ps 78:39), and so every man should love his spirit as much as he loves himself, because they are the same.

Again, it appears that a man should love himself more because he is a spirit than because he is a man, because in so doing he is more like an angel, more in conformity with the good, and so better and more worthy of love.

Here we need to make a distinction about love: some is absolute, and some is properly relative. There is no absolute love unless there is a willing of the good that is loved, and thus every man should love God infinitely more than himself. I say infinitely more, and not infinite in intensity or with an infinite love, since no creature can love infinitely, but the majority of loving should be measured by goodness in willing so that, just as I ought to will God to be infinitely greater than myself, so I should love him proportionately that much more. And so logicians agree that I ought to love God as much as he loves himself, not in regards to my act [of loving], but in regards the good willing [behind it]. And so in speaking of love more simply, I should love any creature insofar as it is good, as [I should love] the blessed in heaven more than myself because I know that God loves them the more; and as I pray to God, "your will be done," so should I desire and love that the will of God be realized. This approach makes one truly humble.

But there is another reason of loving, which is relatively appropriate to the order by which it is caused. Because any love of man has man as its origin and is caused time and again by him and not by any other creature, so according to this reason of relative propriety a man should love himself all the more, even though in the [absolute] order of loving described above, he should love the greater good. But God himself ordains this loving before I myself do, though it is not directed to some other creature. I ought to love any creature according to two reasons, namely, according to the reason by which any creature is good in itself or according to the reason by which any creature is good for me or likely to lead to my own perfection. And by this reasoning, I surpass any other creature [in being good for myself].

Because of this, the response to the first argument is that it is well reasoned that man should not love himself first after loving God. This is how some understand Moses to have loved his people more than himself, "Either forgive them this trespass, or if you do not, strike me out of the book that you have written" (Exod 32:31–32). So it can be said that the loving of God exemplifies both of these loves in man: the first most generally, and the second more specifically. God loves himself first and commands that human love be caused according to such a priority of ordering. It would be easier just to admit that a man ought to love what is more proportionately lovable as it is good, and since equivocally there is no contradiction here, and since these loves are equivocal, it is not contradictory that a man loves himself more than the blessed, and yet loves the blessed more than himself.

Regarding the second, the love by which a man loves his spirit and the love by which he loves himself are not enumerated according to some sort of diversity of objects because the object is the same thing. To say otherwise would be to think that there is a difference between a man loving himself as a whole human being and loving himself as a complete spirit. This is like the case in which Porphyry says that Socrates in the theater is a different Socrates from Socrates in the forum. Hence, the highest degree by which a man can love himself would be the reason by which he loves himself as blessed. This is why the damned are said to hate themselves most and love themselves least, since they will that which is the least good for themselves.

Regarding the third, it is false to assume that a man, a composite of body and soul, is more like an angel in perfection and fully blessed in whatever way, whether he is a spirit conjoined to a body, or a spirit separated from a body. For if this similitude were real, since God is simply more perfect than a creature, then a soul and others like it lacking mass, taken together, would be much more perfect than any body of the world. God forbid! A man, Jesus Christ, is more primary to us and to the angels. Insofar as we are similar to him, we are more perfect; however, he is more perfect than any created spirit.

This is why Augustine says that, in choosing whether to adopt humanity or angel, Christ chose to be a man. If this body were imperfect in itself and could in no way be perfected, God would not have gone on to perfect man to a full beatitude of the soul joined with a body, nor would blessed souls affect the bodies they rejoin. It would be a work of evil, and not of nature, for God to have composed man of body and soul. Just as the body of the blessed has an appropriate, finite beatitude, so God himself could make a blessed man imperfect in the same beatified body, or in a part, by taking a piece and leaving the rest. The corrupt body in this life bespeaks the imperfect virtue of man, but while reason says that there is a more perfect soul in this clay vessel, man would not be imperfect in this life unless he did not have as much body as soul as he has in the composite of them.

A third doubt is how the body and the soul are equally worthy of love, since the human soul is more perfect than the body in its nature. Just as a man loves his soul more than a neighbor, or his body, a good God would not command or warn man to be willing to destroy his body on behalf of his neighbor, because this would be a change from the better to the worse that would make the devil laugh.

Philosophers and theologians wallow helplessly in equivocation here. The soul is often taken as an abstraction for the animation by which a natural, organic body is in act. Averroes says, as do others, that the human soul is corruptible along with the body, like the souls of beasts and their own animation. Since it is necessary that the body return at the resurrection, a man should give himself for his neighbor—indeed, as the gospels say, he should hate himself, that is, hate the actuation of the body according to the vital reasons of living that impede him as punishment. Those who live luxuriously according to bestial desires love their souls, but these are the people who love their animation more than they love God. It is fitting that a man hate himself, that is, he should make light of or dampen this affection because of love of God. One who does not hate the soul in this manner does not live in love, hope, or faith.

But in another sense, the soul is taken concretely, or personally, for the person that it animates, and by giving animation to the body, this same soul—that is, the person animated—is perfected and preserved for sanctification. This is the sense it seems Averroes had in mind by holding the same soul to be the whole man, not because it is the person of any particular man or a part of him. Instead, it is one spirit joined with the whole of the corruptible [sublunar] sphere and is differentiated according to the disposition of the human power of thought in the way it arranges an appropriate and mortal soul to be joined with an individual man. This is why one man understands more than others do.[3] The faithful hold that the soul is not joined to a lesser understanding, but to the highest Spirit, which will satisfy and illuminate it when it enters in, and gives the soul spiritual gifts.

The error among the philosophers regarding the immortality of the soul rests partially in their equivocation and partly in their hesitation to believe in the resurrection. They do not know the person of a man, that it is the immortal spirit joined to a body in time for a determined period, during which it looks to heaven, and after this brief period, it remains either in beatitude or punishment. And in the last judgment it is reunited with the corporeal atoms, wherever they had been dispersed, and this union of spirit with body is an indissoluble union; according to its desert this same, perpetual person is beatified or punished.

Bearing this equivocation in mind, it is clear that a man loving his own animation, that is, that he is animated in a body, is the same as his loving that this body is his body. The identity of the spirit is not corporeal unless it enters into the body. So this man who loves that a body is his body for a brief time faithlessly loves ownership, instead of loving the fact that his or his neighbor's soul might be saved for all time. And many of the faithless love this ownership when they seek the goods of fortune at the expense of their abbey or their sect, instead of living with other followers of Christ according to his established law.

Regarding the first doubt [that is, how can every man love God more than himself?] this is a natural instinct, but to the second [how a man can love a neighbor as himself] something is simply a satanic instinct, so that the Apostle calls greed "a serving of idols" (Eph 5:5). Observing God's commandments leads one to love of God and of neighbor at the same time, so that the Truth says, "You are my friends if you do the things I command you" (John 15:14). Those who have their souls taken up with obeying the commandments have realized Christ's way of life. And a friendship is taken up now according to simple benevolence (as is clear of Judas in John 18) on both sides.[4] According to Aristotle, friendship is a mutual benevolence extended into the present unconcealed, so it is clear that this friendship is not complete until it is in heaven.[5] This will be seen in every word, act, and *habitus* of good men, but of necessity many secretly ignored it in this life. Christ reveals the greater familiarity to be enjoyed in heaven, "I will not now call you servants, for the servant knows not what his lord does" (John 15:15).

One might well be astounded about this, because according to philosophers friendship is between equals or near equals, but here it is between Christ and his apostles. The simple response is that humanity is in its nature equal. It is a near equality, insofar as grace is concerned, since Christ says to them that whatever they ought to have done at his request is different from servitude. But a doubt can arise: the apostles as a rule called themselves servants of the Lord, and Christ saying particular truths beforehand says that he would not speak to them as servants. This problem is addressed in a distinction about servitude. Contractual servitude is that in which someone serves his lord in fear and not in brotherhood. While this is how things are in human affairs, it is also how things are with the damned and with people weighed down under the burden of guilt. Ministerial servitude is when someone is subject to his lord with a brotherly respect, freely doing his lord's will; this is how the apostles conceived of themselves as servants of the Lord.

Since Christ revealed his desire as well as his reasoning to his apostles, it is clear that they are above the lowly contraction of servitude and are friends. "I have called you friends because all things, whatsoever I have heard of my Father, I have made known to you" (John 15:15). Although Christ himself heard from the Father, since he is all in all, by knowing himself he taught them individual truths in a particular manner; by expressing hidden truths formally in their reasons, and by treating the apostles as his dearest disciples, he showed how they are not servants. And by explaining that this friendship does not remove them from subjection, and does not detract from the divinity of the Lord, he joins with them. "You have not chosen me, but I have chosen you" (John 15:16). For in human affairs, subjects choose their king through the hands of their ministers, but it was otherwise for the apostles regarding Christ. For "he was born into this," as said in John 18, and was master and Lord before the apostles were born. They literally did not choose Christ, but he chose them. Nor are they included because of this in a contractual servility for ministry, since he chose them for this duty, and they went into the world preaching the gospel and bearing its fruit for the conversion of the people and for their merit, and this fruit stays with them in heaven. Since, for the apostles, "whatever they will ask of the Father, he will give to them," as Christ's words affirm, it is clear that they are kept out of the burden of contractual servitude. Servants immediately would seek freedom, just as the apostles have done in the Lord's prayer. In concession to this, Christ removes them from this sort of servitude.

This sermon should be adapted for the people, adding to what has been said here, as is suitable.

2. The Six Yokes[6]

Wyclif's 245 sermons fill four volumes. These are in Latin and were intended for an academic audience. Wyclif may have intended that they serve as a resource for preachers who would follow him, and the Wyclif Society edition reproduces the order into which Wyclif seems to have collected them. One clue indicating that this collection was intended to be a resource for Wycliffite preachers is the small treatise *De Sex Iugiis*. This began as a standalone treatise but was divided up and incorporated into five Latin sermons: numbers 27 (Matt 5:1), 28 (Matt 4:18), 31 (Matt 10:16), 32 (Luke 10:1), and 33 (John 12:24). This "treatise" runs through these five sermons and also was collected in four manuscripts edited by Gotthard Lechler in 1854. The readily remembered six pairs of human relationships that Wyclif describes as drawing Christ's plow might easily have provided the grist for extemporaneous Wycliffite preaching to farmers and townspeople alike. References to antichrist throughout this section are not to any one individual, group, or to the papacy in particular, but to any force of the world working against the church militant. In other works, Wyclif readily identifies individual popes and other prelates with antichrist, as well as whole groups of people, most notably, the mendicant friars.

[27] So that the simple priests with zealous souls may have material for preaching, there are six yokes that draw Christ's plow

along in our age.[7] The first is between Christ and the simple, faithful viators, the second is between spouses joined together by the law of the Lord, the third is between the parent and the natural child, the fourth is between the master of the house and his bondsmen and servants, the fifth is between the secular lord and his subjects or tenants, and the sixth is generally between those who are neighbors. The dove of the church should choose and sing a song of love and peace for all of these. Since these yokes can be grounded in scripture by their lightness and sweetness, evangelists animated by God ought to preach this with zest and strength. The yoke that should be a priest to Christ or the people is either joined in the law of the Lord, or split through the perfidy of antichrist.

The first yoke of the whole church to Christ rests in the observation of the commandments, for every Christian who keeps them will be saved. And "this yoke is sweet," not wearing down those who bear it, and "it is light," not burdening those who carry it, as is said in Matthew 11[:30]. For in the old law they had observed the decalogue with responsibilities beyond Christ, but now that they are unburdened, through the comfort of Christ and the multiplication of his ministers, it is lighter now than it was. It fits that the law of God was more burdensome with the old, ceremonial law, as Peter says in Acts 15. Since all this weight is removed in Christian freedom, this first is clear. But, oh, how antichrist confuses the law of grace through his caesarean tradition, which makes the old law more bearable.[8] The simple and prudent Christian should wisely put those traditions away, since it is poisonous to be regulated by keeping them. The comfort of Christ certainly exceeds all the oppression of antichrist, since the faithful in Christ always remember that holding onto his law and condemning the traditions of man is a greater reward than sin. It is clear that although the ministers surviving are few indeed, yet the ministers militant are multiplied throughout the church triumphant in the end, so that today the team of God is greatly enhanced. Thus it is that there should be much rejoicing because the Lord is in the church militant.

And regarding all the sophistry shouted by the imposters, it is clear that all Christ's teaching facilitates keeping the commandments. Those [that is, the friars and monastics] who foolishly and privately exempt themselves from this superior teaching without any authorization, disgrace themselves. Nor is it fitting to beg of Christ that he correct the one who is his yoke-mate, since we firmly hold by the faith that he cannot split this team. Of the keeping of the commands of the decalogue, the first part above is clear.

[28] Regarding the second yoke, following what was introduced in the first sermon, we should understand the "voice of the turtledove" of St. Paul [in the letter to the Colossians (3:17)]. Although generally Christ would be the turtledove, combining light with joy, "Blessed are they," he said, "who mourn, for they shall be comforted" (Matt 5:5), yet his members may be called turtledoves, since the Baptist was a great turtledove when he said, "The friend of the bridegroom who stands and listens with joy rejoices because of the bridegroom's voice" (John 3:29). Paul the apostle was a great turtledove when he echoed, "The Spirit himself asks for us" (Rom 8:26). From which it should be gathered that the Spirit itself was a turtledove. The Apostle teaches that everyone among the faithful should act in the name of the Lord Jesus Christ, "Everything that you do in works or speech, do in the name of our Lord Jesus Christ" (Col 3:17). It is reasonably clear from this principle that the voluntary or natural life of every man ought to be meritorious, and so should be in the grace of our Lord Jesus Christ. His is the primary nature and the grace in which it is fitting that a nature subjected to sin be [made] natural as it was created. Take away, I say, the burden of sin, and any creature is in his virtue and grace; one who is selected specially in the ministry of Christ will display this particularly well.

The Apostle says, with this principle, so that it may help the faith, "Women, obey your husbands as one would the Lord; men, love your wives and do not be bitter toward them" (Col 3:18–19). Women should be subject to men by their nature and from the command of the Trinity, in whose sign they are ordained to be inferior essences. This is why philosophers call them defective men in their natures.[9] In Genesis 3, we read how the first woman was formed from the rib of the first man: not from the foot, not from the head. Both teach how a woman ought to be united with a man in matrimony with a particular subjection. With this, it is natural, says the Apostle, that women are suited to be subject to their men, but importantly modifies it, they should be subject in the Lord. Wives should devotedly serve their man as a lord, as Peter teaches of Sarah and Abraham. If, however, men drive their wives so that they are separate from God, then they should not be subject to their men in this way, because then they would not be subject to the Lord.

From this topic to a greater: if a superior or a prelate of the church were to command his subject in any way that disagrees with the law of Christ, then that subject should humbly rebel, because of the obedience owed to Christ and to this prelate. When two prelates, of whom the one is inferior and the other superior, command contradictory things, the superior should reasonably be obeyed. Since Christ, then, is superior to anyone ordained by man and cannot command anything unless it is reasonable and just, it is clear that whoever would strictly command his subject contrary to Christ's will, whether pope or any other sort of prelate whatsoever, his subject ought to rebel strenuously against him. For in doing otherwise he would sin very gravely.

So it is clear that a prelate should consider the good pleasure of the Lord Jesus Christ just as much as a subject, for one can be saved without obedience to someone superior, since obedience does nothing unless it leads one in reason to obedience to the Lord Jesus Christ. But without obedience to Christ, no one can be saved. Thus, those ordained in the ordinary fashion should devote themselves first of all to teaching the rule of Christ. If they are so foolish that they cannot regulate themselves by using the rule of Christ, then they should consult a superior wise in charity who can mercifully direct them in their actions. But if perchance they were commanded to do something cursed, or strange, they should instantly break their tie with this fool, and either live prudently by the guidance of another, or simply hold to the Christian religion purely according to the universal abbot, the Lord Jesus Christ. And while there is danger in a foolish spouse, there is even more in a foolish prelate who leads the greater part of his flock into ignorance of the good pleasure of God or instructs them in ways contrary to his commands.

Whenever a given prelate commands someone to do what is not expedient to his spiritual path and the pleasure of God, he sins gravely. But what does one who is ignorant of place or life, who is even unaware of his own ignorance, know of this? Thus according to the law of Christ, which cannot be contradicted, every viator should be led continuously to merit in the spirit of Christ, for this rule lacks nothing, unless a sinner introduces an obstacle into it. Thus a hard judgment will come to that prelate who blindly commands himself and those subject to him (Wis 6:6).

It is fitting not to be bound blindly by the ties of marriage, though. The man should bear in mind the commands of God, and the wife should, too, either from the advice of the husband or from Christ. Thus Christ commands through his Apostle that men care for their wives in love and not be bitter toward them (Col 3:19). He treats his wife bitterly who treats her disrespectfully, as a servant, at one time beating her, at another mocking her, and at another causing her to sin. This ill treatment notwithstanding, it does not seem to me that the marriage should be dissolved, since often a faithless man is saved through a faithful wife, and a woman finds salvation by not consenting to sin, by living meritoriously despite such ill treatment, in true matrimony, as one should do.[10] The practical and spiritual nature of the chain of love should be preached to these spouses. When particular terms are introduced in the betrothal, priests should examine them with their special conditions and gospel advice.

Regarding the third yoke, namely between parents and their children, either boys or girls, know that, according to the laws of God, parents are expected to provide for their children more spiritually than corporeally, although the corporeal care is more immediately appropriate from the parents. This is because perfect love requires it, and they are held to care for their children with a perfect love. God holds the interior spiritual love of man in a higher regard than the corporeal kind. Why, then, should not a parent, who ought to care for the child only in God, love with an interior, spiritual love?

Again, since advancement in morals is more useful to a child than is the nourishment of the body, should not their sincere love compel parents to hunger for this greater advancement for their children? For loving the lesser good in the being one produces would be a preposterous arrangement, not a love, indeed, but a poisonous hatred. Likewise, a man should hunger all the more for this to be in one whose absence would bring him sorrow. But who would not find more sorrow in damnation, more [sorrow] indeed from the stain of sin than from the hunger of the body or from mortal need? These, after all, rarely, if ever, occur. Therefore, he should strive much more for the greater, spiritual good. From this it is clear that many parents care poorly and improperly for their children; indeed, many even delight in nurturing them in sin, and either care not that they corrupt them, or correct them with too much lenience, which is a sure sign that they love God as improperly as they love their children. They ought to love their neighbors, however foreign, according to a transverse ordering of the law of love; therefore, they should love their own children all the more. But the worldly bear this reasoning heavily and with great indignity, saying that by these lights men should allow not only those near to them, but their own children, to die. Since this contradicts the laws of nature, it is manifestly against the command of God. Nobody knows whether someone who is physically nurtured will sin mortally or will be ethically impaired.

Here, a logician says that it is never fitting that a father dismiss the death of a loved one or a newborn, but he should endure it, as is clear of David, who cheerfully withstood the death of a newborn (2 Kgs 12). This does not contradict but is consonant with the fact that an able parent should provide the necessities of a child's life, but whenever the child would press forward to an evil beyond the intent of the parent, the parent should prudently and moderately regulate his child. [He ought to provide] not because of the beauty or carnal power of the child, or because of fornication, or to enhance by reputation the secular magnificence of the parent, but both to the honor of God and the intended advancement of the church. And if in evil times a child is taken away because of the misdeeds of the parents, the parent should not be castigated on that account, since according to the reason of Augustine, nobody would then do any work whatsoever. In such cases, one should turn toward prudent thought.

On the other hand, though, it is necessary that the child be encouraged, so that he might most fully honor and obey his parents, as is clear in the matter of the first commandment of the second tablet. It is right, though, that a catholic could modify this [commanded] obedience as above, as the Apostle says, "Children obey your parents in all things, this is the will of God; fathers do not seek to provoke your children to indignation, that they not have pusillanimous spirits" (Col 3:21). Children should obey their parents not only in work with their hands, but especially in spiritual matters, which speaks of the salvation of their souls. So since everything is spirit and body, the Apostle notably says, "Children should obey their parents in all things." He does not say, though, that children ought to obey absolutely everything a parent might be going to command, because it remains that he might command unreasonably, and as consequence, then, they should obey by the reason that is the superior father, the Lord Jesus Christ. Such an irrational rule does fall within the number of the commandments. Fathers should not treat their children with undue harshness, lest afterward they be inadequate to bear what they should. Just as Christ introduced his assumed humanity to deity by degrees, as is clear of the Baptist and his close association [with Christ] for thirty years, thus parents ought to introduce good habits to their children by degrees.

[31] In Sermon 27 there were six yokes in which the harmony of the church stands within the secular arm, and since there has been superficial treatment of three, the fourth yoke is between the master and his servants or householders. It is indeed right that there be faith, hope, and charity among these, and as a consequence, it is right that there be faith between the yokemates of masters with their contracted servants for managing together reasonably and for the due handling and faithful payment of what is due. Just as fraud in buying and selling is damnable, so with a faithless mastery and [faithlessness in] the other two [yokes] following, it is clear the reasoning is the same in each case. So regarding the third [that is, paying wages], in the old law it is said, "Do not say anything against the work of your servants among you until the morning" (Lev 19:13). This is commonly explicated by saying that after the completion of the labor, the work that remains for the laborer is not his responsibility through the night hours, yet to meet the laborer's needs, one should pay his wages at the end of the day's labor. God, the exemplar of human justice, always graciously anticipates the servant and pays more generously than his laborer's merit. And as far as due treatment, the world knows how many laborers are unjustly treated, by the denial of payment for labors for long stretches of time, because of the quality of the work, and for other reasons. Thus there should be a rule of equity in such things according to this: "All things therefore whatsoever you would that men should do to you, do you also to them" (Matt 7:12). We should understand this rule to be the principle of moral interaction. Whatever one justly wills to do to one person, one ought to do similarly for another in similar cases. And all of this is understood in this saying, "Thus, do

you also to them." All men ought proportionately to do to their neighbor as they would wish the same done to them. So in this principle is founded the fifth petition of the Lord's Prayer, when we pray, "Forgive us our trespasses as we forgive those who trespass against us."

On the part of the laborer, though, many deceits are possible, beginning with entering into service as a laborer, in the deceptive execution in the fullness of the work, and finally fraud in the goodness of the work. The Apostle spoke against this, commanding that they would not be "serving to the eye, as pleasing men, but in simplicity of heart, fearing God. Whatsoever you do," he says, "do it from the heart, as to the Lord, and not men, knowing that you shall receive of the Lord the reward of inheritance. Serve the Lord Christ. For he that does wrong shall receive for that which he has done wrongfully. And there is no respect of persons with God" (Col 3:22–25).

These words show that everything that any of the faithful might do should be done in the presence of God, so long as it appropriately serves God. They should not serve only in appearances, under the gaze of the master, and shirk in his absence because then they would serve with duplicity of heart; this is worthless in the eyes of the God of truth. Second, it follows that laborers should faithfully do their work continuously in their places, because they should serve God at all times, whose presence they should always believe to be near, perfectly knowing the whole quality of their work along with their hearts' intentions. When someone works faithfully under the gaze of his master, how much more so under God's watchful eye, the infinitely greater master, who comprehends the true quality of the work? Nothing within reason, save absence of faith, could excuse shirking then. Third, it is clear that ministers should think of their work according to the reason by which they serve Christ. This reason is very compelling and worth careful attention because if they serve Christ faithfully, whatever their station, they cannot lack the payment of Christ. And this is why those ministering to the faithless or to the disagreeable in whatever way should do so as faithful laborers, because they serve Christ and receive his payment without fail. How much the more we priests, servants of Christ, are especially directed by his admonitions.

[32] But about the fifth yoke, which is between secular lords and their tenant subjects: each should be enjoined to observe charity. Lords should treat their subjects as brothers in lordship and do

nothing to their subjects save what they would desire to be done to themselves in a similar situation. Every work of a viator ought to be done from love, whence Col 4[:1], "Masters, do to your servants that which is just and equal, knowing that you have a master in heaven." This is why civil trivialities and matters not supportable in this matter ought to be put aside, since it should be certain from the faith that lords should not treat their subjects save in love and defense against the world's impediments on the road to heaven.[11] Thus in Ephesians 6[:9] it is said, "And you, masters, do the same things to them, forbearing threats; knowing that the Lord both of them and of you is in heaven. And there is no respect of persons with God." Since God frees and accepts anyone according to virtue or humility, and not according to a place in the world, it is certain that a more humble and virtuous subject is much more acceptable to God.

So it appears to many that the subjection of the lower classes is a harness of pride keeping secular lords from virtue and, frequently, impeding them. They should provide their subjects with the necessities of life as is fitting with their state. Second, they should defend them from predators, ecclesiastical as well as secular, and from their mad calumnies. Third, they should treat them with love in word and in deed, as is clear from the aforesaid moral principle.

Subjects should not grumble against their subjection, as the Apostle says in 1 Corinthians 7[:21], "Are you called a servant? Do not let it be a care to you." And the reason is, as is clear in both testaments, the command of God is that a subject serves him better in punishment for his sins. And often this estate is more suitable than secular lordship, since a servant of God may merit more fully because this kind of servitude is consonant with God's law, so the Apostle writes in 1 Timothy 6[:1], "Whosoever are servants under the yoke, let them count their masters worthy of all honors, lest the name of the Lord and his doctrine be blasphemed." Christ indeed commanded his kind to be led in servitude for many years (as is clear in the narrative of Genesis and Exodus), but because there are two kinds of lords, namely, the just and the unjust, the Apostle declares that just as neither the servant's nor the lord's state precludes reward, servants of whatever type of lord ought willingly to subject themselves to him.

"But they that have believing masters, let them not despise them, because they are brethren; but serve them instead because they are faithful and beloved who are partakers of that benefit" (1 Tim 6:2). The reasoning of the Apostle is that subjects should faithfully serve lords, whether faithful or unfaithful, because their primary service is to the Lord Jesus Christ; and briefly, since everything of the like can be done without consenting to criminality, they ought to serve both faithfully to mitigate evil. And it is clear just how those who exhorted subjects or house servants to rebel spoke with unthinking malice: because tyrannical lords reign over them. For according to the law of the gospel, as much of Christ as of his apostles, subjects and household servants ought to serve tyrants humbly, not for the reasons the tyrants give, but on the reasoning that they serve the Lord Jesus Christ.

And the disciples of the devil object to this forbearing patience and champion rebellion and revolution so that they might consent to crime.

Again, subjects have the power to resist their lords, so why should they not resist injuries, as the Lord teaches all as [one resists] serpents?

Again, God causes conquest because of an absence of merit among the conquered; why then would he not cause subjects to kick back against those who would keep them down? Just as anyone naturally desires to live, so he naturally hungers for freedom.

But here it is said to the students of the devil that nobody instructed with the law and grace of the Lord Jesus Christ should rebel in such injurious cases, but humbly endure. The reason for this is [the following]: in cases when two alternatives are contrary to one another—the first difficult and morally ambiguous, the other simpler and certain—the law of grace is that the first should be rejected and the other chosen. The law of humbly enduring injury is simple and sure, and the law of rising up and rebellion is difficult and ambiguous; thus the teaching of the devil would be to reject the first and embrace the ambiguous.[12] And Christ himself teaches this as much in works as in preaching, for by grace he endured the most horrible death, and taught his disciples this lesson. "In your patience," he said, "you shall possess your souls" (Luke 21:19). Anyone who teaches this kind of [patient] resistance shows himself an expert in the wisdom of scriptures. But it should be said to secular lords and any Christian that they should not consent to the evildoing of priests who rebel against the law of Christ, which is as inseparably evil as is consent [to such]; individual Christians should be instructed thus, since a subtraction of assistance is not an action, but a rejection of action about the same. And this is the reason why a priest should be free in his almsgiving ministry and not coercive.

To the first instance, the response is that because nothing is certain from violence, so that one could resist evil but at the same time, by doubting in this way, one will foment crimes as much in the agent as in the one to whom violence is done.

Regarding the second, although subjects may have enough mediate power to attack other Christians, this power is, from the first, infected with criminality. So one should insist upon rejecting one's inclination according to the law of endurance through grace. I do not excuse secular lords in these violent depredations or conquests, but I recognize the possible legitimacy of the action because of the excellence of God in his chief lordship. Nor do I perceive evidence that this comes from diabolical prompting.

Regarding the third argument, those with special revelation from God are able to rebel freely, but they ought to test their spirit to see whether it comes from God. Indeed, it is conceded that God gives to sinners and rebels a natural power and instinct toward all kinds of criminal acts, but when it comes to a king's pride, they have to bear in mind the dilemma involved. It is conceded that every man naturally desires freedom, especially from sin. But because there is a more secure way of holding fast to this freedom, and violence generally always brings about alienation, the desire for freedom's continuing power compels one to reject violence and accept the law of patience. Nor does it follow that if secular lords tyrannize their subjects, they should be repaid in kind, because the teaching of Christ is that one ought to return good for evil.

[33] Because the teaching of Sermon 27 is that there are six yokes in which the priest especially should exhort viators to observe mutual love, and five have been explained, the sixth ought briefly to be treated, which is the love between neighbors. Although the Apostle describes sixteen conditions of love by which, in comparison, our discussion is as nothing, we are hypocrites to imagine that we fulfill the love that leads to salvation. Who, indeed, is sufficiently patient (1 Cor 13:4–8) with injuries and annoyances?

Who, second, is so kind as to mourn another's injuries, so that it could truly be said along with the Apostle, "Who is weak, and I am not weak?" (2 Cor 11:29). It is more likely one rejoices at the frustration of one's neighbor.

Who, third, does not envy the successful sects, and the sects unfortunately opposed to one's own, and so rob oneself of relation to the sect of Christ through pride? One is certainly false in supposing that such charity envies not.

Who, fourth, does not turn away from the commands and counsel of Christ, dealing perversely?

Who, fifth, is not puffed up by the abundant goods of fortune or nature, either truly or apparently given by grace? Touch the mountains to find out the truth, and they shall smoke (Ps 143:5).

Sixth, is the capacity of charity of the viator not ambitious? One should judge whether the propriety of conscience strives after worldly honor, secular fame, or material goods. If it is thus twisted in this primary rule, how can it not decline from observing charity?

Seventh, charity seeks not to her own, but (here I leave out the cupidity of seculars) what priest's charity is not extinguished by this sin? For the possessioners [monks] work more for property than for blessedness; the mendicants work for many kinds of damnable property, the better to elevate their cult or themselves, so that they acquire a bounty of temporal goods, resulting in their own appropriate honor. This way, while it builds up God's honor, it also supplements their popularity. And this is the judgment of rectors, of vicars, and of any kind of viator. Who would act so that all were done in common, just as in the state of innocence, and the apostolic state ordained by Christ?

Who, eighth, is not provoked to anger by words—not by admonition but kindly—spoken to them truly of such vices? This touches the preacher inasmuch as he will have been charitable in his will, only to see that all viators of every kind, even friars, might succumb from a want of charity.

Ninth, love thinks not how evil might be brought upon one's neighbor in vengeance or blame. But who is there that, free of all other faults in love, yet perceives himself to be immune in this? We idly think how to wreak vengeance upon the enemies of Christ and of the church, and we think it preferable to pray for this vindication rather than for a merciful way by which these injuries may lead to salvation.

Tenth, love rejoices not in iniquity, as do the evil who emulate the devil; they delight in vengeance upon neighbors and in the defamation of those whom they envy, joyfully listening for the sins of neighbors and joyously proclaiming their evil by lying rumors.

Eleventh, well-formed love rejoices in the rightness of the justice of neighbors, so that whenever one hears of a zeal for justice, without exception of persons (1 Pet 1:17) he approves and rejoices in it. By stirring up this kind of charity, rumor and defamation are obliterated.

Twelfth, love bears all things, whether good or evil, with immoderate joy. Can we believe violently impulsive men to have this property of charity?

Thirteenth, love influences the good as much as the evil, so that all the truths of faith might be believed. But those who wish to believe what is favorable to them, and to discredit what displeases them, even though it may be a truth ordained by God, are guilty of a want of this charity.

Fourteenth, love hopes for the joy of the blessed as well as the joy of the damned; it does not fall into the heresy, that particular people will be saved, but it wills joy for anyone, either predestinate or foreknown. There may not be awareness that one is damned, and it would be certain that "to all who fear God everything works together unto the good" (Rom 8:28).[13]

Fifteenth, love endures all things, the justice ordained by God as well as the injustice brought about by one's neighbor. But those who harbor zeal for proper vengeance are not described here, that is, the kind of people who contend for what is theirs beyond the limits of reason, who combat with a foreign king for justice, whose dreams cloud their understanding, or who rebel against their lords and regularly disobey them because of the injuries they have done to them. And lest it appear that this condition would crop up with the twelfth condition, know that the perfect in charity bear everything in works and in words, not only insofar as their injuries, but regarding everything that happens to them. They know that God brings justice into all things, and he directs singular things for the completion of justice. Thus, love leaves one undisturbed in such things.

Sixteenth, love never falls away, because if it were to fail with regards to anything, it would be through an enemy's violence. But the charitable sustains every such injury with patience (as is clear from the foregoing conclusion). So it is easy to see that, when someone describes himself as being charitable, he is usually lying. Love does not endure that which is mortally sinful in itself; indeed, whenever someone will have understood himself to be in mortal sin, he has ignored his love because of this final condition, unless perhaps it were revealed to him. And, if I may be brief, I do not see how anyone could persist in love who would not give himself in martyrdom on behalf of any of his neighbors. Someone who would shrink from this does not embody his love for his neighbor, and as a consequence, in this he is evilly perverted from the rule of love. And it is clear that love of one's neighbor can be better judged from life and works than from proper words, however solemnly confessed. And it is obvious, as much of the clergy as of the laity, how today their love has frozen over; if, indeed, they have such a *habitus*, then it would incline them to acts appropriate to charity. I am certain that the aversion from the observation of the laws of Christ introduced by the new sects is contradictory to the observation of the sixteen conditions. And since everything resounding against love is as damnable as a heresy, the church should take great care in searching out these sorts of novelties introduced fallaciously from the counsels of antichrist.

3. On Love[14]

This short work takes the form of a letter addressed to someone "faithful in the Lord" who has asked five questions about love; it is one of a number of short pieces in epistolary form that Wyclif seems to have written, most of them taking the form of an answer to a question or list of questions posed by a friend in faith.[15] All of these letters were circulated to a wider audience—a common phenomenon for medieval works in epistolary form, whose addressees may indeed sometimes be a convenient fiction.[16] *On Love* seems to have achieved the widest circulation of any of Wyclif's letters; there are seven copies extant in manuscripts in Prague and Vienna, and the probability that the letter circulated in England as well but does not survive is supported by fragments of the text preserved on the remnants of a torn out booklet in a manuscript that originally belonged to Peter Partridge.[17]

While the questions posed in *On Love* may indeed have been put to Wyclif by one of his followers, we should recognize that they are also the same five questions posed by Richard Rolle at the beginning of the second half of his *Form of Living*, and that Wyclif's response here, and the translation and adaptation of his remarks in item 7 below, the *Five Questions on Love*, are replies to Rolle's claims about the best way to love and to live in the world as developed in the *Form of Living*.[18] Rolle develops the answer to question five, in what state in the world one can best love God, into an extended description of the virtues of the contemplative life. While Rolle does briefly address the situation of men and women living in the world who cannot devote themselves to contemplation, it is clear that an ecstatic beholding of heaven is, in his view, the highest form of love available in this life. Wyclif, in contrast, emphasizes that all the forms of living ordained by God (in contrast to the four newer sects founded by the devil) are suitable to those who belong in them, and God guides each person toward his own best state. Everyone in every state should study the gospel to learn how to love Christ best. And in answer to a sixth, added question, it may be that the best state attainable in this life is not contemplation, but martyrdom.

One faithful in the Lord asks in love that I address five questions: first, what is love; second, where is love; third, how should God truly be loved; fourth, how can the faithful know that he loves his God; and fifth, in what state can a man appropriately love his God.

So far as the first question is concerned, it is clear love truly ordered to its object is an act or habitus of loving of the willing power. And thus, since the place of love is not sought, but its subject is, it is clear that its subjective basis is in the willing power and its objective end in the object of love that is loved. And so love in this life comes about for a number of imperfect reasons. But that love which truly finds its end in God is arranged for the heavenly love that is wholly good.

Regarding the third question, the response is clear through John 14[:21], "He that has my commandments, and keeps them, that is the one who loves me." Thus the most effective means of realizing the love of God in this life is in one's careful study of God's law, since in Psalm 1[:1–2] nearby it says, "Blessed is he who does not abide in the council of the wicked and does not stand in the way of the sinners, and sits not in the seat of pestilence. But his will is in the law of the Lord and on his law he will meditate day and night."

So far as the fourth question is concerned, it is clear how the faithful can easily know after careful study of the law of Christ whether he will have preserved this law, because if he will have kept it is clear from the word of the Lord in John 14 above. He can know with certainty and security that he loves his Lord God, because as steadfast as he is in obeying the decalogue or any particular law of God, in that way can he be certain that he loves his God. Just as the commandments of God are connected, so also are obedience to them and the love of God, which is object of these laws.

Regarding the fifth question, it is clear that the state of the viator is instituted for him by Christ, whether it is the state of priesthood, the state of knight, or the state of laborer, in which one is generally virgin, married, or widowed. The most perfect state for a viator is the state of priest and virgin, since Christ had these and will remain so, in holiness, in heaven. One state is suitable for some viators, while another is so for others. God cannot fail them and assigns them to a more suitable state, so long as they do not place an obstacle to this by sinning.

The status of the four sects who were brought in not through Christ but through the devil appears to be dangerous and should be avoided by catholics. So it is beneficial for many viators to study the gospel carefully in the language in which the reasoning of the gospels is most clear, because the faith requires that all the faithful ought to follow the Lord Jesus Christ, and from as much as they have followed him, likewise and more, and meritoriously, do they love him. So because the stories as much as the teachings of Christ are described more in the gospels, it is clear how much careful study of these books benefits the faithful.

But in addition this man faithful in the Lord asks, What is the sense intended by the Psalmist in these two verses of Psalm 116[:16–17], "Lord because I am your servant, your servant and the son of your handmaid, you have broken my bonds, I will sacrifice to you the sacrifice of praise, and I will call upon the name of the Lord"?

Here I say, as it is likely to me according to the faith, that any martyr of God can rightly say to God these words. This may be admitted to the Lord, because God from his grace has established two kinds of service [in martyrdom] to him and to his son in holy mother church, the bride of Christ. O Lord God, here I freely confess, because you have made me your servant in your grace; especially, I say, because not only do I hope but I believe really before death that in serving you I may merit beatitude after this death. And because such is a twofold martyrdom, because body as much as soul serves God, these words do not come forth without warrant, "I am your servant," and "I your servant," and because martyrdom is not possible unless one has been a son of mother church in life, thus the martyr humbly confesses that he is "son of your handmaid," which is the mother church, Christ's handmaid in this life, just as is said of Mary in Luke 1. And since she is bride of God in heaven, this faith should not be formed in pope or cardinals but generally and commonly in Christ and any of those whom he has predestined to glory, "you have broken my bonds," which are the chains of sinners and the chains of a disordered love between body and soul. This love is broken during this life for martyrs. Afterward, martyrs make confession to the Lord that "they have sacrificed the sacrifice of praise," since they have freely offered up their lives in defense of the law of the Lord. Nor does it appear that a greater sacrifice of praise or offering to God can be offered that is more pleasing to the Lord here in this life. And the invocation of the name of the Lord in this deed of the holy martyrs appears to be a more pleasing invocation of viators. Thus Christ and his apostles, along with other more devout martyrs, have invoked the name of the Lord, and since it is necessary to break the chain of love binding the soul to the body in any viator, let us ask God that we might break this chain to his glory in such a state of suffering.

4. On the Divine Commandments (Selections)[19]

Wyclif's fullest treatment of the moral basis for the Christian life begins in the ninth chapter of a treatise that contains a philosophical analysis of the basis for just human law, an extended study of the Ten Commandments and their relation to our understanding of right and wrong, and several smaller chapters, including those translated here. This was not a treatise written for the unschooled, and Wyclif assumes a comprehensive understanding of his philosophical theology as the basis for his description of what should be preached about the Christian moral life. Wyclif seems to have envisioned several levels of education among his readers. Another of his works, *Trialogus*, is a Latin summary of the whole of his intellectual system patterned on the standard text of theology in the schools, Peter Lombard's *Sentences*, and Thomas Aquinas's *Summa Theologiae*, but in a language that assumes very little understanding of the material. *De Mandatis Divinis* is at a higher level and likely was intended for well-educated preachers.

The two chapters prior to the selections printed here include a philosophical account of the relation of moral theology to metaphysics and a discussion of the relation of fear to love. The law of God embodied in the decalogue and fully developed throughout scripture, Wyclif begins, is perfectly summarized in Christ's commands in Matthew 22:40 to love God and one's neighbor. Love may not seem to have a bearing in the commands prohibiting murder, theft, adultery, and so on, while commands enjoining love of one's parents and keeping the Sabbath appear to coerce behavior without involving love. The right method to resolve confusion about this requires an appreciation of how God's understanding contains the perfect idea for each and every created being. Wyclif developed a complex description of the divine ideas, which he believes to be central to any understanding of God's law. The ideas, analogous to Plato's forms, "exist" within God's being as eternally intelligible but distinct from the creatures to which they correspond. The divine being is the ultimate goal for all creatures' love, so the perfect ordering of creation that the ideas provide is a part of this goal. The prohibitive commands correspond to what God wills we ought to do, the neglect of which we name with words like *theft* and *murder*. These do not refer to things in the world, but to absences, as Augustine had argued. God's understanding of these privations is itself a distinct issue in Wyclif's thought, which he here simply says is what God understands that we should avoid doing. The affirmative commands correspond to the idea of justice and what is due. God's understanding encompasses all created acts, so the relations within it are complex. For instance, God understands the universal justice contained in the command to keep the Sabbath, but this is distinct from God's understanding of whether people actually keep the Sabbath. God understands that whether or not people keep the Sabbath is up to them and also understands each case of their obedience or disobedience. That this is not so deterministic as to rule out human freedom is another issue that Wyclif explores very fully in other works but not in this chapter.

Wyclif passes from the divine ideas in chapter 9 to the motivation for human behavior in chapter 10. In the selections to come, Wyclif occasionally makes references to the divine ideas as the highest authority for law. It is important to remember that many of his opponents, disciples of William Ockham and the Moderni movement, had rejected the place of divine ideas in explanations of human morality, and Wyclif clearly expects his disciples to champion his philosophical explanation of their importance in their preaching. But preaching the gospel is not an academic exercise, and Wyclif switches to how to understand the proper Christian approach to the law in the next chapter.

The prologue to the Ten Commandments, beginning "I am the Lord your God, who led you out of Egypt," teaches us that two precepts may guide us in obeying these commands. The first is fear, and the second is love. There are many kinds of fear, a list of which Wyclif borrows from William Peraldus, OP's *Summa de Virtutis et Vitiis*. These include a natural fear of bodily injury, a worldly fear of misfortune and peril to one's goods, a fear of doing evil, a fear of punishment, and a fear of losing grace. While this last fear is ethically good, a servile fear of the divine forestalls charity. Other fears, namely, those that are concerned with losing temporal goods, may well tempt one to break the commandments, but no good comes from breaking God's laws, even if it seems that one might acquire the kingdom of heaven by doing so. Because God is the supreme lord of creation, his laws take priority in every case. A concern for temporal goods, and a fear of poverty should never lead one away from obedience to God's laws. A fear of confusing temporal goods with spiritual ones is justifiable and will likely follow us until we die, but any fear beyond the proper fear of God is reprehensible and should not motivate our obedience of God's laws.

Chapter 11: The Delightful Treatise on Love

After having discussed fear's compelling power to keep one from evil, which naturally precedes doing the good, the more delightful Treatise on Love remains. And since love varies according to who loves, and the object of one's love, I will here limit myself to the love by which one loves his Lord and which is the highest power of one's soul. Since the whole Christian religion is founded in this love, this treatise should lead the faithful to learn the art of loving wherein lies reason's rest and man's salvation. For in Matthew 22[:37] it is written, "You shall love the Lord your God with all your heart, and all your soul, and all your mind; this," says the Truth, "is the first and the great commandment." It is first, I say, because any man will have learned that by omitting it, all other learning is not simply empty, but evil; while by preserving it, everything else may go by the wayside. All who observe it will have learned more in so doing, while those who pay it no heed are all the more fools. It is highest in value because anyone following it cannot wander off the path, since "for those fearing God" as his children, "in all ways agree with the good" (Rom 8:28). It is the most certain map for seeking the kingdom of heaven. Where is there a greater wisdom than prudently to enter into communion with the Lord and to commit oneself to such a friendship that one serves him as a son as much as a subject? This commandment, then, is the first in worthiness and the highest in value that the Lord and Master deigned worth teaching to his disciples.

But it must be remembered that in scripture this teaching varies in four ways. In Matthew 22[:37], the way is taught by which we should love God according to the triad already mentioned (heart, soul, and mind). In Mark 12[:30], "and with all your virtue" is added. In Luke 10[:27], "and with all your strength" is added, which is the same thing. This precedes "with all your mind" in Deuteronomy 6[:5], and is added to "with all your strength." This shows that there is no contradiction but omissions and additions to how we know the holy mystery.

Fear and love lead one to such a love; fear, insofar as he is "the Lord your God," for in Malachi 1[:6], "If I am the Lord, where is my fear?" Since, then, inasmuch as the Lord has the power of punishing, insofar as God has knowledge of all evil and regarding you, he is your cause, in assistance of which there is no possible co-agency, but that he may punish since you fall short; all of this shows that as Lord he ought to be feared, and because he is the good Lord, he should be loved. He is, I say, a good Lord, because he demands nothing from his subject except what is useful to his subject, since he has subjects not to satisfy his own needs but to satisfy those of his subjects.[20] Further, he is a good Lord because he cannot unduly hinder what should occur. He prevents all his subjects from giving more than they need to for hope of reward. Third, he defends and commands his subjects against every possible opponent. Who would not follow such a lord? The goodness that he has in himself can stimulate one to love, for he is the Lord your God. Through this it is clear that he is Father, Son, and Holy Spirit. The heart corresponds to the Father, the soul to the Son, and the mind to the Holy Spirit. Just as the heart is the first thing formed in the soul, from which every other body part is formed, so the first that is within the interior man is the intellective power from which proceeds the volitive and mnemonic powers in effect. Correspondently, in the uncreated Trinity, the origin is the Father, of which Psalm 44 says, "The good word burst forth from my heart." The true soul of God is understood as a person in the form, the art, or the wisdom by which God is animated to act outside himself. Isaiah 1[:14], "My soul hates your feasts and solemnities." The mind in which God remembers the good and the evil is the Holy Spirit. Luke 1[:51], "He sends away pride of mind from his heart," that is the Holy Spirit, "who flees from doing your teachings," and against whom one might commit the unforgivable sin. So from the intellect in man the affect arises, and from this the act of memory [arises]. If the human soul understands the truth, then it gives consent to it and remembers the good.

So if someone asked how Augustine and the other saints say that there are three things in the soul that are the same person, that correspond to the uncreated Trinity, the answer is that they are memory, reason, and will. But here the order is reversed, and there are powers that are distinct from the essence, through which the soul cognizes things in the world. First, there is the cognition of the true, and following this, the willing of the good, and from these, third, the power of memory proceeds. And when the love described in scripture is toward another, it is a sign of the powers of the Trinity. But

91

since nothing is loved unless it is cognized, the true order of the knowledge of God leads the reason into loving him. While one can philosophically gain knowledge of God from creatures, as is clear in Wisdom 13[:1] and Romans 1[:20], the way by which one ascends to God through exemplary reasons and the intelligible being of creatures is so much fuller and more certain. He who turns away from the appearances of what is perceptible and sets them aside as fantasies, according to the greater part of the soul, in favor of their source, instantly has what he loves, just as a man's eyes are shut and all fleeting perceptions are blocked. He who puts audible voices aside gathers all his powers to apprehend the reasoning of the book of the world's life with its hidden wisdom. So just as when as two people perceive a very sumptuously made book, one unencumbered by understanding stares at its signs and the other looks past the signs to what is signified, so it is for the lay man and the contemplative philosopher perceiving the perceptible world.

So the best teaching for me and those like me is not to dwell on transitory things in thought and desire, except insofar as the spiritual can be contemplated in them. I have learned from experience that the smallest hindrance these things cause in the understanding and the affections impedes contemplation, and hence, the love of God. This is why the prophets, and Christ and his disciples, taught in both word and action not to dwell upon transitory concerns, whether for good or ill, but to move forward through wise meditation and constant enjoyment, to their source, the uncreated Trinity. So if my human soul asks what I love when I love my God, the interior man answers by saying that in everything that I love, I love the one that is every good. Just as, by the force of the words, "God is all in all things," so without a doubt he is every good. Just as he is intelligible being, so he is the intelligible good of every creature. Although he may be every good, he is not each created good, but infinitely earlier, greater, and more profound. So he should be loved wholeheartedly, as the highest Lord. It is foolish to love anything before him, or against him, for what opposes him cannot prevail. Just as we ought to do everything in the name of the Lord, as the Apostle teaches in 1 Corinthians 10[:13], so ought we to love every creature through the reason by which it has intelligible being within him. In God, power, wisdom, and goodness are one and cannot be separated in operation. His power wisely creates through goodness, his wisdom conserves through good power, and his goodness governs powerfully through wisdom. The creation's immensity manifests his power; creation's beauty, his wisdom; its usefulness, his goodness. This shows that the created universe is the natural book written by the finger of God, in which the foolish admire only perceptible beauty with their brute senses, while the wise meditate on its maker, and on the interior man made in his image and nurtured to his likeness.

The layman can easily call to mind the work of the Lord as he considers things in themselves, so long as the preacher's words explain it. But it is difficult for a cleric to understand how all things created exist according to the exemplary Word of God. So this difficulty is explained through the word *miracle* and terms of coming to be, and the focus of the grace to which perceptible knowledge is ordered so that "I will remember from the beginning of your miracles" (Ps 77:11). But because there should be a quiet contemplation running through all of this, it follows, "And I will meditate on your acts" (Ps 77:13).

The weary viator runs aground in such things, because he has such a confused knowledge of the God he ought to love. It appears to the materialistic man that his God might be palpable or perceptible, just as it seemed to Moses in his sorrow, who said "Show me your glory" in Exodus 33[:18]. God said to him, "You are not able to look upon my face; indeed, no man may look upon me and live." Elsewhere I have explained how God cannot be seen by flesh after the fall save through faith, or discursively through analogous knowledge of his creatures. It is necessary to have knowledge of the Trinity and of ideas, and the matter of universals, for knowledge of this sort.[21] The ideas are so necessary that without knowledge of them, nobody could be wise or virtuous, as Augustine says in *83 Questions*, Q.47. God may be seen in three ways, then, and loved proportionately. These are by intuition, as the blessed enjoy in heaven; by discursive reasoning, as by the philosopher in this life; and by faith alone, as by the simple Christian.[22] And love follows as a result from these imperfect kinds of knowledge. One who does not know to lift up the understanding to recognize that the deity is not some other creature, but something beyond individual, species, or kind, is an infidel.

So according to the venerable Anselm, God is a being greater than which cannot be conceived, which is shown to be so by a *reductio ad absurdum* against anyone brazenly ignorant of his logic.[23] First, he posits that the fool recognizes that a thing has a proportionate intellectual being. This is clear through the way of speaking in Aristotle's *Metaphysics* VII, how a house comes into being from a house in the builder's mind. Next, suppose that every living thing having real and intellectual being has a being that is greater than if it only had intellectual being. Third, one holds that, according to the definition that describes the name of God, that than which nothing greater can be thought, it is suitable that there must be something to which so great a sign points. There is no trickery in this, because the name is nothing more than a significative sound that signifies, insofar as it is suitable. Those supposing that God would be in the understanding are asked whether God has only this intellectual being or has real being as well. If God has real being as well, the conclusion [that is, that there is no God] is negated. If in the first way only, then according to the second premise, God could have a greater being, if, in addition to having intellectual being he had real being as well. It follows from the third premise, then, that what only has intellectual being is not really an idea of God.

It seems to this saint that, given this, God may be most manifestly cognizable by abstractive knowledge made more evident and complete through a reduction to impossibility against the fool than through demonstrative, Aristotelian arguments from effect. From this, it likewise follows that God would be the most useful, the most beautiful, and the most delightful of anything that can be conceived. From these things, whether taken from the understanding and reasoning from what is impossible or based in a pure and simple Christian faith, it is clear that it is necessary for the faithful to lift their understanding above the whole created universe to conceive of and to love God. This knowledge is not in itself useful, but is suitable for a continuous meditation, night and day, in addition to good works. So just as the knowledge that an intemperate philosopher is said to have been overcome by his passion to fornicate, so that as he does so, he is foolish and unknowing, in just the same way, every Christian who flies from meditation on the eternal law of God in favor of the temporal goods that so enflame his appetites commits spiritual adultery against his spouse, the church, and acts the fool.

So one should contemplate upon the fact that from his most fruitful omnipotence, God is most useful; from the wisdom of omniscience, he is most beautiful; and from the benevolence of willing, most kind. It is necessary that, with this in mind, the viator extend his constant contemplation and love to God in faith and in argument. Who does not adhere to God with his whole heart, while believing that God in his watchfulness charitably supports his servant with his commands, and in his omnipotence does not abandon his servant? The Apostle imprints such reasoning in his words, "If God be with you, who could be against us?" in Romans 5[:31]. This is especially so if the adhesion through love is most simple, most prudent, and most delightful. Not in the contemplation of the cares of the world's tumults, not in colliding with the phantasmata to which the spirit is subject, which endlessly run into one's mind, nor indeed in the body's passions, but the highest good is contemplated in speculative quiet.

This, I think, is "the One" that Truth says is necessary in Luke 10[:42], not because it is best to prefer entrance into the joys of contemplative life, but because adherence to the most simple One is the most useful thing. And so far as the most Beautiful and the true Good are concerned, it is clear that not only the highest but the whole of its beauty rests in the Word. If beautiful things can be produced in their kinds in creation, where they have the shadow of the splendor of the first light, and are all equal in their capacity to be perceived by us, how much greater are their eternal exemplars, where they are all equal with the first light, and exist really with the source of light in the perception of the Lord? That which rests in the Lord is infinitely more beautiful than the accidental, extrinsic being that is infinitely more imperfect, in which man cannot find rest. The existence of things in their kinds is perplexing and foul in comparison to the primary being they have in God, since the home of the soul is more beautiful and delightful than the exterior, material body for which they provide the exempla.[24] The soul ordered from within and arranging everything outside it is more beautiful than the exterior matter without. Truly, there is a proportionality here, for just as the form of a thing within the soul surpasses the corporeal figure [perceived in] its outward home, so the exemplars within the divine, from which created singulars are formed, are infinitely more beautiful as well.

Here, I imagine that, because the heights of beauty of the created universe are gathered together most beautifully within the divine Word, this same Word says, "The beauty of the field is within me" in Psalm 49[:11]. A certain physical beauty of flowers growing in the earth excites the soul of man, but spiritually it recognizes that the beauty within their source infinitely surpasses this, which in Jeremiah 31[:23] is called "the beauty of the just." When you wish the fullest enjoyment in usefulness and honesty, ascend beyond the whole of the created universe and contemplate the reason within your God, wherein all things are in him, united from within rather than from without.

And it is clear, third, that God is to be adored above all, not least because he is the most useful and beautiful good, but also because he is the delightful and honorable good. So he is the safest haven for rest, where all that is perceptible is combined without being confused, without contrariety or defect of ordering, for in him is the highest reason of every good. How would the interior man's powers of understanding, willing, and enjoying not find its complete peace upon comprehending this good according to the comprehensibility of every possible reason? It would have the greatest peace in the greatest proportionate object, not piecemeal, by whichever reason is most helpful in allowing it to grasp its proper object here in this life, but comprehensively according to many reasons, according to the intelligible being proportionate to the division of its powers. So all our perceptible delights in life are mixed in with sadness and punishment, as is obvious with the taste of what we eat and the touch that accompanies lustful acts. One body part finds delight in its titillation while the others mourn sorrowfully, and the same part now feels delight, now sorrow. The brevity of the sensual delight is as much a cause of disgust for the individual stealing it as is its punishment. The natural desire for the highest good shows that whatever a man loves beyond God simulates a desire that, at its end, is frustrated, like an eccentric planet wandering out of its orbit, or an empty stomach.

So it is suitable for such willing to feel a different sweetness than that associated with perception, apart from all temporal goods.

This is why in Exodus 33[:20], after the Lord has spoken amicably and familiarly with Moses in the form of an angel, he says that "man will not look upon him and live," meaning that he may not be perceived in his essence by any man living. Thus man often appears in scripture, as in 1 Corinthians 3[:1], "Since there is envy and contention among you, are you not of flesh, and walk amongst men?" Spiritual sweetness should be sought, as is clear in 1 Corinthians 2.

Chapter 12: Seven Arguments against Those Who Oppose Wyclif

Now we can refute the materialists, who object to the words and judgments that follow upon describing how we profit from loving in this way. When they say that all of this is but a fiction, or a phantasm, the materialists speak like "expert" judges of color who are born blind.[25] There is no resolution in contentious argument with these infidels; resolution comes in leading them into love from the kindness done to humanity by our Lord Jesus Christ, as the Apostle says in 1 Corinthians 2. The wisdom of the divine nature with its [exemplary] reasons and the capacities of the soul, these should be treated by those with understanding. So, since the baser, more delectable things can collude to assist belief and are demonstrable through philosophical ethics, they should be trusted because of their concomitant good and lend credence to what is superior to them.

1. Aristotle places man's happiness in speculation upon the highest cause in *Ethics* 10, and the Commentator [places it] on the intellect's understanding within us as what is most noble and agreeable of all that exists, in *Metaphysics* 12, Commentary 39. But who doubts that the power of our understanding is nobler than the power of perception, and further, that the most excellent object of our understanding is God himself? From this, it follows that contemplation is the greatest delight possible for us. Gentile philosophers and the wiser Christians have not simply invented this, especially given the faith in the reward attendant upon the assisting works of the glorious martyrdom of Christ, whose first fruits they tasted in this life. Since the philosopher clearly perceives God's existence, and the fact that God includes within himself every most perfect reason of the good, it is likewise obvious to [the philosopher] that he is the supreme object of love. Goodness and lovability follow from one another. But

God is most finally deserving of our love in himself, and anything else that is in the ordering of loving him is given its ordering by him. God is more the object of our love than anything else.

Further, given this, it appears that I should love God first of all things, and nothing that is not suitably ordered to him. I know that God is infinitely the object of love because he is infinitely good and the first good. Insofar as he is the object of love, he loves himself; otherwise, his lovability would be for naught. So I know that the first of all beings loves Itself, yet I also know that his ordering of love is the most reasonable, because God only loves every being insofar as he is good. So I reasonably ought to will good for the first being, and to other beings according to the order in which God loves them. The love of God should be my exemplar for loving my fellows, because nothing can have a rationale for good unless it is appropriately in measure with the divine love.

It is clear, second, that there is no possible good that can be acquired, no habit that can be fostered or any evil avoided, that can justify a man in sinning mortally.[26] God cannot will a man's sinning, since there can be no good reason for it, so the love by which a man desires to sin is a voluntary act displeasing to God. So much the more is it displeasing to God to hold fast to such a false good because of some "possible good."

Third, it is clear that in all things, every man is expected to be in conformity in every act of his willing with God's willing. Whenever a saint wills something that he does not have, he should ask for it on the condition that it is pleasing to his God, as Christ clearly taught when he prayed, "Father, if you will or if it is possible, take this cup away from me; yet not as I will but as you will" (Matt 27:39; Mark 14:36). And the holy exercise their wills this way as well. If they did not do this, they would not subject themselves humbly to the divine ordering and would risk willing what is contradictory to God's will or incurring offense if they will some "possible good." When Mary wants Christ not to suffer, and when Abraham wanted to sacrifice Isaac his son, along with other such examples, they willed conditionally, as I've said elsewhere.[27] This willing was in conformity with the divine willing. It is also clear that everyone ought to submit wholly to the divine will and not grumble against the Lord about what happens. A spouse should not argue so in reasonable things.

98

The soul espoused to Christ, knowing that he would permit nothing to befall it unless it were within reason, or useful, is not upset by such things for fear of jeopardizing his love.

Fourth, just as I should love God foremost, and other things insofar as they have their own natural order, so I should have a greater love for things that are more common, and chiefly God, because these are more useful to me.[28] This is because I should conform my will to the divine will by willing the greater good as God orders the greater good. And the more common is greater than the less common. Further, if I should love God chiefly because such a love is good for me, then I should love myself even more, because it is naturally prior that I exist before something else that may be good for me. This means I should love myself more than some other thing that is good for me, because what exists as such is greater than what is caused to be. Just as God's being good is prior to his being good to me, or some other creature, so I should love God first in the order of greater commonality, perhaps simply because he is the good, rather than because he is good to me, because otherwise I would not love him first above all.

Fifth, it is clear that although all three arguments for good loving, namely, the arguments for the enjoyability of the good, the good's usefulness, and its truth, do not correspond equally in a proper human love for God [in that the object of love far exceeds the capacity of the lover], yet as regards loving other men, they regard one another equally, respectively tied to another. This is because nothing is useful to the divine, so all utility is with respect to creatures, which means the argument for the good of utility is only temporal, but since the other two are eternal, it appears that the first [the good] and the last [the true] correspond to the love by which a man loves God. So if I am not mistaken, the argument from the simplicity of the good corresponds to God the Father, and the argument for the beautiful and the delightful to the two other Persons.

God is not my God save insofar as he is good, useful, delightful, and beautiful to me. He would not be my God unless he created me, sustained me, and governed me, and so can give to me whatever good I might need. Accordingly, he would be beautiful, wise, and true, indeed, enjoyable, to me. So far as I grow in the knowledge of God according to the logic of his utility, beauty, and enjoyability, I grow in his love also. Every man loves just as he naturally knows his God, but not in proportion to his command, and regarding his beauty and enjoyability, God is evident to him only in a confused proportionality. It is clear to me that however beautiful the eternal reason of some creature is to me, its utility exceeds the object that it exemplifies by the same amount, but without God, nothing can exist. So I am bound to love God infinitely more than any other creature. He gives beauty to the whole universe through the beauty of his essence. So those who suppose that these exemplary reasons are useless to us, or that their existence in their kinds is more useful, sin shamefully. A creature cannot do any good in any way save through the power of its exemplar, and that intelligible being is no diminished being, as the being an act of the intellect has when it exists in somebody's mind or perception. An honest cognition of a human artifact is more beautiful than the artifact alone, something made by the artist, even though the work of nature that is its substratum is indeed beautiful.

Sixth, if it were fully and rightly observed, the commandment of the love of God that should naturally be obeyed by any man would bring sufficient rectitude to the whole church. This is clear, first, because man naturally has with himself the power of loving God. The most powerful natural reason establishes that God should be loved before all else; indeed, the complete love of God is the end to which men are naturally ordained. How, then, might the love of God be impeded in man? Indeed, the moral reasons proceeding from the principles about the good teach quite effectively that the commandment of the love of God should be valued more dearly than anything. Next, this commandment, duly observed by a single person of the church, would exculpate it, making it the most effective means of preserving the health of the republic. Because of this, it governs not simply the whole church militant but the church triumphant also, not to mention any blessed nature, human or angelic. This is obvious, because mortal sin is impossible unless it is something that offends God, falling short in loving him. So, as is clear elsewhere, loving God, keeping his commandments, and being loved as his children all amount to the same thing. If all guilt were taken away from the church, she would behold herself most fully in her life and works, as she should, because sin amounts to any defect in the conduct expected of her. One man would not be injured by another, or overtaken, but would be inclined to his neighbor without offense to God or man. Christ signified this by saying, "This is the first and great commandment," Matthew 22[:38], because truly, as is said in Luke 10[:28], "Do this and live," namely, without the blame of God or man in this life, and blessedly in heaven.

This helps to show the sufficiency of the law of Christ, which is the best teacher of the love of God. How incorrectly we proceed whenever we place some other law before this one! We go along without any use at all to ourselves or to society, relying on the goodness of some other, substitute good. This must always be in vain, because the teaching of the law of God is most natural, simple, most fundamental, succinct, and useful of all. This is the reason Christ cast aside the cares of the world, whether the study of human traditions, inquisitions into astrology, or other natural sciences or crafts. Solomon and others sought this law in wisdom, being led by the Spirit of God, and "every good will come to them equally along with it" (Wis 8:11).

It seems to me that this is what we Christians should learn. It is the same for any scholar who struggles to learn metaphysical conclusions by logic before knowing the rudiments of the arts. The first fundamental of the faith is to believe in God, to adhere firmly to God through love; without this, nobody grows in learning. A second example is of willing and entering the house through the open door so that one may rest in the house's bed most suitably; yet the fool digs in the earth to break through the impregnable stone foundation to get to the bed for which he yearns improperly. The bed is the peace of contemplation to which we ought to be introduced through the teachings of Christ, the door; he is our master, who instructs, "First, to seek the kingdom of God," Matthew 6[:33]. However much we recognize the logic of this argument, the blindness of the soul too frequently leads us to abandon this necessary art of love through weakness of faith.

Seventh, the commandment of God is connected to every other commandment, so that whoever duly obeys it, obeys all the others. If one breaks any of the others, then he does not love God in so sinning, as is already clear. Likewise, if someone duly loves his God, then he likewise loves the ordering such a love demands; anyone who flouts so beautiful and reasonable an order of loving the church's bridegroom does not truly love him. Loving in accord with this order means willing it as well, and so one wills the beloved to be in the order of goodness, just as God does. In this way, everyone loves the greater good, since loving involves willing the beloved to be well. Similarly, if one does not love another, say, an enemy, when he knows that the other loves God—for otherwise, he could not recognize his enemy's nature having any being—it follows that his will is different from the divine will. The third conclusion, then, leads to his being wanting in the love of God that is his duty. And the blessed John has this in mind in 1 John 4[:20]: "He who does not love his brother whom he sees, how can he love his God, whom he cannot see?" So, since he knows that God loves any of his neighbors as much as [God loves] him because of the equality of the species, it follows that he is obliged to conform his will to God's. Further, since the seven commands of the second tablet are included in loving one's neighbor, and all the commands of the first tablet are contained in loving God, it follows that all ten are connected with the single commandment to love God.

Augustine pursues this in his letter to Jerome discussing James 2:10, "Whoever would observe the whole law, and offends in one, has done the same in all," proving the sweetness of this conclusion, "Whoever has one virtue, has them all, and whoever lacks one, has none."[29] Nor can there be a moral virtue where there is no charity, as is clear in 1 Corinthians 13. And if charity is present, there is no mortal sin. Thus, so-called virtues in the infidel are nothing save the habits of good action and peace in this life's public affairs, but they merit no salvation.[30] Whoever possesses happiness injures no one, for otherwise, he would not love God or his neighbor as he ought, and be neither prudent nor just. And since he could not love himself unless he is temperate, it follows that the three cardinal virtues are added to charity. And since "Love is as strong as death" [Song 8:6], it follows that fortitude is added to charity. Augustine explains this in three ways: either because nobody overcomes him, for according to the Apostle [in the letter] to the Romans 8[:35], "Nobody will be able to separate us from the love of Christ," just as nobody conquers death but that his time would occur. Or, second, because charity to death is exercised in love, as in John 15[:13], "Greater love than this no man has, than to give his life for his friend." Again, third, just as death removes the soul from the perceptible flesh, so does charity remove the soul from carnal concupiscences. And it is clear how the four cardinal virtues are connected to love. Nor do I doubt but that love is connected to the two other theological, and the twelve moral virtues, of which Aristotle wrote in the *Ethics*. Although love does not have to fight corporeally as a habit [as with courage], neither does it have to distribute temporal goods [as with justice], and so on of the other virtues Aristotle describes in *Ethics* 3 and 4; [love] has the infused habit of carrying out all things like this, if it is fitting, and even greater things.

So Augustine says that, in general, moral virtue is the due love of a beloved, which is commonly called piety. This is either the religion by which God is loved, which the Greeks call *theosebia*, or it is the love of one's neighbor, which is called *eusebia*. This saint holds the virtues to be so connected to one another that no sinner is wise, but only the good [are], because all who sin are blinded by foolishness. Because of this, the Stoics do not dare call themselves wise, but philosophers or lovers of wisdom. Love, and wisdom, and other virtues are connected to one another in their complete being, and love fully carries with it all the other virtues, but to speak plainly, any worldly abuse will develop a likeness sharing the name of a virtue, despite being a vice.[31] Sadness or coldness is called prudence, and being stubborn is called temperance, and a lust for vengeance is called justice, and being dishonorable, strength. This is how the prevarications are connected as vices. Every virtue of man is exemplified from the ordered loving by which God necessarily loves what is precious, and so, every prevarication from a preferable love in this manner is the very common habit of personal prejudice. The blessed James gives the example of loving the more excellent of one's neighbors because of his wealth, or ornament, or blood, or some other thing that is not virtue, from which alone a man is better and more useful to his brother. The church and its prelates conferring benefices are very much blinded by this kind of thinking.

So according to James, prevaricators break all the commandments because they do not love God properly, knowingly departing from the due order of loving him, nor do they love all their neighbors as themselves. They neither give those who are foolish what they deserve, nor do they honor those who do. Even though they consider them more able, they do not love them as they love themselves. One should make provision for one's household and do good to those closer to one, yet one ought to love all the more those who are farther away, thinking of the greater good and what is useful in serving God, or else one risks losing God's love. After all, God would offer such a love. If not, God's love would be less useful to the church, and then one need not love mother church, or oneself, either.

By contravening the law of love, a man abuses himself and the one whose flesh he desires, thereby hobbling love. God and all of mankind would be affected by someone made ignorant by being blinded by appearances, who imagines himself to be benefited by them.[32] In fact, he is subtracting from the greater good and causing a greater harm. The more useful, which all men consider to be more valuable as well as what is more beautiful and enjoyable to any person in the church, assists God in making what is lovable into the good. So all such blind love is not love at all, but hatred, which is why the blessed in heaven rejoice at the damnation of their parents, for they love the soul of their brother much more than they love the body, and so in general imitation of God, they love the greater good more. If there were no defect in love in this life, then without a doubt there would be general agreement about all of this. Every just man is thereby the more right by being closer to what is right. So there is no possible good by which a bishop ought to obey a pope improperly bestowing offices within the church because injuring mother church is against the first commandment of the second tablet....Since, then, this would be against the command of God and the law of love, it is clear that such obedience is offered up for no possible good. And in the very rare case in which there is an equality of persons eligible for a divine office, it should be determined on the spiritual part of counsel, without personal differences [coming into play]. But oh! how personal exceptions and the neglect of the common good throws inquisition into confusion, blinds elections, and impedes the execution of justice!

Chapter 13: Gradations of Love (excerpt)

An objection: All charity begins at home; indeed, I should love more those things that I know and recognize to be more useful to me. In response, I say that this is assumed to organize teaching the fundamentals. Certainly, nobody can exist unless he first love himself. In fact, there are three kinds of love in all men: the first, substantial; the second, natural; and the third, accidental. Since every man is the same personally as his spirit, and this spirit is in three things, of which the third is love,[33] and so, since the essence along with the spirit does not precede this love, it is absolutely clear that this love precedes every love by which someone loves God. All love of God follows upon the created spirit just as a passion or accident does to a subject.

In this gradation of love there ought to be a double ordering, namely, to what is most base and to what is [ontologically] foundational. The first order is from imperfection, which ascends to its goal from what is inferior and more imperfect in nature to what is more perfect, as from the less common to the more common. The second ordering, on the other hand, descends from the more common to the person loving, and so, in the ordering of what is most basic, all charity of a man begins in himself. Understand, though, that every error of loving lies in the love of singulars, for every singular of a species and a genus should be loved equally in species and genus insofar as it pertains to a nature. In their natures they are equal and only better individually by accidents, just as the more virtuous man should be loved more in proportion [to the man's virtues]. When the love of particulars is scattered among men, then error enters. There is a threefold division in this, in which the first is with respect to consanguinity; the second, affinity; and the third, virtuosity. In the order of consanguinity, the father loves the son more than the reverse, and the son loves the father nearby more than farther away. In that of affinity, the first degree is marital, in which "the two are in one flesh," as the Apostle says of Christ and the church. After the marital bond the order is divided according to bonds of affinity. And in the order of virtues, the most virtuous should be loved, both in the more universal, and in the particular, [in cases] when it is in particulars. These three degrees of loving can bring peace to society, if they are ordered according to their proper arrangement, because in Ecclesiastes 4[:12] it is written, "It is difficult to tear a threefold cord."

When this threefold cord is twisted, I am not surprised if the peace of society is dissolved because of disordered love. I ought to love my spouse more for the good of my spouse, my parent more for his or her good nature, and the virtuous more because God's church profits from his virtue. [I ought to] love nothing because it is preferable either for worldly dominion or some other enjoyable good of the flesh, save insofar as it resonates in a good that is useful to the universal church, making it an honest good commensurate with the divine nature, a good that ought to be enjoyed by me.

So it is not unsuitable that one's neighbor be loved more in one ordering and logic of love, and less in another. An ordering and logic of loving in which God and the common good have precedence should always be observed. Making exceptions for people regarding the goods of fortune brings unrest to society. The law of love demands that we aid those nearest to us in material benefits. So runs the natural order, demanding that we give bodily assistance to our neighbor according to our natural ability, just as the earth tends more toward the center and what is near to it. Even though at first one may have tended toward somebody close at hand in time and place, one still loves God, the angels, and the morally virtuous, all the while favoring one's neighbor with physical gifts as an effect. Hence, the order of loving is in effect, and in affect.

Second, there is an order of loving simply, since the blessed in heaven love themselves and God without any disruption in effect, so they affectively desire the greatest good without any envy for a better. So the blessed one loves the better more than himself or his parents [and loves] the soul of his neighbor more than the body. We should apply ourselves to developing this in life, just as Christ loved the church more than his own body. Had he not, he could not have given it over for her salvation, nor would anyone martyr himself for the salvation of his neighbor, which would frustrate the law of love.

The remainder of this chapter is exegesis of Bernard, De Diligendo Deo, Liber seu Tractatus ad Haimericum. *Chapter 14 recounts Anselm,* Proslogion *25, on loving God. Wyclif describes the contemporary understanding of Anselm as varied and corrects several misunderstandings. He then explains how those who love God can find delight in loving, specifically exploring the joys experienced by the blessed in heaven, as delineated by Anselm.*

Chapter 15: The First Commandment

The prohibition of objects of idolatry perceptible to the five senses is clear; second, the act of idolatry is prohibited; and third is the reason for these prohibitions....These three commands, along with the command against swearing falsely, and that about the Sabbath, make up the five commands of the first table.[34]

This commandment is divided into three parts. First, one should not make similitudes of celestial bodies for worship, such as planets, stars, or the heavenly constellations. Second, [one should not make] images of earthly things; and third, images of things in the waters, of which the Apostle in Romans 1[:23] [says] that "they changed the glory of the incorruptible God into the likeness of the image of a corruptible man, and birds, and beasts, and creeping things." Some worship human images, such as Jove and Hercules, "just as the Assyrians worship the image of Beli, father of Nyn their king." Others worship moles and bats, as is said in Isaiah 2[:20]; so, according to Haymo, "the Romans have worshiped geese, the Egyptians hawks, the white cow, and the crocodile, and the Babylonians, dragons," as is clear in Daniel 14[:22].[35] They imagine the spirits that they call gods to be united with such beasts, and because of them, the cults of their followers are favored in proportion, just as we Christians worship images. So although images have been introduced after the stability of the early church to assist in the worship of God, as were the books of the laity and the recollective signs for individual Christians [for example, the sign of the cross], in the Old Testament this was prohibited for three reasons. First, because this people, not as well versed in the faith as Christians, tended to idolatry, as is clear from the narrative of the Old Testament. Second, because God was not then corporeal, as after the incarnation, nor had the holy dead yet entered into heaven, as happened after Christ's ascension, but were all in limbo, so they did not worship either the divine nature or any angelic ones through images. There was no likeness for depicting an incorporeal nature in any image. Third, the marriage of the hypostatic union of humanity to divinity was not yet celebrated in the virginal womb, nor was the marriage of Christ to the church made on the cross, nor prepared through Christ's conversations with his disciples. After his departure, his bride, the church, instituted the images that remain by which the bridegroom and his family are remembered. In the early church there was no such multitude of images, even though the blessed Sylvester was chosen by the emperor to portray images of Peter and Paul, and many miracles were recounted because of the flourishing of these images in the church.

It is clear that images can be made for good or ill—for good, in stirring up, aiding, and reviving the minds of the faithful to nurture their devotion to God; and for evil, as an occasion for one to begin imagining counter to the faith or to provoke undue pleasure because of the excessive beauty of the image. The laity faithlessly portray the Trinity, as if God the Father were an aged paterfamilias having his family, both God the Son crucified and God the Holy Spirit, a descending dove. So it is with many likenesses by which not only the laity but also their ecclesiastical superiors err in the faith, supposing the Father, or the Holy Spirit, or the angels to be corporeal.

Second, many err by supposing something spiritual to be present in the image, and so one image is more affected by their worship than another. This is, without a doubt, idolatry, as shown in Baruch 6 through ten arguments, and in Isaiah 44. A tree trunk, a statue, or some other human artifact should not be worshiped, since it does not do the miraculous, but the devil deceives many at moments of faithlessness, when they imagine something to be miraculous, which is a deception. And the people of Christ continue to be blinded by this deception, which encourages adulteration of the faith by seeking portents.

So there should be sermons against the costly, the fraudulent, and other sophistries with which we mislead seekers for the purpose of attaining wealth, rather than foster the religion of Christ among the people. No image is helpful in this, unless it awakens a man's mind and attention to stretch up to the heavens, so that if, when he does so, enriched in what is naturally good, he is all the more aided with images. God would certainly deem this meritorious if it were done with love. Insofar as the human imagination is freed up, then, after awakening to the heavenly realm, it puts aside the accidents of the images themselves, for in the habits of the imagination lie the enticing poison of idolatry. In Exodus 20, "You shall not make for yourselves any graven thing" of a creature for worshiping. This is taught as a morally indispensable first commandment. If you say that you only worship in the name of the saint of whom it is a likeness, in the time of the Old Testament this is what was called infidelity. So the histories of nations tell more of the wondrous miracles that have been attributed to their idols than we attribute to our own images. Further, their gods of the heavens, or angels, have said that there is one great god, by whose power the subject gods labor; hence, he should receive the most worship.

Since in the first and great commandment we are forbidden to worship the works of human hands, to the extent that Jews were not even permitted to craft such images, it follows that we should be wary of poison in the honey of the idolatrous worship of a sign in place of what it signifies. While the freedom of crafting images is most lovingly explained to the laity through the authority of scripture, not only when saying that such work can be done properly—because in this way it can be a handiwork that is against the third command against working on the Sabbath—but also because it is good carefully to set out the uses and dangers of them in particular.

This is what Epiphanius of Cyprus wrote to John of Constantinople in a letter that Jerome translated and placed among his letters: "I have discovered," said the bishop, "a sheepskin hanging in the church forum, painted with a depiction of the crucifixion. Since I have seen some men hang images in the church of Christ against scriptural authority, I have torn it asunder and sternly suggested to the keepers of this place that they use it for a shroud for a dead pauper." And it goes on, "Pictures that run counter to our religion should not be hanging about in the church of Christ like this."[36] Either this was said before images were permitted to be brought into the church or because of a people prone to idolatry. It seems to me that the danger is quite effectively explained, especially when so-called Christians today cast aside the faith of spiritual believing as if they were animals or beasts, practically ignoring the sense of the faith, so that they can be the more readily moved in their other senses. The visual extravagance of highly ornamented churches, hearing the bells, organs, and the new ways of telling the hours through bell ringing, all are spurs to irreligiosity.

It cannot be denied that church images can be well made. So Bede in explaining the Temple of Solomon in 3 Kings 6 [said]:

109

"There are those supposing that the law prohibits our sculpting or painting likenesses of either men or animals or of things in the church, because in the decalogue it is commanded, 'You shall not make graven images unto yourselves.'" They would in no wise think this were they to consider the work of Solomon. He made numerous paintings and sculptures showing our images, such as Moses being commanded by the Lord in the Tabernacle, from Exodus 25. But even he [Moses] made a copper serpent in the desert, the perception of which saved the people from serpents' poison. How much more legitimate to set up the figure of Christ on the wood of the cross, so that we might rejoice by calling to mind how his death brought an end to the poison of the ancient serpent. Likewise the images of the twelve cows, and other temple ornaments, may be displayed in the church to depict the apostles and other saints, such as we make quite reputably in our own churches. So if we attend diligently to the word of the law, we are not forbidden from crafting images of things, but only from making them for idols. To show this, he first says, "You shall have no other gods before me." And after forbidding graven images, he follows with, "You shall not worship them," as if it were simply put this way: You shall not make such things for worship. Otherwise, upon seeing the image of Caesar on the denarius, the Savior would not have commanded that it be given to Caesar but instead would have condemned it as idolatrous."

Although the venerable Bede's reasoning is quite catholic, still there are those who do not let it prevent the manufacture of images that put aside the love of God and abet idolatry, whether from curiosity, pride, or some other kind of sin. It is the same with those who wield incantations for the magical arts and other forbidden calculations such as illicit exorcisms. In these things, the teachings of the church have delineated what is licit, and what is not.

Returning to the text, it is clear, second, that the act of idolatry is chiefly forbidden. It is said, "You shall not worship them" (Exod 20:5). Worship can be manifold, as much in work as in words. In work, [it is done] by bowing the head, bending the body, genuflecting, extending the arms, spreading wide the hands, prostrating the whole body, removing the hood, and with incense, offering, making sacrifice, or by other variations that human beings may invent. Prayer, though, might be adoration, confession of sin, now by asking and another time by giving thanks, and another by praise. The first would be made to remove a bad habit, the second for acquiring a future good, the third in response to having a good, and the fourth a proper warm praise to God for continuing good will, and it can be through music, meter, and prose. One might object that it is permissible to worship a creature, as is clear in Genesis 27:[29], "And let peoples serve you and tribes worship you," thus Abraham worshiped in Genesis 23[:17], Joshua worshiped an angel in Joshua 5[:15], and in the same way we communally show public devotion to prelates and secular lords, as both scriptures permit. The agreement of doctors is that worship and reverence are suitably offered in three ways: namely, *latria*, which is due God alone; *dulia*, which is reverence due to a creature; and *hyperdulia*, which is reverence due Christ who, according to his double nature, is at once creator and creature.[37] Just as some things are incommunicably in God, such as omnipotence, omniscience, and the most efficacious omnivolence, along with the other properties that God alone has, so there are some honors that are most suitable to him alone. And from another perspective, there are others that are analogically suitable to him and to others, such as domination, power, dignity, and the like. So correspondently there are two ways of worshiping a worthy person: the first, suitable only for God, is called *latria*; the second is called *dulia*, suitable secondarily to creatures, insofar as they reflect the image of God, but suitable primarily to God in whose image man and angels were created. But the honor due Christ's humanity is called *hyperdulia* and the superior *dulia*, and since all such honor given to a creature is suitable only for him, since he is made in the image and likeness of God, it follows that such reverence is primarily for worshiping God and secondarily for rational creatures, just as they participate in the virtues and dignities.

Second, all theological virtues and, as a result, all moral virtues are prescribed in this commandment. One breaking this commandment offends any of them. If one should not worship a creature with the *latria* due God, one ought to love God before all things, and so believe that he should be my prime object, which cannot be done without faith, hope, and love.[38] And by offending this way in love, I love nothing as I should, neither myself nor my neighbor as myself. Humility and every kind of virtue follow the observance of this greatest commandment, and every kind of vice follows upon its breaking. So in it, all things mortally dangerous are forbidden and all virtues are prescribed, even though idolatry is chiefly forbidden and the worship of God chiefly prescribed.

Third, according to Hugh of St. Victor, the text of this commandment is directed against the evil of the Saracens and the Jews when it says, "You shall have no other gods before me." [This is against the] Saracens, because they believe their prophet to be Mahommet, and the Jews [because they believe] their prophets to be the greatest, or the Messiah to be antichrist to come. Also, the foolishness of heretics rejects this clause, "You shall not make graven images for yourselves." The heretic crafts a lie from God in this fashion. All heresy is based in lies, so that the greatest heretic believes nothing of God save what lies under his own imagination or fantasy. Against such it is said in Isaiah 40[:18], "Whom have you made like God? Or what image have you invented of him?"

Christian idolatry was intended when it was said, "You shall not make graven images for yourselves." From what has already been said, as Jerome and others have contended, whatever someone loves the most is his god, so we so-called Christians make gods for ourselves from creatures. He cultivates the images of things that are in the heavens above through pride or ambition, because like Lucifer, he loves being first before all things or some other dignity above his station. He cultivates the likenesses of things that are in the earth through cupidity, for in 1 Corinthians 10[:14] it says, "Fly from the service of idols." He cultivates the likenesses of things that are in the waters through carnality, that is, in slimy delights; so in Philippians 3[:19] it says, "Their god is the belly and they glory in confusion." Correspondently the evangelist speaks of this in 1 John 2[:15], "Do not love the world nor those things that are in it."

While we [clergy] may hypocritically prosper [like wolves] wrapped up in sheep's skin, still it would be useful for us to examine whether we balance our words faithfully with action. The rule of the obedience of the commandments is the basis for discerning this. The love of God and the observation of the precepts of the decalogue are convertible, as is clear elsewhere. In 1 John 2:3–4 it is written, "In this we know in what way we will know him, if we keep his commandments. He who claims to have known God and does not keep his commandments is a liar."

So we should consider whether we keep the first and great commandment, chiefly in revering God. And since inward reverence is not a suitable subject save through the witness of the one being reverent, we should look at the ten expressions of worship made in one's works to see whether we pay our God what is his due. Without a doubt, the commandments we keep and the service we render show whom we love. Our cares for the world, shoving aside the commands of God, show too well how we are worldly idolaters. We [clergy] travel around the world, sailing over the seas for ecclesiastical benefices as if we were priestly merchants, just as lay merchants labor to carry their merchandise, and traveling such wide distances, which we should only do in obeying God's commands. Oh, if only our clergy would expend as much loving effort in obeying God's commands and benefiting the church as they do in seeking the *temporalia* that dominates them so!

So, of all the physical penalties and wounds that soldiers bear that they may gain riches and honors, with what great power would the kingdom of heaven burst open were lower doors barred shut! But, oh! The road to hell is a broad and well-trod path, while narrow and empty is the way to heaven. The reason for this is important. Men faithlessly love what they can see much more than what [things] they cannot, and what is most damnable, they revel in buildings, vestments, ornaments, and other man-made follies, much more than in the uncreated exemplars.

Lincolniensis says that as distant as something is from the highest and best being, that far should it be reckoned to be evil, apart from the honor of the highest good, and displeasing to perfect justice.[39] So among the sophistic responses that I have heard from the worldly attempting to justify so much variation in ornament and ritual, one thing they say is that this is important because they do not wish to go begging for the inventions of others, so they themselves authorize their own innovations in ritual. If they are more solicitous in these inventions than they are in keeping God's commands, I conclude that they faithlessly tend to their graven images and so drop away from those truly called Christians. A variety of apparatus, of homes, utensils, and of other things made by the pride of inventors is a book or sculpture of the devil, by which mammon and others are worshiped. The whole church, or a great part of it, is infected with this creeping idolatry because the works of men's hands are valued more in effect than God.

The seculars who put aside the commands of God craft ornaments for the body, indeed, stuffing cloaks with down and feathers to make their chests swell, so that they may seem to have the chest of a lion rather than what was made for them by God. They seem so strong and brave, and never in so doing do they praise God with a whole heart. In showing the greatness of one's heart by falsely enhancing one's chest, one makes a graven image of oneself, a likeness against God's commands in Exodus 20. And this is also true for women, who sin in a similar hypocritical way.

As is clear elsewhere, everyone pertinaciously defending his guilt is truly a heretic and blasphemer, as is said in Isaiah 40[:25], "And to whom have you likened me, or made me equal, says the Lord." So by abusing these natural and artificial things, "they have changed the glory of the incorruptible God into the likeness of the image of corruptible man," insofar as he [God] is in these, as the Apostle says in Romans 1[:23]. The idolatry of impiety lies in denying the infinity of God and supposing him to have a likeness to things subject to change, which destroys the religion of Christ. If, indeed, we declare the opposite with our mouths, but do not conform ourselves faithfully in religious worship and works to match our words, we admit our guilt through our deceit. Truly, since the faith rules out all fear of believing, our works reveal the weakness in our faith. Otherwise the infidel's works would not appear good to us, nor would we mourn the loss of temporal goods over that of virtue, nor would we dread deception in delightful worldly things more than pretense in obeying the law. For love and sorrow correspond with respect to their own times, just as do desire and fear, which all give evidence of care. Where there is the greatest care, there is the greatest affection.

Chapter 16: The Heart's Love of God

Whenever we introduce any creature that we regard as the equal of or superior to God into our heart's chamber, we commit serious spiritual adultery by introducing a most vile paramour in the place of the most excellent spouse, now abandoned. Hence Isaiah 57[:8], "You have discovered yourself near me and have received an adulterer."

The bond of this spiritual marriage is based sufficiently in the love of God. God does not require worldly goods of you nor bodily strength nor a puffed-up knowledge; [he requires] only to love the bride and this is enough. Concord alone makes this marriage, so that it is only dissolved by hatred of God. So neither poverty nor worldly obscurity, nor infamy nor weakness, nor absence of worldly knowledge may impede; one can have, and should have, this bond. Nothing is more simple in the power of man than the love of God, nothing more delightful than this, nor is anything so steadfast. So you have, everywhere and always, an object for your love. It is placed in the most delightful number in nature, because it resonates within every visible beauty, every melodious harmony, and every delight in the self-moving, living Word. Indeed, it is most fixed in weight because, as its part, the bond of love cannot be torn asunder. It is invariable within all things as present in its excellence, and in the pliability of its love. So where any other object of love may be lacking, God is there; where they become vile, God remains beautiful. Where the love of any other thing wilts, God's stands strong.

If we grasp for honors due God, or devote ourselves to some other creature, or conspire to do one or the other, do we love God? Chiefly it is the doctors and priests, who have the responsibility of teaching the law of God to the people, who are guilty of this. In the final chapter of John, Christ charges Peter under a triple interrogation, understood as conditional, that [if he loves Christ,] he should feed his sheep [John 21:15–17]. How do those of us with this charge love God but neglect the sheep? Not only do we not feed them spiritually but care for them by wallowing in the mires with sinners.

Lincolniensis gives arguments against man's ingratitude in his treatise on the commandments. Regarding this commandment, he says that God is incomparably better, more venerable, and more lovable than any other creature. So, handing over to a creature the worship due God is an incomparably more serious sin than taking away the reverence due a creature.[40] All happiness or created beauty is only a vestige or a shadow of the beatitude of the uncreated. If we were to believe this, as we should, we would not exert ourselves to attain temporal goods. If I were to exert myself for something in hope of attaining some end, and in the midst of my exertions I chanced upon something I believed more excellent, I would not exert myself any

115

further, since I would already have something greater than what I had been hoping for. This is a happy analogy for worldly aspirations. Those blinded by temporal things faithlessly imagine a limit, because if they were to regard the highest good beyond this through faith, they would raise their intent to attain this, trampling upon what they had formerly sought. They love a God who is a liberal giver of shoddy gifts, and hate him who, in his justice, takes away the goods they abuse. And in this way they reveal retribution, but blaspheme God's justice.

Through possessing or acquiring whatever we may love more than God, we commit an offense against his commandment. So Lincolniensis says that this is similar to us having been given a temporal gift from extraordinary grace, as in the service of a king, judge, or priest. Having been given the gift, we throw it violently away from the throne, thereby spattering it with dung, which the king would abhor.

The soul would be more perfected by thinking of a thing through the most perfect idea. And since the divine idea of a creature is the most perfect because it is eternal and identical to the divine essence, the soul is thereby perfected by knowledge of a creature when it knows the creature according to the idea by which God knows it and not according to the existence it has in its proper kind. So as I have often said, the promise that we have in this life is when we know and love God through our contemplation of him through his creatures by means of their eternal ideas. If we would first clearly behold the divine essence, and through it the eternal ideas, and finally, the creatures, then we could be fully beatified from a vision within the Word. So, if we wish to perceive the divine nature in heaven, we must consider his creatures according to the reasons by which they are known and given order by him. In this way we are turned to the horizon of eternity under which is hidden the secret light, for in Isaiah 45[:15] it says, "Truly you are the secret God." For as we are turned away from God by understanding creatures as they are in their kinds, by knowing these perceptible things from without while seeing within, we can taste the kernel of sweetness. And since, according to the reasoning of the Savior, Where your treasure is, there your heart is also, we ought to meditate upon the reasons of these goods, turning ourselves constantly, respectfully to God (Matt 6:21).

We have been mystically taught ordered love from the properties and accidents that nature has given the material heart, under-standing the heart, as the blessed Bernard understands it, as the power of loving according to Proverbs 23[:26], "Son, offer your heart to me." The heart is anatomically differentiated from the other body parts especially in these three things: in its substance; in its primary, absolute accidents; and in its secondary, respective accidents. Aristotle holds in 15 *De Animalibus* c.6 and elsewhere that the heart is made up of seven parts, composed of seminal substance like a muscle, because of its framework and strength. Hence, "Put me as a seal upon your heart," Song of Songs 8[:6]. Second, the heart is con-structed in every part with fibers running longitudinally, latitudi-nally, and transversely. Likewise love has the power to attract what is necessary, to retain what is precious, and to expel what is extraneous. Third, the heart has cartilage in its base, assuming the form of a bone in the aged, as is obvious with older stags. Likewise, the Apostle speaks of ancient charity that has the solidity of bone in Romans 8[:35], "Who will separate us from the charity of Christ?" This is the foundational rock stronger than bone. Fourth, the heart has engen-dering, blood-making flesh, just as the faithful have had removed a heart of stone, as is said in Ezekiel 11[:19], and have been given a heart of flesh, and believe all things necessary for salvation, as the Apostle says in 1 Corinthians 13. Fifth, just as the heart has three kinds of fibers, so we subtly contemplate love's inflow, retention, and outflow. But even with all things above, below, and beside it, it pro-vides its proper value. Sixth, the heart has pumping veins and arter-ies; thus, love has organs of mercy, through which it enlivens and comforts, as in 2 Corinthians 11[:29], "Who is made weak without me being weakened?" Seventh, it is enveloped in thin membranes, just as love finds support in the hope of reward from all the tribula-tions it will face, because in 1 Corinthians 13[:7], "Love bears all things," and these thin membranes appear to be justice, because Proverbs 12[:21] says, "The just man mourns not anything that hap-pens to him."

Regarding the seven primary or absolute accidents of the heart, it [the heart] has a quantity that is measured insofar as mass, but a power that is sufficiently large in the manner of other things more fundamental. Likewise, love, in the manner of the mustard seed, to which the Savior compares faith in Luke 17, is not buried in boastful

117

words, nor is it hampered by a poverty of virtue in the fruit of its works. Second, the shape of the heart is pyramidal, and to some extent rounded, and so love, in a likeness of this shape, pushes through troubles like an arrowhead or a burning flame. But it always remains solid as rock in faith, nor is it weakened from the angle of impact by dangers from without, because in Acts 5[:41], "The apostles went rejoicing from the face of the council, because they were accounted worthy to suffer reproach in the name of Jesus." Love touches *temporalia* only at the point, and above it, all spiritual good rests secure. Third, the apex of the heart is positioned against the left side, from which the vital spirits flow, nor does its size cause it to rub up against bone, but it is there to allow it to refine the spirits in such a narrow space. Similarly, love is content in the difficulties that arise from lacking temporal goods, as the Apostle says in 1 Timothy 6, to avoid sticking against the gospel like hard, worldly bones; but it flows back upon those inclined to material things with a spiritual support according to the teaching of the Apostle in Romans 12[:17], "returning no evil for evil."

Fourth, the heart's base is on the right, so that it may receive the blood, which flows out again and may move by beating. It has two ventricles in its base, of which the large one on the right receives the greater blood from the head, and guiding it along, directs the lesser blood to the entrance in the middle left, which directing further transmits the spirit to the higher ventricle on the left, and there are within this ever thinner channels for the blood. Yet there are in the two entrances at the base two additional little things, like golden shells, through which on the right the blood comes in from the head, and on the left, air that is cooled by the lungs, so that they are moved this way continuously through the arteries. Meanwhile the heart, in accord with the attractive power, broadens itself from the veins, and according to its expulsive power, constricts itself, flowing into the parts that are beyond it. Likewise, the widest way of love is stretched out for the more powerful good of grace, while the left, sinister path is narrower for the medium, or lower, lesser good. For both it is suitable to mark the path in this way, in Song of Songs 2[:6], "his left hand is under my head, and his right hand shall embrace me." It receives spiritual nourishment from reason, and the mouth opens and breathes in a purified spirit, without which [knowledge of] the world will not be created in the heart. And by binding [reason and grace together] in this way, the entire food for the soul is infused into a whole containing every living reason comprehensible according to diastole and systole, that is, through a flowing in from the uncreated spirit, and an outflow to the powers and organs that is spiritually life giving.

Fifth, the heart is situated in the middle part of an animal, as a king in the midst of his kingdom, fortified on both sides by chest, ribs, and spine. Likewise, love is fortified by the virtue of faith or justice in the chest, by the virtue of hope of attaining prosperity and fleeing adversity, like ribs. Third, love builds up patience or perseverance like a spine; this is required for the reward. So the heart of the interior man is situated most securely, bound by these stays, or by the four cardinal virtues, as if by the strongest ties. Sixth, the heart of man has within it three small chambers, ventricles, with openings or blood vessels. The heart alone makes blood; the other parts have blood in veins that is sent to them by the heart, its source. In the first chamber blood is generated, in the highest chamber it is sublimated by the vital spirit, and in the middle chamber the blood is mixed together with the temperate spirit. In a proportionate way, the heart of the interior man is first a chamber in which a faithful meditation is conceived, a higher one in which it ascends through contemplative prayer, and a middle in which both are tempered by the holy operation of willing.

But beyond the quantity, position, and shape of the heart, it is obvious, seventh, that the heart is the warmest of all the body's parts, since it has a naturally mediating spirit, with which it warms and guides, along with the inner spirits, the blood within and the members without, just as the water in a bath is warmed by sulfur from within the earth. Likewise, love forms every accompanying virtue and advances in every movement to salvation, for it awakens all men to the height of affection, as is clear in 1 Corinthians 13. But, oh! In Matthew 2[:12], Truth foretells, "The charity of many will cool."

There are seven secondary accidents that are, from the two already mentioned, in the heart in seven ways. First, it is the part first formed in an animal from which it naturally forms all the other parts of the animal, enlivening and conserving them. Likewise, the uncreated nature, beginning from love, forms from it the whole body of acts meritorious of eternal life, and it vivifies and conserves those near death, as is clear in 1 Corinthians 13. Second, the heart is continuously moving in attracting the aerated spirit, sending forth life and movement to the other parts of the body. Thus, love cannot abide idleness. "If it exists, it does treat works," according to the blessed Gregory, receiving inspiration from the common uncreated spirit, Matthew 10[:20], "It is not you who speak, but the spirit of your Father that speaks within you." Just as the lung surrounds the heart, so the Holy Spirit [surrounds] the power of loving; this reflects love and merit into the superiors above it, into the subjects inferior to it, into friends on the right, and enemies on the left. So it prompts those who are colder to be more [warm], like the heart, it directs the thoughts of the dying to earlier times, and the thoughts of one in childbirth to times yet to come. Third, the heart nourishes the growth of heat in things that are like it in nature. Likewise the power of the will's nourishment is not a lubricating phlegm or a cold melancholy, as in the beasts and birds, but a smooth and warm reasoning that we may inhale, lifting us heavenward. Fourth, the heart is the most certain test there is for life and death, since the heart of the living is joined to its life from first to last. Likewise, love is the herald of spiritual life and death, since in Matthew 15[:11], "But the things that come out of a mouth come from the heart, and these things defile a man." And since man cannot have a spiritual life without love, it is clear that first he comes into life and then recedes into death, insofar as he does not drop from the life of those always predestinate. Just as the heart rejects even the slightest weakness, thus love suffers no fault within it. Fifth, every other part of the body has been created for the heart—the spleen to the left, the liver on the right, the brain above it, and the lungs for tempering the air like a fan for it and receiving vapors—so that the whole man may be steadied by a temperate heart. Likewise every power of the soul and virtue exist because of the potency and act of the willing power. Patience gathers together melancholic injuries just as does the spleen in times of trial. Temperance delights virtuously in prosperity, as does the liver. Humility perceives the love of God in the highest degree, as does the brain. Finally, the kindness of sweet and prudent words tempers the passions of the heart, just as the lungs do.[41]

Sixth, according to Aristotle, every human condition, insofar as the natural habitudes of the body are concerned, takes the heart as the origin. Just as a large heart with paucity of blood makes one naturally fearful, on the other hand, a heart abundant with good blood—so long as an enlarged brain does not prove an impediment—does the opposite. It is the same with singular conditions appearing in nature. Likewise, those with loving hearts are also caring in the cause of God, having a surfeit of love, while those lacking in love are cowardly, either because they are constructed so that their heads fearfully regard the temporal humors, or because in themselves they are wanting the love that restores the soul to life. Seventh, falcons, eagles, and other birds have a natural appetite to feast upon hearts. Likewise the spiritual man, elevated from the terrestrial to the heavenly in contemplation with the eagle, hungers in his soul for the bread of life, since it would be the whole heart, because as is clear in 1 John 4[:8], "He that loved not, knows not God, for God is charity." Thus the Truth speaks signifying what results from this meal in Luke 17[:37], "Wheresoever the body shall be, there will the eagles also be gathered together."

However many properties of the heart they may be, we can learn to love God from them and to discern whether we love him with the whole of it. To this, it is suitable that lances balanced upon a heart appear in lessons on the cross. The church cannot address the spiritual weakness of any person except in cases of the indisposition of the heart or the soul in someone while another preaches. When the heart is overturned or regards the other body parts out of proportion, the whole composite is weakened. And when a prelate or a prefect, who should be the heart of a people, is overturned from the described order in quantity, shape, position, or quality, the people are necessarily weakened by it. So we should regard the opened heart of the crucified Christ on the altar and conform ourselves to it according to the three sevens described of the soul's heart. This is how we show him our hearts.

The following two chapters were likely not a part of Wyclif's original commentary on the decalogue but were inserted to help explain his understanding of the proper use of the Sabbath. The extended quotations from Hugh of St. Victor (d. 1141), Robert Grosseteste (d. 1253), and Innocent III (d. 1216) illustrate Wyclif's typically Scholastic attitude toward authoritative voices from the past. It is no coincidence that these theologians wrote before the dominance of Aristotelianism and of the friars. Wyclif habitually favored citing theologians from before the

121

middle of the thirteenth century. Despite his antipathy for many aspects of the papacy, Wyclif recognized that some popes, like Innocent III, contributed importantly to authoritative Christian theology.

Chapter 19: On the Virtue of Praying

Keeping the Sabbath can be more acceptable to God if we pause for a time and discuss the method and virtue of prayer. Every catholic ought to be especially taken up with prayer and the sabbath, because according to Augustine in his book on praying to God, frequent prayer is necessary to keep the practice of devotion from flagging; and so, every adult is required to know the Lord's Prayer.[42] It is through speaking and enacting this prayer that the human mind is elevated in devotion to God. Hugh of St. Victor famously divided vocal prayer into three parts, which are supplication, postulation, and insinuation.[43]

Supplication is without the determination of humble petition and devout request. Postulation is a determined petition included within a narrative. Insinuation is without petition through the sole narration of the will made through signification. There are three kinds of supplication: captation, extraction, and pure prayer. Captation, which occurs in three ways, is what occurs before postulation to prepare or incline the soul of the hearer. The first is when something is said that commends a person or cause of prayer, such as his merit or need or something similar determined ahead of time. The second mode of captation is when we lift up something in praise for which we pray. And the third is when we put forward a person or adverse cause as worthy of the hatred of the one to whom we pray. Scripture has these species of captation, showing in one place prayer for those in need, in another, exalting the excellence of God, and in another, listing the machinations of the devil, so that we may render in our own supplications something worthy of the ears of God. Exaction is what usually is done after postulation, lest the petitions be forgotten by the hearer. Thus, indeed, as I will say, we engage in a certain relentlessness or urgency for remembering the prayer in three ways, namely, when we express something about his person, about our person, or our cause to help with the memory. Although this kind of reminding may seem importunate to men, it is agreeable and praiseworthy to God.

Pure prayer occurs when the mind ascends from an abundance of devotion so that it turns away from itself to God in love of his greatness so that what is sought is forgotten, and allows him to see that he had only emptily desired that for which he had asked before, in comparison to the love he enjoys now. This uniform and undivided kind is the most perfect of the three kinds, so that captation suggests fear; exaction, hope; and pure prayer, love. Understand that supplication occurs only through terms such as these: "Have mercy upon me, my refuge, my guardian, my liberator, my God, my hearer"; at other times, when these words are used, "Provide for, have mercy upon, attend to, appease, and do," sometimes combined, as in "May your ears hear my words, Lord." Nor does he attend more to polished, flowery rhetoric, but when the interior affect is more devout and thereby more fervent, as when the voice is particularly rough. Thus the kind of prayer resonating in joy, which is called pure prayer, is set forth with pure names, simple prayer at once words and names, but captation, the least perfect, with words alone.

Postulation is a distinct petition contained in a narrative, such as "My heart cries out within me, God." This happens in three ways, namely, by beseeching, entreaty, and simple request. Beseeching is when a more pressing necessity compels us to insist with a more devoted supplication; in less pressing things, entreaty, and in small things, we make simple requests.

Insinuation is narrative only, without petition, a statement made indicating one's will, which happens in three ways, namely in fear, trust, and contempt. Fear, when the person or reason is great, as when Martha says in John 11[:25], "Lord, had you been here, my brother would not have died." She wished that the Lord had rescued her brother from dying, but because of the extent of the reason and reverence for the person, she became afraid and decided to ingratiate rather than make a demand, so that the will might be understood and her temerity not be rebuked, and so that from ingratiation prudence might guard against the opprobrium of refusal, but that on perceiving, the effect of willing might be reached.

Trust occurs in insinuation when either the cause is easy or the person asked is of good will; and here, what is desired does not vocally need to be expressed, as it is with Mary, lacking wine at the marriage in John 2[:3]. "They do not have wine." Here, she insinuates with the privilege that is due her maternal reverence, that she may reasonably ask anything from her Son by insinuation without receiving refusal, although because of irrelevant invocation in the name of a woman, Christ teaches that it is not from the nature that he assumed from her that such miracles shine forth. Third, insinuation can be from contempt, either when the person being asked is humble, or the cause tiny or contemptible, and this is in two ways, either by the thing, or by reputation. And thus the first insinuation includes the fearful, the disorganized, and the imperfect, while the second, arising from the confidence of love or desert, agrees with what is more perfect. And the third, arising from contempt, is suitable only for evil. Only the proud insinuates his God in petition with contempt.

So we are all sinners in praying so viciously....And it is clear that every psalm, every divinely inspired scripture, indeed, every work done in grace are all like prayers devoutly offered to God. It certainly aids in the elevation of the soul to God when we alternate with appropriate interchanges in this type of prayer, so that first we read the accounts of God's power, mercy, and vengeance, showing each to be most kind, boundless, and just, and then offer petitions useful to us according to another of these new methods, and then read the books of wisdom and the prophets that draw forth wisdom, by which we can regulate our works according to the limits of charity.

Vocal prayer has the fire of love within it, reaching forcefully to God, and the consideration of our misery and elevation to divine mercy as its alarum. But if it lacks love, prayer does not rise up, and if it lacks the holy meditation that brings peace, and the devotion that enkindles, the prayer is just so much stinking smoke. According to the philosophers, a flame is caused by the incorporation of the heat of fire into subtly rarefied air, mixed together with an oily moistness. The subtle fire is the fervor of love, the rarefied air is the meditation of heaven, and the oily moistness is the grease of devotion, which, if accompanied by almsgiving and fasting, is a perfect mixture.

The highest directs us to think on our suffering with sorrow, so that we may be brought to demand the assistance of the mercy of God, according to Psalm 6[:3], "Have mercy upon me, Lord, because I am weak." About this, Lincolniensis says:

> The stimulus to pray to be freed from our infirmity is the perception and consideration of that same infirmity. Which, as Bernard says, excites the spiritual state of a man more to the study of prayer than suffering and disasters and such evils as oppress us now. The psalmist declaims the touch of this good, and its effect, "Have mercy upon me, Lord, because I am weak" (Ps 6:3). Just as it is necessary for man to be freed from this weakness, and be freed by prayer, so indeed should he pray movingly about the specific weakness that moves him to consideration of his spiritual state. We should first consider what true purity is, the better to expose our weaknesses; in perceiving ourselves to be far distant from it, we may see how deeply sunken in our infirmity we really are. True purity is what man had in the time in paradise before the fall, although a more perfect kind is to come in the state of glory.
>
> In paradise, man was predisposed to happiness, so that there was nothing whereby his internal or his external senses felt the prick of sadness or were fatigued by work or confounded by shame or blighted by undue warmth or frozen by coldness or were shocked by the horrible. There was nothing between the moist and the dry, the warm and the cold in his body against which something contrary

could stand, so no discord or contradiction could arise, and no disease or sickness could be born that might conquer the body's vigor. There was a due consensus of all the parts of the body in no way lacking through discrepancy, but yielding a proportionate temperature throughout. So he was never pressed by the weakness of imbecility or age into confusion in his perceptions: he was there with a vivacity lacking dullness, and so could acquire knowledge there without any labor. There was no opposition between the law of the flesh and the law of the mind there, but complete respite from the rebellious appetites of the spirit, because the honesty of paradise did not permit anything untoward, nor did one experience anything upsetting. There was a memory that never flagged, with a reason that never erred, in the free use of which one could not sin, and in the free concord between the two there never was disagreement. So there was no mistake in this happiness of cognition, a blameless consent in action, and a rightly ordered obedience to the eternal law. This, then, is the state of the first man before the fall: a true purity from which experience well shows that we have fallen because of sin.

Our senses, both within and without, feel the prick of sorrow because of this weakness, and are made weary by labor, confounded by shame, blighted by undue warmth, frozen by coldness, and are shocked by the horrible; they hold no peace within us, leading to the overcoming of the body's vigor, and the rise of diseases before which the most able physicians are helpless. An absence of proportionate balance of integral parts has everything to do with the loss of purity, along with ill health and disgrace: a dullness and tendency to learn very slowly accompany this, a rebellion of flesh against the spirit, forgetfulness in memory, errors in reasoning, and—what is much worse and by far the more sorrowful—an impotence in cognition and a disharmony of action regarding sin, a disobedience of the eternal law. Did not Isaiah speak of this, signifying sickness, in 1[:6], saying, "There is no purity within me from the soles of my feet to the top of my head"? There is nothing more manifest or true in the literal sense, or if in the mystical sense you identify the top of the head with the height of reason, and the soles of the feet with the lowest appetite, since there would be such immoderation in appetites, and obfuscation of ignorance in the highest reason, not to mention an enigmatic appearance in all powers in between, either through defect or disorder: is there not an absence of purity within the inner man? The newborn immediately cries because of this pitiable sickness, and the aged in their dotage give proof of it as well, giggling in this illness when they should be crying miserably; thus Wisdom 7[:3], "And being born I drew in the common air and fell upon the earth that is made alike, and the first voice which I uttered was crying, as all others do."[44]

Such is man's sorrow at birth, as he lives, and at death; and so the life of man is short, miserable, and inconsistent, so that because of these three defects, it can be said of man the wayfarer, "Woe, woe, woe to those living upon the earth" (Rev 8:13). Thus Innocent [III] says of the misery of the fallen man:

When one considers the creatures of the water, [he sees that] God made the fishes and birds from the water, but he made man from the foulest and lowly earth. If he considers the air, he discovers himself to be more foul, for the special spirits of the air far surpass our bodies. But third, if he considers fire, of which kind are the planets and the stars, he discovers himself to be the foulest of all things. And thus man is made of clay and ashes: clay from a state of innocence because some clay or slime was made from water and dust, both remaining, but after the fall he was made from dust or ash, brought about from fire and earth both losing their consistency, as is clear from Genesis 3. Thus Job says of human nature, "I am compared to dirt, and am likened to embers and ashes" And since this is a double conception, the first with a seed and other things with natures, obviously both are holy. The first is from the fervor of the flesh, the heat of desire, and the stench of

127

both persons in lusting, thereby wandering far from the state of innocence. The conception that occurs from the union of the body and soul stains the conception from what is fitting with original sin. And thus the rational power is corrupted through the ignorance in which one does not know the difference between good and evil, the irascible force by anger, which in blindness to the good does not know to resist the evil, and the appetitive power, by which the illicit never ceases to be desirable. So in the first transgression there is an act that is doing what ought not be done, and in the second, the sin that is not doing what should be done, and in the third, the guilt that includes both. And so just as through carnal seduction the work of reason is lulled to sleep in these deeds, so that ignorance is begotten, the heat of desire is stimulated so that anger is propagated; the affect is unbalanced by desire, bringing on the blindness of desire. And so just as from a tainted vessel the liquid within is spoiled, so from a tainted seed and generated in sin's commission the fomes of sin are brought in. This is the law of body parts, the weakness of nature, and the nourishment of death. Indeed, a clean spirit is produced from God at the natural instant lost not of time, before it is united with such matter, but after the hypostatic union sin immediately enters in.

The fetus is nourished in the womb by the foulness of menstruation, the flow of which ceases because of its delimitation to this duty. Crops do not grow that come into contact with menstrual matter, orchards wither, plants die, trees bear no fruit, dogs that eat it become rabid, and those conceived in its flow mixed with semen become lepers, contract the elephantine illness, or other hereditary diseases. This is the reason why, in the law of Moses as well as in prophetic teachings, men are forbidden to come near a menstruating woman, as in Leviticus 18 and Ezekiel 18. But since birth is twofold, the first in the womb, which is the union of natures, and following conception, and the second is out of the womb, in which the conceived comes forth into the light, it is certain that just as the first is miserable, so the second is worthy of tears because of the ugliness and the production of groans, from the weakness and her removal from the heaviness of pregnancy, and from the penalty of the mother, which is not a similar sorrow, so all of us are Bennoni, that is the sons of pain, for our mother Rachel was hastened to her death from the pain of childbirth; all [are] Icaboth, that is inglorious, born by the wife of Phineas as she died. These stories are in Genesis 29 and 1 Kings 4. So to specify, in the sorrowful suffering of the newborn boy, he cries with more force, according to his strength and voice, saying "A, a" upon leaving the womb. The newborn girls, less strong and weaker in voice, proclaim "E, e," hence the rhyme,

They say E or A, all those born of Eva.[45]

As to giving the form, the weakness and deformity of the infant coming naked into the world from the womb, this is clear from much experience. "Naked I came," says Job 1[:21], "from my mother's womb and naked I shall return." And if it is suggested that an infant coming forth is clothed in a mantle [*i.e.*, of blood], it is certain that then he takes it off forthwith; that clothing is filthy to speak of, even fouler to hear about, but foulest of all to see. It is a loathsome skin stained with menstrual blood, and with such a garment, a jealous man's love is chased away with vigor through the tricks of the physicians. This is the partition of which Tamar speaks in Genesis 38[:29], "Why is this partition divided for you, and because of this, the name of her first born was Phares, that is, a breach." Although the newborn is first raised up in a partition, yet it falls away from him before birth,...it exits the womb with its head between its knees, palms lying above the knees and face, it leaves backwards against the back of the mother. This does not suggest the great excellence of man in his setting out, but teaches a mystic weariness in the words of the Apostle, "deliver me from this body of death" (Rom 7:24).

We should reflect on the second state of man in life. How the earth produces from itself, giving birth to leaves, flowers, and stalwart seed, while from you come nits, lice, worms, and dung. They bring forth oil, wine, and balsam, while from you come sputum, urine, and the stink of feces. Indeed, man is an upside-down tree, since in Mark 8[:24] it is said, "I see men as it were trees walking," for the hair of man is like roots, the head as the base, the chest as the trunk, the arms and legs as boughs, the fingers and toes with the joints as leaves, which every part reversed gives witness to a heavenly nature. This is the soul hypostatically joined to the body. And thus it ought to grow within the interior man, in strength of parts proportionate to the exterior man's aging; to do otherwise is a hateful abuse, for in Ecclesiastes 11[:3] it is said, "If the tree fall to the south or to the north, in whatever place it will fall, there it will be." That is, if a man end his life with an earthly chill within rather than an expanding heat as regards the spiritual, like the planets, he falls into hell, with his master, who placed his seat "in the sides of the north,"(Isa 14:13).[46] But if, on the other hand, he is always turned to the sun, he will awaken to glory. Hence 2 Corinthians 4:16, "But though the outward man is corrupted, yet the inward man is renewed day by day."

Reflecting further upon the flourishing state of the ancient fathers, the abundance of the fruit of the earth, the pleasures from concord of the elements with peaceful society and as a consequence, the purity of their longevity, [there are] but a few, evil days in us, having within them all that is opposite; so it is no wonder if we mournfully claim this from Job 14[:1], "Man born of a woman, living for a short time, is filled with many miseries."

We grow old if we pass sixty years, for whoever reaches old age soon finds the heart to weaken, a shaking head, a failing spirit, stinking breath, wrinkles upon the face, a curved back, clouded vision, trembling touch, a running nose, falling hair, faltering joints, rotting teeth, failing confidence, and dirty ears. An old man is easily provoked but restrained with difficulty, quick to believe and slow to disbelieve, stingy and greedy, dejected and grouchy, loquacious but slow to listen, prone to anger, commending what is old, rejecting the new, disparaging the present and praising the past; he sighs and is anxious, tormented and enfeebled. Hear the poet, "Many discomforts beset an old man." But the old man should not glory against the young, nor should the young be insolent against the old, "for we are what he was, someday he will be what we are."[47]

We should reflect finally how many worldly affairs choke one with anxiety, afflict with worry, disturb with cares, frighten with deathly fear, shake with horror, stir up sorrow, depress with disturbances. If any are near to worldly delights, at once their sharpness scatters them, as Solomon gives witness in Proverbs 14[:13], "Laughter shall be mixed with sorrow, and mourning takes hold of the ends of joy." For the watchful, inasmuch as he lives, is constantly subject to unforeseen dangers regarding the parties of the world, to insult and misfortune regarding his neighbors and the goods near to him, and to an unhealthy imbalance in his inward parts. In sleep, he is shaken with tremors, now disturbed by humors, now bewitched by fantasy, and so befouled; and what is worst, whether he is awake or asleep, his soul is imprisoned in the body with the warmest temptations and the dangers of sin always arrayed before it. And since nothing is more certain than the final terror of death, and nothing more uncertain than its moment, it is clear from the signs of its coming with which we are constantly afflicted how we are constantly tortured by the internally moving causes of terror to fear the horrible, and have a horror of the doleful. For as our life passes on, death grows near, and so while we are continually dying, this mortal life is truly a living death. So it is unsuitable always to live as if death were standing in the doorway.

Further, one ought to meditate upon the foulness and horror of the cadaver to which death finally leads, for with the external portion rotting by small degrees the heart finally bursts, and thus one imagines the soul freed from the body, as if a body encrusted with harsh, stinging thorns covering the whole of it were lifted out of this transfixed and bleeding mass. Experience most certainly teaches how foul and horrible is the body that remains. Its stink makes kinsmen rather more touch deadly poison than it. Hence it is entombed swiftly in the earth, lest the survivors and the environs are infected by the poisons that seep from it. In the meantime, in the imagination, the ghost frightens the neighbors through diabolical shaking and terrifies with a choking horror, thus Sirach 41[:1], "O death how bitter is the remembrance of you to an unjust man." Thus, "Jesus wept" over Lazarus's stinking for four days, John 11[:35]. This meditation on death is a particular antidote in resisting the temptations of the flesh, the darts of demons, and the enticements of the world. According to Gregory, nothing subdues the desires of the flesh so well as thinking about how the desired will look when dead.[48] This reflects the words of Augustine in *De Vita Christiani* how "one cannot die ill who lives well, so God helps any who faithfully obey his commands and precepts." So every adversary cannot vex or frighten such a one at the time of death. It is clear that when we struggle with so much care to avoid sinning, in so doing we act so that we may follow his commands. Sirach 7[:40] signifies this, "In all your works remember your last end, and you shalt never sin." Meditating with care on such suffering and hellish punishments and attentive contemplation on the rewards and joys of heaven is the medium that gives rise to the release of heartfelt prayer.[49]

So the blindness of our sin leads us faithlessly to ignore our suffering. This is the greatest reason we neglect prayer. When an enemy's phalanx threatens, and can only be resisted with assistance from without, who would not seek help for the looming struggle? Who would not beg for help in the lesser struggle to overcome some internal weakness in hopes of a remedy? Experience daily teaches that nobody can proceed without seeking the help of his fellows. So, since we should be in such danger and suffering, surrounded by so horrifying an enemy, both within and without, and yet remain silent in seeking help, what could cause this silence but our inability to see the danger? God, to whose kingdom the minds of infidels are blinded by the veil of pride, prevents the proud from perceiving the danger. Eventually, with the wealth of iniquity stupefying the senses, these sufferers cannot perceive these punishments, and thus dead from spiritual lethargy, the gaze of the eye and the stupor in the sense of the interior man makes them fear neither God nor due punishment but turn away from God.

In addition to meditating on just sufferings and celestial rewards, it is necessary to contemplate the teaching of the mercy of God carefully, lest the mind be lukewarm in prayer, hesitating from fear and enticed by love of self. Nor should it be timorous from despair in gaining that mercy. So we should reflect, then, on the expanse of divine mercy, only a small part of which is enough to dispel all our suffering and every supposed reason for despair. Since the mercy of God is the will of God relieving the suffering from their misery, it is clear that this thing intrinsic to God is eternal and is not diminished by its work of mercy. So it is infinitely greater in scope than created suffering; otherwise, it could be diminished by its works and God would become merciless, which is madness, since God cannot be changed in any way. There is no greater act of mercy than the incarnation, although great works of mercy occur as a result of it.

How, I ask, could there be shown a clearer sign of mercy, since the whole human nature would be inimical to God because of the gravity of sin, than to reconcile us to him through the passion, crucifixion, and death of his only begotten Son? Since God could hate nothing aside from sin because of the inexpressible love by which he loves our nature, he took it upon himself, and since the same sinful nature was crucified along with his Son, he destroyed it and "blotted out the handwriting" of sin, as the Apostle says in Colossians 2[:14]. Since a nature sinning in this way could not be reconciled from itself, God transfixed the sinful nature with a sword, punishing both his Son and the mother, not that these had sinned in their proper persons. As immense as was the presumption of man in usurping God instead of serving him, as was appropriate, so also was God's humiliation in accepting a servitude to man that is appropriate only for a creature. So then does the conscientious father beat the dog to chasten the fierce lion. Since, then, "no person is acceptable to God"

(Rom 2:11), it is clear through the place of the greater that there is no reason for despair unless one would shrug off grace with the willful obstinacy of the devil.

To such a one the mercy of God extends itself so that none of the damned can be punished without mercy, which some call punishment beyond what is due, because it gives the damned being and more benefits than they deserve, through grace.[50] Indeed, if I am not mistaken, no one is damned who wants to be converted to the Lord, and if he can be, God would joyfully accept him to his mercy. This is clear: God could not hate his creature without the cause of sin. Since, then, every sin consists in the free choice of the will, it is certain that, with the damned wishing to be converted to God through a fruitful penitence, God would accept him lovingly to grace. But [the damned would] not will this, because the height of pride in the damned is the greater punishment inflicted; thus there would be nothing, either within or without, that would compel him to such penitence. In this life we rise up from ignorance because of sins, displeased because of the knowledge of new punishments, and beg for mercy from the Lord. The damned freely ignores this reasoning from the blindness of pride and is perturbed by obstinate grumbling. Elsewhere I have spoken on this at length, where it was explained according to the fashion of the schools.[51]

From this it follows that misery is a useful treacle through which[, if one affixes his hope with all created confidence in the Lord, by ultimately paying back the service due to him,] none of the aforementioned suffering should depress him but instead exalt him. The love of God and complete fulfillment of his service consists in the observation of all his commandments. And of this it is said in Ecclesiastes 8[:5], "He who keeps the commandments shall find no evil." Whoever would hold himself in the keeping of the commandments has the most powerful castle, with all the necessary armaments, and has any good the prudent could desire, all this from one thing. And this is what the psalmist has in mind in Psalm 26:1, "The Lord is my light and salvation; whom shall I fear?" A light to the intellect because "the declaration of your words gives delight" (Ps 118:130), a consolation to every catholic, and a salvation giving respite to one's feelings, which is the peace of souls. Let us offer up prayers, turning aside from the cares of the world and the treachery of friends, that we may hope in him and what he can do. We should render to the earthly lord or governor every currency or service, for either it will only appear to free us from trouble or obtain what does not help us, or will be left wanting in defending and preserving what is given us. So we should abandon the world and its desires and not subject ourselves to the heavy and manifold service of men against God, because the riches of the age run counter to the salvation that more deeply nourishes the soul. Indeed, the viator who loves physical affliction because of God everywhere has inspiration, while those who love the delights of the world and the flesh never have rest or peace, and this should be said of the objects of every vice and virtue. God is the medium that inspires, the consummation of the end, and the fruit that gives rest within every created virtue.

Chapter 20

Having numerous reasons for praying, we should discuss the place, time, and form of praying. The place is the church, the time is holy days, and the form is the Lord's Prayer. In the church, because of this in Psalm 67[:27], "In the churches, bless the Lord," and elsewhere, "Praise the Lord in his holy court" (Ps 95:9). There are six reasons for the church being the place for prayer. First, because prayer coming after travel involves greater effort, and every work of merit should involve penitence. Second, because what is done in obedience is more acceptable to God and so more broadly meritorious. Third, because in his house the soul is more withdrawn from work and the cares of allegiances, and more devoted. Fourth, the presence of other faithful provides a reciprocal assistance in the example and encouragement of praying. Fifth, because a particular holiness in the material building is said to remain following sanctification by a bishop, weakening the efforts of the devil's temptation of those praying. Where devils are overcome, they flee the place. Sixth, a sojourn at a place of prayer is representative in a mystical sense. The material church represents the pure world, mystically it is the heavenly Jerusalem, and walking into the church signifies this life's wayfaring.

It is clear how, after the building and dedication of the temple, the glory of God completed the home of the Lord. From such words and reasoning I say [that] the church has obviously authorized that, after the construction of a church, the bishop should dedicate it to its duty, and the people should gather there on the Sabbath for prayer and devout reception of the sacraments. More important, the prayers made in a church dedicated in this way are more acceptable to God. But [this is so because of the] meritorious obedience to the church's precepts and the avoidance of the world's cares that normally call for one's concern, with which one deals at home, along with the family and possessions. And this is taught in Matthew 6[:6], "When you pray, go into an interior room, and with the door shut against the enemies, the senses and the tumult of the perceptible, pray to your Father in secret," because the tumult of the age and the jumble of cares about what is perceptible block the fruit of prayer.[52]

The devoted prayer of a neighbor provides an example and inspires others desiring to pray; so Christ commands in Matthew 5[:16], "So let your light shine before men, that they may see your good works." For this reason the clergy sometimes use plainsong and sometimes musical instruments so that the prayer of the clergy and laity is made more flavorful through what is extraneous to prayer. It is well known that the clergy enunciate distinctly, giving every sylla-ble its own time, every pause, both within and at the end of a sen-tence, its due, and they especially await the silence that comes at the end of a complete sentence. If we stammer along together like dogs in a bag, with a mind on the marketplace and a body in the pew, the hymn on our tongue and our interest in the dance, we are very poorly disposed to move toward God. When we do not gather the minds of the laity together with him, we scatter them about as if we were his adversaries. On the other hand, in 2 Esdra [Nehemiah] 8[:8] it is written, "And they read in the book of the law of God distinctly and plainly to be understood, and they understood," distinctly in enunciation, plainly in volume, and so they understood the sense. Thus the Apostle declares "that with one mind and one heart you glorify the Lord" (Rom 15:6). Otherwise the harmony is mockery, and discord against God grows; thus it is with the hypocrites, who in the manner that has just been described are divided within the church, and with the ignorant who sit dumb as statues during praise of God, and especially with the chatterboxes who corrupt themselves and one another with gossiping, boasting, or worldly tales. They all break the Sabbath, corrupt the people, and sully the holy space. They clothe themselves with the cloak of Satan, just as they accuse and condemn their brothers [of doing].

Second, they overturn and scatter the law of God and the church's commandments, because where God has commanded that Christians gather together in churches on holidays, so that they may improve one another with the example of good works, instead they scandalize themselves and others with empty, even hateful, words. They should think about what Christ taught in Matthew 18 about the punishment for scandal, and they should look to see whether they are not wholly entangled within their own sins.

Third, by making a mockery of the Lord's Sabbath they invite the anger of the Lord for themselves and the people on judgment day. Since all books will be opened then, and the Book of Life will make necessary restitution for even the least word, what will we believe of words of scandal in a holy time and place, by which one's neighbor is defamed and the Lord is mocked? God expects anyone to help his neighbor on the Sabbath in obtaining the endless reward. Does one do this by making a mockery of a place made for adoration, by making excuses, praying blasphemously, or leading others into the mental habits of the enemy? These traitors to their people muster in the ranks of the enemy of humanity and, dressed as sheep, treasonably hand Christians over to the squadrons of the devil; thus the whole community ought to rise up against them.[53]

Fourth, regarding the time, it is clear that one should be praying at every time, with every thought, word, or deed, particularly on holidays, and most especially on the Lord's day. I always speak prayerfully, because there is never emptiness in a good work, just as a knight fights vigorously against enemies. So the rhyme that says we Christians should always proceed in this manner:

You should learn or pray, teach, recite, work.[54]

Prayer should conform to the careful meditation of the state of innocence. In Deuteronomy 6[:7] it is commanded, "You will meditate upon the word of the Lord in your house and walking along the way, on going to sleep and awakening." So it should not be imagined that a Christian is limited to praying only on holidays and in church; he should pray always and everywhere, but for these particular times

137

and places he should be more attentive. So the Apostle teaches in Romans 12[:12] and at the end of Colossians [4:2], "We should be instant in prayer," and "Pray without ceasing" (1 Thess 5:17), and James 5[:16], "The continual prayer of a just man avails much." And scripture shows the way with Elijah, at whose prayer the rain that had fallen for three years and six months in Israel ceased, and afterward, at whose prayer it rained again, as is clear in 1 Kings 18. And if one objects based on Matthew 6[:7] where Christ, when giving the form of prayer, allowed, "When you are praying do not speak much, as the heathen do, for they think that in their much speaking that they will be heard," it is certain that it is not Christ's intention to prohibit long-lasting prayer; he himself was in prayer every night, as in Luke 6[:12]. Instead, he destroys the error in which one believes that the more prolix the spoken prayer, the more effective it would be. The Pharisees imagined that there was a proportionate relation between the greater oblation and its worth, and that its secular ornamentation improved it. Mark 12[:43] overturns the prior error, teaching that "this poor widow has cast in more than all they who have cast in the treasury."

So far as meriting reward, Luke 12[:15] refutes the second, saying, "Take care and beware, for man's life does not consist in the abundance of all things that he possesseth." An abundance of virtue makes a life as such more honorable and good, but not a wealth of money, save in the least part, or perhaps by accident.

Next, Matthew 6 destroys an error that otherwise could easily be believed, namely, that Christ spoke against brief prayer. Christ does not rule out simple speaking, but specifies "as do the heathens." The Gentiles were mistaken in four ways about this. First, they would argue that if daily prayer is good, then twice daily prayer is doubly good, and so on. But they failed in their reasoning, forgetting that all the things should be in moderation. Vocal prayer insofar as it stirs up the inner man to pray is useful, and if it distracts, it is poisonous. Second, they suppose that vocal prayer is in itself meritorious, just as foolish Christians do today. But it remains that unseemly prayer is poisonous, as what is prayed while sinning, or when the praying mind does not concentrate on the prayer. Hence, Augustine in Epistle 47 to Probus mentions that Christ does not prohibit daily disposition, since he passes the night in prayer of this kind. And

Psalm 33[:2] says, "Bless the Lord at all times, and praise him always in prayer," but it forbids empty superfluity. "Still," Augustine says, "abstain from too much spoken prayer, but do not abandon frequent praying, if it concentrates the mind. Much prayer is something we do daily within the beating of our hearts. Generally this happens more with painful sighs than with words, more with weeping than with utterances."[55] This saint means to demonstrate that vocal prayer is only meritorious by accident, insofar as it regards the prayer of the mind. This is clear from Moses praying on the mountain, because of which the people of God conquered the Amelikites, as in Exodus 17. And in Exodus 14[:15] we see how the magnitude of Moses's faith in establishing his people's bravery in the face of Egyptian insults made him worthy of hearing, "Why do you cry to me?" (Exod 14:15). "Faith," according to the Apostle in Hebrews 11[:23–27], "prays well." The same is clear, third, from Anna praying "in her heart and by moving her lips, but her voice was never heard," as it says in 1 Samuel 1[:10–13], making Eli believe her to be drunk.

Third, the idol-worshiping Gentiles superstitiously believed that gods are better moved to respond to prayers by incantations or persuasions, or that an absence of loud voices insults the god, or that the god may be led unawares by ambiguous words. Elijah alludes to this false opinion in 1 Kings 18[:27–28], saying to the Gentile prophets of Baal, "Cry with a louder voice; he is your god, and perhaps he is talking, or in an inn or on a journey, or maybe he is asleep and should be awakened." We should not imagine that the holy prophet is speaking in jest, but in the fashion of the person and opinion of those to whom he speaks, as is clear when dealing with heretical works in order to destroy them.[56] So it follows in the text...that these Gentiles believed the prophet was right, and that by louder voices their god would be more prone to be moved, and that by drenching him with blood, whereby they might summon demons through magic, they might convince him. Chrysostom describes these errors in Homily 12.[57]

Fourth, they are wrong to make many petitions for the many temporal things they love because of a gross misunderstanding. Indeed, often their prayers go on and on, where if they had prayed for the common or spiritual good, as Christ taught in the prayer that he himself spoke, they would make greater headway. Thus in

Matthew 6[:33], telling how the people sought vigorously after jewels and good food, he told his disciples not to care about such things. "Seek first the kingdom of God, and its righteousness, and all these things shall be added unto you." To show that Christ intended to eradicate these four errors, he adds, "They think that in their much speaking they will be heard. Do not be like them." And to shatter their heresy's position about God's omniscience to cause them not to worry, he says, "Your Father knows what is needful for you, before you ask him." Behold the powerful destruction of the superstitious heresies of the pagans. "Your ear has heard the preparation of their heart," and the penultimate chapter of Isaiah, "Before they call, I will hear" (Isa 65:24).

While all that is going to be will happen of necessity, still, God wills that the good things that happen to his servants occur through the medium of prayer. For it is suitable that human voices offer God due honors, not because he might be moved by them, so that he grant their petitions through grace, but so that they may be devoted to offering the adoration due him for their own betterment, because otherwise there would not be the complement to the justice of God in his kingdom. The second reason is that prayer shows a creature the fullest goodness of the Creator, and third, by prayer, devotion and affection are more fully kindled within the creature, who is then better able to be lifted to his creator. So there is no sense in which God's need or a good that would suit him prompts him to desire our praise, but [the good lies in] the utility of praying and its complement to the beauty of justice in the created universe

So it is clear how it is necessary and useful to pray. It is necessary because God has eternally ordained that it be so, and this is called "necessary by supposition."[58] There are five reasons in particular why it is useful. First, prayer occupies the person praying, keeping the person from evil. Second, it stimulates the attentions toward God, so that one can do good; these are the two parts of justice. Third, it organizes the prerequisite good of virtue. Fourth, it procures a just petition. Fifth, it communicates the petitions of others, thereby exemplifying and disposing one to improve the self. Regarding the first, one who speaks with God in prayer does not generally fall into temptation; thus the prayer by which the devout confides in the Lord is a spiritual treacle against the devil. For in

Mark 9[:28] it is written, "This kind can go out by nothing save prayer and fasting," for one should pray humbly because of diabolical sin, just as one should pray on behalf of an ill-disposed superior. Regarding the second, John 4[:23], "The Father seeks those who adore him," and doubtless this is useful, since God cannot define the duty of a rational creature to whom he would not provide aid. Regarding the third, Matthew 21[:23], "And all these things whatsoever you shall ask in prayer believing, you shall receive." Hence, repeated prayer is like a hammer striking a key. For the fourth, Matthew 7[:7], "Ask and it shall be given to you." And for the fifth, James 5[:16], "Pray for one another, that you may be saved."

Such is the power of prayer that it is not possible for a man to ask anything of God and not receive it. For in Luke 11[:11] this is most effectively shown by taking as known that a powerful and benevolent father would not give a stone to a respectful child needing bread or a serpent or a scorpion to one seeking fish or an egg. "If you, then, being evil, know how to give good gifts to your children, how much more does your father from heaven give the good spirit to them that ask him?" He gives in one contained spirit, which is the bread of life, the water of wisdom, and everything that is required by the worth of the one who asks.

A request can be refused in five ways. First, because of the unworthiness of the person asking, as with the Pharisee boasting that he was not like the others because of the greatness of his merit in Luke 18. Second, because of the unworthiness of the person on whose behalf the request is made, as is clear in 1 Samuel 16, where Samuel's prayer on behalf of Saul was denied. Third, because of the usefulness of what is sought, as in Matthew 20[:22], when the sons of Zebedee desired worldly regard, and heard the Lord's response, "You do not know what you ask." Fourth, because of the absence of devotion in the one praying, as in Isaiah 29[:13], "This people honors me with their lips, but their hearts are far from me," and as the Savior says of the Pharisees in Matthew 25. Fifth, because of a flaw in the abbreviated form of the request, or because of some other, greater utility, or some such reason. Thus, the response to the Canaanite woman was delivered for the continuation and concentration of devotion, and as an example for others, as is clear in Matthew 15. Thus the Apostle in 2 Corinthians 12[:9], "Whoever asks for the removal of the pricks of the flesh will have the divine response, 'My grace is enough for you, for power is perfected in suffering.'" Having knowledge of the enemy's practices to attain victory is much more useful than not having it; thus in Romans 8[:26] the Apostle says, "We know not what we should pray for as we ought, but the spirit himself asks for us." We should only ask for beatitude and the means that are necessary for it; so John 16[:24], "Ask and you shall receive, that your joy may be full." Otherwise asking would be unreasonable, and so could not be made in the name of the Word of God; in John 14[:14] it is said, "Whatever you ask of the Father in my name, he will give to you," and in 1 John 3[:22], "And whatsoever we shall ask, we shall receive of him," including that we pray in whatever manner without defect.

The defects can be reduced to three, namely in the one praying, in that for which one prays, and in the prayer itself. When there is unreasonableness or something wanting in any of these, the prayer falls short. Hence, James 4[:3], "You ask and you receive not, because you ask amiss." From this it follows that whatsoever we ask beyond the limits of the Lord's Prayer should be sought conditionally, namely, insofar as it is useful to us, and pleasing to God. Otherwise it would be unworthy for a pious Father to give it to us.

Regarding the third, namely, the form contained within the Lord's Prayer, know that this prayer surpasses all others in five ways: in worth, in completeness, in utility, in subtlety, and in every kind of goodness. It surpasses in worth, because the author of the created universe himself unmediatedly constructed it and taught it. Since, then, the authority and worth of a prayer comes from its author, its worth is evident. By reason of its worth we should not say or name him with polluted hearts or lips, because this would mock his authority, which is the truth. Since etymologically prayer is so called because it is like "reasoning by the mouth," if it lacks the intentional voice of the rational mind, it is not prayer but the strange echoes of a dead voice.[59] For this reason, musical instruments do not pray, although they will form sounds like prayer; nor is the sound of a man a voice as such, unless it brings the word to life in the imagination. Lacking this, says Aristotle, the sound is only a sound, and not a voice. Otherwise, a man making sound is a nonsensical organ of God, like a musical instrument, and an instrument does not vocalize according to *On the Soul*, even though it makes noise.[60] Likewise, according to Augustine the human voice is not praying if it lacks the mind's words; the same imperceptible word is believed to lead to sound within the mind, and so to be the perceptible voice without, just as with the eternal Word of God the Father, which upon assuming humanity was graciously made our brother. Although the speech of the mind and external sounds are two disparate things, the individual vocalization is a miraculous union of the two, which is naturally prior and temporally is the word of the mind rather than the voice of the mouth. When a nature is without a voice, it remains the same individual hidden away within the mind. This appears to be the reasoning of Augustine on true living cognition in *On the Trinity* 15, chapter 12. So it is obvious how praying to the Word of God, which is Truth, with false, or duplicitous, or dead prayer is a mocking blasphemy.

A prayer should be pure, not mixed with extraneous mortal words, and especially not with shameful mental words of the kind found in dishonest thoughts about temporal things. These sorts of words mixed into spoken prayer befoul it, just as garish colors and horrible expressions disfigure appearances. Thus the smoke of burning prayer does not drift upward, but blinding the eyes of its speakers, it makes people to walk in darkness, as in Psalm 108[:7] it is said, "May his prayer be turned to sin."

A prayer should be ongoing, so that when there is no sustained vocal expression, at the least the absence of a break in the prayer may concentrate the devout intention. Discontinuity or mangling degrades the perceptible object, but discontinuity or blank spaces between mental words degrades spoken prayer much more. They are in error who say that it is enough to begin the prayer properly, intending one's entreaties with piety and devotion, even though the mind may wander a bit, thinking of other things. All such empty wandering is sin; so it is difficult, if not impossible, for us who are fallen to offer up even the shortest prayer without a venial sin, especially for those devoted to the flesh and the world. So we sin continuously when we pray. At the least, I fear this is true for me, which I report with sorrow. I am someone who is insufficient in serving God; if I do serve, it is filled with defects.

Second, this prayer surpasses every other and is more complete with the reasoning it contains than any other, and I think this was instilled into it by the wisdom of God the Father, so that nobody given the wherewithal to say it by God may be absolved from using it because of laziness; instead, he should say it repeatedly. I believe the middle Person in the Trinity to have balanced the prayer in this way, so that if it were increased even a little, it would be excessive, if not the cause of sin in mankind. And if it were any shorter, it would lack what is necessary. Christians can shorten or prolong this prayer in their locution, as is suitable for their devotion and capacity; it is suited to be the exemplar, fully formed to be the measure [of prayer] so that right instances of praying may be formed from it. This prayer that Christ gave us is the exemplar for every other prayer we might offer up, whether on our own or through an intermediary. Further, the reasoning of Christ, which is the same thing in the one who is praying, is the praying mind of God itself, because it is a prayer from the mind of Christ. So the same prayer is common to every Christian. While a prayer that is agreeable to me might properly be called a Lord's Prayer, not only because the Lord prayed it as his instrument, but also because he is entreated in it, my own deformed version is not the Lord's Prayer save equivocally. From this it appears that since common things are better than things that are not in common, the common prayer is better for the whole family of man than is a private one, which lacks the commonality.[61]

Third, this prayer exceeds every other in utility, because its seven petitions contain everything that is necessary for the soul and the body, both in this life and the next. So we can safely direct our petitions to God without any condition. Further, it has a special utility in that it instructs the understanding and the affect so that we might chiefly desire the good. Since Christ did not teach us to pray for civil lordship, material comfort, or the goods of nature, it is clear that we ought to put aside these goods for what he taught us to seek. He would be an imprudent master indeed who would teach [us] to pray for the lesser good instead of the greater and more necessary one, especially when praying to so magnificent a king, whose giving cannot be drawn to the lesser good. Indeed, the honor of his greatness keeps him from giving anything to man unless he will have given it through the Holy Spirit, and so, through the highest good. Luke 11[:13] refers to this, saying, "The Father in heaven gives the Holy Spirit to all who ask for it." This prayer also has a special utility in that every man naturally loves his work and, because of this, loves the influence of his work. Thus, every poet loves his song, every schoolman his argument, and parents their children. Without a doubt, this is the way for Christ, who loves this precious prayer just as much as he loves the proper reasoning by which he composed it. So he will gladly hear the words of those who love the Lord's Prayer for the same reason. This prayer is better than all the others in subtlety in matter as in form, so that no one has the wherewithal to comprehend its smallest part while living in this life. From this it is clear, finally, that this prayer excels in every sort of goodness, because it is structured by reason of goodness, utility, delightfulness, and honesty. He says in Matthew 6[:9], "So shall you pray, Our Father who art in heaven."

Throughout the treatise, Wyclif emphasizes that each of the seven petitions of the prayer is itself a prayer and deserves consideration as such. He describes the opening as perfectly catalyzing the theological virtues of faith, hope, and love. It is "an invitation informing the faith, inflaming love, animating hope, inclining to reverence, inspiring imitation, instilling humility, inviting acceptance of grace, and teaching in brief whatever is necessary to be sought in prayer." What follows is his summary of the petitions that appears at the end of this treatise on prayer, which emphasizes the relation of the petitions to the three theological virtues (faith, hope, and love) and the four cardinal virtues (fortitude, justice, prudence, and temperance.) Next he describes how the petitions combat the seven deadly sins. This comparison was a familiar medieval technique of describing the theology behind the Lord's Prayer, and was used when catechizing the laity.

The first petition ["hallowed be your name"] expresses the stability of the faith, which cleanses the heart. The second ["your kingdom come"] expresses the loftiness of hope, which is to await the kingdom. The third ["your will be done"] expresses the love of affection, which is to conform in all things with the divine willing. The fourth petition ["give us this day our daily bread"] expresses the solidity of fortitude, which strengthens the pilgrim on the journey. The fifth ["forgive us our trespasses"] expresses the equity of justice, which is to yield up to each what is right. The sixth ["lead us not into temptation"] expresses the sagacity of prudence, which is to foresee possible evils. The seventh ["deliver us from evil"] expresses the austerity of temperance, which is simply to rule out the threefold evils of the enemy. And so the first petition is against the pollution of lust; the second against the eager greed of the earthly kingdom; and the third, about doing the will of God, is against sloth. The fourth, since bread is enough, is against gluttony; and the fifth, since it sends away rancor, is against wrath. The sixth is against the "foot of pride" (Ps 36:11) by which all who first fell away from God were first led into temptation; and the seventh is against envy, by which one seeks and hungers for another's evil. And so the complete fecundity of the Lord's Prayer is evident, which God put into a sevenfold order so it could be learned quickly, remembered better, and repeated more frequently, to shut out loathing, and to facilitate understanding that no one may be excused because of ignorance. It also strengthens trust for a swift answer to prayer, and allows the virtue of prayer to show the devotion of the mind through an economy of words. Understand that in every one of the seven petitions, every good is included and all evil is excluded, since the virtues and vices are connected together in a like manner.

5. On the Lord's Prayer[62]

Wyclif wrote five studies of the Lord's Prayer, in each examining the logic of and relations among the petitions. In the interest of providing a slightly broader sampling of the range of Wyclif's writing on this subject, what follows is a complete translation of one of the shorter, and certainly the most polemical analysis, *De Oratione Dominica*. While its criticisms of the friars give evidence of having been written later in Wyclif's career, it represents only one facet of his analysis of the prayer. He had written about it in his *Postilla* of the Bible earlier in his career and composed at least one sermon summarizing it. The second book of Wyclif's four-volume gospel commentary, the *Opus Evangelicum*, is devoted to his most sustained examination of the Lord's Prayer. It follows a book devoted to analysis of the Sermon on the Mount, and together the two books illustrate Wyclif's conception of the theory and practice of the Christian life. After having completed this prolonged commentary on Matthew 5–7, Wyclif turned to "the little apocalypse" in Matthew

23–25, which provided him with the opportunity to examine the relation of the Christian ideal to the reality of the fourteenth-century church and, finishing this, began to write a sustained commentary on the "priestly sermon" of John 13–17. The whole of the *Opus Evangelicum* lacks the polish of a final product and is laden with extended quotations from Augustine's *De Sermone Domini in Monte* and the pseudo-Chrysostom's *Opus Imperfectum*. Wyclif would certainly have pruned these quotations and edited his own words before being satisfied with the work, but he died on December 31, 1384, shortly after beginning the fourth book. So while what follows likely was written after the contents of *De Mandatis*, following his 1381 exile to Lutterworth, it was written before Wyclif's final, exhaustive analysis of the Lord's Prayer in *Opus Evangelicum*. In it, Wyclif's sharp tongue and choleric temper are more evident than in the previous work.

Something should be said about the heretics in these most recent, more dangerous days, who openly contradict the catholic faith, unashamedly attacking the Lord's Prayer and the symbols of God's saving grace. For as is clear from the teachings of those who are wise in the church militant about what is probable, in their heresy of the nature of the church, the friars seem to necessitate our Lord to be betrothed to the devil. This is because, as they say, any pope or prelate they might select is some head of the holy mother church, and since it is likely that one or many of these is greater than Iscariot, indeed, the very devil, the conclusion is clear. Believing that however much God has dignified the holy church to be called his spouse by grace, and seeing that many of its prelates stray from the track of Christ's life in their Lucifer-like pride, in the greater breadth of their greed, and in their active persecution of Christ in his limbs through instituting diabolical rules against the church, and with the permission of the faith of the holy Catholic church, the Lord's Prayer should be examined somewhat, supposing as an element of the faith that it surpasses all other prayers in authority, in brevity, and in needed subtlety.

I say that it surpasses all other prayers in authority because Christ—God and man—spoke and taught it in his own person, which I do not think that I have read is true of many other prayers.

For God composed many other prayers through the saints as catholic members of his body. But he composed this prayer in his own person, as is clear in Matthew 6. If, then, a prayer takes its authority from its author, it appears that this prayer surpasses all others, just as Christ surpasses all his members. And regarding brevity, it is clear that this two-part prayer fully encompasses every other prayer offered to God. It contains seven petitions, of which the first three, in allusion to the Trinity, seek the excellence of the praise of God for the utility of the church. The four others briefly teach both what and how much is necessary for the utility of the church militant, so that it is impossible to take away one iota or syllable from this prayer without taking away something necessary for praying. And it is clear how this prayer, teaching according to a form expedient to the church militant, surpasses every other in necessary subtlety, since nothing is true that does not either expressly or tacitly allude to it. In short, no other prayer is faithful or sound save insofar as it is reinforced originally in this one, nor is another sound save insofar as it leads the one praying to pray this prayer.

The first petition, which is in a certain way proper to God the Father, is contained in these words, "Our Father, who art in heaven, hallowed be your name." Here, because of the solidity and holiness of God the Father, who is the source of the other Persons [of the Trinity], the faithful expresses hope that the name of his God will be made holy in the church militant. But because a general prayer lovingly made is more powerful, and certainly humbler, when considering the excellence of the one receiving the prayer, its three terms are sent in an optimal order. Faith, hope, and love are contained by the fact that he is called "Father" by adoption. Through "our," understanding the universal church praying together, the prayer is bound to individual members of the church militant. The humility of the one praying is emphasized through the fact that he is so excellently "in heaven" and we are miserably relegated into this valley of tears. We ask that the "name" of the Lord be "hallowed" in his church, because just as it is a necessary name, so it is necessary that the church's faithful pray this, and since the name of God finds powerful strength in the faith of the elect, the first catholic virtue, faith, is subtly implied in this petition. For although the faith might exist "in heaven," through the clear vision of the blessed of holy mother church, the disposition of grace causes it also to be in the church militant, preceding the faithful vision in heaven. It is fitting, and not inappropriate, to pray for that which will happen of necessity. Thus the humanity of Christ and the blessed in heaven burst forth in praise of God for his gracious arrangement that they perceive as having been ordered from the beginning of time. This is what the blessed James says: while many petitions may reasonably remain secret, one should still postulate that "let him ask in faith, nothing wavering" (Jas 1:6) so one should adapt his petition for reasoned submission, as well.

But here the heretic grumbles, saying that from such a disposition of things that you call necessary for the appropriate prayer request, it follows that the gospels would inspire none of the foreknown to pray according to this form, since none of them will be in the final state of grace in the end. So these "sons of God," as you call them, pray in vain. Indeed, since all viators remain ignorant about this matter of final grace, there is no praying without doubt for any in this life. I say here that any Christian, just as he should continue to persevere toward final grace, should also have faith and not waver in praying the Lord's Prayer. He should be strong in faith, which is beyond observable knowledge or direct perception and is a hindrance to hesitation. So sound judgment suggests to me that anyone predestined praying in this way perceives infinitely better fruit in his prayer than does the foreknown. The foreknown benefits from praying so, and proceeds well enough in this life, as can be seen from virtue's temporal goods, and ultimately he squanders himself through an evil absence of merit into a lazy damnation.

The second petition follows, in which something of Christ's is made one's own upon saying "your kingdom come." The kingdom of Christ is the church following its continuously wandering path, in which we ought to choose to triumph with Christ in heaven. Christ is this man of nobility who comes into our realm to accept its kingship for himself and to return. Everyone should long with Paul "to be dissolved and be with Christ" (Phil 1:23). This would be better than this life's suffering service, bearing in mind the condition that while we ought to make pleas to God in this life, these should not overtake the progress of the church militant. Thus, James teaches that we always should include "God willing" in all such petitions (Jas 4:15).

And it is clear in this petition how greatly the friars' heresies contradict the faith of holy mother church as well as the creed, through which the faithful ought to believe in the church. For we should hold the church militant, which is the kingdom of Christ, to be of the holy Catholic church, and in every way immune from the church of antichrist or the body of the devil, so that Christ does not teach us to the devil's benefit. Nor should we suppose another to be damned, since the faith establishes that it would be empty to pray for a church with such an inevitability present to it. Christ teaches us to pray for the coming of his heavenly kingdom, and not for the coming of the host of the damned of antichrist. The reign of the Word of God is to come from a necessary renewal, and just as pride is excluded by the first petition of Christ when the pious pray, and humility is implied, and especially just as faith is necessary to the first petition, so in this second petition envy is taken away and charity is implied, and hope is necessary to this petition.

The third petition follows with these words, "your will be done, on earth as in heaven," which appears appropriate to the Holy Spirit, which is the eternal willing of the Father and the Son. "Everything the Lord wished, he did" (Ps 113:11), in the heavens and the earth, as the sacred psalm says. So it is reasonable and pious for the faithful of the Lord to want this. Considered in itself, the will of God can only be eternal and cannot not be. Still, one's choice is about the effect of the divine willing, that it be so, just as it would be in heaven. For not only is the willing of God realized without the resistance of the sinner in celestial spheres, but also in the elect who are pondering the heavenly life, and especially in the blessed, so we too choose that the will of God effectively be done on behalf of the whole church militant on the earth just as it is regularly done in heaven.

St. Stephen would say that the reprobate resists God's will, as in Acts 7[:51]. Still it is certain that God wills them all to be damned and does not wish that these foreknown be among the blessed in heaven. So as the more subtle minds, with an understanding of logic, know, God wills that those foreknown to be damned be made blessed, since he wills all people to be saved and commands and counsels that it be so. But he does not will that these people be saved, because then this necessarily would come to pass.[63] So they resist the Holy Spirit, which the Holy Spirit wills that they do, and those foreknown in their sinning would obstruct this, lest it be done. So it is suitable to learn the difference between these two sentences diligently: God wills this to be done, or that this be so, and God wills that this should be. The aforementioned contradiction depends on the first. And this is why the friars fall into heresy. In their Earthquake Council, they made definitions on the efficacy of prayers, saying that it is heretical to say that "special prayers put into practice by one person through prelates or the religious are not more useful for that person than the general prayers for that person, all things being equal."[64]

Just as the Holy Spirit, or love, communicates through its goodness, insofar as it is needed, so whenever one directs a prayer, it should also be for the willing of the one praying. Nor do I doubt but that with the condition of good willing having been met, the Holy Spirit moves to the greatest improvement sustainable for the person on whose behalf one prays, rather than moving simply as a result of a special prayer on behalf of another. After all, praying in the first way is not envious seeking for things that might come to one, which pleases the Holy Spirit greatly. Yet these heretics imagine that by restricting prayer and their attentions to but a few, willing that God help only that few, God would go along with such an ignominy.

The second part of the Lord's Prayer follows, with four sections. The words are turned to us and our needs, just as before it directed us to "you, God." The first of these four petitions follows in these words, "Give us this day our daily bread," which can be understood, according to Augustine, in three ways. First, the bread stands for the necessary nourishment of the whole church for this life, in the manner of food and clothing, which we need every day; thus some call these "daily bread." The second catholic sense that the Holy Spirit recognizes in these words is the spiritual bread, namely, the teaching of the word that "comes from the mouth of the Lord," and this bread is more necessary than the first, just as the human spirit is more worthy than the body, and the nourishment of the word of God is more useful to the human family. The third catholic sense is the understanding of daily bread as the holy viaticum or the consecrated host, which we need in the form of bread daily, and because of these two senses, Matthew 6 is believed to have called this the "supersubstantial bread." Nor is it an affront to the Holy Spirit to lay such a burden of meaning upon the word of scripture in the catholic sense. The "daily" is given in the request, because we need to ask for God's help daily regarding things needful to us, and this is why the Baptist, Joseph, Mary, and others of the elect gradually were instructed in the necessary knowledge. Had Eve not heeded the serpent, she would have had it too; he would not have seduced her through lies to have no thought of the Lord.

And we are afflicted with heresies about this, especially by the pseudo-friars. First, I say, they cut knowledge of the nature of the consecrated host away from the church by holding without foundation that it is accident without substance, the which they cannot possibly understand. They faithlessly deny the truth of scripture in saying this. The friars spread a second heresy of the mediated bread [that is, scripture], that it would be impossible that the word of God be expressed in the greater part of scripture, which gravely injures the faith of scripture and condemns the law of God. And in a third, the friars imagine properties and ceremonies for the bread, for which they fashion the name *latria*, that is, honor and majesty beyond the *latria* minimally suitable for a perceptible sign of Christ having been founded in the power of the Holy Spirit. And these three heresies along with their accoutrements throw the church militant into confusion.

The second petition, in which the good useful to the church militant is sought, follows in these words, "Forgive us our trespasses as we forgive those who trespass against us." Here it appears that we ask to be freed from the due penalty because of the execution of an act of mercy that we should be doing in any case. We are obliged to do this because we ought to be merciful to our neighbors, brothers, and those far away, in teaching, giving counsel, and reprimanding, and in being consoled, forgiving, and suffering the impetuosity of our brothers, since we make common cause with them and pray. Those who are not wanting in any of these seven acts, I warrant that they do not sin. So Augustine calls these trespasses "sin" since there would be prescribed rules in which the man sinning be punished. The added importance of the condition of mercy in this petition is clear in Christ's parable in Matthew 18[:22]. So it is suitable for salvation that everyone forgives his brothers' debts. But just as this does not follow: This is the church of malevolence or the church of antichrist, therefore this is the church, since the preceding term qualifies it, so this does not follow: I, or someone other than Christ, forgives the sin that this person commits, therefore he is simply absolved from the sin.

It is enough to verify the antecedent that I perceive his charity and not look for vengeance because of the injury done to me. And it is clear from this fifth petition [that is, the second petition of the second group] that the friars have planted heresies in the church. They say, publish, and defend this, no doubt because of a hearty affection for the honor and temporal comfort that accompanies the connection in which someone may absolve with a perceptible sign, but without thought, meaning that God must simply and wholly absolve likewise. So they construct a heretical explanation for the belief in the forgiveness of sins. Instead, this belief should be that forgiveness comes first and foremost from God. There are many who are swept up in this heresy, even some eminent figures. But truly, just as a part of loving another as a brother involves the eradication of corporeal debts in the appropriate manner, so another part of that love involves exhortation, chastising, and punishment for spiritual debts. This is especially so when a man desires to resolve one in the appropriate manner, as for the completion of the law or the betterment of the church. This should be in speech, because it dismisses this rebuke and awaits the merciless vengeance of God, and preserves the debt, not avoiding paying what is due.

So in all things it is suitable for the faithful to have an eye to the church of Christ and its success. First, what this petition asks from God is simply grace, and second, it is expressed because of the speaker's own sin; otherwise, God does not forgive the sins of the debtor who does not himself forgive those of his neighbor.

The third petition of this [second] part of the Lord's Prayer follows in these words, "And lead us not into temptation." While it is permitted to tempt and be tempted, since God tempted Abraham, and Christ our God was tempted by the devil as an example for our church, still, to be led into temptation is always an evil punishment, and this, along with the tempter, should always be fled. Being led into temptation appears to be a sin with diabolical roots, which in the end is hardened into culpable evil. God permits this, though, as is clear with Pharaoh's heart, since just as one rooted in earlier sins naturally hardens, so is clay or some other natural body to harden because of its previous natural disposition. So the faithful need not murmur about a good God leading the foreknown into temptation. One is tempted who thinks on a moral lapse prior to his own death. But one is led into temptation who is so deeply mired that before and after the actual tempting he is still inextricably bound up within temptation. This is called diabolical temptation, but the prior species is called human temptation. So the Apostle says, "Let no temptation take hold of you, but such as human ones" (1 Cor 10:13). It is human nature for someone predestined to glory to give in to temptation, as is clear for Peter, but it is diabolical for someone to remain in temptation until death.

And the four capital sins can be applied to these four premises along with their opposing virtues. This petition, "Your will be done," touches the sin of wrath and the virtue of kindness, since the spirit of the Lord is gentle and mild, as the scriptural faith asserts, and as Christ showed himself the gentlest and kindest of men in Matthew 6. The fourth petition, "Give us this day our daily bread," touches the sin of sloth, along with the virtue of fruitful perseverance, because only the slothful is denied his daily bread. The fifth petition, "Forgive us our trespasses as we forgive those who trespass against us," touches upon the sin of greed or avarice, along with its opposing virtue *theosebia*, since only the greedy are rightly not forgiven and are duly damned.[65] But the sixth petition, "Lead us not into temptation," touches the sin of gluttony, wherein those for whom their gut is god are immersed, and it can touch the opposing virtue, parsimony or fruitful abstinence, or temperance. Just as deep burial in vice hardens a person to diabolical temptation, so does a deep immersion in the flesh lead one into an indestructible gluttony. In this petition looms the friars' heresy that they have introduced from their lying and secrets. They insist that their order is more powerful than any order that Christ thought worthy to confer upon the person of a man.

The final petition of the Lord's Prayer follows with these words, "But deliver us from evil, Amen." From this, it appears that the evil of an impenitent death should be understood. This is the greatest and worst evil that can befall a person, for God never rests in fighting against this evil. So, since every sin might be, in a certain way, infinite, however evil this diabolical sin of final impenitence may be, while God leads one into this because of antecedent desert, God does not bring about this evil, just as he causes no one to sin. Still, he makes the sin consonant with its penalty, made necessary from the many media and methods by which sins unfold. Thus God wills that those foreknown be damned, just as he wills that they lack love and the grace of final perseverance. Yet there is no contradiction in saying that God wills that another person merit grace and salvation; nor from this does it follow that some things in God's willing are frustrated. Just as God wills that this person be damned, so it is done, and just as God wills that this other be saved, so salvation, or at any rate the meritorious path that leads to it, is effected. So this perpetual obligation remains standing: sempiternal damnation follows from the impossibility of its implementation by God, so the interjection of truth, "Amen," follows upon this petition. It suggests that this seventh petition truly be realized. It touches upon lust, since a perpetual divorce from the church comes about from the evil of this spiritual lust. But all who have been swept up in such evil were never really a part of holy mother church; it is only known publicly in the death of such men regarding the church triumphant. Some call this a divorce by extension of meaning, in the same way they call the moment of death a liberation from evil, even though every one of the predestinate was freed from this evil in his conscience. Nor do I intend to argue about the propriety or lack thereof of this kind of term. And here the heresies of the friars creep in, along with their influence on papal power to absolve anyone who wishes from punishment and guilt. And the generally promulgated heresy about absolution, in which such calumnies are included, is left untouched, infecting and blinding the whole church. But still, it would be wrong to say that nobody is truly contrite, makes confession, or does any virtuous works unless he is eternally predestinate of God, because then the pope would not administer anything sacred, nor could he recognize that a man could do anything worthy of praise.

PART II
English Wycliffite Writings

FORMS OF LIVING

6. A Short Rule of Life[1]

The *Short Rule* is a comprehensive guide to daily conduct. It begins with a general section addressed to all readers that lays out a daily routine for meditation and prayer, then follows that with specific recommendations about proper conduct for members of each of the three estates. It draws on the *Speculum Ecclesie* or *Mirror of the Church*, a guide for religious written by Edmund of Abingdon and produced in various Latin and Anglo-Norman versions from the early thirteenth century, then translated into Middle English in several complete and excerpted versions (some of them plainly influenced by lollard ideas) in the fourteenth century. In its later recensions the *Mirror* appears to have been popular with lay readers because it combines catechetical instruction on the basics of faith, advice on how to behave, and a how-to guide for contemplative devotion, all within a single text.[2] This short alternative rule similarly gives its readers advice on how to feel, what to think and when, and how to act, but extends the scope of its advice on conduct to address all three estates.

A short rule of life for each man in general, and for priests and lords and laborers in particular, and how each man shall be saved as befits his status.

First, when you rise or fully awaken, think about the goodness of God. Out of his own goodness, for no other need, he made all things from nothing, including angels and men and all other creatures good in their nature.

Second, think about the great passion and willing death that Christ suffered for mankind. When no man might make reparation for the guilt of Adam and Eve and others besides, and there was no angel that could or ought to do so either, then Christ, out of his endless charity, suffered so great a passion and painful death that no created being might suffer so much.

Third, think how God has saved you from death and other misfortunes while he has allowed many thousands of others to be lost that night, some in water, some in fire, some in sudden death, some to be damned forever without end. Thank God with all your heart for this goodness and mercy. Pray to him to give you grace, that day and evermore, to use all the powers of your soul—mind, reason, wit, will—and all the powers of your body—strength, beauty, and all your five senses—in his service and his worship. In no way go against his commandments, but always be ready to perform works of mercy and give a good example of holy life, both in word and in action, to all around you.

Take care, next, that you are well occupied, and at no time idle and receptive to temptation. Take food and drink moderately, neither too costly nor too delicious, and avoid being overly concerned with them. Rather, take what God sends in such measure that you are fresher in your mind and wits to serve God. All the while thank him for his gifts.

Beyond this, be sure that you act justly and equitably toward all men, whether sovereigns, equals, subjects, or servants. Guide all men to love truth and mercy and practice justice, peace, and charity. Allow none to be at odds, but bring them to accord, if you can, by any good means.

What you should fear most is God and his wrath. And what you should love most is God and his law and his worship. Do not ask for worldly reward as the most important thing, but with all your heart desire the bliss of heaven through the mercy of God and your own good life. Think often about the dreadful judgment and the pains of hell, to keep yourself from sin, and about the endless great joys of heaven, to keep yourself virtuous. To the extent of your knowledge and ability, teach others to do the same.

At the end of the day, think how you have offended God, both how much and how often. Feel wholehearted sorrow for that, and amend it while you can. Think about how many God has allowed to perish in many ways on that day, some to be damned forever without end, and about how graciously he has saved you, not because you deserve it but through his own mercy and goodness. Therefore, thank him with all your heart. Pray to him that by grace you may remain, and end your life, in his true and pure service and true charity, and teach other men to do the same.

If you are a priest, that is to say, someone having care of souls, live in a holy way, excelling in holy prayer and holy desires and thoughts, in holy speech, counsel, and true teaching. May God's commandments, his gospel, and his virtues be always in your mouth, and may you always despise sin, to draw men from it. Your actions should be so rightful that no man can reasonably blame them—an open book displaying truth to all subjects and lay men, showing how to serve God and keep his commandments. For a public and long-lasting example of good living is better guidance for lay men than true preaching by words alone.

Do not waste your goods in great feasts like those of rich men, but live a simple life, on poor men's alms and goods, as regards food and drink and clothing. Give what is left over to poor men who have no livelihood and cannot work because they are weak or sick. In this way you will be a true priest, faithful to both God and man.

If you are a lord, make sure that you yourself live a rightful life, with regard to both God and other men. Keep God's commandments, do the works of mercy, govern your five senses well, and act with reason and equity and good conscience toward all men. Second, govern your wife, your children, and your household well in God's law. As far as you may, allow no sin among them, whether in word or in deed, so that they may be an example of holiness and rightfulness to all others. For you will be damned for their evil living and your evil negligence, unless you amend it as much as you can.

Third, govern your tenants well and maintain them in right and reason. Be merciful to them about their rents and fines, and do not allow your officers to do them wrong or extort from them. Chastise, in a good way, those who are rebels against God's commandments and virtuous life, more than you would for rebelliousness against your interest or person. For otherwise, you love your own interest more than God's, and yourself more than God almighty. Where is there a worse traitor to God than that? Love, reward, praise, and cherish the truth, and virtuous life, more than if they do only what brings you profit and honor. Maintain truly in rest and peace, to the extent of your knowledge and power, God's law, its true preachers, and God's servants. It is for this that you hold your lordship from God. And if you fail in this, you offend against God in all your lordship, in body and soul—most especially if, out of blindness and covetousness and worldly friendship, you maintain antichrist's disciples in their errors, and help to accuse and persecute true men that preach Christ's gospel and his life. Warn the people about their great sins, and about false prophets and hypocrites that deceive Christian men, in faith and virtuous life and worldly goods.

If you are a laborer, live in meekness, and truly and willingly do your labor, so that if your lord or master is a heathen man, by your meekness and willing and true service he will have no reason to complain against you or to speak ill of your God or of Christendom, but rather be guided toward Christendom.

Do not serve a Christian lord with complaints. Serve him truly and willingly not only in his presence, but even in his absence, not only out of worldly fear or for worldly reward, but out of fear of God and conscience and for reward in heaven. For the God who put you in this service knows what status is best for you and will reward you more than all earthly lords might, if you do it truly and willingly as he commands. In all things beware of complaining against God and the adversities he may impose—great labor and long, great sickness, and other adversities. Beware of anger, or cursing and reviling and vituperating of man or beast. Always maintain patience, meekness, and charity toward God and man.

Each man in these three estates should live in this way, and save himself, and help others.[3] By this means there may be good life, rest, peace, and charity among Christians, and they may be saved, and heathens soon converted, and God greatly praised among all nations and sects that now despise him and his law because of the wicked living of false Christians.

7. Five Questions on Love[4]

This text is a translation and adaptation of item 3, Wyclif's *On Love*, which is itself a response to the second half of Richard Rolle's massively popular *Form of Living* (see pp. 84–85 above). Rolle wrote the *Form of Living* in the first instance for a solitary enclosed religious woman, Margaret Kirkby, but it seems to have achieved a much wider audience among spiritually ambitious readers of the vernacular. Wyclif's response to it and this adaptation in their epistolary form and their claim to answer five questions posed by a "friend in God," similarly present themselves as a personal communication now also circulated to a wider audience.

A special friend in God asks in charity these five questions of a meek priest in God. First, what is love? Next, where is love? Third, he asks how God should meritoriously be loved. Fourth, he asks how a true man may know whether he loves his God in the form that God asks that a man love him. Fifth, he asks in what status in this life a man may best love his God, to gain most merit for coming to heaven. All these questions are hard to explain truly in English. Yet charity drives men to explain them as well as possible in English, so that men may know by this exposition what God's will is.

To the first question that is asked, men answer in this way. Love is a kind of work, that comes of a man's will, to will good toward a loved thing. And so love is in a man's heart, and [a man, in another way, is in love].[5] To the third question Christ answers in John's gospel. Christ says, *"He that has my commandments and keeps them in this life, he is that one who loves me"* (John 14:21). And thus his will is intent on loving God, who studies well God's law, as the first psalm says (Ps 1:2). As to the fourth question, a man may know by himself whether he thinks on God's law and loves it and keeps it, and then, Christ says, he loves God. As concerns the fifth question, it is known by God's law that there are in the church three estates that God has ordained: the estate of priests, the estate of knights, and the estate of commons.[6] Alongside these three there are three others, common and lawful by God's law: the status of virgins, the status of wedlock, and the status of widows. The status of virgins is highest, by witness of Christ and saints in heaven. One status is good for one man, and another for another; and God moves a man to his own best status if he does not hinder this by his sin.

But four statuses, of the emperor clerks, of monks, of canons, and of friars, seem perilous, and not ordained by God, but endured as a result of man's sin. And therefore men should beware about partaking in these four statuses. For other statuses that God has ordained bring men to the bliss of heaven better; and he is a great fool that leaves the better and chooses the worse. Thus, it is helpful here to Christians to study the gospel in that language in which they best know Christ's meaning. For our belief teaches us that each

Christian man is required to follow Christ here in his manner of living, some more remotely and some more closely, insofar as Christ gives him grace. And he who follows Christ most closely loves him most and is most loved of God. And since the life and works of Christ, and his teaching, are in the gospel, it is clearly to the benefit of men to study this book, in order to love Christ.

But in addition to this, the friend of God asks, what David intended in these two verses that he says in the psalter—and they are commonly known in Latin—*O Lord*, I confess to you that *I am your servant*, in body, soul, and I am *son of your handmaiden*, for I am a true child of holy church. *You have broken my bonds*, of sin, and bonds by which my soul loves my flesh; *to you I shall sanctify a host of praise*. And thus *I shall call* in to me *the name of the Lord*, to dwell in me (Ps 116:16–17). Martyrs may say these words, those who love God's law so much that they will suffer the pain of death for love and maintaining of this law. God has never shown a better cause of martyrdom that was more pleasing to him. Since a man must needs die, and God's law has now many enemies, a man should wisely put him forth to suffer now in this glorious way.

> Beware, man, stop not for sin,
> Priest, knight, yeoman, nor page,
> If you will of God have large wage
> Amen, amen, amen.

8. The Two Ways[7]

This treatise develops an extended exposition of the "two ways" of Matthew 7:13–14 and Luke 13:23–25, the narrow way that leads to the bliss of heaven and the broad way that leads to the pain of hell. It does so by means of a commentary on the commandments, showing that all those who keep the commandments are in the narrow way, while all those who break them are in the broad way. The struggle to keep the commandments is lopsided, not least due to the effects of original sin: "Our flesh always has the sickness that it tends toward madness if it has all that it desires" (p. 172). The solution, according to this author, is to live humbly. Eat, drink, and dress in moderation; suffer the wrongs of others; and do not fall into evil company, into gossip, or into lustful thoughts: this is the way of Christ, whom the text envisions as a model for righteous suffering and whose life it narrates briefly. While some scholars have contended that there is nothing lollard about this treatise, in the context of the selections in this volume its rejection of claims to religious perfection, and explanation of how all can and must follow the commandments, can be compared with similar preoccupations in other Wycliffite writings. The incipit of the single extant copy attributes the text to Sir John Clanvowe, one of the "Lollard knights" and a companion of Richard II and imitator of Chaucer.

Sir John Clanvowe, knight, wrote this following treatise on the last voyage he made over the great sea, on which he died. Jesus, have mercy on his soul. Amen.

The gospel tells that once when our Lord Jesus Christ was here on earth, a man came to him and asked him *if only a few men will be saved* (Luke 13:23). Christ responded and said, *The gate is wide and the way is broad that lead to loss, and many go in that way. But how strait is the gate and how narrow is the way that lead to life, and few find that way* (Matt 7:13–14).

By these words of Christ's, we may understand that the way that leads to the pain of hell is a broad way and that the way that leads to the bliss of heaven is a narrow way. For Christ calls the pain of hell loss and the bliss of heaven life, and therefore it would be very good if we tried to avoid the broad way and go on the narrow way, for every day we are heading very quickly toward another place and we do not know how soon we will leave this world. And when we pass from here, he who is at that time found on the broad way will go straight to the pain of hell, and he who is found on the narrow way will go straight to the bliss of heaven. And that bliss is so great that *no eye has seen, no ear has heard, nor has it come into man's heart the joy that God has prepared for those who love him* and will come to him (1 Cor 2:9). And that joy is not like the joy of this world. For all the joy of this world is temporary and is soon over and is foully mixed with fear and many other miseries and afflictions.

But the joy of heaven increases and increases, and it contains neither fear nor affliction nor misery. It does not lack anything that the heart may desire, and it lasts forever. Therefore, he who is found in the narrow way when he passes out of this world is fortunate, for he will dwell with God in everlasting bliss. And he who is found in the broad way when he passes out of this world is wretched, for he will have the pains of hell. And that pain is unlike any pain of this world. For every pain or torment in this world must have an end, either by death or in some other way. But the pain of hell is greater than any heart can imagine, and it will never end but always increase and increase. And he who is there will never die but live forever among the fiends in darkness and in torment without end.

Therefore, let us cry out to our Lord God and pray that of his endless mercy he may teach us his narrow way and give us grace to leave the broad way. But we must be meek and cry to him with a meek heart, for the Prophet says that God will teach his ways to those who are meek. And therefore, let us cry meekly to him with the Prophet, who says, *Lord, show me your ways and teach me your paths* (Isa 2:3; Mic 4:2).[8] But if God teaches us his ways out of his goodness and we sinfully leave his ways and follow other ways, then we will be much to blame and will deserve much penance. And the greater harm is that many do so because although they know the ways of God, nevertheless they leave them and follow the ways of the fiend, on account of the lust of their flesh or the desires of the world. Truly, they are greater fools than those who will not give up their weapons for all the king's treasure.[9]

For a weapon is an instrument that is made out of something worth little, with which a fool beats other men and with which other men often beat him in return, so that he both beats and is beaten with it. And though it serves no other purpose, yet a fool will always have it near him and will not give it up for any reason. And men say that when a fool loves his weapon this much, then that is proof that he is a natural fool. But they are proven to be even more foolish who will not let go of their wicked desires, which are worse than weapons, with which desires they both hurt other people and are hurt themselves. Yet they will not exchange them for all the treasure of the king of heaven. And therefore by their example men may know that the word of Christ is verified: *the wisdom of this world is folly before God* (1 Cor 3:19).

Therefore, for the love of God and of our own souls, let us not fall into that folly. But instead, when we know the ways of God, let us pray heartily to him that he may give us grace to remain steadfastly in them. And let us cry yet again to him with the Prophet, who says, *Lord, make perfect my goings out in your paths so that my footsteps may not be moved* (Ps 17:5). And if we busy ourselves and meekly ask God to help us, than we will learn his ways and walk in them and have the blessing that David speaks of in the psalter where he says, *blessed be all those who fear our Lord and who walk in his ways*, which is to say, blessed be all those who go in at the strait gate and wish to walk in the narrow way (Ps 128:1).

This narrow way is the keeping of God's commandments. This we can see and know from the words of Christ, when he spoke to the man who asked him what he should do to have everlasting life. Christ answered him: *If you want to enter eternal life, keep the commandments* (Matt 19:17). By these words and many others in holy writ we may well understand that there is no other way to heaven but by keeping God's commandments, so the commandments of God are the narrow way that leads to heaven. And the strait gate is the fear of God, through which we will leave our evil desires. This we may understand from holy writ, which says, *the fear of God is the beginning of wisdom* (Ps 111:10). There is no wise thing we can do that does not lead us toward the bliss of heaven. Thus the fear of God is the beginning of the narrow way that leads to heaven. Because it is the beginning and the entrance to that path, it is called the gate. Thus we may see by reason that keeping God's commandments is the narrow way that leads to life, and the fear of God is the strait gate of that way.

And just so, in the opposite way, the breaking of God's commandments is the broad way that leads to the pain of hell. For as the Prophet says to God, those who turn away from the commandments of God are accursed. And the wide gate of that broad way is carelessness in keeping God's commandments, through which we follow our evil desires and fall into the broad way to hell. May God in his endless mercy keep us from it and give us grace to go in through the strait gate and remain in the narrow way until it is his will to take us into the life to which that way leads. Truly, if we are wise, we will cry to God day and night to grant us this. Let us trust fully in him, that he will grant us all that is good for us, if we pray to him with a true heart. Therefore, let us go through the strait gate, that is to say, let us fear our Lord God, for he is the beginning of wisdom. Truly, we

167

ought to fear him indeed, for we have neither being nor life nor health nor wit except from him and by him. And when he so desires, he may take that from us. Also he is and will be our judge, and he knows all that we do and have done. There is nowhere we can flee from his judgment, for he is everywhere and almighty. Also, we have been sinful, and sin must be punished, in this world or another. Though our Lord God is full of mercy, he is also full of justice. Therefore, let us fear him more than anything, and that fear will make us leave our idleness and evil desires. This will be to our great profit if we are wise merchants.

For those who are considered wise merchants in this world, no matter how much they love money, when any of them sees that he may gain a hundred pounds by spending twenty pounds, he is more willing to spend those twenty pounds than to obtain forty or fifty pounds. And also, if a merchant knows that he may with twenty or thirty pounds avoid a loss of a hundred or two hundred pounds, he is more eager to spend twenty or thirty pounds for that reason than to receive freely fifty or sixty pounds. Truly, we should be much more glad to put aside our evil desires and our evil deeds, for by getting rid of them we may without any hindrance gain the bliss of heaven and avoid the pain of hell. And if we do this, we are wise merchants; and if we do not do this, no matter how much honor and comfort and wealth we receive in this world, we are fools.

But when our Lord Jesus Christ spoke of these two ways, he commanded them that they should strive to go in by the narrow way and the strait gate. Truly, if we wish to enter, we must do so. For we have three strong enemies that will not permit us to enter there without great strife. One is the fiend; the next is the world; and the third is our flesh. These three enemies are always trying to lead us through the wide gate into the broad way to hell and stop us from going through the strait gate into the narrow way to heaven. The fiend is always busy trying to stop us with falsehood and his tricks. Our flesh tries to stop us with lustfulness and frailty. And the world tries to stop us with folly and vanity. This is a very difficult struggle. But we may well take the example of the saints in heaven, who despite these enemies have passed through the narrow way to the bliss of heaven. They have left their words and their teachings to show us how we should come to heaven after them and withstand our enemies as they did, if we wish. Therefore, it is for us a great shame and endless harm if we do not keep to the way as those saints did. For with the grace of God we may go in that way as well as they did, if we want to. For among those saints, some were old men and old women feeble of body, some were young children, some innocent maidens, and some were strong in body, both men and women; some were rich and some poor. All these kinds of people wanted to leave their desires in this world in order to go through the strait gate, and therefore they are now in bliss and are much honored, both in heaven and on earth. Just so we must do, if we want to love and fear our God and not be careless about him. For the Wise Man says that each man *should turn away from evil through the fear of God*, and also the Prophet says that *God is near those who fear him* (Prov 3:7; Ps 85:9).[10]

But as it has been said before, the fiend will hinder us, in every way that he can, from fearing God. For he will suggest to us that there is no need to fear God so much, because God is full of mercy and because with the smallest cry for mercy that we are able to cry, God will forgive us. So if we are going to live a long time, we might as well enjoy physical comforts and desires until we near our end; then we can cry for mercy and have forgiveness. So we may enjoy our desires both in this world and also in heaven. The fiend also says that no one knows if heaven and hell exist as men say; therefore we should take what we can from this world, for of it we are certain.

And our flesh will suggest to us that it cannot suffer because it is tender, and that unless it has its desires it will fail us, and that comforts and desires exist so that we might enjoy them, and that it may not be happy without them, and that it would rather be dead than give them up. And thus will the flesh complain.

And the world will suggest to us that it is neither beneficial nor honorable for us to set aside our desires, and that all wise and honorable men work to gain physical comforts and desires and honor and great renown in this world, and if we did otherwise, men would blame us and scorn us and think little of us, and therefore it is wise and honorable for a man to conform himself to the world. And also he may be sure of the way of life that his position in society requires while he is alive. These are the arguments of the world.

But against all these enemies we have plenty of good and true arguments taught by Christ in his law. With these we can keep ourselves from these three cruel enemies and warriors. As regards the fiend, St. Peter warns us and teaches us in this way. He says, *Brothers, be serious and watchful, for your enemy the devil, roaring like a lion, goes about to seek whom he may swallow and destroy; but withstand him strong in faith* (1 Pet 5:8–9). By this apostle's counsel we will withstand him with faith. That is a true counsel. For our faith teaches us that the devil is a liar and is always trying to beguile us with falsehood. For we were created to pray to God. And if we do, and keep his commandments, and die so doing, we will be partakers in his bliss. And if we neglect God and break his commandments, then we will go to the pain of hell. And no matter how long a life the devil promises us, we will not live any longer for that. Even if we might live many thousands of years, still in the end we must die and be judged according to our deeds in this life. Therefore, if we have lived well, it is good that we continue to do so until we die. And if we have lived in evil, it is time we repented before our end.

Although God is merciful and good, that is not a reason to be bolder in sin, but it should make us more careful to refrain from sin. For the better the lord is, the better he should be served. Surely, there is no lord who would not be dissatisfied if his servant hurt him even more because of his trust in the lord's goodness and meekness. For that might make a lord very stern to his servant. Therefore, we may well feel that the fiend's teaching is false and wicked, against our true belief. Therefore, with our true belief, we should steadfastly withstand him and his lies.

For St. James says, *Withstand the devil, and he will flee from you* (Jas 4:7). Thus with the grace of God we will make the strong enemy flee. But we must be very cautious, for though he may flee at one time, he will come back again with another deception. For he is full of deceptions. Also, if our flesh or the world attacks us, the fiend will always be with them, to see how he may help to deceive us. And if he cannot do anything to us in this way, he will assail us on his own in other ways, or by other means, like these:

He will often try to bring a man into gluttony, and if he cannot, he will try to bring him to excessive abstinence. Or some men he will tempt to be covetous and too concerned about worldly things. But if he cannot overcome them in this way, he will try to bring them into the sin of sloth. Some he tries to bring into despair, but if he cannot do that, he tries to make them sin even more out of trust in God's mercy. Thus the fiend is always busy with many sins and temptations to draw us into the broad way to hell. Therefore, we must always be ready to withstand him with strong faith. For our belief teaches us about these temptations: neither gluttony nor excessive abstinence is a virtue, but instead the mean between these is a virtue, that is, moderation in food and drink, as nature requires.

And also, desiring to have too many worldly things is a vice, and sloth is a vice, but the mean between these two is a great virtue. That is, to labor truly for what one needs, and if a man gets more than that, to help his needy brothers and neighbors with it.

Also, it is a great sin to mistrust the mercy of God, and it is a great sin to sin more out of trust in God's mercy. Yet the mean between these two is a great virtue, that is, to reject evil out of fear of God and do good out of love of God.

Therefore, in this way our belief will teach us the middle way of virtue between the extremes of vice. The fiend wants to draw us away from virtue and lead us into vice. Therefore, we must walk in virtues and strongly withstand the fiend with our faith, in these temptations and all others. Then, by doing this, we will have our reward from God and victory over our old enemy, the fiend.

Also we must strive strongly against our flesh, for if we follow the lustfulness of the flesh or obey its frailty, it will lead us by the wide gate into the broad way of hell. For as St. Paul says, *The flesh desires against the spirit, and the spirit against the flesh; these two desire against each other*, but the works of the flesh are vices and the fruits of the spirit are virtues (Gal 5:17). Therefore, Paul teaches us that we should *not walk according to the flesh, but according to the spirit,* for he says that *the wisdom of the flesh is death and that the wisdom of the spirit is life and peace. The wisdom of the flesh is enemy to God and is not, and cannot be, subject to the law of God.* Therefore, he says to us that *if we live according to the flesh we will die,* that is to say, we will be damned. But *if through the spirit we make dead the deeds of our flesh we will live,* which is to say that we will be saved (Rom 8:4, 6–7, 13).

Therefore, let us follow this true counsel of the gospel and deaden the vices of the flesh. For as the Apostle also teaches, God, out of his goodness, does not want us to deaden our flesh but to deaden the deeds of our flesh, which are vices fighting against the spirit. For God of his great mercy wants us to let our flesh have all that it reasonably needs: enough food and drink and clothing. God wants us to take these things in such measure as is best for us. God is not pleased when we take so much of these things that it does us harm, just as a good doctor is not pleased when a sick man takes more than will do him good, although the sick man often desires to have more than is good for his life and his health. And therefore if we are to enter at the gate, we must rightly rule our flesh, just as men keep a sick man who is disposed to fall into ravings, hoping to bring him back to health.

For our flesh always has the sickness that it tends toward madness if it has all that it desires. If it is in this madness, then it would readily harm its nearest and best friends, for it is that kind of madness. Therefore, with good discipline from the spirit let us deaden the vicious lusts and deeds of the flesh and let us give the flesh all that is good for it and no more. Then the flesh will live and be whole. And so we will live together forever in endless bliss and our good hope will make us rule our flesh well and keep it from this unreasonable lustfulness while we are here in this sorrowful world, in good hope that the least thing that we willingly suffer now in our flesh will turn into much more bliss than anything we could imagine here on earth. In this way, through the grace of God and through good hope, we will subdue the flesh and walk according to the spirit through the strait gate into the narrow way that leads to heaven.

We must also strive very hard against the world, which with folly and vanity tries hard to bring us into the broad way that leads to hell. And therefore let us do as St. Paul teaches, for he commands us that we should *savor those things that are above and not the things that are here on earth* (Col 3:2). Truly, if we take heed, this is a true counsel. For if we look at the things that are above, we will find there our Lord God and his blessed mother, his angels, and his saints, with endless rest, joy, and peace. And if we look at the things that are here on earth, we will find that there is nothing without toil or fear or anger or some other misery. As anything that is gained here soon passes away, therefore, for the love of God, let us not set our hearts so much upon the foul stinking muck of this false, failing world. Instead, with good reason we should have great relish in those things that are above and love them with all our hearts. For they are good, delightful, certain, and lasting. Certainly we should despise and hate the vain things of the world, for they are evil, unpleasant, uncertain, and ephemeral. Also they are opposed to the things above.

St. John says, *Do not love the world or the things that are in the world. For whoever loves the world, the love of God is not in him. For everything that is in the world is the desire of the flesh, or the desire of the eyes, or the pride of life, which is not from the Father of heaven but from the world* (1 John 2:15–16).

And St. James says that *the friendship of this world is an enemy toward God, and that whoever wants to be a friend of this world becomes an enemy to God* (Jas 4:4). What could be more foolish for us, then, than to love this wretched world, since we see well from the teaching of these saints that loving the world will bring us from the love of our Father in heaven and make us his enemies? Let us pray heartily to our Lord God, the Father of heaven, to give us grace to love him and despise this world. For certainly, we may not love him as well as we should if we love the world. For this world is full of falsehood, vanity, and folly, and all this is contrary to God. Also, those who put their trust in this world are all deceived, and those who put their whole trust in God and in heavenly things above are always secure and will lack nothing that is good for them. And also the world can give nothing to those who love it, though they please it ever so much. For to those that best love it, the world can give nothing except such things as it calls riches and worship, which are falsely named. For if these things were truly named, men would call them sorrow and shame. For it requires much work to acquire that which is called riches, and much fear to keep it, and great sorrow to lose it, so that from the first gaining of wealth to the last abandoning of it, everything is sorrow. And they who have great fortunes in this world are as often incensed as they are fearful and sick, and they die as soon as those who had no such riches, and when they are dead, their wealth hinders them from coming to heaven more than it helps them. For Christ said that it *was hard for a rich man to enter the kingdom of heaven* (Matt 19:23).

And therefore the filth of this world that is called riches should be called sorrow, and not riches, for when we have the greatest need it can do nothing for us. And so by reason we ought to despise such riches and work hard *to build up treasure in heaven*, as Christ commands (Matt 19:21; cf. Mark 10:21, Luke 18:22). For that is true, delightful treasure that will never fail, but treasure here on earth is false and ephemeral and foolish. Therefore, as St. Paul says, and as it has been said here above, let us take delight in those things that are in heaven above. With the delight of them we should despise the false, unsavory things that are here on earth, which if we took delight in them would bring us into the broad way of hell, for there the delight of earthly things has led many people. Thus St. Paul witnesses when he says that those who wish to become rich have fallen into temptations and into the devil's pantry and into many unprofitable and envious desires that draw men into manslaughter and also bring men to the loss of their body and their soul. Therefore, by this and by many other authorities, and also by right reason, we may well see that these things that men here call riches are not true riches but rather worthless things that prohibit men from gathering for themselves the fair riches of heaven, which are true riches. Therefore, let us take delight in the riches above and despise all that is here on earth that would prohibit us from going in the strait way that leads to the bliss of heaven.

And also, the honors of this wretched world that men desire so greatly are not honors, nor ought they truly to be called honors, if we are well taught. We may be certain that before God, who is himself the truth, they are neither riches nor honors. For before God all virtue is honor and all sin is shame, but in this world it is the reverse. For the world considers honorable the great warriors and fighters who destroy and conquer many lands, who waste, and who give much to those who already have enough, and who spend outrageously on food, drink, clothing, buildings, and living in ease, sloth, and many other sins. Also, the world greatly honors those who revenge themselves proudly and mercilessly for every wrong that is said or done to them, and of such folk men make books and songs and read and sing of them in order to keep the memory of their deeds alive longer here on earth. For that is a thing that worldly men desire greatly: that their name might outlast them here on earth. But whatever the world thinks of such people, let us learn well that God is sovereign truth and a true judge who considers them shameful before God and the whole company of heaven, for in them is all sin, shame, and dishonor.

But such folk who wish to live humbly in this world, away from this riot, noise, and strife, and live simply, and eat and drink in moderation, and dress modestly, and suffer patiently the wrongs that other people do and say to them, and consider themselves paid well enough with few worldly goods and desire neither a great name nor many goods, such folk the world scorns and calls them lollards and rogues, fools and shameful wretches.[11] But in truth, God considers them the most wise and most honorable, and he will honor them forever in heaven while those whom the world worships will be shamed and punished forever in hell unless they amend themselves before they pass out of this world. Therefore, let us take delight in the things that are so good and honorable above and let us never pay heed when the world scorns us or calls us wretches. For the world scorned Christ and considered him a fool, and he suffered everything patiently. St. Paul says that Christ suffered for us, giving us an example that we might do the same, following in his footsteps. Therefore, let us follow in his footsteps and suffer patiently the scorn of the world, as he did, and then he will give us grace to enter by the narrow way into the honorable bliss where he reigns. And if we follow the honors of this world, as God forbids, they will quickly bring us by the broad way into the shameful place where the fiend is, which is to say the pain of hell.

Also, it behooves us greatly to be watchful that we neither follow the evil company of this world nor conform ourselves too much to that company, for that is something that may quickly bring us into the broad way of hell. For oftentimes evil company encourages men to sin when the fiend, the flesh, and the world would not encourage them if they were not in such evil company, and thus oftentimes men go to the tavern and get drunk or to the brothel and commit lechery. And they sometimes fight and commit other sins to please the evil companions whom they follow, yet if they were not in that evil company they would not do these things, either because of the fiend's temptations or the desires of the flesh or the vanity of the world. Therefore, it seems in such a case that evil company is worse than any of these three enemies, and this the devil knows full well. Therefore, he does as a fowler of birds would do, who first takes a bird and makes it a watch-bird and sets it to sing beside his net; and then, when other birds see it and hear it sing, they all come down to it, and then the fowler draws his net and captures them. Some he slaughters, and some he keeps to make watch-birds of, in order to beguile everyone with the watch-birds. Thus the fiend acts: when he takes a lecherous man, he often feeds him with the foul desires of the flesh and of the world, and then he takes him and makes him into a "watch-man," so that he may by his enticing and his evil example cause more men to fall and be caught in the fiend's net. And he does this again and again until at the end he takes them all to a foul death, unless it so be that through the grace of God they break out of his net and fly up to heaven. Therefore, it is necessary that we pray diligently to God that he preserve us from evil company, lest we fall down with them and be caught by our old enemy, just as he caught Adam, our forefather, by enticing Eve, his wife, and by overcoming Adam the fiend gained power over all mankind until our blessed Lord Jesus Christ suffered a painful death in order to capture mankind back from the fiend's power.

But now, sinful men and the "watch-men" of the fiend are called good fellows by the world, because they waste the goods that God has given them. In worldly pride and the lusts of their flesh they go to the tavern and the brothel and play at dice and stay awake long into the night, and swear loudly and drink and gossip too much, scorning, backbiting, complaining, boasting, lying, and fighting. They are a fetter to their fellows. And they all live in sin and vanity and are considered good fellows, and because of such cursed fellowship there is now more harm in the world. Truly, all such fellowship walks in the broad way that leads to the loss of the body and of the soul. And as the gospel says, few men find the narrow way that leads to bliss. Yet of those few, when they come among those who go the narrow way, they speak to those who remain on the broad way and counsel them to turn to the narrow way that leads to bliss, but those on the broad way frequently hinder them and scorn them, insult them and blame them and hold with others who maintain their evil deeds, and they become weary of fellowship with those on the narrow way. Yet despite all this, the narrow way is the way of God, and the broad way is the way of the fiend. Nevertheless, the world calls them fools who follow God's ways, and men call them good and honorable fellows who follow the fiend's ways, and so in this world the service of the fiend is honored and praised. Therefore, it is true, as St. John says, that *this whole world is turned to evil* (1 John 5:19). Since this is so, let us follow St. Paul, who commands us that we should *not desire to become like the world* (Rom 12:2).

Therefore, let us despise this wretched, false world that is turned to evil, and let us take delight in the good things that are above. And in this way, as it has been said above, let us withstand the fiend with strong faith and let us subdue the flesh with good hope, and let us despise the world with the charity of God and the bliss of heaven; and then we will with God's grace go in through the strait gate and go forth in the narrow way, which with God's mercy will bring us to the bliss of heaven. And when God, of his great goodness, has given us grace to enter onto the narrow way, then it is good that we remain there and not fall away into the broad way; that is, it is good that we keep the commandments of God and break them for no reason, for it has already been said before that the narrow way is the keeping of God's commandments and the broad way is the breaking of the same commandments. And therefore we should understand that there are ten commandments, which are these that follow:

The first is that we should have no other God but our
   Lord God of heaven.
The second is that we should not take the name of our
   Lord God in vain.
The third is that we should hallow our holy day.
The fourth is that we should honor our father and
   our mother.
The fifth is that we should kill no man.
The sixth is that we should commit no adultery.
The seventh is that we should not steal.
The eighth is that we should bear no false witness against
   our neighbor.
The ninth is that we should not covet our neighbor's house.
The tenth is that we should not desire our neighbor's wife
   nor his servant nor his maiden nor his ox nor his ass
   nor anything of his.

And of these ten commandments, the first three pertain to the love and worship of God, and the other seven pertain to our fellow

Christians. Therefore, let us take very great care to keep these commandments and not to break any of them.

For all those who hold any false belief or commit idolatry or witchcraft, or who love or fear or worship anything more than God, they break the first commandment. And all those who take the name of God falsely or in vain, they break the second commandment. And all those who on the holy day do not commit themselves to the service of God and refrain from all earthly works that are in their power, or who spend holy days in worldly business, in the lusts of the flesh, or in the mirth of vanity, they break the third commandment.

And all those who do not honor their father or their mother, or who do not help or comfort them in body and soul in their time of need, as it lies in their power, or who do not honor their spiritual mother, holy church, as they ought to do, they break the fourth commandment.

And all those who kill any man in thought, in order, or in deed, they break the fifth commandment, unless they are men who have authority by good reason to put to death men who deserve death according to God's law. And all those who commit lechery in any degree, naturally or unnaturally, they break the sixth commandment. And all those who rob or steal or take their neighbor's goods by force or extortion, or by any deceit or falsehood, they break the seventh commandment. And all those who bear false witness against their neighbor or slander or injure them falsely break the eighth commandment. And all those who covet their neighbor's house, land, or anything of his only for the sake of coveting it break the ninth commandment. And all those who desire their neighbor's wife or household servant or maiden, even if they do not achieve their desire, nevertheless just by their desire break the tenth commandment.

Also, all those who break any of these commandments remain in the broad way that leads to hell until they repent and fully desire to keep all of the commandments, as it lies in their power, until the end of their lives. So it is very perilous to break the commandments and very profitable to keep them. Worldly and fleshly men think that the commandments are very hard to keep, but in truth, those who are spiritual and love God well think them not difficult to keep. For St. John says that it is *the* charge *of God that we keep his commandments, and his commandments are not burdensome* (1 John 5:3).[12]

Therefore, if we love God as we ought to do, we should always keep these ten commandments, loving and fearing God as our Father and our Lord, and loving our neighbor as ourselves. And this we may well know from the words of Christ, who said to a man who asked him *what was the greatest commandment of the law.* Jesus answered and said, *You shall love the Lord your God with all your heart and all your soul and all your mind and all your strength; this is the first and the greatest commandment. The second is similar to this: you shall love your neighbor as yourself. And in these two commandments is all the law and the prophets* (Matt 22:36–40). Since we may keep all the commandments of God by loving God and our neighbor, we ought not to consider it burdensome to keep these commandments, nor should we complain about keeping them in that way.

For truly, it is reasonable, delightful, and profitable to love God above all other things, and to love our neighbor as ourselves. It is reasonable because God created us out of nothing in his own image and likeness and ordained us, if we ourselves we wish it, to be partners with him in the bliss of heaven. He has ordained everything that is here on earth for our help and our comfort. He gives us everything we have that is good, and he grants us everything fitting that we ask of him with a good, true heart. And when we had lost our share of paradise through the sin of Adam, for love of us he came and took flesh and blood of the blessed maiden Mary and became man for us and was born of that blessed maiden without the loss of her virginity. The time of his blessed birth was in the coldest days of winter and in a poor and cold hut, and when he was born his blessed mother wrapped him in a few poor clothes and laid in him a manger, between an ox and an ass, to keep him warm. There were no finer clothes, and he came into this world as poor and humble as possible in order to give us an example of humility and willful poverty. And on the eighth day after his birth, he was circumcised and shed for us some of his precious blood.

After that, he remained here on earth more than thirty-two winters and preached and taught the people the right way to heaven and worked many wonders and healed many people, both physically and spiritually. He suffered heat and cold and thirst, wetness and dryness, and evil lodgings, scorns, reproofs, injuries, rebukes, wrongs, and many other spites and great ills.

And at the last his own disciple betrayed him for his goodness, and afterward they took him and bound him as a thief and led him to their bishop.[13] There they accused him falsely and struck him and blindfolded him and scorned him and spat on his blessed face as they would have done on a dog. After that, he was led before Pontius Pilate, and there he was falsely accused and imprisoned and afterward stripped naked and bound to a pillar and beaten with sharp scourges until his whole blessed body, which never sinned, ran with blood. Afterward, they set on his blessed head a crown of great sharp thorns and clothed him as a fool and scorned him, and after that they condemned him falsely to death and ordered him to hang between two thieves. As weary and bloody as he was, they made him to carry on his own back the heavy cross on which he would die, in the sight of his blessed mother, his kin, and his other friends. And when he came to the place of common justice, they nailed his blessed feet and his hands with great coarse nails and drew his holy limbs upon the cross. Yet in all his great pains, this innocent man prayed for his enemies and said, *Father, forgive them this guilt, for they do not know what they are doing* (Luke 23:34). For spite, they hung one thief on his right hand and another on his left, with him hanging between the two. Then he was very thirsty on account of the great pains that he had suffered and the bleeding that he had bled, and they gave him easel and gall to drink. But when he learned what it was he would not drink it, but bowed down his blessed head and gave up the ghost. Then there came a knight called Longinus, who pierced him through the heart with a spear, and out came water and blood. All this he suffered for us, and afterward his blessed body was taken down from the cross and buried. Then he went down to hell, and from there he brought out all those whom he loved.

The third day afterward, he arose from death to life and showed himself to many men and women in many ways; afterwards, in the sight of his disciples, he ascended into heaven. And now, in his great goodness, he keeps us from many perils and we sorely aggrieve him every day, yet he spares us, to see if we will amend ourselves over time. And though we sin ever so greatly, yet he forgives us gladly just as soon as we are sorry for our sins and fully desire to sin no more. Therefore, when we reflect on these things, which God out of his great goodness has done and does every day for us, and on the hard pains that he has suffered for us, we may well know that it is reasonable to love God above all other things, as it is said before.

And also it is reasonable that we love our neighbor as our self, for it is the will and the commandment of God that we do so. Also, our neighbor is of the same form and nature that we are, and therefore naturally we should heartily love one another for good reason.

It is also delightful for us to love God above all other things and our neighbor as our self. For he who loves God over all things may well delight in thinking that he loves him who surpasses all other things in goodness, in fairness, in wisdom, and in power, and that God of his great goodness will love him in return a thousandfold better than any heart can think or imagine. He will have the love of the whole company of heaven and of all good folk on earth, and that will not pass away as worldly love does, but it will last forever without end. And to love our neighbor as our self is joyful for the body and the soul. So the love of God and of our neighbor is full of joy and is of greater delight than any other thing.

It is also profitable to love God above all other things and our neighbor as our self, for he who does so will have the bliss of heaven that will last forever, and that is the greatest profit that ever can be. Therefore, since the love of God and our neighbor is so reasonable, delightful, and profitable, as it has been proved here above, we would be great fools unless we keep ourselves in all our strength in that love, for that is the narrow way that leads to heaven, which has been spoken of heretofore. Therefore, we pray heartily to our Lord Jesus Christ that of his great mercy he may give us grace to come into that way and remain there.

But there are many people who say that they are in that way when it is not so. For everyone says that they love God above all other things. But whatever they may say, Christ, who cannot lie, says thus: *Those who love me will keep my words and my commandments, and my Father will love him, and we will come to him and make our dwelling with him; and he who does not love me does not keep my words* (John 14:23–24). Also Christ says: *He who has my commandments and keeps them, that is he who loves me* (John 14:21). And St. John says that *we know that we know God if we keep his commandments* (1 John 2:3). And whoever says that he knows God but does not keep his commandments is a liar, and the truth is not in him.

And also St. John says that we do not *love with word nor with tongue, but with deed and with truth* (1 John 3:18).

And therefore we may well know from these words of Christ and of his apostles and by many other authorities of holy writ that no man may come to the bliss of heaven unless he desires to keep the commandments of God, which are fully kept by those who love God and their neighbor as themselves, as they should do, as it has been said before.

And therefore all those who love God and love their neighbor as themselves are in the narrow way that leads to the bliss that will last forever.

And all those who do not love God and their neighbor in this way are in the broad way that leads to the death of hell and the pain that will last forever.

Therefore, let us lift up our hearts to our Lord God almighty, who has made us and has redeemed us with his precious blood, and let us pray heartily of him, of his great goodness and his endless mercy, that he give us grace to keep out of the broad way that leads to the hideous pains of hell, and grant us grace to go in the narrow way that leads to the bliss of heaven, until we come to that bliss that he has ordained for those who love him. Amen.

9. On Holy Prayers[14]

On Holy Prayers focuses on prayer and is more polemical than many of the selections here, devoting extended discussion to the inefficacy of the false prayers of sinful priests. Yet it is also a commentary on the Pater Noster in disguise and draws extensively on mainstream commentaries on prayer in order to develop its unusual emphasis on how any Christian may *pray without ceasing* (as Paul enjoins in 1 Thessalonians 5:17), regardless of his or her occupation or social position, through keeping the commandments in daily life in the world. The efficacy of one's prayer is closely connected to one's moral standing, and the best prayers are those made sincerely, in the name of Jesus, for spiritual rather than worldly goods. In contrast to lengthy, new-fangled, and complex sung prayers, this text ranks the Pater Noster above all others; it "contains all things which are necessary and profitable for the body and soul" (p. 184). More than half of the text is devoted to an analysis of the prayers of wicked men; not only does God not hear them, according to a long series of citations from the Old and New Testaments, but also the law of the church proscribes obedience to the wicked. Like the author of this text, many Wycliffites sought to hold the clergy to the standards of behavior they found in the Bible, rather than (as earlier commentators have suggested) to eliminate the clerical estate altogether.[15]

How the prayer of good men is of great benefit, and the prayer of sinful men displeases God and harms themselves and others.

Our Lord Jesus Christ teaches us to pray at all times for all the things that are necessary to both the body and the soul. For in the gospel of St. Luke, Christ says that *it is necessary to pray at all times,* and St. Paul commands Christian men to *pray without ceasing* and without delay (Luke 18:1; cf. 1 Thess 5:17). This means the prayer of charity, and not the prayer of a man's voice, as St. Augustine explains well, for otherwise no man could fulfill the command to pray at all times.[16] As long as a man lives a just life, keeping God's commandments and charity, then he prays well, regardless of what he is doing; and whoever lives best, prays best. Also, St. James says that the diligent and *continuous prayer of a just man is worth much* (Jas 5:16). Therefore, *when Moses* was on the mountain and *held up his hands* and prayed for his people, *his people had victory* over their enemies; *when he* ceased to pray, *his people were overcome,* as the second book of scripture teaches (Exod 17:11).

If priests dwell on the hill of a high spiritual life, keep watch for the deceits of the fiend and show them to the people through true preaching, and hold up their hands, that is, their public good works; and if they persist in these and pray with a burning desire to do the justice of God's law and commandments, then Christian people will have victory over the fiend of hell and over cursed sin, and calm, peace, and charity will dwell among them. But if priests cease their holy life and their good example and their desire for justice, Christian people will be greatly overcome by sin and have much pestilence and wars and woe and, unless God helps them, endless woe in hell. Also, King Hezekiah was given remission of his sins *and fifteen years of life on account of his holy prayer and weeping* and sorrow; *and the sun went back*, or turned again, *ten lines on the clock*, as the book of Isaiah witnesses (Isa 38:5, 8). Also, the sun and the moon stood still all day on account of the holy prayer of the noble leader Joshua to give light to pursue God's enemies, who wished to do away with God's name, his law, and his people (Josh 10:12).

Therefore, Christ says to his disciples, *if you ask my Father for anything in my name, he will give it to you* (John 16:23). We ask in the name of Jesus when we ask for anything necessary or profitable to the salvation of men's souls. We ask this devoutly, out of great desire, and knowingly, humbly, and continuously, through serious faith, just hope, and lasting charity. And whatever we ask for in this way, we will have from the Father of heaven. Also, Christ says in the gospel: *If you evil men know how to give good things to your children*, which good things have been given to you, *how much more will your Father in heaven give a good* spirit *to men who ask him?* (Matt 7:11). Then, if nature teaches sinful men to give goods to their children, how much more will God, who is the author of goodness and charity, give to his children, whom he loves so much, the spiritual goods profitable to the soul? Therefore, ask God for heavenly goods, such as grace, will, knowledge, and the power to serve God at his pleasure, and not for worldly goods, except insofar as they are necessary to sustain life in the truth and service of your God. For Christ teaches us that whatever we pray and ask for, we should believe and trust without any doubt that we will have it and that it will be done for us. And *if two* or three *of you agree together on anything on earth that you might ask for, it will be done to them* (Matt 18:19).

This is why Christ taught and commanded us to pray the Pater Noster, which is the best and simplest and truest prayer of all.[17] For it contains all things that are necessary and profitable for the body and soul, but no error or any single thing against God's will. Jesus Christ composed it and commanded us to say it in few words, in order that men should not be burdened or made weary by saying it or be overburdened with learning it. And therefore a saint blames men who neglect the Pater Noster, which was taught and commanded by God, and instead choose the private prayers composed by sinful men.[18] Thus it is clear that holy men who live in charity toward God and toward all men living on earth, both friends and enemies, Christian and heathen, profit much by devout prayers, but most by a holy life and the desire for justice.

See now how the prayers of wicked men displease God and harm themselves and the people. God himself says this to evil men who pray to him in need: *I have called, and you have forsaken me and have shown contempt for my counsel and reprimands, and I will delight in your perishing and will scorn you when the thing that you fear comes to you. Then they will call, and I will not hear; they will rise early in the morning and will not find me, for they hated my discipline,* that is, my teaching and chastising, *and they did not have the fear of the Lord. And they did not pay attention to my advice, and rejected and ignored my correction,* that is, my reproving, warning, and chastising them for sin (Prov 1:24–26, 28–30). By the prophet Isaiah, God says this to wicked men: *You princes of Sodom, hear the Lord's word; you people of Gomorrah, listen with your ears to the law of our Lord God. Your incense is an abomination to me. I will not stand for your holy day,* that is, your principal feast, *and the Sabbath and other feasts. Your guilds are evil; my soul has hated your feasts of the calends and your solemnities; they are burdensome and annoying. And when you hold forth your hands, I will turn my eyes away from you, and when you make many prayers, I will not hear, for your hands are full of blood,* that is, of the wrongful deaths of men and of foul sins (Isa 1:10, 13–15).

Also, God says that the prayer of the man who turns away his ear, so that he does not hear the law, is abominable or cursed. God also says by the prophet Malachi: *And now to you, priests, I give this commandment, if you will hear. And if you will not give glory to my name with your whole heart, says the Lord of companies or hosts, I will send among you famine and put a curse on your blessings; and I will curse them, for you have not set this commandment on your heart. Lo, I will* send armies against you and *spread all over your face the dung, or dirt, of your solemnity.* By the same prophet, God says to priests and ministers of the temple: *Who is among you who will sit and incense my altar willfully and freely, without a reward?* None will say it. The Lord of hosts says, *There is no good will toward me among you, and I will receive no gifts of sacrifice from your hand.* By the same prophet God says to priests, *You have covered the altar of the Lord with tears and weeping and mourning,* that is, of the widows and the poor men whom you oppress and deceive, *so that I will look on your sacrifice no more, and I will not receive any pleasant thing from your hand* (Mal 2:1–3; 1:10; 2:13). Therefore, David says, *if I have held wickedness in my heart, the Lord will not hear* by his grace, that is, if I knowingly and gladly do wickedness (Ps 66:18). God says to the sinful man, *Why do you talk about my justice and take my covenant in your mouth?* (Ps 50:16). The Holy Spirit says of Judas Iscariot, *His prayer is turned into sin* (Ps 109:7). And our Lord Jesus says, *This people worships me with their lips, but their heart is far from me. They worship me for no reason, teaching the laws and commandments of men*, that is, of such men who teach and believe men's laws, traditions, and commandments rather than scripture and God's commandments, vainly and falsely worshiping God (Matt 5:8–9).

Also, Jesus says to wicked men: *Why do you say to me, "Lord, Lord," but fail to do the things that I commanded?* (Luke 6:46). For Jesus says, *Woe to you, scribes and Pharisees, hypocrites, for you devour widows' houses, praying your long prayers; therefore you will receive the greater judgment* (Matt 23:14). In the gospel of St. John is written thus: *And you know that God does not hear sinful men, but if any man worships God and does his will, God hears him* (John 9:31). When a priest says his mass without being of good and charitable life, and consecrates the sacrament, he eats and drinks his own damnation, not discerning wisely the body of our Lord, as St. Paul teaches in scripture (1 Cor 11:27–29). Therefore, Chrysostom says on the gospel of Matthew: "As a thing may be without odor or savor, but odor may not be without a thing, so a good deed without prayer is something, but prayer without a good deed is nothing."[19] St. Augustine says on the psalter, "If you eat more than your fill of meat and drink and live in gluttony and drunkenness, then whatever your tongue might speak, your life blasphemes God."[20] Therefore, St. Paul says, *many men claim that they know God, but through their deeds they deny God* (Titus 1:16). And St. Gregory writes in many books, "A man who is implicated in grievous sins does not do away with other men's sins while he is weighed down with his own. For it is known to all Christian men, that when someone who is despised is sent forth to pray, the hearts of those who are angry are provoked to greater wrath and vengeance."[21] Truly it is written, the sacrifices of wicked men are abominable to the Lord; the vows or sacrifices of just men are pleasant. For in the judgment of God almighty, it does not matter what is given, but by whom. Therefore, it is written in scripture, *the Lord beheld Abel and his gifts* (Gen 4:4). When Moses wished to say that the Lord gave a reward for gifts, he diligently set down the way God beheld Abel, from which it is clearly seen not that the offerer pleases God by his gifts but that the gifts please God on account of the offerer. Indeed, God almighty does not approve of the gifts of wicked men, nor considers their offerings, nor will have mercy on their sins, on account of the multitude of their sacrifices. Also, the Lord is far from wicked men, and he will graciously hear the prayers of just men. All this St. Gregory says in the pope's law.[22]

Now see how strict man's law is against the prayer of sinful men. The pope commands in his law that no man should hear the mass of a priest whom he knows without doubt to have a concubine or a lover, and this law is confirmed by the holy council under a great penalty. On this Pope Alexander says, "We command and require that no man hear the mass of a priest whom he knows without doubt to have a lover or a woman whom he married clandestinely." The holy council confirmed this law, and says, "Whatever priest, deacon, or subdeacon keeps and publicly marries a concubine, or fails to leave her after he has married her, we command, by the statutes of St. Leo the pope, and Pope Nicholas, on the chastity of clerks, and on God's behalf and by the authority of Peter and Paul, and notwithstanding any contradiction, that he sing no mass nor read from the gospels or epistles at mass, and that he not remain within the choir at divine service with those who have obeyed the law of chastity, and that he receive no portion of the church's goods."[23] Also, Pope Gregory says this: "If there are any priests, deacons, or subdeacons who are living in the sin of fornication, we forbid them, on God's behalf and by the authority of St. Peter, to enter the church until they do penance and are reconciled. But if any of them would rather remain in their sin, then none of you should presume to hear their office or divine service, for their blessings turn into curses and their prayer turns into sin, as our Lord witnesses by the prophet Malachi: 'God says, I will curse your blessings.'"[24] Truly, those who will not obey this most wholesome precept fall into the sin of idolatry, that is, the worship of false gods: so the prophet Samuel and St. Gregory witness.[25] It is the sin of witches,

187

of men who are outside the Christian faith, not to be obedient, and it is the sin of idolatry to will not to assent.

Also, it is written there that if any bishop, priest, or deacon henceforth takes a woman, or fails to leave her if he has taken one, he falls from his order until he makes satisfaction, and he shall not remain in the choir with men who sing God's service, and he shall not take any part of the goods of the church.[26] Also, if any bishop consents, whether by prayer or price, to the fornication of priests or deacons in his diocese, or if he fails to denounce those who commit such sins, he will be suspended from his office, that is, deposed, as the law says.[27] Also, Augustine says that, truly, no man does more harm in the church than he who acts wickedly and bears the name of the order of holiness or priesthood. For no one will presume to correct him when he sins, and his sin will give an example, as it happens when a sinful man is held in reverence because of his orders. And so the bishop who fails to correct the sin of such men is more worthy to be called an unchaste hound than a bishop.[28]

Now, since lechery makes priests unable to enter into holy church, and to say mass, and to have their part of the tithes and offerings, and men should not hear their services when their sin is public, there should be much greater penalties for greater sins, such as pride, envy, covetousness and gluttony, usury, the theft of God's word, and simony, which surpasses all other sins. For the more serious sin deserves the greater punishment. Pride makes men forsake God, the king of humility, and take Lucifer as their false king, as God says in scripture. Envy and wrath make men forsake the God of charity, mercy, and patience, and become children of Belial, as God's law, reason, and the saints all teach. Covetousness and usury make men forsake the God of truth and justice and worship false gods, as St. Paul says (Eph 5:5). Gluttony and drunkenness make men worship false gods and forsake almighty God in the Trinity, who is the God of moderation and reason. For Paul says that gluttons *make their stinking belly their god* (Phil 3:19). And the theft of God's word and giving an evil example to Christian men are worse than the bodily sin of Sodom, as God's law and Grosseteste witness, since God's word and man's soul are better than the seed of man's body. And thus curates and priests commit theft and the spiritual lechery of Sodom when they do not truly teach the scriptures by word and good example, as the wise clerk Grosseteste shows.[29] Manslaughter is committed not only by the hands but also by consent, advice, and authority. And since priests consent to false wars and many thousands of deaths, they are cursed murderers and unfit to perform their duties, by God's law and man's, and by reason as well.

Simony is such a great heresy that all sins count for nothing in comparison with it, as the law says. For each sinful priest may say mass and consecrate the sacrament, though he does it to his damnation, with the exception of a priest who received his orders through simony. But since no man receives orders or a benefice without simony, nearly every clergyman may fear that he is unfit and fear being deprived of his benefice, losing his salary, and being degraded. They should fear that their prayer is cursed, and that they are on the way to damnation, on account of this cursed simony. For whoever receives priesthood or comes to a benefice on account of a gift of money, by prayer or service, does so by simony, as St. Gregory and the law teach.[30] And whoever comes to this order or benefice must seek the worship of God in humility, and the help of Christian souls, and the piety to live in holiness and to give a good example. But to live in pride and in the lusts of the flesh, such as idleness, gluttony, drunkenness, and lechery, is inspired not by Christ but by the devil. Anyone who does is a traitor to God and a heretic until he amends this fault and performs his spiritual office well, as Christ taught. Very few are worthy to pray for the people, because of the greatness of their own sins in receiving their orders, and their evil countenance, because they remain in and condone their own sins, and other men's sins, for money and worldly honor, against God's just judgment.

But against these laws, both God's and man's, and against reason, and against the saints, the fiend teaches his disciples a new gloss, to say that though men may not be worthy to be heard in their prayers on account of their own good life, yet their prayers are heard on account of the merits of holy church, for they are the procurators of the church. Certainly, this is a foul sophistry, a foul and subtle deceit of antichrist's clerks, to cover up their sins. For this gloss is foul, and contrary to God's words, and none of the great holy doctors ever heard the false subtlety of these words until the fiend was loosed.[31] Why should God graciously hear the prayer of such a cursed man, who despises the holy service of God and wrongly takes the honor of the priesthood against God's commandment? For God commands through St. Paul that *no man should take honor for himself except he who is called by God, as Aaron was* (Heb 5:4). The people desire to find a true servant of God, one who is pure of life and devout, to help them overcome their sins and throw off the encumbrance of the fiend. If a clergyman is not such a man, then he foully deceives the Christian people.[32] For God commands his priests to be holy, for he is holy; and he commands that no priest with obvious filth in his body should minister to the people. That is, no priest having the filth of horrible sin in his soul should presume to say the divine office, for if he does so, he does it to his own damnation, as St. Paul says.[33]

These sophisters of antichrist should know it to be true that a cursed man fully administers the sacraments, though it be to his damnation, for they are not the authors of these sacraments, but that dignity is God's alone. But where prayers are concerned, it is entirely the contrary, as the citations above from scripture and the saints have shown. For if the prayers of cursed men were heard by God, why would God not say so in his law? Instead, he makes clear the contrary. Why should the popes punish men and suspend them from the mass when they are well-known lechers? Why should God say that the prayer of such as sinful man is abominable and that God curses their blessings? These wayward hypocrites gloss directly against God's word, for they fear that the people will become aware of their cursed life and reject their prayers and not obey them and cease to admire them and support them financially; and that the people will hound them to live well, and will give alms to poor and needy men, as Christ teaches, rather than to such hypocrites like this, who blaspheme God.

It is surprising why men praise this new style of prayer so much, with its loud words and elaborate singing, and leave aside the silent prayers that Christ and his apostles made. It seems that we would rather have our own preferences and pride in this kind of song more than devotion and understanding of what we are singing. This is a great sin. For Augustine says in his *Confessions*, "As often as the song pleases me more than that about which it is sung, so often I know that I am trespassing greatly."[34] Paul says, *I would rather have five words in my mind than ten thousand on my tongue* (1 Cor 14:19). Paul's mind is devotion and true understanding; his tongue is a man who does not understand and has no devotion. One Pater Noster said with devotion and right understanding is better than many thousands without devotion and understanding. But these new prayers take up so much time that men have no space to study and teach scripture. Augustine asks, "Who may excuse himself from preaching and seeking the salvation of souls because he loves contemplation, since Jesus Christ came from heaven into this wretched world to seek souls and to save them, by the public example of his holy life and true preaching?"[35] And Gregory says in his *On Pastoral Care*, "They who have the fullness of the virtues and the knowledge of God's law, and who go into the desert to seek contemplation, are guilty of as many souls as they might help by teaching men who live in the world."[36] How will this new song excuse us from learning and praying the gospel that Christ taught and commanded? Therefore, you priests, live well, pray devoutly, and teach the gospel truly and freely, as Christ and his apostles did. Amen.

10. Of Wedded Men and Wives (Selections)[37]

While the Wycliffite affiliations of *Of Wedded Men and Wives* have been cast in doubt by some scholars, the excerpt from this treatise given here shows what kind of instruction in Christian faith, and what sort of Christian behavior, its author thought appropriate within the domestic sphere of a family or household.[38] While the text's sternly traditional patriarchy, drawing heavily on the letters of Paul and Peter, may be uncongenial to many modern readers, research on lollard families and communities based in the analysis of heresy trials tends to corroborate that many lollards did share these attitudes.[39] Nonetheless, even if this text reinforces Pauline prohibitions against female teachers and women in leadership roles in the household, the writer also admonishes husbands who drink too much, visit prostitutes, and abuse their wives and children. The close engagement with biblical evidence and means of its expository deployment found in this text are certainly characteristic of Wycliffite writings elsewhere in this volume, and so is the text's strong emphasis that instruction in God's law, that is, in the commandments, provided both through word and example, should be the center of Christian teaching and is an obligation for all parents.

See now how the wife ought to be subject to the husband, and how he ought to govern his wife, and how they both ought to govern their children in God's law. First, St. Peter commands that *wives be subject to their husbands, so that if any do not believe because of the word of preaching, then they might be won without the word of preaching because of the holy living of women.* These women *should not outwardly adorn their hair, nor wear garlands of gold* or precious stones, or over-precious or strange *clothes,* but they should have a *pure soul, gentle, meek, and kind, which is precious in the sight of God. At one time holy women who hoped in God,* honored him in this way and *were subject to their own husbands, as Sara, Abraham's wife, obeyed Abraham, calling him lord, and women who do well are the spiritual daughters of Sara.* All this St. Peter says (1 Pet 3:1–6).

Also St. Paul speaks in this way about husbands and wives: *I wish that men pray in each place, lifting up pure hands, that is, pure works, without wrath and strife. Also I wish that women dress in appropriate attire, adorning themselves with modesty and seriousness and making themselves fair, not with braided hair, nor with gold nor pearls, nor in precious cloth, but in that which becomes women who pledge themselves to mercy, with good works. A woman ought to learn in silence, with all obedience and deference* (1 Tim 2:8–11). And Paul says: *I do not permit a woman to teach, that is, publicly in the church,* as Paul says in a letter to the Corinthians, and *I do not permit a woman to have lordship over her husband,* but rather to be in silence and stillness (1 Cor 14:34–35). Paul says in many places that *the husband is head of the wife,* and Paul gives this reason, that *Adam was made first and Eve afterward, and Adam was not deceived in faith but the woman was deceived in faith,* by trespassing against God's command (Eph 5:23; 1 Tim 2:13–14). All this Paul says in various places in holy writ. Paul also commands that bishops and priests teach wives to love their husbands; *to be prudent and chaste and sober; to take responsibility for the house; and to be gentle and submissive, or subject, to their husbands, so that the word of God is not blasphemed against* (Titus 2:5).[40] *And old women should have a holy appearance, not accusing others falsely of crimes or sins, nor serving too much wine,* and teaching well by teaching prudence (Titus 2:3–4).

Paul also teaches that *women should be submissive, or subject, to their husbands, as they are to the Lord. For the husband is the head of the woman, as Christ is head of holy church; he is the savior of its body*, that is, of the great multitude of all who are worthy to be saved. But *just as holy church is subject to Christ, so women should be subject to their husbands in all things. Husbands, love your wives, just as Christ loved holy church and gave himself willingly over to* pain and death *for holy church to make it pure and holy. And he made it pure by the washing of water in the word of life, in order to give the glorious church to himself, neither having blemishes nor being marred by any filth, but to be holy and without spot or stain. Husbands ought to love their wives as their own bodies, for he who loves his wife loves himself. For no man ever hated his body but nour-*ishes and strengthens it, *as Christ does holy church. For we are mem-bers of his body*, his flesh, and his bones. *For this reason a man will leave his father and his mother and will cleave to his wife, and they will be two in one flesh. This sacrament is great*, Paul says, *both in Christ and holy church.* But truly, you husbands, *let each man by himself love his wife as himself, and let the wife honor her husband. Children, obey your elders*, father and mother, *in the Lord, for this is virtuous. Honor your father and mother; this is the first command-ment with a promise, that it will be well with you and that you will have a long life on earth. And you fathers, do not stir up your children in anger, but nourish them and bring them up with instruction, or teaching, and the discipline of God.* All this says St. Paul.[41]

Paul commands in another epistle: *Women, be deferential to your husbands, as it is proper in the Lord. Men, love your wives and do not be bitter toward them. Children, obey your elders in all things, for this pleases the Lord. Fathers, do not stir up your children to indig-nation*, lest they offend or trespass against God or man, lacking knowledge (Col 3:18–21).

Here fierce husbands and those who fight cruelly with their wives without reasonable cause are rebuked by God. Many, when they are drunk, come home to their wives—sometimes from their cursed prostitutes and their drinking companions—and scold and fight with their wives and household, as if they were Satan's brats. They permit neither rest, nor peace, nor charity, to be among them. But they will pay dearly for this wickedness, for if they wish to have mercy from God, they must show mercy to other men—even those who deserve beatings—and correct them in a fair manner.

193

Thus married men and wives may know how they ought to live together and to teach their children God's law. For at the beginning of life a child may easily be taught, and good works and good manners according to God's law may easily be imprinted on his heart; then he may easily demonstrate them and increase in goodness. Therefore, Paul commands that the father nourish his children in the teaching and discipline of God. God commands in the old law that fathers must tell their children God's commandments and the wonders and miracles that God did in the land of Egypt, in the Red Sea, in the water of Jordan, and in the promised land. And much more now must the father and the mother teach their children the belief of the Trinity and of Jesus Christ—how he is truly God, without beginning, and was made man through his most ardent love to save mankind by a fierce penance, hard torment, and a bitter death. And also all common points of the Christian faith, but parents are most beholden to teach their children God's commandments, the works of mercy, and the points of charity; and to govern well their five wits; and to fear God before all other things; and to love God most above all other things on account of his endless power, endless wisdom, endless goodness, mercy, and love. And if they trespass against God's commandments, parents ought to rebuke them sharply for this and discipline them a thousandfold more than for spite and unkindness against their own person. This teaching and discipline should in a few years make them good Christian men and women, especially from the good example given by the holy lives of men and women of old, for that is the best teaching for children and for other Christians.

Many priests command godfathers and godmothers to teach children the Pater Noster and the Creed, and this is a good thing. But it is most necessary to teach them the commandments of God and to give them a good example by their own lives. For even if they are baptized and know the common points of belief, they will not be saved without keeping God's commandments but instead will be violently damned deep in hell, deeper than heathens. *And it would have been better for them never to have received Christianity*, unless they end their lives truly in God's commandments, as St. Peter plainly teaches (2 Pet 2:20–21).

But some teach their children stories of battles and false chronicles not necessary to their souls. Some teach them novelties of songs, which encourage men to revelry and harlotry. Some assign them vain and unnecessary trades, on account of pride and covetousness; and some permit them to live in idleness and debauchery, thus giving birth to prostitutes and thieves. Some at great cost train them in the law, for the sake of financial gain or worldly glory, but yet this costs them in many ways. But in all these things God's law is put behind, and as a result it is only with great difficulty that a man can speak to glorify God and to save men's souls. Some teach their children to swear and strike out and fight and curse at all other men, and at this they have great joy in their hearts. But truly, these are Satan's children, teachers, and procurators, to lead them down to hell by their cursed example and teaching, and by nourishing and maintaining them in sin. They are the cruel murderers of their own children—indeed, crueler than if they had hacked their children as small as morsels for their pot or mouth. For by their cursed teaching and their continuing in it, their children's bodies and souls are damned everlastingly in hell. And even if their bodies had been hacked ever so small, both their body and soul would be in the bliss of heaven, so long as they truly keep God's commandments.

And about such negligent fathers and mothers, who do not teach their children God's law and do not discipline them when they trespass against God's commandments, St. Paul speaks a dreadful verdict: *He who does not take care of his own, especially those in his household, has forsaken the faith and is worse than a heathen man* or a woman without Christianity (1 Tim 5:8). And such fathers and mothers who knowingly maintain their children in sin and teach them wickedness are worse than the cursed fathers who killed their children and offered them up on altars to false gods. For those children in their youth were dead and committed no more sin, but these children of cursed fathers and mothers who teach them and maintain them in pride, theft, lechery, wrath, covetousness, sloth, and gluttony, these children live long lives and increase in sinfulness, to the damnation of each party.

And thus it is little wonder that God takes vengeance on our people, both old and young, for all regularly show contempt for God and take much joy and mirth in despising and rejecting him. And God must punish this sin on account of his righteous majesty.

EXEGESIS AND COMMENTARY

11. The Our Father[42]

Translation of the Lord's Prayer into English, accompanied by commentary on its content, was a very frequent topic of pastoral teaching in medieval England. The seven petitions in the prayer lent themselves well to systematic exposition of the fundamentals of Christian faith. These were taught predominantly through lists of seven items, as for example in John Pecham's influential syllabus of 1281: fourteen articles of faith (seven on the Trinity, seven on the humanity of Christ), seven works of mercy, seven deadly sins, seven principal virtues, seven sacraments. Among Pecham's required teachings, only the Ten Commandments and two gospel precepts could not be conveniently accommodated to this scheme.[43] Much of this pastoral teaching also passes through Anglo-Norman; many English works that treat the prayer are related somehow to Laurent d'Orleans's massive *Somme le Roi*, for example.[44] But commentary on the Lord's Prayer is a favorite topic of clerics writing in Latin as well. While Wyclif's five separate commentaries display an unusual level of interest and engagement for a single author, the list of 1,261 extant commentaries produced between 1100 and 1500 found in Bloomfield's index shows that Wyclif was far from alone.[45] Even if many of these Latin commentaries aim to provide some sort of learned epitome of thinking about prayer, rather than the sort of basic introduction to Christian teaching that is the focus of the vernacular commentaries, still, it is clear that most writers of vernacular commentaries knew, and drew extensively upon, the Latin tradition as well. The movement of topics, materials, and conventions between commentaries is extraordinarily fluid, to the extent that some examples seem to be not much more than patched-together commonplaces.

The Wycliffite commentaries on the Lord's Prayer are no exception to this habit of extensive cultural borrowing; each one quotes extensively, and without acknowledgment, from a range of previous sources.[46] This is perhaps one reason why some scholars have found it difficult to see what is Wycliffite about them.[47] However, if some commentaries on the Lord's Prayer seem unoriginal, others refashion existing materials and discussions in less expected ways. Some of this sort of rethinking is visible here, in ways that readers of this volume will be able to appreciate more easily than has been possible in the past. For example, the exposition of *"your kingdom, or realm, come to you"* incorporates a characteristically Wycliffite understanding of the church "as all angels and men and women who will be saved," with Christ as its leader, while "all those who will be damned" are the devil's church, just as in *The Lantern of Light*. In explaining *may your will be done on earth as it is in heaven*, the author seamlessly incorporates a Wycliffite understanding of *prayer without ceasing* as the work of conforming one's will, understanding, emotions, and actions, to God: "We pray that we may do the will of God without error and *without ceasing*, as the blessed angels always do in heaven, and that we may do God's will with full understanding and with great desire and joy and delight."[48] And while this commentary does also develop a rather perfunctory pastoral scheme treating the seven virtues and seven sins, it emphasizes that the center of the moral life is "God's will," "God's word," "God's law," or the place where all of these can be found: "God's commandments."

This is the Pater Noster:

Our Father, who is in heaven, hallowed be your name. Your realm, or kingdom, come to you. May your will be done on earth as it is done in heaven. Give us today our daily bread, and forgive us our debts, that is our sins, as we forgive our debtors, that is men who have sinned against us. And lead us not into temptation, but deliver us from evil. Amen, so be it (Matt 6:9–13).[49]

When we say, *"our Father, who are in heaven,"* we are taught to love each other as brothers of a single earthly father and mother do, and much more, since God is our Father who created us from nothing. We are taught to live in meekness with one another, to desire heavenly things like virtues and a holy life, and to do all our deeds, privately and publicly, for the honor of God and the bliss of heaven. Our life ought to be "in heaven" in this way, through holy desire and perseverance. Thus at the beginning we must be meek and loving to all men, both Christian and heathen, and to friends and enemies, otherwise we are not worthy to pray the Pater Noster.

When we say, *"hallowed be your name,"* we pray that we may be made holy and steadfast in virtues by the holy name of God and by his grace and virtue—that we may be holy by grace as God our Father is holy in himself. In this petition we devoutly ask for steadfastness of faith, without which faith we cannot please God. We pray that all kinds of pride, in thought, speech, deed, and all kinds of actions and appearances, be kept away from us, for such pride makes men into the children of Lucifer. And we pray that all kinds of true meekness ground us against pride, for true meekness makes us God's children.

When we say, "*your kingdom*, or realm, *come* to you," we pray that all men and women living in this world who will be saved, and all those who have died, come to the bliss of heaven as soon as God wills it, in order to see our blessed spouse Jesus Christ and have endless joy with him and his angels and saints. For all angels and men and women who will be saved are God's kingdom and holy church, and our Lord Jesus is king of this realm and head of this holy church. All those who will be damned to hell are the devil's church or synagogue, and the devil is their false prince and king, or rather their tyrant. Here we ask for true hope and perseverance in order to have the bliss of heaven by the mercy of our God and by our good life and by dying in perfect charity. In this petition we pray that all cursed envy and hate be kept away from us and that all fervent charity toward God and our fellow Christians be so steadfastly rooted in us that it never fails in this life, no matter what.

When we say, "*may your will be done on earth as it is in heaven*," we pray that we may do the will of God without error and *without ceasing* (1 Thess 5:17), as the blessed angels always do in heaven, and that we may do God's will with full understanding and with great desire and joy and delight, not with complaints and heaviness of heart. In this petition we ask that in all things our will may be conformed to God's will, so that nothing may separate our will and our love from God, who is endlessly good and just. And here we pray to acquire the high virtue of charity, without which all other things are not sufficient to bring us to heaven. And here we pray that in every way God will keep us from wicked desires for worldly goods, so that we do not offend against God's commandments or good conscience either by acquiring or keeping worldly goods. For he who gets or keeps his neighbor's goods by breaking God's commandments—for instance, by false oaths, false measures or weights, or any deceit—

does not do God's will but is a thief and traitor to God and his neighbors, according to God's law.

When we say, "*give us today our daily bread,*" we pray for the sustenance necessary for our body, and to understand and keep God's word, and especially God's commandments, which are spiritual sustenance for our soul. And we pray that we have gotten this sustenance by true means, not by robbery or extortion or deceit; and that it be used in the service of God and the fear of God; and that we humbly give thanks to God for all of his grace and the gifts that he gives us out of his great generosity. In this petition we pray to have the virtue of prudence, in order to know what sorts of sustenance are necessary and appropriate for us, and what we ought to do in return for God, and in what measure we should take this sustenance, in order that we may put aside all kinds of gluttony, drunkenness, daintiness, and waste of food and drink. For gluttony and drunkenness make men love their belly and their gullet more than God almighty, *for they make their belly their* false *god,* as St. Paul says (Phil 3:19).

When we say, "*and forgive us our debts,* that is our sins, *as we forgive our debtors,* that is men who have trespassed against us," we pray that God may have mercy on us as we have mercy on those who have angered us. Certainly, if we have no mercy on those who trespass against us, then we pray against ourselves that God condemn us for our sins. Here men must forgive their neighbors for their rancor, hate, and ill will toward them, but they may lawfully pursue worldly debts, so long as they do so by just means and retain their patience and charity. And if men are poor and live justly and would gladly pay their debts, and if they work hard in truth to do so, and if they do not waste their few goods, then this prayer wishes that such poor men should not be imprisoned or punished but rather tolerated in patience and mercy until they can pay. In this petition we pray to have the virtue of justice, to put aside unreasonable wrath and vengeance and to keep ourselves steadfast in true mercy and patience against anger and unreasonableness, so that reason and mercy may govern well all our stirrings of heart, speech, and actions.

When we say, "*and lead us not into temptation,*" we pray that God may not allow us, by withdrawing his grace and his help, to be overcome by the temptations of the devil, the world, and fleshly desires and evil delights. It is beneficial to be tempted and to withstand temptations by the help of God and his angels, for thus is our merit and joy restored. But it is evil to be overcome by temptation, and that will only happen by our own negligence, sloth, and false desire for sin. Therefore, in this petition we pray to have the virtue of spiritual strength, to be strong by the help of the Holy Spirit against all temptations, and not to be obstinate in sin but to be diligent in holy prayers and good work and to bear in mind the shortness of the delight of sin and the bitter punishments of purgatory and hell. And if we wish, we will overcome all our temptations with diligence and by remembering these things, since God's grace and help is available, and we will acquire our crown in heaven forever.

When we say, *"but deliver us from evil,"* we pray that God may deliver us from all the evils of sin and punishment, both of body and soul, in this life and also in purgatory, and especially from the punishment of hell, and that we might not despair of God's mercy on account of our having been used to sinning in the past.[50] In this petition we pray to have the virtue of temperance, to take worldly goods and joys in such a way that we do not forget God in heavenly bliss. And we pray to temper the stirrings of our flesh, so that we do not touch any woman except in true and lawful matrimony and in fear of God and not like beasts without reason, who set about their lusts and forget God and all his works. For the archangel Raphael taught Tobit that the devil *has power over such men who dishonor the order of matrimony and act only according to their lusts and forget God* and the fear of God *and act as beasts without reason* (Tob 6:16).[51]

May God deliver us from all evil of sin, both hidden and public, especially from enduring in sin and despairing of God's mercy, and from all bodily conflicts and vengeance and punishment, both in this life and in purgatory and hell. And grant us, by correct faith, to receive heavenly bliss through true and perfect charity. So be it, Jesus, for your great mercy.

Certainly, this Pater Noster surpasses all other prayers in authority, wisdom, and benefit to both soul and body. It is of the greatest authority, for our Lord Jesus Christ, God and man, composed it and commanded Christians to say it. But other prayers are composed by men and contain no other meaning than the Pater Noster, unless it is error. Therefore, since Jesus Christ is more worthy than other sinful men, the Pater Noster is of more authority than prayers composed by other men, even if their prayers are good. This Pater Noster is more profound than other prayers, for it is made of the endless wisdom and charity of Christ and contains all topics for thought that are necessary both for body and soul in this world and in the other. Our Lord Jesus made it in few words and much wisdom, so that men should not be weighed down by it nor excuse themselves from knowing and saying it. It is of the greatest benefit, for if a man says it well, he will lack nothing that is necessary and profitable for virtuous life in the world to bring men to heaven to have endless bliss in body and soul. Lord, how much they are to blame who busy themselves with prayers made by sinful men and neglect the Pater Noster, which is the best and easiest of all and contains all goods for the body and the soul. Blessed be this endlessly good lord, who out of his endless wisdom and charity taught this short prayer. Amen.

12. The Ten Commandments (Selections)[52]

This is one of the longest and most important of lollard commentaries on the Ten Commandments, of which there are a large number. These may be found embedded in longer treatises as well as in a number of freestanding texts. There are two similar, related versions of this long commentary, each with unique added contents; this, the longer one, appears in a single manuscript, while the other version appears in three closely similar copies. The opening sentence of these two Wycliffite versions is also found in a much larger group of Middle English commentaries on the commandments with no especially Wycliffite characteristics. There is extensive influence and crossover and borrowing across the whole of the corpus of commentaries on the commandments, so that it would be hard to say anything definitive about what these related openings suggest.[53] The commentary presented here is noteworthy for its extended engagement with Wyclif's *On the Divine Commandments*, as detailed in the notes; cross-references to the excerpts from *On the Divine Commandments* printed here (item 4) are provided for comparative purposes.

All kinds of men should follow God's commandments, for without following them no man may be saved. And so the gospel tells how someone asked Christ what he should do in order to go to heaven (Matt 19:16–19; Mark 10:17–21; Luke 18:18–21). Christ told him that *if* he *wanted to enter into bliss*, he should *keep God's commandments* (Matt 19:17). Jews keep these, as all sorts of people should. For we should all be Christians and truly serve God. But we may never do this unless we keep these commandments.

O Lord, if a king commands all his liege men to do something on pain of death, then how busily they would keep this commandment. But our belief teaches us that God is a greater lord than any earthly lord may be in this world. And we know well that to the extent that a lord is greater, so much more his command should be kept and revered. Who does not know that God should be loved the most? And Christ says that *whoever loves* him well shall *keep* his *word*, that is, his command (John 14:23). You may say that a king's commands are more severe, and men who break them are more severely censured than they are for any breaking of God's commandments—for anyone who teaches another person is following the commandments of God. But think wisely of the Lord's wisdom, and that he wants his commandments to be kept of a person's free will. There is no merit in keeping them unless it is done willingly.

Know well that he has commanded you under threat of a great punishment to keep these commandments—that is, on pain of damnation in hell. He may not forget or fail to give this punishment to whoever does not keep his commandments. Nor may anything bend him from his purpose, for that would be expressly against his own word as it is read in the holy gospel. There, he says himself that he will give appropriately to every man, just as he has deserved (Matt 16:27). Our belief says the same. Just as he wants us to live in hope of heavenly bliss, so he wants us to believe that all men who do not keep his commandments will be damned. For they *are not burdensome* (1 John 5:3). But this great Lord, since he is full of mercy, has given us time to keep them, throughout the time of our life, and especially at the end of our life, if we want to be saved. For only the one who at the time of his death is found in God's service will be saved.

Know well that it is little enough to keep God's commandments continuously in order to make a good end at the point of death. For St. Augustine says that our last day is unknown to us, and so we should spend all our other days well.[54] We should keep in mind that all of us will pass through the gate of death. For St. Augustine says that all men that live on earth will undergo bodily death at the day of judgment, and then, when Christ descends for judgment, they shall suddenly arise again.[55] St. Bernard says, "It is certain that you will die, but it is uncertain when, or how, or where. Death awaits you everywhere, and if you are wise, you will await him."[56] Therefore, the Wise Man warns you, saying, "*Be mindful*, for *death will not delay*" (Sir 14:12). He does not give this advice only to men who are old, feeble, and sick, but also to men who are young, bold, and strong. Every day a man approaches nearer and nearer to his death. The more a man grows in days and years, the more he diminishes. For as saints say, the first day in the week that a man is born is the first day of his death, for he is dying every day while he is in this life.[57]

That is why the gospel says, "*Be vigilant, for you never know when* our God *is coming*, whether in your youth, or your middle age, or your last days; whether secretly or openly" (Mark 13:35). Take care that you are always busy in his service, and then, whenever he comes, you will be ready for him. For the servant should await the lord, and not the lord his servant. Especially when there is great haste, whoever is not ready is worthy of blame. But no man knows of a greater haste than there will be at Christ's coming. In this way you may know well that it is little enough to keep God's commandments continually in order to make a good end. Your spiritual enemies, and especially the fiends, are eager to tempt you at the hour of death. But since God cannot ask of you anything that is not reasonable and easy (Matt 11:30; 1 Cor 10:13; 1 John 5:3), we know well that we are capable of keeping these ten commandments. For just as he who breaks any one of them offends in all of them (Jas 2:10), so he who keeps any one of them well, keeps them all.

Chapter Two

Priests should teach these commandments of God and make them generally known to the common people with all their might. For this is the greatest honor that we do here for God, and the greatest benefit that we do here for his church. But I fear that we are stewards of error for these commandments. So that they are easy to remember, they are divided into ten. God spoke them as they are written in the second book of holy writ, where the book says this:

203

God has spoken all these words: "I am your Lord God who has led you out of slavery in the land of Egypt. You shall have no alien gods before me. You shall not make an image carved by man's hand, nor any likeness of what is in heaven above and what is in earth beneath, nor of what is in the waters under the earth. You shall not worship nor praise them. I am your Lord, your God, a strong, jealous lover. I visit the wickedness of fathers upon their children, up until the third and fourth generation, for those who hate me. And I bestow mercy up to a thousand generations on those who love me and keep my commandments.

"You shall not take the name of your Lord God in vain; truly the Lord God will not consider guiltless the one who takes God's name in vain.

"Remember to make holy the day that is God's Sabbath. For six days you shall work and do all your own works, but on the seventh day is your Lord God's rest. On that day, you shall do no servile work, nor shall your son or daughter, your servant or maid, your beast of labor, nor the stranger that dwells in your house. For God made heaven and earth and sea in six days, and all that is within them, and rested the seventh day. Therefore, he blessed the Sabbath and made this day holy.

"Worship your father and your mother, so that God may grant you long life upon earth.

"You shall not kill.

"You shall not commit lechery.

"You shall not commit theft.

"You shall not bear false witness against your neighbor.

"You shall not covet your neighbor's house.

"You shall not desire your neighbor's wife, nor his servant, nor his maid, nor his ox, nor his ass, nor anything that is his" (Exod 20:1–17; Deut 5:6–21).

These are the Ten Commandments that God spoke, as it is said here. But all men do not understand them correctly. So take heed, with a pure soul and good intent, and often read or listen to the writing that follows, so that with the help of God's grace, you may be brought to good understanding of them. God's will would be for lords, ladies, and other men and women of rank to pay attention to them, and have them willingly and freshly in mind, to honor God and help all true Christian people, that is, holy church. They should teach them to their children and servants, and share them with lay people who cannot read. For in the fifth book of holy writ, the Holy Spirit says this: *"These words that I say to you this day should be in your heart, and you should tell them to your children. Think of them sitting in your house and going in your way. Wind them round your hand as a token, sleeping and arising, and place them between your eyes. Write them on the doors of your house"* (Deut 6:6–9). And thus all men, by God's command, are required in their speaking, seeing, hearing, going, sitting, standing, and everything they do, to have God's commandments freshly in mind and to govern themselves by them, for the good instruction of their children and of all others dwelling around them.

If each man would busy himself to learn and share with others God's commandments, as Christian men should do, as busily as many men learn and share follies and vanities that never do any good, but rather lead to harm and wasted time, then the people would not live in so much vice, against God's law, nor would their children be so rebellious and disobedient to them as they have become. So do as the Wise Man advises, and follow him. He says, *"Let all your telling,* all your diversion, *be the commandments* of almighty God"* (Sir 9:22).

And then see the goodness of him who puts all his commandments in ten, so that you should easily learn them and have them in mind, as I said before—and in two, as well. Indeed, they are all gathered into just one, as St. Paul teaches, for if you keep yourself in charity, you keep the Ten Commandments (Rom 13:8–10). Charity has two branches: loving God as you should, and loving your neighbor (Matt 22:37–40). That is why God gave Moses two tables of the law. The first table teaches men to love God and contains three commandments, as God's law teaches. The second table contains the other seven commandments and teaches you to love your neighbor as you should. These seven, and the other three in the first table, make ten commandments. We cannot adequately tell the authority of these commandments, or all the reasons why men should keep them. But we should know one thing about our good God; he does not ask any man to do anything not to his own advantage or anything that he cannot accomplish. For Christ himself says that his *yoke is soft and* his *burden light* (Matt 11:30). And St. Augustine says,

"If we want to deserve the reward of everlasting life, then let us hasten with all our strength to fulfill God's commandments."[58] For his commandments are burdensome to those who do not want to keep them, and easy for those that do. And so, wisely attend to what it would be best for you to know and do, and that is what your Lord asks you to do.

Blessed be this mighty Lord, gracious in his commands. He is mighty because he has no need of our service. And he is gracious because he asks from us what benefits us most. Who would not want to love such a lord and serve him with good will? Bear in mind that we are children and often yearn for things that would be bad for us, for we do not see all things. Therefore, we need to be grounded in belief, and see far through belief, to the end of the world. In this way we may know what would be good for us. For men often desire what does them much harm, like willful children or men in a fever. And so many suppose that worldly honor and riches would be the best thing for them to have. But if they saw the end of their life, and God's commandments, and how these things prevent them from keeping God's commandments, they might well see that such things harm many men.

Chapter Three

The first commandment of the ten that God himself spoke says this: "I am your Lord God who led you out of Egypt, from the house of slavery." But before we pass any further here in this commandment, you may ask a question: why Christ in God's law is called by these two names, "Lord," and "our God," and why this name "Lord" comes first. And I may answer that he is called by these two names with respect to two different things, that is, the fear and the love that we should have for him. For this reason God asks in the book of his prophet, "*If I am lord, where is my fear? And if he is God, where is his love?*" (Mal 1:6). Furthermore, the reason "Lord" is put first is that in this name "Lord" is understood "fear." St. Augustine says that fear brings love just as a needle brings in thread, and therefore God's law puts this name, "Lord," first.[59] You must love your God and fear him, for Augustine, the good clerk, says, "Understand the power of God. Understand the mercy of God. Fear his power. Love his mercy. Do not presume so much on his mercy that you disregard his power, but do not fear his power so much that you despair of his mercy. For in him is power, in him is mercy, and all goodness."[60]

For this reason we should gladly keep in mind that our gracious Lord God, by means of his power, wisdom, and kind and merciful grace, led the children of Israel out of Egypt, from the house of slavery, from the power of Pharaoh. How he leads us, too, by his power, wisdom, and kind and merciful grace, from Egypt, from the house of slavery, and from the power of Pharaoh. By this word "Egypt" is understood "darknesses." By deadly sin, God, that is, the light of man's soul and all knowledge, passes from man's soul. Then man is in "Egypt," meaning, in the darkness of ignorance, not able to recognize what things might help him. His soul, as the gospel says, is the house of an impure spirit (Matt 12:43–45; Luke 11:24–26). Then he is under the power of "Pharaoh," by whom is understood the devil, who is lord and prince of all men and women who know that they are subjected and enslaved by deadly sin.

The holy clerk Augustine says that a man is the servant of as many lords as he does sins.[61] Christ in the gospel says that *he who does sin is servant to sin* (John 8:34). For the desire and pleasure that many men and women have in their sin, they bring themselves by their own free will into the house of the devil of hell, that is, a house of great slavery. John Chrysostom, the renowned clerk, says that all of us, before we fall into sin, have a free choice about whether we will follow the devil or not. But if once, in sinning, we bind ourselves, he says in his works, then we may not by our own power escape his bonds. Just as a ship when its tiller, by which one steers it, is broken, is driven wherever the storm may wish, just so a man that by sin has lost the help of God almighty's grace does not what he himself wants, but what his lord the devil may wish. And unless God, he says, may unbind him with the strong hand of his mercy, straightaway to death he goes, where he will dwell in the bonds of his sins.[62] Just as a fish enters a wicker trap whenever he wants, but when he is in, cannot come out when he wants, so a man, before he sins, has free choice of whether he will be under the devil's kingship or not. But when, through sin, he has put himself under the devil's kingship, then he may not by his own power escape him.[63] That is why God speaks through his prophet, and says, "You, man, *your loss comes from your-*

self, but your only help comes from me" (Hos 13:9). And so, when a man forsakes his sin by contrition and confession, and does satisfaction as much as he can, with the wholehearted intention of keeping himself from deadly sin; when he meekly thanks God, acknowledging that it is not by his own power, but by God's freely given grace given beforehand, that he has escaped and forsaken the filth of sin; then he says, as did Paul, "*by* your *grace I am what I am*" (1 Cor 15:10). Further, he asks for God's grace to continue his life in good works so that he may say further with Paul, "*and his grace in me was not empty*" (1 Cor 15:10). To all that continue in life in this way, by the grace of God, we may say with the apostle, "*By grace you are made safe*" (Eph 2:8). And so a man who because of sin is in the power and kingdom of the fiend cannot get free by his own power, but only by the merciful hand and power of God. For it is *not through our righteous works*, says Paul, *but through his mercy* that *he has made us safe* (Titus 3:5). He continually leads mankind out of Egypt, from the house of slavery, and from the power of Pharaoh.

The book tells how clerks say that a child, before it is christened, has a wicked spirit dwelling in its soul. This wicked spirit is overcome and defeated through the grace of God and the prayer of the priest before the church door when the child is to be christened. This sacrament of baptism is the ground and beginning of all sacraments, as was truly signified in the passion of Christ by the water than ran from his side when all his blood was gone. By this sacrament of baptism the child is delivered from the fiend's power and made God's child. He receives a share of the passion of Christ, and of all sacraments and prayers that are done in holy church, and of all good deeds that are done among all Christian folk. In the making of the covenant that he makes there with God, when he forsakes the fiend's pride and all his works and by the grace of God acknowledges himself God's child, God, by his power, wisdom, and kind and merciful grace, leads him out of Egypt, from the house of slavery and the power of Pharaoh. In this way our Lord God has led us graciously from the land of Egypt.

All these works and goodnesses that our Lord God continually shows to us should teach children that have discretion, to make them love their God better and learn and keep God's commandments more eagerly and earnestly, as the Holy Spirit teaches us. So it is written in the fifth book of holy writ, where after rehearsing the Ten Commandments he exhorts you to teach your child, he says, "*When your child asks you what all these precepts, statutes, and laws that our Lord God has enjoined upon us mean* for him, *you should answer* your child and tell *him* this: '*We were Pharaoh's servants in Egypt, and our Lord God, with a strong hand, has led us out of Egypt*'" (Deut 6:20–21). Further, he should tell him about the plagues, signs, and great marvels that God showed to Pharaoh in Egypt and the goodness that God promised to them if they would keep his commandments.

Here we should take good heed of how our good Lord God wants to draw us into his love, as a good father does his child. For we should freely, without servile fear, keep his commandments and truly serve him. For this reason, before giving the commandments he recounts the good things he has done for us, and says, "*I am your Lord God who led you out of Egypt, from the house of slavery*" (Deut 5:6). In these words are understood more good things that he has done for us than man's wits may suffice to show or understand. Next, he commands and says: "*You shall have no other gods before me. You shall not make an image carved by man's hand, nor any likeness of what is in heaven above and earth beneath, nor of what is in the waters under the earth. You shall not worship them nor praise them. I am your Lord God, a strong, jealous lover, etc.*" (Deut 5:7–9).

Many men think that they keep this commandment, and yet in many ways live contrary to it. We should know, therefore, that whatever sort of thing a man loves most, he makes it his god. Since all sin consists of a deficiency in love, every type of sin entails the breaking of this commandment. For all deadly sins are forbidden by this commandment, and whoever does any deadly sin breaks this commandment and makes a false god for himself. And so the Ten Commandments are like ten mirrors in which men may see themselves, examining whether they please God or not; for if you keep any of them, you please your God. Since there are three sins, as St. John says, that encompass all other sins that any man can tell, therefore a man may break this commandment in three ways. These three sins consist in these three wrongful loves: love of flesh, love of eyes, and pride in this life (1 John 2:16). Desire of the flesh is our particular enemy, as St. Bernard attests, speaking of it in this way: "I may not flee my body nor drive it away. I must bear it about, for it is bound to me. It is not lawful to kill it. I am constrained to sustain it. When I make it fat, I nourish my enemy against myself."[64] And so this enemy guides man's soul into love of two fleshly sins: gluttony, and the lechery that stems from gluttony.

To covetousness of the eyes our second enemy, the world, guides us—and so into the love of two other sins, covetousness of worldly good and sloth. For commonly rich men are slow in God's service, and delight in the pleasures of their possessions, as a sow or a swine does in mire and muck. To pride of life, which consists in love of worldly honor, the fiend of hell stirs us—and so into two other sins, wrath and envy. In the love of these three sins are enfolded all kinds of sins that are forbidden in this commandment, where God orders you that you should have no other gods before him or make any likeness of what is in heaven above, what is in earth beneath, or what is in the waters under the earth: you should not worship them or praise them. This is understood in this way: because nothing should be loved most except what is best and most worthy to be loved, that is, God alone, therefore God should be loved most. And so whatever thing any men or women love most, they make it their god.

Gluttons and lechers break this commandment. Paul says that these great gluttons *make their belly their god*, because they love it (Phil 3:19). By the same reasoning, foul lechers make the fleshly belly of a lecherous woman their god. God tells you to love him above all things, but every man and woman who loves something more than God, breaks God's commandment for that thing, whatever it is. In this way they may know that they do not love God above all things. Since God only asks us to do what is good and most profitable for us, we should put what he asks before all other things and all other requests. For whoever's bidding a man puts first, in doing so he loves him more than he does the other whose bidding he puts second, and he serves the first one first.

Now, God asks you to feed yourself the appropriate amount of food and drink and other sustenance. If you exceed the appropriate amount because of your belly's desire, then the inducement and the desire of your flesh impel you more to do what your flesh asks than what God requires. Thus, when you consent to do the will and desire of your flesh, and put God's commandment and desire second, you falsely make your belly your god and act against God's commandment, in which God asks that you should not make likenesses of the things that are in the waters under the earth. For these are understood to be fleshly lusts, what gluttons and lecherous men and women love most.

In the same way, covetous men and women make false gods of worldly goods, since they love them most, and most set their heart and trust on them—as, for example, on land, rents, gold, silver, or any other possession for which, whether out of desire or profit, they break God's commandment. Or upon wife, child, or any other creature for whose pleasure they act against God's commandments. And so all misers and covetous men sinfully make these worldly goods their false gods. For this reason Paul says that *covetousness* in such things *is service to idols*, and so of false gods (Col 3:5). All such people break this commandment, where God asks them to make no likeness of a thing that is on earth, by which is understood earthly goods.

All the more do proud men and women make the devil their god. For the devil is king of all proud children, and insofar as a man or woman gives himself to pride and abandons the meekness of heart that Jesus Christ asks him to learn (Matt 11:29), he makes the devil his god and forsakes Christ. And so, those who set their hearts most on worldly honor and on vainglory and social status break this commandment. Lucifer, the high angel of heaven, sinned in this sin of pride when he thought in his heart in this way: "*I shall go up into heaven and shall raise my seat above the stars* (that is, the angels of heaven) and *I shall be like the one who is most high* (that is, God himself)" (Isa 14:13–14). But because he wanted to make himself so high, therefore he fell to the lowest place, into the deepest pit of hell. Therefore, St. Gregory says, in a book, "If Lucifer, through pride, fell down out of heaven into hell, how shall you, through pride, come up into heaven?"[65] Trust well, it will not be. As sure as God is in heaven, the higher you make yourself through pride against God's will, unless you make amends in this life in time, you will in proportion to your pride be nearer Lucifer and deeper in hell. And therefore, learn from Christ, who is humble and meek, to set your heart in humility. For the lower you hold yourself, the higher you are in God's sight. And the higher you hold yourself, the lower and fouler you are in the sight of God. All such proud men and women forsake Christ, who is humble and meek, and make the proud fiend of hell their god, and follow him. In this they break this commandment, in that they act against God's bidding where he says, "*You shall make for yourselves no likeness of what is in heaven above.*"

All kinds of witchcraft, enchantment, and all other various incantations that are done through the counsel of wicked spirits are forbidden in this commandment.[66] St. Augustine tells true priests to warn the people that works of this kind are no help to sick men, or to sick beasts, lame or sore. Rather, works of this kind are harmful traps for the foolhardy laid by our old enemy the fiend, through which he plots to beguile mankind. Whoever uses these, he says, if he is a clerk, he is to be expelled from his order, and if he is a lay man or woman, he is to be excommunicated.

Also, Augustine says that we should not observe days called "Egyptians," also known as "bad luck days."[67] Christians should not avoid these days in beginning any kind of work or journey. Nor should they observe the first of January, when people give gifts to one another to mark the beginning of the year with an enchantment of good luck gifts, as though they said or thought, "We believe and trust that through this good luck new year's gift we will benefit all the year following." And if they have no good luck gift at the beginning of the new year, they expect to do worse all the following year. Into this type of sin fall all those who believe and trust in the taking of good luck gifts in any dealing. Even though someone might say that he knows some men benefit or do better through such gifts, he knows well that it is not true, but it is a trick of the fiend to bring them into misbelief. Here you should understand that good Christian folk may give gifts to one another to nourish and increase love, that is, charity—but not in the mistaken belief I mentioned before or in order to get a greater gift back, for that would be usury.

Also, St. Augustine says that we should not observe times, years, days, or the course of the moon or sun (meaning, for the beginning or completion of any beneficial and lawful work, or for weddings). Nor, in gathering herbs for any medicine, should we say any charms or put written words on any man or beast to cure sickness, unless it is the Creed or Pater Noster. For those who observe, or heed, or consent to those who observe such times, the things already mentioned, or any kind of divinations, prognostications, or enchantments, or who believe in them, or ask them for things that are lost or stolen or to know what is to come, or lead them into their house, in these matters they forsake God, erring against Christian faith. And unless through penance of holy church they are reconciled to God, they incur God's everlasting wrath in the pains of hell without end.

Therefore, let us follow the holy apostle Paul where he says, "*Whether you eat or drink, or whatever else you do, do it* in the name of our Lord Jesus Christ in whom we live and die" (1 Cor 10:31). Otherwise, we act against God's commandment and err in the faith of holy church, making the fiends of hell our gods. For if we steadfastly believed that God of heaven is almighty, we would not for the health of our bodies or beasts, for any worldly goods lost or stolen, or to know things to come, or for any reason, ask the help of these things already mentioned, that are variously and subtly accomplished through the work of certain fiends. For as the Prophet says, *all gods of the people are fiends* (Ps 96:5),[68] and they are called strange gods, or alien gods, because through pride they make the people aliens and estranged from God. If you, a misbelieving man or woman, worshiped any such false gods, no matter how hidden from the world it was, it would be openly known and seen by God, to whom all things are open and from whom nothing is hidden. Therefore, he says, "*You shall have no alien gods before me. You shall not make for yourself an image carved by man's hand*" (Exod 20:3–4; see Deut 5:7–8).

Some men perhaps think that this commandment means that it is forbidden to make any images at all. The noble clerk Bede discusses this in explaining the temple of Solomon, where he says this: "It should be known," he says, "that there are some men who think that it is forbidden by the law that we should carve or paint the likeness of men or beasts or other likenesses of any other things in church, since in the Ten Commandments it is commanded that you should not make for yourself any carved image or likeness. They would not think this was forbidden if they recalled the work of Solomon. For Solomon, in the temple of the old law, made various paintings and carvings that are figures for the images that we have now in holy church, as did Moses in the tabernacle, by God's command. And just as Moses, at God's command, also made a brazen

213

serpent, so that people who had been envenomed by other wild fiery serpents, beholding him, should be healed and live, much more it is lawful for us to have the image of Christ on the cross. By this means we may be mindful of the death of Christ, and overcome the temptations and venom of the fiend, the old serpent. And as figures of the twelve images of the twelve oxen and of other things that entered the temple, it is lawful to paint in holy church images of the twelve apostles and of other saints, as we do in holy church, in honorable and praiseworthy ways. If we diligently take heed of the words of this commandment, we will understand that we are not forbidden to make images. As evidence of this, he says first, 'you shall have no alien gods before me,' then after prohibiting images and likenesses, he says, 'you shall not worship or praise them.' It is as if he said, openly, 'You shall not make such images in order to praise them or worship them as God.' Otherwise, truly," says this great clerk, Bede, "Jesus Christ our Savior, seeing the image of Caesar the emperor on a penny, should not have commanded, '*Give to Caesar the things that are his*' (Matt 22:21, Mark 12:17, Luke 20:25). Instead, he would have censured the image of Caesar because of the idolatry that might be done to the image in a penny."[69]

But here, we should understand that images may be an occasion of good and also of evil. For a great clerk says that images may be made well, and also badly.[70] They are made well when they are to enlighten and leave an impression in and stir or move the souls of good Christians so that they more diligently and devoutly worship their God. They are made badly when because of images someone errs from the truth of faith so that that same image is worshiped as God, as for example if anyone should trust finally to be helped or relieved by them in any sickness or any other need or disease, and should therefore offer and pray to them and worship them with the kind of worship that is appropriate only to God, and nothing else.

Therefore, St. Gregory in a letter that he wrote to a bishop offers this teaching: "Dear brother, recently it was revealed to us that you saw some people worshiping images, and therefore you broke the images and cast them out of church. We praise your zeal, or love, that what was made with man's hands should not be worshiped. But we think that you should not have broken them." For Gregory says, "This is why paintings are placed in a church: so that those who

214

know no letters shall read in walls what they may not read in books, and so if a clerk shall worship his book, then another man may worship an image."[71] In another letter the same Gregory says, "Whoever will make images, do not hinder him. But in every way prevent them from being worshiped. And warn all men diligently that they should derive warmth and love (that is, love from compunction) from the sight of things that happened; but that only in the worship of the Trinity should they kneel down or prostrate themselves."[72]

For this reason a great clerk says, "I do not worship the image of Christ because it is a tree, or because it is the image of Christ; instead, I worship Christ before the image of Christ, because it is the image of Christ and moves me to worship Christ."[73] And so, when we come into any church, we should kneel meekly on the ground, and if you understand that the holy sacrament of the altar—that is, Christ's body in form of bread that was born of the virgin Mary and redeemed us by death on the cross (if we keep his commandments) from the pains of hell—is present, above the altar or on the altar, worship it with all your heart, soul, and mind. And when you see the cross, think with great sorrow and compunction of heart of what kind of death he suffered for mankind. And so, before the cross that moves you to devotion, worship Christ with all your might.

And in this way, by images and paintings made by man's hand, you may see and know how holy saints of heaven loved almighty God, and how great and how various were the passions that they suffered for the love they had for him. Consider for example the image of St. Laurence, painted or carved holding a griddle, symbolizing and showing how Laurence was roasted on a griddle, or the image of St. Katherine, painted holding in her hand a wheel and a sword, to show what passion the holy virgin Katherine suffered. And so, from the images of other saints, you can to some extent know what they suffered for the love they had toward almighty God. And thus, through seeing visual representations, as Gregory suggested, we should kneel to worship the Trinity alone. And this should be a great honor to the saints in heaven, that in seeing their images our devotion is excited toward more devout worship of God. And if we offer to and worship their images in ways that are only appropriate to God, we not only offend God, breaking his commandment, but we offend all the holy saints of heaven. For they hate it if such things are

215

done, as St. Augustine attests.[74] They do not want to usurp for themselves things that are only appropriate for God. All the more, then, do they hate it if such things are done to their images, that are but their shadows, made of tree or stone. For holy writ provides evidence that the angel of God would not allow John the evangelist to worship him, but ordered him to worship God (Rev 19:10, 22:8–9). And if you want to worship his true image, do as Tobit advises and *eat your bread with the hungry and needy* (Tob 4:17). That means, give part of your sustenance, as far as you can, to those who are needy, and especially to the meek, true, poor man that is the true image of God and may help you greatly with his prayer. For the holy apostle St. James says that *the devout prayer of a righteous man is very worthy* (Jas 5:16). For this reason the Wise Man tells you to *hide your alms in the poor man's bosom, and these*, he says, *will pray for you* (Sir 29:15).

Many men and women pay little attention to this image of God, and befoul this noble image in many ways with various filthy sins, to God's great displeasure and offense. For this reason the holy clerk St. Bernard speaks to this image and says, "O my soul, if you want to be loved by God, arouse your image in yourself, and he will love you. Restore his likeness in you and he will love and desire you. Truly," says St. Bernard, "by reference to the holy Trinity your maker made you in his own image and likeness, an image and likeness he gave to no other creature, so that you would love him the more fervently, so far as you know yourself to have been miraculously made by him. Therefore, understand your noble nature. Just as God has fullness and wholeness everywhere, making all things live and moving and governing all, so your soul is full and whole in each part of your body, making it live and moving and governing it. And just as in God there are three Persons, Father, Son, and Holy Spirit, so you have three attributes, understanding, will, and mind. Just as the Son is begotten of the Father and from the two of them (that is, the Father and the Son) comes the Holy Spirit, so from understanding is beget will, and from these two (that is, understanding and will) comes forth mind. And just as the Father is God, the Son is God, and the Holy Spirit is God, yet there are not three gods, but one God that has three Persons, just so understanding is the soul, will is the soul, and mind is the soul, and yet there are not three souls, but one soul that has three attributes with which we are ordered to love God, with all our understanding, all our will, and all our mind. For understanding of God on its own is not enough for heavenly bliss, unless there is a will intent on love; and these two are not enough unless there is a mind always understanding and willing, and unless God dwells in the mind. For just as there is no hour in which a man is not sustained by God's pity and mercy, so there is no moment in which a man should not have him present in his mind."[75] And so a man dwelling in charity is the living image of God. "For just as your maker," says Bernard, "who made you according to his likeness, is charity, good, righteous, sweet and meek, patient, and merciful, just so you are formed for having charity, and so that you should be pure, holy, fair, meek, and humble. The more that a man in God's image has of such virtues, the more that image is like God."[76] For the great clerk Chrysostom says that he is not a true disciple, who does not follow his master, and it is not a true image, that is not like its maker.[77] For that reason, whatever man or woman has most virtue is the image most like God. "And therefore," says St. Clement, "if you will truly honor the image of God, we will show," he says, "to you, what is true, so that you may do well."[78] This means that you must do alms deeds, and reverence and honor to man, who is made in the image of God. "Minister, or give food," he says, "to him who is hungry, drink to him who is thirsty, clothing to the naked, service to the sick, housing to the pilgrim or wayfarer, and minister or give needful things to him who is in prison."[79] This is an offering and a pilgrimage so highly pleasing to God that as he himself witnesses in the gospel, whatever we do to the least of his, he considers it done to himself (Matt 25:40). But we do not read in any place in all of holy writ that Christ says he considers everything done to him that is done to any image made of man's hands. St. Clement also asks, "What honor is it to God," he says, "to run about between images of stone or wood and despise man or consider him as nothing, when in him is found the true image of God?"[80] But this is not said so that any man should despise images of holy saints and consider them as nothing, but so that they should truly worship God in the true, meek, poor man who is a living image of God, serving him, as I said before, and not allowing him to be naked and cold, hungry and thirsty and in other discomforts, while they clothe, visit, and feed dead images that neither feel thirst nor hunger nor cold nor suffer discomfort. For they may not feel, nor see, nor hear, nor speak, nor look, nor help any man in any discomfort, as the holy prophets attest.[81] And so, whoever trusts in them, worshiping them with the worship that only belongs to God makes false and alien gods for himself and breaks God's commandment. No man should do that, for life or death or any other worldly good. For God says in the first commandment, "*I am your Lord God, a strong, jealous lover. I visit the wickedness of fathers upon their children, up until the third and fourth generation, for those who hate me. And I bestow mercy up to a thousand generations on those who love me and keep my commandments*" (Exod 20:5–6; Deut 5:9–10).

We must understand, as the book says and as clerks may show by authorities,[82] that our almighty Lord God agrees to be the spouse of man's soul. For through the prophet Hosea he speaks to man's soul and says this: "*I shall marry you* or wed you *to me in righteousness, in judgments, in mercy, and in faith, and I shall wed you forever*" (Hos 2:20, 19). As a great clerk witnesses, just as much as a man or woman in this life increases in knowledge and love of God this worthy spouse, so, proportionally, he receives more plentiful foretastes of the dowers of heavenly blessedness that as a queen he will receive in heaven.[83] But this marriage is better than a bodily marriage. And God and the holy souls of true men are better than men's bodies. And so, this marriage is broken, for a time, by the breaking of faith and lack of righteous living. And this is why God says often, through his prophets, that his people engaged in fornication and adultery when they worshiped false gods.[84] And St. James says that men who love this world are spiritual adulterers, for he says this: "*You adulterers, do you not know that the friendship of the world is an enemy to God?*" (Jas 4:4). And thus all men who love worldly honor or worldly goods more than God and his law and true living are spiritual adulterers, if they were Christian before. This is why men should fear the power of this spouse, who says this: "*I am a strong lover*," knowing well that his power is so strong that he may not desist from putting such adulterers into the everlasting prison of hell, unless they are reconciled to him in this life (Exod 20:5; Deut 5:9).

But here they should understand the humility and meekness of this spouse, who is a jealous lover, and meekly turn back to him. For out of great love he calls them to be reconciled, as the book records in many places. In one place he speaks to a sinful man's soul through his prophet Jeremiah, and says, "*You have fornicated with many lovers. Nonetheless, turn again*" (Jer 3:1). This is as if to say, "You have loved many things more than me, and broken my commandment many times for love of them. Nonetheless, forsake the love of those things and come back to me, loving me above all things, and I will receive you." For as a great clerk says, a strong and jealous lover is someone who wishes all love to be turned toward him.[85] It follows that he wants nothing to be loved except himself or something else for love of him. And the noble clerk Chrysostom, according to the gospel, says, "You shall love God with all your heart, so that you will not be inclined toward the enjoyment of any thing more than of God." Afterward he says, "If your heart's love is occupied with any of these earthly things now, you do not love God with all your heart. Truly, your heart is so much less with God, in as much as it is united by love to another thing. He that least loves earthly things loves God most, and he that most loves earthly things loves God least."[86] And so, when they receive in love into the inmost chamber of their heart any created thing, loving it equally with God or more preciously than God their spouse, they are spiritual adulterers and so, living in adultery, produce and rear bastard children. Good, meek men who labor to live in truth and soberness, keeping the commandments of their spouse Jesus Christ, produce law-abiding and spiritual children and bring them up in virtue by the example of their own consistently good conduct to make them true heirs of the everlasting kingdom of heaven. Conversely, lovers of the world, spiritual adulterers, produce proud bastard children and by the example of their wicked way of life, bring them up in pride, anger, envy, sloth, covetousness, gluttony, and lechery. And they teach them false and subtle worldly imaginings, such as great deceptive oaths, lies and other false frauds, to make themselves great and rich through false worldly goods, bringing about the damnation of these fathers and of the children that follow them. This is why God says here in his commandment that he *visits* (that is, punishes with pain) *the sins of the fathers on their children, up to the third and fourth generation, of those who hate him and will not keep his commandments* (Deut 5:8). For Christ says in the gospel, "*He who does not love me does not keep my words,*" that is, his commandments (John 14:24).

But the prophet Ezekiel says that *the son shall not bear the father's guilt, nor the father the son's guilt,* and in this commandment

God says that he punishes the sins of fathers in their children into the third or fourth generation (Ezek 18:20). This, as a great clerk explains, is how long fathers remain upon earth with their children.[87] So insofar as the children, through their fathers' misbelief and lack of chastisement, take part and share with their fathers in sin, following their fathers' habits, so by God's righteousness they take part and share in their fathers' distress and punishment, more or less, in proportion with how much they share in their fathers' sin. But where the prophet says that the son shall not be punished for the father nor the father for the son, you should understand that if the father is a righteous man, keeping God's commandments, and hates sin and loves virtues, and teaches and chastises his child as far as he is able according to what God's law teaches, then, if the child rebels against his father and will not live as he teaches him but follows his own desires against God's commandments, in this case, as the prophet says, the father will not be punished for the child. If the father is unrighteous and breaks God's commandments, but his son, seeing and knowing his father's wickedness, does not follow his example, but fears God, forsakes falseness, and hates sins, following virtues and in all his actions keeping God's commandments, then the child who does this, as the prophet says, will not bear his father's guilt, not unless he follows his father in wickedness. God punishes the sins of fathers upon their children, into the third and fourth generation, of those who hate him, and punishes them accordingly. "*But,*" he says, "*I give mercy up to a thousand generations on those who love me and keep my commandments*" (Deut 5:8). This word of our Lord God is packed with much more meaning than we can expound. But we should take one thing from God's law: he mixes together words of love and fear. For by love and fear he leads his children and chastises them with these two, as with rod and staff. Since man should naturally be led by love, God mixes in more love than fear; this is why he extends vengeance only to the third or fourth generation, while his words of love extend to a thousand. And so God mingles wit and strength together as a token that every man is required to love him and none may escape knowledge of him, or if he does wrong, the pain that he deserves. And so this commandment symbolizes God the Father, for unity is properly associated with the Father, and this commandment bids you to have only one God, for Father and Son and Holy Spirit are the same

God. The three commandments of the first table each symbolize one of the three Persons of God, as is revealed by their words. Since nothing may be true God except one, whoever makes many gods for himself must have some false ones. And since this is alien to the nature of our God, these are appropriately called alien gods.

O Lord, since no man loves his God except insofar as he knows him, since knowing is proportionate to love, we should labor diligently to know our God and flee all errors that are associated with this knowing.[88] This is why St. Paul says that if the Jews had had this knowledge they would never have put Jesus, king of bliss, on the cross (1 Cor 2:8). This is the reason children of the old law were forbidden to worship God through images. This is why God manifested himself to Moses in a bush (Exod 3:2). We should understand through reason that things that cannot be sensed surpass in goodness things that can be sensed. For example, health, something we cannot see, surpasses palpable things, just as life, which we cannot feel, surpasses coarse bodies. Likewise God, whom we cannot see, surpasses worldly things. But since we know him little, we love him less, and according to our belief, we should know him and love him.[89] For we must believe that he is the best thing that may be, the wisest man and most just that any man may think of. He is everlasting, without beginning or end; knowing all things, he may not forget, nor may anything escape his notice. For evermore he ordains all that is good. Since he has power to know himself, and from this power his knowing is engendered, while from these two things comes rest in himself, he must be three things and all one God.[90] Power is first, the Father of heaven. Knowing or Wisdom is the second Person. The third is Good Will, which we call the Holy Spirit. From this holy Trinity come all kinds of created things. Since the holy Trinity cannot fail in any place, it also cannot fail in any measure. But since these words are far from bodily wits, men should be careful to keep them soundly, for bodily things distract men from keeping them correctly. This is some part of a full account of the first commandment.

The second commandment pertains to the Son, the second Person in the Trinity,[91] and is written in the law in these words: "*You shall not take the name of your Lord God in vain,*" either in words or in manner of living, "*for God shall not consider that man without guilt who uses the name of his Lord God without cause*" (Exod 20:7; Deut 5:11). The name of God is the wisdom of the Father, for, as philosophers say, the proper name of a thing is the form that is found in that thing and in no other, and this wisdom of God is the form of God alone.[92] This is why St. Paul says that Christ, the second Person, is *in the form of God* as a son is in his father (Phil 2:6). So, this second commandment has to do with Christ. But we should note that God's law calls Christ "Lord" and "our God" for two kinds of things, as I said before in the first commandment. They are the fear and love that we should feel toward him. This is why God asks in the book of his Prophet, "Since *I am Lord, where is my fear*? And *if* he is God, where is his love?" (Mal 1:6). But Augustine says that fear brings in love, as a needle brings in the smallness of the thread.[93] This is why God's love puts fear first.

Each man takes God's name in vain that swears by his name more than is needed. Christ teaches us in the gospel to arrange our words like this: "*Yes, yes, no, no*" without any oath (Matt 5:37). For no man shall speak any kind of truth unless he says "no" or "yes." Because Christ wants our understanding and our word to match in speaking to our neighbors, therefore he doubles these words, as if he were saying, "If it is 'yes' in your soul, say 'yes' in your words and make these two conform; and if you say 'no' in your soul, say 'no' with your mouth, and be true men." And so "*yes, yes*" and "*no, no*" should be what we say, for if we swear anything, it *comes from evil*. Christ did not say that all swearing is evil, for God himself swore, and Christ with his apostles.[94] But Christ wisely says that the evil comes either more from the one who swears or from the one to whom he swears. For as God teaches through Jeremiah the prophet, it is lawful for men to swear with three conditions. First, that they know they are swearing to the truth, and [second] that the cause of the oath is to reveal what is right, and [third] that through deliberation there is a need for them to swear (Jer 4:2). Otherwise, all men should keep themselves away from oaths except, as I understand God's judgment, oaths of the kind holy writ delimits.

Great swearers think to excuse themselves, but they accuse themselves before God, who knows all truth. They say that no man will believe them unless they swear in this way. In this way, by their lying, they increase their sin. For the world bears witness that such heavy swearers are more false in their tongue than men who swear very little. For this reason, if you want to be considered true of tongue, take care that you are discreet in words and speak nothing but truth or what you know you can accomplish. When your wise words are spoken from your heart, take care to fulfill them, and do not make it false. This should show your reputation and make you a true man.

It seems to me that three reasons should impel us to keep this commandment and take the name of God with great honor and fear. One reason is because there was never a man or woman that did sin that might attain salvation except in the power of his name, nor will there ever be, as St. Peter witnesses in Acts. *"There is no other name,"* he says, *"under heaven, given to men by which* they may *be saved,* except this name, Jesus Christ"* (Acts 4:12). But how shall any sinful wretch be bold enough to stand before Christ at the dreadful day of judgment, with his hands and feet and sides and wounds wide open, and wait to be saved in that dreadful hour by the power of Christ's name and by his terrible wounds, when he has so horribly despised that name and those wounds all his life, through the swearing of vain and horrible oaths, and would not then repent. Let him trust well, it will not be unless he repents in this life.

The second reason that should impel us to abandon great and unlawful oaths is that the name of Jesus is so honorable that, as St. Paul says, *"In the name of Jesus every knee of heavenly creatures, or earthly, or of hell is* bowed"* (Phil 2:10). For it is so high and so honorable that the cursed fiend in hell should tremble to hear it named. And therefore it seems that the man that swears so horribly by that blessed name despises that name more boldly than the cursed fiend of hell might ever dare.

The third reason that should impel all men to leave their great oaths is this: it seems that such swearers, who so dismember Christ, swearing by his heart and his soul and blood and bones, suppose that the cursed Jews did not torment Christ enough. For with their horrible and cursed oaths they tear Christ limb from limb, as the cursed Jews never did. Unless this sin is amended, it will incur harsh vengeance. For the Wise Man says that *vengeance will not depart from the house of a man who swears a great deal* (Sir 23:12).

But perhaps here you will say that what you see contradicts this, for you see that often such great swearers have a great deal of worldly prosperity, while others who are peaceable and do not swear suffer great worldly adversity. You need to understand that scripture does not speak only of the material house that we live in. This is why St. Paul says that *"we have no city of dwelling here,"* that is to say, in comparison with the city or house that will last forever. *"But we seek,"* he says, *"one that is to come"* (Heb 13:14). Therefore, when the Wise Man says that *vengeance will not depart from the house of a man who swears a great deal,* he is speaking especially of the house that the Prophet speaks of in the psalter book, when he says, *"their graves"* (that is, of hell) *"will be their everlasting house"* (Ps 49:11). And all that shall dwell in that house shall feel everlasting vengeance. So vengeance shall not depart from the house of that man or woman who swears a great deal, unless he should amend himself here. For fear and love of this blessed name Jesus, therefore, let us leave such oaths, and take this name with all honor and worship.

Since keeping of the commandments banishes every kind of sin, and if you break one, you break all of them, we need to know how broad the scope of this commandment is. We should know, first, that both prayer and speech have more to do with action than with words spoken by the mouth. Every man on earth bears the name of God printed in his soul, for otherwise he might not have being. So when any man abandons what he should do, or does what he should not do, on pain of the hate of God, he takes this holy name in vain. For no man is ordained for any purpose but to serve God, and he must take his name if he has being, and so he takes his name in vain when he fails in achieving his proper purpose.[95]

God has ordained this purpose for everyone that has his name, just as God has ordained speech of mouth for the purpose of communing with your neighbor in truth and love, as beasts do by their nature. If you fail in this purpose, you blabber all in vain, more falsely than beasts or birds in the air. O Lord, your soul is made in the image of God, and therefore Augustine teaches, and Bernard too, that it is three things, understanding, will, and mind, and all are one substance.[96] And so, as the gospel teaches, you should worship the name of your God in three ways in keeping with these three: You should *love your God with all your heart,* and also love him in *all your soul,* and also you should love him in *all your mind* (Matt 22:37; Mark 12:30; Luke 10:27). You love God *with all your heart* when your wit and your power are set only on him—not that you may not lawfully do worldly things, but look that the purpose of your work is worship to God. You love God in *all your soul* when you arrange your life around worship of your God. You love God with *all your mind* when you do not forget in any way to think on God—but thinking takes place through actions as well as in your mind. This is how the Trinity should be worshiped; then, you do not take in vain the holy name of God, necessarily printed within your soul.

Since God *has arranged his house* (Prov 9:1) for you to *wander wisely* in his service (Prov 9:6; Col 4:5), idleness is damned both by God and by nature. God has ordained duties for each limb of his church, and so every man in Christ's church takes God's name in his office, since he is God's officer in virtue of his name. So each Christian man takes God's name in vain who fails in the service that belongs to his office. Each prelate or priest of the church takes God's name in vain who does not know the office that God's law has designated for him, and who does not perform it. God has given three kinds of office to his church: clerks and knights and laborers.[97] Clerks should be the highest, and the least in expenditure, and the busiest in God's law, and the furthest removed from the world; if they deliberately abandon this way of living, no man in this world takes God's name more falsely. Some say that antichrist has changed all these offices, for he claims to be king of the church of all wicked men.

Knights should show the power of the divine and maintain God's law using worldly power. If antichrist has conquered these lords by his hypocrisy and the falseness of his priests, then these are dangerous men, capable of destroying Christ's church. These knights should truly know God's law, and the officers in his church, and their duties, and through their power they should constrain them to labor in their office. They should use force to expel idle men in the church who were not put there by God, nor given the office they pretend to have, and assign them to labor. And then Christ's church would be purged of shirkers and rightfully grow to heaven as a well-proportioned tree. For bastard branches hinder the growth of this tree, and the burden of worldly goods knit together with greed makes these boughs bend and stops this tree from growing.

The foundation of this house consists of laborers, who are the least idle of any, thanks to their manual labor. For they are required to work and to support the other parts. As they should be taught by clerks to keep God's law, so should they be defended in their right by

225

lords. For it may happen that priests will prey on them through hypocrisy and turn the business of the labor God asked them to do toward hidden theft, as antichrist teaches them.

O Lord, if charity were widespread in the church, and each man labored truly in the office God has assigned him, how pure the church would be, *without spot or wrinkle* (Eph 5:27). And then neither clerks, nor knights, nor laborers would take this holy name in vain and without cause, as false Christian men often do now, breaking this second commandment.

13. Sermon 57[98]

This selection from the *English Wycliffite Sermons* adapts Wyclif's *Sermon 29*, presented in this volume as item 1. In the hands of its adapter(s), this brief sermon explains how Christ's injunction to the apostles to love one another is compatible with sharp criticism of those who are living in sin and offers Christ's comfort to those the world hates and persecutes for keeping his word. It develops these points through a systematic verse-by-verse explication of John 15:17–25, in the style of an ancient homily rather than of a "modern" sermon, which would typically confine itself to expounding one or two verses. It finishes with a strongly worded condemnation of the Jews, and especially their priests, for pursuing Christ—one that is not (or at least, not overtly) provided with an allegorical interpretation that applies it to the author's present day.

This gospel speaks sharply, as Christ often does through John's gospel, about how men should love one another and put away hindrances to this love, for the beginning and ending of God's law is love. Christ begins in this way, commanding his disciples, "*I command to you these things: that you love one another*" (John 15:17). Nothing is commanded more by God than this love. Whatever man abandons it, despises God. The craft of this love should be wholly mastered. Loving something and willing good toward that thing are one and the same. Each thing should be loved insofar as it is good, and so God should be loved the most, and better men more than worse men. Out of love for God we should love evil men, and evil common people, and for his love busy ourselves to give them what will make them better. As far as we can we should do good to every man, to some as a way to make them better, to others as a way to make them less evil. We should give one kind of priority in love to ourselves, and to our father and mother, yet preserving the proper order of God's law.

The first hindrance to this love that Christ recounts here is the hatred of this world toward men who maintain this love. For the world is so blind that it calls hate love, and love hate, for it errs in belief. All our love should be grounded in the love of God, to maintain his law and encourage others to do so as well. But many, out of lack of faith, consider this foolish, for men who behave in this way do not gain worldly goods.

This is why Christ says, *"If the world hates you, you should know that it hated me before"* (John 15:18). This worthiness in Christ, who suffered for man in this way, should encourage true men in God to suffer for Christ. If you complain about poverty and covet worldly lordship, you should know that Christ was poorer than you are, since in his humanity *he did not have a place to rest his head* (Matt 8:20). If you complain that your subjects will not give you goods, think about how Christ's subjects would give him neither food nor shelter, and yet he did not curse them for this, but did much good to them. If you complain that the world does you any injury, while you in return do good in the world in love and meekness, think of how Christ, before you, did much greater good in the world, though he suffered far greater wrong from his subjects than you are able to suffer. And thus, if you were to think about Christ, how he suffered for the love of mankind, it would be the best possible example you could have, of how to be patient and cease complaining. For as Augustine says, no man in the world may sin except by abandoning what Christ taught or complaining about what he suffers.[99]

This is why Christ says next, *"If you were of the world, the world would love what is his"* (John 15:19). For this rule is consistently maintained among both good and evil; each man loves what is like himself, indeed, even if they will be damned for it. For example, one sinful man loves another, because of their likeness in sin, even though they will both suffer harm in hell for this likeness. So it is no wonder that limbs of the fiend hate limbs of Christ, since they are so different from one another, both here and after the day of judgment.

This is what impels many men to hate new religious orders, for this new diversity quenches love and creates hate. Yet the members of religious orders themselves have a fiendish custom, in that they hate their own brethren and torment them because they hold with God's law against that of the order. And certainly they love others outside far too little, but only pretend to do so, to despoil them of their goods. This is why Christ says to his disciples *that because* they *are not of this world, but* he *has selected* them *from the world, for this reason, the world hates* them (John 15:19). If you learn from the world to hate in this way, your love will be quenched. But if by Christ's law you hate men of this world for this sin, and withdraw them from the world, then you love these men in God. For "the world" is understood here as men overcome by the world, those who love worldly things more than God's law, or the good of the virtues. And Christ says that "the world" hates these disciples.

Because this teaching is better than all others in its benefits and its holiness, Christ asks them to *think on* his *word that* he *has said here to* them (John 15:20). For then they will overcome the world. This is why John the evangelist says, "Brothers, *what man is he who overcomes the world? None, certainly, unless he believes that Jesus is God's son*" (1 John 5:5). If we hold with this foundation of faith, that Christ is truly God and man, and beyond this, if we believe in his life, and all the words that he said, then we shall overcome this world and all the helpers of the fiend. For as Christ truly says, "there is *no servant greater than his lord*" (John 15:20). So Christ is greater, both in virtue and in worthiness, than any other man may be. Since Christ suffered in this way and taught Christian men this lesson, what man should we believe or follow in our life but Christ? Neither the world nor the fiend may harm a man in this. And so Christ comforts his members with two intertwined truths: *If men of this world have pursued Christ, then they will pursue* his members; and, *if they have kept* his *words, then they shall keep* his disciples' *words* (John 15:20). This is easy to know if all that shall be, shall necessarily be.[100] For it is more difficult for enemies to pursue the person of Christ than to pursue his members, and so, they will do the easier thing. But there is a comfort here: just as Christ converted some who were men of the world, so shall his disciples. And so they shall not work in vain to keep his law as he commands. For each man that works must have hope of some result, for despair of this would prevent him from working.

But the blindness of the world, which torments Christ along with his limbs, is ignorant in belief. They do not know Christ's Father, for if they knew him well, then they would also know his son, and that these two are one God. And who would strive against this God? Lack of belief, and ignorance that men have, brings about all evil deeds, and thus each sinner is a fool. If men knew God's power and wisdom in these two persons, and how he may not forget to punish sin when the time comes, then men would fear to sin because of their knowledge of these two persons. But this faith is either lacking, or asleep. Christ reproaches this lack of belief, saying *if* he *had not come and had not spoken with them, they should not have had this sin* (John 15:22). For since Christ necessarily came in his humanity, as he came, and necessarily did all the actions he did for men, just as he did them, this great sin of the unkind disloyalty of the Jews should not have been. It was very unkind of them to treat their brother in this way, who nonetheless was so kind to them in return, and it was openly disloyal to hate their god in this way. But *now* these Jews *have no excuse for* this *sin*. This is why Christ says that *whatever man hates* him, *hates* his *Father also*, because they are one and the same (John 15:22–23).

Because in every kind of things one is the first and the measure for all the others in that kind, therefore among sins there must be one that is first among all other sins and the benchmark for the others. That one is the sin of the priests against Jesus Christ. This is why Christ says that *if* he *had not done things* for *them that no other man has done, then they would not have had this sin*. But *"now they see* this faith, *and* yet they still *hate both me and my Father"* (John 15:24). Still, this sin was not done without an important reason, for God allows no sin that has no advantage. And so *what is written in their own law was proven true: that* the Jews *willfully maintained enmity* toward Christ (John 15:25).

14. Commentary on Psalm 87[101]

This excerpt from the single copy of the longest of the versions of the lollard-interpolated *English Psalter* by Richard Rolle draws the scaffolding of its allegorical framework from Rolle's much shorter commentary. The foundation is the church (or Christ), the hills are apostles and prophets, the gates are the righteous (or the saints). The city of God is the church, while Raab and Babylon signify the sinful, as do the foreigners of Tyre and Ethiopia, who may become citizens of the spiritual city if they call out to God and turn to him. Much of this might also have been drawn from the *Glossa Ordinaria*, and much of it appears in Bodley 554, a heavily glossed Wycliffite psalter.[102] However, in the lollard interpolator's hands this framework is developed into an exposition of several key Wycliffite concepts: how we may guess (but not know for sure) who is part of the church understood as those that shall be saved, and who is not; the proper disposition of the emotions, will, knowing heart, and actions in a Christian; how sinners may return to God; and what is promised to those who do.

The foundations of it are in the holy mountains; the Lord loves the gates of Sion above all the tabernacles of Jacob.
The foundations of it in holy hills; the Lord loves the gates of Sion above all the tabernacles of Jacob (Ps 87:1–2).[103]

This psalm is short in number of words and long in wisdom. It mentions heavenly Jerusalem, that is, holy church, a spiritual city, one part of which fights on earth while one part reigns in heaven. Here are showed true flashes of knowledge about who in this life is part of God's church and who is not. Through all the time of this life, one or the other or all together—that is, either the devil or the world or man's own flesh—strive against man. Those who are found fighting against this assault show themselves not to be consenting to their adversary, and so, to be members of holy church. Just so, each man has these same adversaries; whoever does not strive against them shows himself either to be overcome by them or to be consenting to them, and so, to be a member of the devil.

The foundations of holy church is mainly Christ, along with holy prophets and apostles, dwelling in holy hills, persisting in high virtue, giving light to low valleys—that is, to meek folk in whom pride or vainglory does not dominate—with beams of pity and charity. Pity belongs properly to Christ, and charity to his saints. The Lord, that is the Father of heaven, loves the gates of Sion. The foundations I mentioned are the gates by which each man enters into bliss. These gates are loved above all the tabernacles of Jacob, for among all men obedient to the belief or trying hard to be, these blessed saints I mentioned strove, putting themselves willingly into battle in the phalanx, shedding their blood to the death for truth, giving example and comfort to those who come after, to go boldly as lovers of truth by the same path that leads most surely to endless bliss. Because each man should desire heaven willingly, mightily, and persistently, striving against his adversaries for this reason, the Prophet says,

Glorious things are said of you, O city of God.
Glorious things are said of you, city of God. (Ps 87:3)

The faithful people of God are his church, in whom he reigns as a faithful shepherd among his flock, leading them into wholesome pastures, defending them from ravenous beasts. And as a bailiff among his servants, apportioning their work to them and giving them food at the right times. And as a husband among his household, giving them good example. And as a lord among his servants, restraining their wicked actions, planting virtue in them through his own example. And as a lady among her maidens, rightfully teaching them meekness and purity. And as a king among his knights, giving each one responsibility as befits his rank. And as a father among sons, diligently, fairly, and generously dividing their inheritance among them—the inheritance, that is, that Christ describes, "*You blessed of my Father, come and see the kingdom that has been prepared for you from the beginning of the world*" (Matt 25:34). So that no greatness of sin should cause any to despair of God's goodness, the Prophet in the person of Christ says,

I will be mindful of Rahab and of Babylon knowing me.
I shall be mindful of Raab and Babylon, through knowing me. (Ps 87:4)

Raab means "hunger" or "hastiness," "large" or "enlarged," "broad" or "spreading abroad." And *Babylon* means "confounding" or "confusion," or "transgressing." These specific conditions belong to lechers and other rebels against God, since among them "hunger" and barrenness of each good virtue is "hasty" and swift to run toward evil, and "large" or "enlarged" to return evil for evil according to the world and evil against good, as the devil teaches them. And so such

231

folk, persisting in their vices, are "broad," holding within themselves all evil, "spreading abroad" their wickedness, "confounding" themselves without shame, bearing their own "confusion," "transgressing" against truth, impelled by foul love of vile lust of this uncertain life.

Raab was a whore dwelling in Jericho—that symbolizes "the moon," now waxing, now waning like the moon. Indeed, the moon first waxes and then wanes, and as much as it waxes, it wanes. These conditions are proper to lechers, and specifically, to lecherous women. For a while in their youth, whores busily adorn themselves, desiring to be seemly and pleasing in the sight of men whose goods they covet. For women who practice whoredom do it more for men's goods than for love of those men, and so they sin trebly (that is, threefold). First, in pride, through their whorish clothing; second, in cursed covetousness for the taking of gifts; and third, in stinking lechery, even if they often have no pleasure in the deed. And so, like the moon, first they wax in the time of their youth, in beauty and great pleasure to fools. But soon afterward, as they age, they wane and are unlovely, and hugely disfigured, and refused by men. And so, often, they receive in their last days as much humiliation and misfortune as they had in their youth of praise and good fortune. And so, by the righteousness of God, beauty of pride, and prosperity coveted and sustained by ill-gotten goods, are witnesses to all of everlasting damnation for those that misuse the goods of nature and fortune in this way. For by the sentence of God's law, everlasting torment shall be given to such people, as befits their manifold wickedness and their evil livelihood. And so, after their waxing here shall come their waning in hell—if, indeed, they do not repent, acknowledging their offense to God with a will to make amends. For neither wisdom, nor strength, nor any thing that may be thought, can hinder God's righteous judgment.

And thus Raab, in whom there was hunger and barrenness of virtues, heard of the wonderful might of God: how marvelously and with what a strong hand he had brought his people out of Egypt, laying waste kingdoms and slaying those kings who opposed his people and denied them passage to the promised land, and was astonished within herself. She feared the hasty coming of God's people over Jordan into Jericho (and this coming figuratively symbolizes the coming of Christ with his saints to judgment). Considering these things and many other marvels of God, Raab received God's messengers, hiding them from their enemies who would have slain them in the cellar of her house, under flax straw that was there. The story does not tell that Raab, hiding God's messengers, led them into her cellar and covered them with flax, but with the straw of flax, showing by this means that although she was engaged in works of hideous sin, still, within her house in her private room were signs of needful work proper to women.

Raab feared that the sudden vengeance of God would come to her, as it was to come to the city that she dwelt in. So she acknowledged God before God's messengers, saying "truly *the Lord your God, he is God in heaven above and in earth beneath*" (Josh 2:11). After this acknowledgment Raab bound the messengers of God by oath, that in the destruction of Jericho God should show mercy to the house of her father, as she had done to them. And they gave her a true sign for use at their coming into the city, a way to save her father and her mother, her brothers and her sisters, and all that were with them, delivering them from death. When they had heard these words from Raab, the messengers said these words: "*Our life is yours*, if you are not safe from the vengeance on this city, *providing you do not betray us*"—that is, providing you are not a hypocrite, but faithful and lastingly true in the things you have done, in a way that pleases God (Josh 2:14). "Now, in this hour coming, in your pity and assistance in saving us, and in the fear of sin that is in you, we see in you a true confession to God. Therefore, according to these conditions, *the red rope* by which you let us escape from our enemies *will be a token* between you and us, *when we* return to destroy this city and its inhabitants. We shall save *your father and mother, your brothers and all your nation.* You will gather them together *into your house*, so that none pass out of your house. *Whoever goes out of your house, his blood will be on his own head*"—that is, vengeance shall come upon him—"*and we are not guilty* of that vengeance" (Josh 2:18–19).

This is a comforting sentence for all sinners, and especially for hideous, stinking lechers and adulterers, if they will cease their evildoing, having within themselves fear of the offense to God, and desist from their sin, as Raab did, for fear of God's vengeance. Then, the charity of such true penitents shall stretch to their neighbors; they will have pity on them, as Raab had on God's messengers, when they are wrongly treated or put in distress. All the other gifts of the Holy Spirit, and the works of mercy to fellow Christians, follow upon true pity. These blessed godly virtues draw their leaders in faithfulness so near God, joining them so fast together, that each delights so much in the other that each is made beloved or dear to the other. Such loving or dearness of God to man and man to God is called charity of God and man, for each wills as the other wills. This charity of God was showed in Raab when, in such great fear on each side, seeing different regions destroyed for her sin, and her city about to be destroyed, and herself impure and sinful, she acknowledged and said to the messengers, "Truly the Lord your God is God in heaven above and in earth beneath." This acknowledgment of truth made her so beloved of God, and God of her, that all she asked was granted to her: father and mother, brothers and sisters, and all things with them. And furthermore, she was ordered to gather together into her house all her nation, and make them dwell within, not going out in the time of vengeance upon that city. They should be safe, if the red rope were seen to hang in the window, by which the messengers went out of her house.

The red rope that Raab was ordered to hang out at her window signifies willing penance, and the various adversities that the followers of Christ suffer willingly for the truth. This red rope is the bloody painful passion of Christ that each man and woman should busily have in mind each day, mortifying in himself or herself the vice of each rebel member, so that nothing but virtue may be seen in each one. All those in whom this blessed sign appears need not be in despair for any sin done before, if by Raab's example they stand faithfully in the fear of God, having pity toward their fellow Christians, acknowledging the truth. Whatever they ask, they must believe, and it shall be granted to them—and more, as it was to Raab, in a display of mercy toward her. This is what he says about Babylon, which signifies hideous sinners transgressing against his commandments. These sinners, whatever condition they are in—that is, whatever vice reigns in them—must come to the mercy of God if they want to leave their sin. They must come to mercy through counselors who know Christ, that is, through counsel of those who are sent by Christ truly to bring his message to the people, and who teach them truly the faith of Christ through holy example of good works—teaching them always to have ready the token of their salvation, hanging out at their window, as Raab did.

This was not a token of vainglory or hypocrisy but a token of proper penance, that is, man's debt for sin, assuaging the wrath of God. This token causes whoever bears it properly to lack the power to sin. For it makes stable and rules each of their wits inwardly, in fear and love of God. This token is the sign of tau that God commanded to be marked on the foreheads of men wailing and sorrowing over all the abominations in Jerusalem (Ezek 9:4). This token is the cross of Christ, that is, his painful passion marked on the forehead of men who believe in Christ, in whom there is remorse at sin, who shame and put out of their mind all impure thinking. In the name of Christ crucified they do not shame his faith but unfeelingly seek his glory, loving it, desiring reproofs of the cross, and by them to be filled with exultation.[104] For whoever shames the reproofs of the cross shames Christ who suffered on the cross. The angel shall smite him with God's wrath, as one who does not have the sign of tau.

The red rope, a true sign of salvation, is the threefold rope that the Wise Man speaks of (Eccl 4:12), binding God to help man and man to serve God. This is the true belief of the holy Trinity, most truly contained in the gospel of Christ. Whoever truly—that is, in works and words—acknowledges this gospel as God's word, acknowledges Christ to be God's son and to have come in flesh. And *"whoever shall confess me before men*, the son of man *shall confess* him before the angels of God" (Matt 10:32).

Fervency of spirit, in whoever faithfully in his heart believes in Christ, must necessarily move him to recognize the friends and enemies of the belief. For whatever the lover of Christ hears or knows has been spoken or done, love moves him to perceive whether it leads to praise of Christ or to dispraise of Christ. If to praise, he gladdens in his heart at this. Sometimes the conditions of men speaking faithfully of the truth are of great fame or wisdom or of fitting estate, such that other simple men and women of lower rank, even if they are strong lovers of truth and great in knowledge, ought not to push themselves forward to speak among them. But if he is called to be among those who speak truth, then let them speak very circumspectly and mildly, with fear, in meek words fitting to their condition, and God will be praised. If at a certain time they are not called, like willful children, to learn sitting under their master, then they should quiet themselves to hear wise men speak. Yet if in companionable fellowship the truth is put forth prudently by the spirit of God, well examined, let them truly speak the truth of Christ in a praiseworthy way, and by this friends will be comforted and enemies astonished. For belief grounded in the heart of a true lover of Christ may not be hidden but must be spoken out at the proper time. The time, I understand, is always proper for the lover of truth, except when he is occupied in hearing one who is wiser than he, or else when he is in company where he perceives that the greater part are despisers of truth. Then, silence, sorrow, and prayer are necessary for the lover of truth.

Whoever confesses Christ in this way, having true belief in his heart and showing it at the proper time, must also conform to truth in his actions. They alone shall be free and exempt from all punishment and blame at Christ's judgment, those who have this threefold rope to show at their end. They received the apostles under threat of various charges and penalties. They heard from them the belief of Christ, forsaking idol worship and other sins and believing in Christ, as was said before. Christ, quieted and pleased by this, said he should be mindful of all such people, of whatever condition, showing them mercy and acknowledging them before the angels of God as faithful and true, and worthy to take from God's hand the crown of everlasting bliss. But because God does not wish any man to despair of his great mercy because of the enormity of his sin, nor his long persistence in it, if he will forsake it and ask mercy, he lists through his Prophet more sinners of various kinds whom he received to mercy, saying

Behold the foreigners, and Tyre, and the people of the Ethiopians, these were there.
Behold, foreigners and Tyres and the people of Ethiopia, these were there. (Ps 87:4)

These foreign folk were far from God, separated from him by hideous sin. But God did not refuse them when they wished to forsake their sin, but gladly, without any scolding, received them into his mercy. By these men of Tyre and Ethiopia may be understood different sorts of people anguished and troubled on every side, made black and dark with every kind of sin in the sight of God, separated far from righteousness and out of belief, living in every kind of fleshly desire, without reason, like mad beasts in whom there is no under-standing. But not, indeed, when they heard the message of Christ's mercy, cried out by his apostles in every land on earth. Christ said generally to all men and women burdened and laboring under sin, *"Come to me and I shall unburden you"* (Matt 11:28). The most hideous sinners turned from their wickedness at this, believing in Christ and keeping his commandments from then on, and they were gladly received by him to mercy. This was in order to make known to us that those who, at any time, will forsake their sin for the love of God—however hideous it may be, natural or against nature, private or notorious—God is more ready to forgive than they to ask forgive-ness, provided they believe in him, and that he alone forgives all sin.

For neither Mary, Christ's mother, nor Peter, Christ's vicar, is willing or able to forgive any sin unless Christ forgives it. Conversely, if Christ does not forgive it, then neither Mary nor Peter will or can forgive it.[105] Therefore, each man should believe that Christ, God and man, forgives sin. Every saint that is in heaven and every man living in earth is, and always was, merely a pronouncer of Christ's forgiveness. This is the belief the apostles taught. Many hideous sinners believed through them in Christ and were brought to his fellowship, strong and willing in belief and patient in every tribulation. And thus holy fathers, inspired with the Holy Spirit before the coming of Christ, believing in Christ's mercy, and languishing after his coming because holy church might not be perfectly unified by his coming, said

Shall not Sion say: This man and that man is born in her? and the Highest himself has founded her.
Whether to Sion a man shall say, "And man is born within, and he the most high founded it"? (Ps 87:5)

Sion means "beholding" or "bidding," and through these inter-pretations it may be called holy church. And thus whoever is part of Christ's church must behold him with the clear eye of soul, that is, with his mind steadfastly upon him. By this means, and without dif-ficult labor, he will know Christ's commands and keep them unde-filed. Whoever busily beholds Christ in this way, following him, may easily know who is a faithful member of Christ's church, who errs in this, and who never came within the church. It cannot be denied that there are some faithful men who truly believe in Christ, following him as far as their frailty allows, hating sin and loving virtues first in themselves and afterward in all others, always in dread rather than hope of falling, loving God above all things and their neighbor as themselves, punishing themselves most austerely if any rebellious feeling rises and would overcome them, and applying the gentlest of remedies to their brothers. Even though their brothers or sisters might sin most hideously, they ask for no more than the leaving of this sin and its occasion. These whole members of Christ are busy in teaching belief in him.

Those who receive this belief and dare not openly acknowledge it, err in Christ's church, even if they have no other guilt. Indeed, they err perhaps enough to be damned for this alone. There is no doubt, though, about those who have received belief and yet still live according to the world and their fleshly desires, governing themselves according to the common course and custom as the greater part of men do and scorning those that do otherwise. Whatever dignity, primacy, or degree they may stand in, higher or lower, they never came into holy church, nor shall they be counted as one of its members, unless they amend themselves. These are enemies of Christ, destroyers of the church as much as is in them. If God's mercy might bend to this, that in any way they might be called back from their blindness, when opportunity of hearing and speech might be hazarded, one should say to them, "Christ, God and man, is born head of holy church, and his members are most like to him, following him after the example he gives. He, the highest of all, founded his church in meekness and charity, in true peace of conscience, in appropriate occupation, in desire for heavenly things, in purity or chastity and in good temperance. And you, to your unutterable confusion, are about to destroy this foundation, in greatness of your wills and hardness of your hearts unexercised in spirituality, since in words and works you overturn that foundation." And the Prophet takes the Lord to witness that all such people are inexcusable, even if the greater part of the world favors them, saying

The Lord shall tell in his writings of peoples and of princes, of those that have been in her.
The Lord shall tell in scriptures of the peoples and of the princes that were in it. (Ps 87:6)

Great is the wisdom in this statement, and of much importance, since the Lord witnesses it. The scriptures that the Lord will tell are the ceremonies, prophecies, judgments, and acts of the apostles. These were written by Moses to other prophets, for the education of the people, and by the apostles, in various places. These scriptures tell plainly of the rebellion and vengeance of those who should have been governors of God's people according to his law, who instead followed the world in pride and covetousness, oppressing the people with many grievous burdens, compelling the people to obey them and drawing them from knowledge of God's law to service to themselves, until they were made so dull and weary that they had little or no memory of God or his saints. For when princes of the people were given to pride and covetousness, they did not occupy themselves with the law of God, which had been entrusted to them by holy fathers, to read and keep undefiled and busily teach to the people. They did not set the love and dread of God in their hearts, or the keeping of his law. And as they wandered away from that, so did the people after them, and do until this day.

So that the princes of the people both secular and spiritual should have no excuse before God for not knowing the law of God or teaching it to his people, the Lord bears witness often in his law that he gave it to his chief princes, and they wrote it and followed it, and busily taught it to the people, as it should always be the obligation of the chief princes to do. As an example of glory to those that should be glorious before God, it is written and witnessed here that the prophets and the apostles of Christ were in their time princes in the church militant among the people—and not princes only in their social rank, but principal among men, surpassing others in the holiness of their way of life. That is why the holy Lord gives witness to their holiness. He tells in their scriptures of their praiseworthy occupation in this life, and their endless glory in heaven, in which those who follow them in their actions shall be partners. But their successors in name who are enemies in their actions shall not receive thanks or merit from God. Not only they themselves, but many by their example—yes, indeed, the greater part of mankind—are drawn into the devil's yoke and made into the synagogue of Satan. Oh, since God complains of the devotion of the people when they *worship him with their lips* and not *their hearts*, what excuse will there be for clerks, who understand what they read, if they had their words in mind? (Isa 29:13). Certainly, whatever they read or say of God's law, their works openly show that their words pass undevoutly away from them, with no memory or understanding.

Whatever man has his mind devoutly engaged in the law of God must know that he is called by God into some type of service to God. Each man should willingly serve God in the social position in which God has called him to serve, and so be made a worthy limb of holy church. But as the works of men openly give witness, few in any social position make themselves worthy in this way, and none so few as priests, as the meaning of this next verse following will openly show. For if priests, who often read this verse, had it in mind and thought on its meaning, they should be astonished at themselves, and with fervent desire they would busily hasten to be in holy church through virtuous living and true teaching, as Christ and holy saints of his two laws have given them example. And so the Prophet shows the excellent reason why each man should desire to be a limb of holy church, saying

The dwelling in you is as it were of all rejoicing.
As of all joying, the dwelling place is in you. (Ps 87:7)

In these few words is much comfort. But they are hastily slid over and soon out of the mind of readers, as their works openly (and into their great confusion) bear witness. For each effectual prayer has this condition and strength in it. First, it prays to be cleansed of all evil done before. And after that, to be defended from all evil to come. Then, it desires and yearns after God's will, to be his heir in the bliss of heaven. And so each effectual prayer to God has in it sorrow and dread, desire and hope, which all together spring out of belief. For whoever does not believe, has none of these conditions. And so it seems that the faith of many men and women is dead, and their prayers void. For they are but naked words, which when they are multiplied stink before God, and he closes his ears against them. No wonder, since the most part of mankind, as their open works bear witness, are stuck fast in hypocrisy and covetousness. Such people receive their reward here, no doubt. Effectual prayer makes the one who prays in virtue stable and constant, drawing him from all unprofitable occupation, inward and outward. Since each man must have some occupation, he that is withdrawn from evil must be occupied well, and vice versa. And since men and women, when they come from their prayers, even priests from their masses, are seen to be occupied in vanity, worldly and fleshly, who may guess their prayers to be said in sorrow and dread. Such people are not praiseworthy according to God, so it is no wonder that they do not rejoice in the untellable comfort of saints dwelling in the church of God, who say "dwelling in holy church is as of all joying," as who says "no joy is greater."[106] For such people dwell in God, and God in them. Let God be in us, then, and let us dwell in him. Beyond that, let nothing be thought and spoken. We shall rejoice in the most perfect joy of all men joying.

WYCLIFFITE DEVOTION

15. The Seven Works of Mercy[107]

This brief exposition of the seven works of mercy differs markedly from most treatments of this topic. Most treatments list the standard seven bodily works of mercy, often the seven spiritual works of mercy too, and commonly provide some discussion of how each work in turn might be performed. For mnemonic purposes they usually reduce each of the works to a single verb, or to a short phrase featuring that verb, for example, "feed, give drink." Instead, the *Seven Works* frames itself as an exposition of Matthew 25:31–46, the biblical source for six of the seven bodily works of mercy. It takes care to provide even the seventh work not listed there, burial of the dead, with a biblical grounding. What is more, it provides each of the seven bodily works of mercy with a new allegorical interpretation and augments God's quoted words from Matthew 25 as well, with the end result that the whole labor of performing the seven works of mercy is reinterpreted as that of knowing and keeping and teaching God's commandments, both through word and through example.

As the explanatory notes explain in more detail, there are three other versions of this text, each differing systematically in ways that suggest considered revision rather than merely accidental variation; in addition, the second half of item 16 condenses and reworks this item's content (see below). Two of the three versions of the *Seven Works* are freestanding, while the third appears in the first part of chapter two of the Middle English manual of religious instruction *Book to a Mother*, whose editor dated it to the 1370s and denied it was in any way Wycliffite.[108] The version modernized here, taken from TCD 245, is the one least like that in *Book to a Mother*. While the Trinity version is in addition plainly corrupt, and its final sentence has been lost with the book's missing final quire, it is of great interest, for it removes an anticlerical digression that follows the first work of mercy in all other extant versions, and more carefully and fully elaborates its explanation of each point; it is the most pastoral and least polemical in its emphasis of the extant renditions.

God will speak about the works of mercy to all his chosen ones, standing on his right side, at the dreadful day of judgment. *"Come, you blessed children of my Father, and receive the kingdom of heaven that has been ordained for you from the beginning of the world.* For you kept my commandments. *For when I was hungry you gave me food"* (Matt 25:34–35). That is, when the least of mine that shall be saved hungered for lack of spiritual or bodily food, you fed them and guided them to keep my commandments. As a result, they are written in the book of life among my holy saints. For the second work of mercy, God will say, *"I was thirsty and you gave me drink,"* both bodily and spiritually (Matt 25:35). For first, a man should know God's commandments and keep them, avoiding all seven deadly sins; that is, give me drink. Just as bodily drink is more easily received than bodily food, so the commandments of God are easier for him, and dependable for any man newly turned to God. For the third work of mercy, God will say, *"I was homeless and you housed me,"* that is, both bodily and spiritually (Matt 25:35). When any of my men poor in virtue from breaking my commandments was separated from holy church—for whoever lives against God's commandments is separated from God and holy church, and whoever lives according to God's commandments is part of holy church, for God is in him and he in God—and when you knew any such men who were separated from holy church through breaking of my commandments, you through your good living moved them to know my commandments and to keep them, and so you housed me in my members, spiritually. For the fourth work of mercy, God will say, *"I was naked and you clothed me,"* both bodily and spiritually (Matt 25:36). That is, when any of my poor were naked of virtues, you through your good living moved them to keep my commandments, and by you, through my grace, they were clothed in virtues. For the fifth work of mercy, God will say, *"I was sick and you visited me,"* both bodily and spiritually (Matt 25:36). That is, when any of my people were bound with the foul bond in their own soul through their unsteadfast way of life, you with good conversation moved them to keep my commandments, and with sorrow of heart you busily prayed for them. For the sixth, God will say, *"I was in prison and you came to me,"* both bodily and spiritually (Matt 25:36); that is, when any of my poor feeble men were fallen into unsteadfast-

ness, and would easily be led to break my commandments, and so
they lay in the devil's prison wrapped in pain. For whoever breaks
God's commandments is bound to the devil tighter than any man
can imagine from the binding men undergo bodily with snares or
chains. And so through your compassion, moved by charity, you
delivered my folk from the devil's power and taught them to keep
my commandments. The seventh work of mercy, burying the dead,
is not openly recounted in the gospel. But it is understood as part of
the third work of mercy, when Christ said he was homeless. That is,
when any of my people lay proudly out of the house of holy church,
here above earth, not humbly knowing themselves to be earth and
ashes, but with a stinking bier of foul lecher's words, you through
your good living moved them to keep my commandments and leave
their wicked life. You through your way of life slew in them the
seven deadly sins, and so through keeping my commandments they
were clothed in the seven virtues. Humbly knowing themselves to
be earth and dust, they followed in charity[109] that *covers*, as St. James
says, the *multitude of sins* (Jas 5:20).

And then Christ will say to those on the left side, "*Depart from
me, you cursed people, into the everlasting fire that is ordained for the
devil and his angels*" (Matt 25:41). For you did not do the works of
mercy, neither bodily nor spiritually.

16. A Form of Confession[110]

Formulas designed to aid lay readers in preparing themselves for
confession are common in a wide range of Middle English manuscripts, as well as in the late medieval Christian tradition more
broadly. This example of a template for confession is unusual in a
number of ways.[111] It makes no mention of any interaction with a
priest, whether in the sacrament of confession or in other circumstances related to confession. Instead, it frames itself as a highly personal interaction with God. The confession it rehearses is not framed
around any form of a catalogue of the seven deadly sins or of the vices,
as was far more common in penitential materials, but around the Ten
Commandments. (Wycliffites do discuss the seven sins, but typically
in a cursory way; they are far more interested in the commandments.)
The first-person confession the text rehearses canvasses each com-

mandment in turn, but it interprets the breaking of each one not as a transgression of specific directives about religious and other conduct, but, through an unusual figurative flattening, as a violation of the properly loving relationship that the sinner should have with his God. The second half of "A Form" is a reworking of the same content found in the text on the *Seven Works of Mercy*, item 15; this material probably appealed to the author because of his similar close focus on the Ten Commandments.

I acknowledge before God almighty and his blessed mother Mary and all his saints that I, a sinful wretch, have often and grievously sinned against his will. I have not reverently feared him, fleeing what displeases him and doing what pleases him. I have not loved him with all my heart, as he commands—that is, as St. Augustine says, with all my understanding without error, with all my soul (that is, with all my will) without contrary impulses, with all my mind without forgetting.[112]

Instead, I have worshiped false gods in my soul, likenesses of the many things that I have loved against his commandments, putting the love of them before the love of my God.[113] I have taken his name in vain, and worse, in the sin of being called Christian without engaging in Christ's works, and also in swearing with my mouth by his heart and soul and blood and eyes and other oaths without number. And so I have not made his Sabbath holy, for I have not made myself holy by ceasing to sin and keeping his commandments. And I have not honored God our Father, or his spouse, holy church our mother. I am killing my soul from the life of grace. I engage in spiritual adultery, separating my soul from my Christ, her spouse, because of my wicked thoughts (Wis 1:3–4). All the more so if wicked words and works are added to those wicked thoughts. And so I have stolen his goods, against his will. I have thievingly and traitorously taken service from his creatures. For I have drawn his servants away from their proper service, established for his true servants, in order to serve the devil, and hold with him under his banner of sin. And we have warred against my king, God, from whom I have taken wages, and to whom I have often made a promise to serve truly. So I have borne false witness against my nearest neighbor, God, who is nearer to me than I am to myself. In this way I have wickedly coveted my neighbor's house, his wife, his servants, his maid, his ox and his ass and his other goods, against his will, for an evil purpose.

I have sinned in pride, envy, and wrath (for David says, *he who loves wickedness hates his soul*) and in gluttony, lechery, sloth, and covetousness.[114] I have sinned with my five wits, misusing them in sin and in vanities: seen with my eyes, heard with my ears, spoken with my mouth, smelled with my nose, gone with my feet, done with my hands, thought with my heart, wrought wickedly with all of my body. Most especially I have misused the five wits that live on with the soul after the death of the body, and not looked toward the last judgment as I should with an eye of true faith.[115]

How hard it will be to see Christ angry and hear him say, "*Depart from me cursed into the everlasting fire that is made ready for the devil and his angels. I was hungry,*"[116] that is, principally for justice, that men should do his father's will by keeping the Ten Commandments, for as Christ says, *my food is that I should do the will of the one who sent me* (John 4:34), "*and so you did not give me food. I thirsted*"—and this refers to the easier things to be done in following his commandments, while food refers to the harder things, just as bodily drink is more easily received than bodily food—"*and so, you did not give me drink. I was homeless* when any of mine who shall be saved was out of the right faith of holy church because of breaking of my commandments and not gathering themselves home to hold my commandments, neither by good living, as every man is required to, nor by good teaching. Also, *I was naked* from virtues because of the breaking of my commandments, when any of mine was naked, and you *did not cover* him with virtues. *I was sick,* easily to be overcome with sin, or all overcome, *in prison,* bound fast with a strong chain of the seven deadly sins"—for they are so closely attached together that one may not be without all seven, as St. Augustine says.[117] In a book of his Confessions he acknowledges to God that from often doing sin he arrived at a habit, and from a habit to a custom, and from custom to necessity, and so bound himself with a great chain of necessity to the seven deadly sins.[118] For this reason he cried out, as did David in the psalter, "*Deliver me from my necessity,* Lord" (Ps 25:17).[119] And Solomon says, "*With the ropes of his sins* every man *is constrained*" (Prov 5:22).

The seventh work of mercy is not openly rehearsed in that gospel for the first Monday of Lent, in Matthew the twenty-fifth chapter. But it is mentioned in the book of Tobit (Tob 2:1), and it is understood in the third work, when Christ says, "*I was homeless.*" That is, when a man who shall be saved sleeps from day to day, spiritually dead in his sins, envenoming others with his evil example. He consents with a stinking breath, speaking foul lecherous words, or horrible oaths, by soul and heart, sides, nails, arms, bones, in contempt of God. He does not meekly acknowledge that he is wretched worms' food, earth and ashes, nor does he ask to be buried from his sins.

Christ speaks of these spiritual works[120] when he cries out often in the gospel, "*He who has ears, let him hear.*"[121] And what I say to you, I say to all, "*Stay awake, for you do not know the day or the hour*" (Matt 25:13; cf. Matt 24:42).

17. A Dialogue between a Wise Man and a Fool[122]

The unique copy of this dialogue is the last and longest of the twelve tracts in Cambridge University Library Ii.6.26. Rather than arguing on behalf of biblical translation, as many of these tracts do, it gives an exemplary illustration of the effects of proper biblical instruction, staging the conversion of the ill-informed Fool's wayward will toward its proper goal. This text, too, frames itself as a commentary on the commandments—in this case, an extended discussion in dialogue form of the precept "do not kill," either bodily or spiritually. Once again, this author uses a distinction between bodily and spiritual interpretation as a framing device; once again, he focuses overwhelmingly on the spiritual alternative. Spiritual murder he interprets as idle speech. The Wise Man teaches the Fool that instead of enjoying tales and fables and indulging in swearing and merrymaking, he should speak God's word, focus his attention on preparing for death, and encourage others to do the same. The text only halfheartedly embraces dialogue form; at first the Fool's possible objections are presented as what the Wise Man thinks he might say, and even once the Fool emerges into speech, some of his objections are spoken by the Wise Man rather than by the Fool himself. Yet even if the text is hesitant about what it may regard as literary artifice, its author is also plainly well acquainted with literature. The Fool names a whole string of romances he would rather hear in place of the Wise Man's sober instruction, and he quotes in rapid succession two proverbs that play a key role in *Piers Plowman* and in Chaucer's *Pardoner's Tale*. He may be evoking these poems themselves. Similarly, in his reference to the souls of an owl and a cuckoo, he may invoke the poetic tradition of debates staged between birds, even perhaps Jean Condé's *Mass of the Birds* or John Clanvowe's *The Cuckoo and the Nightingale*. This text includes an especially extensive definition and explanation of what a "loller" or "lollard" is, asserting that the best loller was Christ.

A dialogue as it were of a wise man and of a fool denying the truth with fables.

WISE MAN

"*Do not kill*" (Exod 20:13, Deut 5:17). This is the fifth commandment of almighty God, commanding every reasonable creature that none should slay another, whether bodily or spiritually. Both these forms of murder are very common among those who are called Christian—especially spiritual murder, which is given least attention of all, but should be the cause of the greatest sorrow. For nowadays, if a man comes among the people, old or young, he will soon hear tales of pride, gluttony, lechery, and every kind of sin. Whoever is able to tell these stories to unwise people most entertainingly, he is greatly commended by them for this foolishness. They swear, by arms, bones, heart, and sides, that he is a good fellow, and that every gathering where he is present is the better for it. But a holy man says in his writing, "Cursed be the mirth with which God is displeased."[123] Perhaps you will say that this is not evil speech, because it drives away heaviness and makes men light and glad. Ah, in this way you want to prove that this vain speech is wise and Christ's words are foolish. This would be foul heresy. For Christ says in the gospel, "*Of every idle word that men speak* here, unless they repent it before they die, *they shall give an account at the day of judgment*" (Matt 12:36). St. Jerome says that all words that all men speak are vain and idle unless they lead to the spiritual profit of the speaker or of the hearer.[124] And thus, lying, flattering, backbiting, slander, swearing, cursing, and ribaldry are proven to be idle, because they are against the command of Christ and his apostles. For St. Peter says, "*When you want to speak, speak like the words of God*," that is, always truth and goodness and never falsehood or wickedness (1 Pet 4:11). For the Trinity hates these and loves the first two. Paul, John, James, and Jude agree with this, who were faithful servants of our doctor Jesus Christ. St. Gregory says, "He slays himself who will not keep the commands of our heavenly doctor Christ."[125]

But alas, if a simple man nowadays, who loves his doctor Christ and his law, wants to show sinners the healing words of God in order to purge these idle forms of speech, right away they despise him, and hate him, and say he is a heretic and a loller. I advise men to be wary of this claim, for it is a foul heresy, openly going against the Holy Spirit, to despise men and women who speak the law of God in order to tear up vices out of men's souls and plant virtues in them. Christ says to the true lovers and faithful speakers of his word, "*It is not you who speak, but the spirit of* my *Father almighty that speaks in you*" (Matt 10:20). Also, he says, "*Whoever* sins *against the Holy Spirit, it shall not be forgiven him, in this world or the world to come*" (Matt 12:32). For this reason, be wise, and do not contradict God's word, for by witness of St. Augustine it is a grievous heresy.[126]

As for where they call men lollers for speaking God's word, I read of two kinds of lollers in the law of grace. Some loll toward God, and some toward the fiend. I intend to talk about both these kinds. The most blessed loller that ever was or shall be was our Lord Jesus Christ, who lolled for our sins on the cross. Wearing his livery and belonging to his retinue were Peter and Andrew and others as well. These were blessed lollers, lolling on the right hand of Jesus with the repentant thief, trusting in God's mercy (Luke 23:40–43), to whom our Lord promised the bliss of paradise on that same day. But good friends, what was the reason why Christ and his followers were lolled[127] in this way? It must be, because of their faithful speaking out against the sins of the people. And especially because they spoke against the covetousness and sins of untrue bishops and of the false, feigned religious.

Now, let us speak of cursed, untrue lollers, who deny God and his law and remain in this wicked state until death. I read in a book of God's law that is called Esther how there was a wicked loller whose name was Aman Amalechites, who hated and despised the word of God and the people of Israel who were teachers of this word. Because of the malice and envy rooted in his heart he got the permission of a king, Assuerus, to destroy these people that God had chosen. And to accomplish his evil intention, he made a pair of gallows fifty cubits in height, in order to hang blessed Mardoche, the counselor of God's people. Then the king of heaven and earth, through his might and mercy, turned Aman's malice upon himself, for he was lolled to death on the same gallows on which he had planned to hang Mardoche.[128] This was a wicked loller who died in his sin. We read of another cursed loller in the gospel and in the Acts of the Apostles, whose name was Judas Iscariot, who betrayed Christ.[129] For this reason he fell into despair, and went and lolled himself to death (Matt 27:5). And in this way he was damned, and so he lolled on the left side, with the thief that blasphemed against Christ.[130]

Now, may God grant us grace to follow the blessed lollers, Christ and his followers, and to flee the condition of these cursed lollers, for example, Aman, Judas, and the thief who lolled on the left side of Christ. Why so? Because their lolling brought them to endless woe. Each man and woman here on earth lolls in the way to endless bliss, or in the way to everlasting punishment. But our Savior says "*Large and broad is the way that leads to perdition, and very many enter by this gate to hell. But very narrow and small is the way that leads to heaven. And very few enter through it into bliss*" (Matt 7:13–14). And therefore Christ says to his *little flock* (Luke 12:32), "*Strive to enter by the strait gate* of tribulation and anguish, and in this way, through your meekness and patient suffering, you will bring your soul to bliss and peace that will never end" (Luke 13:24).

Dear Christian friends, do not be ashamed to speak God's word and to live according to it. For Christ says, "*He that is ashamed of me and my words* before men, I *will be ashamed of him* before my Father and his angels" (Luke 9:26). Do not be surprised when sinners despise you and call you lollers for loving Christ's gospel. For Solomon says that those who *walk in the right way* to heaven by loving God and his law are *despised* by those who live wickedly, wandering in ways contrary to God and his law (Prov 14:2). And our exemplar Christ says, "*If they have called the husbandman of faithful souls 'Beelzebub,' then they will much more readily despise his household servants*" (Matt 10:25). And this true husband, Christ, says to his faithful servants, "*Learn of me.* Take my example. Follow me in meek suffering.[131] *Pray for men who pursue and* hate *you, so that you may be the* true *children of your Father who is in heaven*" (Matt 5:44–45).[132]

But perhaps you will say,[133] "I would gladly speak God's word and

250

live according to it, leaving this and words of ribaldry. But I am very reluctant to lose the possessions I have worked so long for. It is well known that if a man speaks crude words, swearing great oaths, and engaging in lechery and other great sins, he will not be punished for this except in his purse. If he pays the summoner and the bishop's officers well, he will be called a manly man, valuable to holy church. But if a man speaks God's word and lives according to it, and does not stop for any persecution or loss of worldly goods, he will be cursed and put out of the church, and burned as a heretic if he can be caught."

I pray you, friend, wait and hear an answer to your words. Christ says to lovers of his law, "*Do not be surprised, if the world hates you,* because *it hated me before you*" (1 John 3:13; John 15:18). And God says through his prophet to all who commend vices and hate and despise virtues, "*Woe to those who say good is evil and evil is good, calling light darkness and darkness light, sweetness bitterness and bitterness sweetness*" (Isa 5:20). Good friend, attend to the words of Christ that follow: "*Whoever* does not forsake house, land, *father, mother, wife, and child, taking up his cross and following me, he may not be my disciple.*"[134] Also he says, "He who forsakes all these and *loses his life* here for me and for my gospel, will *receive a hundredfold reward* and have lordship and everlasting life."[135] Also, he says to the patient sufferers for his law, "*You shall be blessed when men pursue you and accuse you of all manner of evildoing while you are living for me and my word. Rejoice, then, and be glad, for your reward is great in heaven. They slew and persecuted holy prophets who were before you in just this way*" (Matt 5:11–12). Let us bear gladly this cross of tribulation, following the example of Christ and his holy apostles, who went forth rejoicing from the sight of wicked princes (Acts 5:41–42). The reason for this was that the king of mercy made them able and worthy to suffer pain and contempt for showing his name to the people. Therefore, let us drink gladly of the cup of Christ's passion, trusting steadfastly in Paul's words when he says, "If you are partners with Christ in tribulation and pain, then do not doubt that you will be partners in his endless bliss" (2 Cor 1:7; cf. Rom 8:17). The apostle also says, "*It is fitting that we enter into the kingdom of heaven through many tribulations,* for *all those who want to live meekly in Christ shall suffer persecution for the sake of righteousness*" (Acts 14:21; 2 Tim 3:12; Matt 5:10). And Christ says, "*You who suf-*

fer tribulation for righteousness shall be forever blessed" (Matt 5:10). And the Prophet says, "*Many are the tribulations of the just, and our Lord shall* graciously *deliver them from all of them*" (Ps 34:19). And our Savior says, "*Do not fear those who may slay you in body, but fear the one that may slay you both body and soul*, and send them either to pain or to bliss as he pleases" (Matt 10:28; cf. Luke 12:4–5). For the sake of these comforting words of our Redeemer and his holy followers, each true soul should take the voice of David, saying "*I shall* gladly *take* the wholesome *cup* of tribulation, *and* in drinking of Christ's cup *I shall* inwardly *call* his *name* to my help" (Ps 116:13).[136]

But men and women who love the world and its lustful living do not savor this wisdom. No wonder. For blessed Job asked God, "*Where shall* we find *heavenly wisdom?*" (Job 28:12). And the Holy Spirit gave him an answer: "This valuable wisdom may not be found in the land of lust and lovers of the flesh" (cf. Job 28:13). This is why Solomon says, "The *wisdom* of God *shall not enter into an ill-willed soul, nor shall it dwell in the body that is subject to sins*" (Wis 1:4). And Paul, speaking of fleshly and worldly wisdom, says that *the wisdom of this world is as folly to God almighty* (1 Cor 3:19). And Christ, the wisdom of the Father, speaking of the worldly wise, says, "*The children of this world are wiser* and more prudent in savoring earthly and fleshly things *in* fleshly *generation than are the children of light* led by the spirit of the Father (Luke 16:8). For this reason, he says to his followers, "*I have chosen you from* this worldly wisdom, and *therefore the world hates you*" (John 15:19). And Paul says, "*Do not conform yourself to the world* in this sort of wisdom of the flesh" (Rom 12:2). For this reason, he says, "*If I* wanted to *please men* with this sort of fleshly and worldly wisdom, *I would not then be Christ's* true *servant*" (Gal 1:10). Christ prayed to his Father to keep his servants from the evil that worldly wisdom brings to men (John 17:15). And St. Gregory says that antichrist shall choose men who are full of worldly wisdom to preach his falseness.[137] May God keep us from this wisdom, and fasten his fear in our souls. For Solomon says, "*The beginning of* heavenly *wisdom is the fear of* our Lord *God*" (Prov 1:7; 9:10; cf. Ps 111:10). This is why David says to God, "Lord, fasten and nail *my flesh* to *the fear of you* that *brings in* this heavenly *wisdom*" (Ps 119:120). For those who have this fear in their hearts are cleansed from worldly wisdom. This is why Christ says, "*Blessed are the* men who are *pure in heart, for they shall see God* in endless glory" (Matt 5:8).

252

Very blessed is this word of God. For it quickens and gives life to his lovers, who before were soaked and spiritually sleeping with sin. This is why Peter says to Christ, "*Lord, to whom shall we go* but to you, for *you have words of everlasting life?*" (John 6:69). And Christ says, "*The words that I speak to you are spirit and life*" (John 6:64). This is why he says to Martha, Mary Magdalene's sister, "*He who believes in me,* turning from sin to good works, *even if he were dead* in sin, he *shall live* by the power of my word without end" (John 11:25). David, describing spiritual virtue, said these words to God: "*Lord, I have closed your words in my heart, so that I will not offend you by sin*" (Ps 119:11). Beyond this, he says, "*Lord, the explaining of your words enlightens and gives understanding to* the meek" (Ps 119:130). That is why he says, "*Blessed are the pure that walk in the law*" (Ps 119:1). "*For your law is without stain, turning souls from death to life. And our Lord's testimony is true, giving wisdom to* men of little ill-will" (Ps 19:8). This is why John says in the Apocalypse, "*Blessed is he who reads and hears* with a good life the blessed and fruitful law of our Lord God (Rev 1:3).

FOOL

But a certain man says, I pray you, stop these speeches, and tell me a merry tale about Guy of Warwick, Beves of Hampton, or Sir Libeaus, Robin Hood, or some well-favored man with the same sort of status and manners.[138]

WISE MAN

Oh, unwise man, in this desire you show yourself to be among that number that Isaiah rebuked, saying, "Rebellious *children, not wanting to hear the law of God,* say '*Tell us pleasant things* even if they are *errors*'" (Isa 30:9–10). Let it be known to all men that these stories and poems about fighters, adulterers, and thieves are coveted by sinners through the idle imagination of their hearts. Also they are powdered over, for the most part, with false lies. The Prophet talks about these sorts of writings and performances, saying, "Lord, *wicked people have told me fables* and trifles, *but nothing according to the law*" (Ps 119:85). Also, he speaks to men who desire these, and says, "*How long will you be of heavy heart, and for what reason do you love vanity and lies?*" (Ps 4:3). Isaiah, speaking about the writers of trifles and fables, says, "*Their actions are unprofitable, and deeds of wickedness are in their hands*" (Isa 59:6). There is no doubt that all who have more delight in such stories and jokes are spiritual adulterers, for in this they forsake their spouse, Christ, and his law that is the bread of life, and they wed Satan, with his lies that are the loaves of lasting sorrow. David speaks a fearful wisdom about such liars: "Lord God," he says, "*you shall destroy all those who speak lies*" (Ps 5:6).[139] The reason why is that they are proven in God's law to be the murderers of themselves as well as many others. For this reason Augustine says, "Man's soul dies from hunger, unless it is fed with the heavenly bread that Christ calls the bread of life."[140] The prophet speaks about this bread, saying "*You have given* your *people bread from heaven*, holding within itself all the delight of grace and mercy."[141] Ecclesiasticus says, "The Lord has fed his chosen number *with the bread of life and of understanding*" (Sir 15:3).[142] St. Augustine says, "Live well, and believe in Christ well, and you will have eaten the bread of life."[143]

"Yes, yes," you say,[144] "I like having tales like these as much as I like having nothing. Let us live as our fathers did, and that will be good enough. They were well loved by tricksters, wrestlers, fencers, by dancers and singers. They welcomed them to drinking parties with good will. Yes, and often on Sundays, for good fellowship, they would dine and drink with song, and go to church afterward. Let us do likewise nowadays, and we shall have the blessing of St. Thomas of Canterbury." Yes, man, and if you have drunk well at home, your stomach will grow warm, even if the weather is cold. And the sweet savor of good ale will rise into your brain and bring you contentedly to sleep. Yes, and however persistently the priest may preach, it will grieve your wits no more than the sound of a merry harp.

Ah, Jesus, your words are true, where you say, "*The mouth speaks* all *the abundance of the heart*" (Matt 12:34; Luke 6:45). And so, unwise man, it seems that in your heart are rooted idle thoughts, in your tongue, vain words, and in all your members, unprofitable works. And so you reveal yourself through your words to be evil and wicked and in no way good. Christ says, "*Wicked servant, I judge you by your own mouth*" (Luke 6:45; cf. Matt 12:35). Also, he says, "*A good man brings forth good things from the treasure of his heart, but an evil man brings forth wicked things from the cursed treasure of his heart*" (Luke 6:45; cf. Matt 12:35). And, "*Each good tree makes good fruit, and each evil tree makes evil fruit*" (Matt 7:17; cf. Luke 6:45).

Every tree is known by the fruits that come of it.[145] This is why the enemies of truth said to Peter in the time of Christ's passion, "*You are one of them,* judging by *your speech*"—that is, "the fruit of your tongue makes you known to us" (Matt 26:73; cf. Mark 14:70; Luke 22:58; John 18:25). Now, friend, beware, for Christ says that *each tree that does not bear good fruit shall be cut down and cast into the fire* (Matt 3:10; 7:19; Luke 3:9).

Where you say we should live as our fleshly and sinful fathers did, this is unwholesome advice. God says that he will punish *the wickedness of* such *fathers and such children into the third and fourth generation* (Exod 20:5; Deut 5:9; cf. Num 14:18; Exod 34:7). I believe that you are among the number of those who speak in this way: "*Our fathers have eaten a sour grape, and the teeth of* [. . .]" (Jer 31:29; Ezek 18:2).[146] Christ on this subject says in his gospel, "*Your* sinful *fathers ate manna in the desert, and* because they did so unworthily they *are dead. But he* who eats the *bread* of life, that is, my word, he *shall live without end*" (John 6:49–59, passim). In another place Christ says to the deniers and haters of his word, "*You are* children *of your father the devil,* for *he was a murderer from the beginning*" (John 8:44). His children are all those who love fantasies, fables, and lies more than the gospel that is the truth. Nonetheless, God says through his prophet, "*The son shall not bear the wickedness of his father* if he does not follow him in his sins, *nor shall the father* be punished *for his children,* if he taught them to believe in and cultivate the keeping of the commandments of God" (Ezek 18:20; see also 18:19). So let us follow our father God almighty, both in thought, work, and word. And let us flee the sinful habits of our fleshly fathers, which do not lead to life, but to everlasting death. For Christ says he is *way, truth, and life* to all that shall be saved (John 14:6). Let us follow our fathers, and all people, in that they follow Christ, but no further, for life nor death. For Christ says, "*He who hears my words and does them, he is my brother,* sister, *and mother*" (Luke 8:21; cf. Matt 12:50, Mark 3:35). Also, he says, "*Whoever does the will of my Father, he shall enter into the kingdom of heaven*" (Matt 7:21).

FOOL

What?! Then by your account we should never be merry but always sorry. It seems that you want all men to speak of God's law, and think about the pains ordained for sinners, and also about their deaths. This would make them die for sorrow!

WISE MAN

This most certainly proves the words of the Wise Man true, for he says, "*Malice* may be *overcome*, but it may not be *appeased*" (cf. Wis 7:30). You show this well in your answers, for they are grounded in folly. Good friend, pay attention to the words of David: "*Blessed is the man whose will is in the law of the Lord, who* shall enclose his mind in his law *both by day and by night*" (Ps 1:1–2).[147] Also, he says, "*Delight in the* law of our *Lord, and he shall give you the* rightful *askings of your heart*" (Ps 37:4). St. Augustine says, "Enclose your mind in our Lord's biddings and be zealous to keep his commandments. Then he will confirm your heart in goodness and give you the desires of heavenly wisdom."[148] Also, he says, "There is no thing sweeter to him who shall be saved than to be held within the commandments of God."[149] This is why he says, "Love the knowing of holy scripture, and you shall not love, or fulfill, the sinful desires of your flesh."[150] It is a very good idea to avoid the things that bring men to hell, and to do those things that bring men to heaven. For holy Job says that there is no redemption in hell.[151] This is why Christ calls it the utmost *darkness, where there is* forevermore *weeping and gnashing of teeth* (Matt 8:12; 22:13; 25:30). As holy doctors say, the pains there are so grievous and great that all the pains of this life are joys in comparison with those in hell. The Prophet, considering the pain of death in hell, said, "*O second death, how bitter is the memory of you*" (Sir 41:1). David, speaking of this, says, "*The death of sinners is the worst* of all pains" (cf. Ps 34:21). But Paul says to the lovers who live according to God's law, "*Rejoice* in your tribulations, for they are nothing in comparison to the world to come."[152] This is why he says soon after, "*Rejoice, and may your forbearance be known to men, for our Lord is near you*" (Phil 4:4–5). And David says about such people, "Our *Lord is near* those who are troubled in *heart* for his law, and if they remain in *meekness, he shall make them safe*" (Ps 33:19). Our Savior says, "*A woman when she is with child has sorrow, but when the child is born the memory of the sorrow is passed*" (John 16:21). By this childbearing is understood a true soul, suffering many tribulations in body, who at his departing is borne by the angels of God into that world where all bliss is enclosed. For this reason, when his soul was going to depart from his body, Augustine said, "Welcome, death, end of all sorrow and trouble and the beginning of all joy and rest."[153] Why did he say this to death? Sir, just as death is the end of joy and beginning of endless pain for all those who will be damned, so death is the end of all sorrow to those that shall be saved, and the beginning of lasting joy. This is why the Prophet says, "Very *precious in the sight of* God *is the death of* just men" (Ps 116:15), but "*the death of sinners is most wicked*" (Ps 34:21).[154] Solomon speaks about these two deaths and says, "*Hold in your mind the last things, and you shall not sin without end*" (Sir 7:40).[155] Moses had the same desire when he said this: "Would God *that men knew and understood and provided for the last things*" (Deut 32:29). It is also wisdom to bear the day of judgment in mind, and by this means to flee the thoughts, words, and works that shall separate men from God into pain. And to love God and his law and live according to it. By this means men shall be received by God into bliss. For Christ says, "*Then, as* a good *shepherd separates goats from sheep, so he shall separate* the cursed from the blessed" (Matt 25:32)—the cursed to endless torment, the blessed to joy without end. For then Christ shall say to the number of the accursed, "Go, *you cursed* ones, *into everlasting fire* of the kind that is *prepared for the devil and all his angels*," according to that sentence (Matt 25:41). He will say to the chosen ones these words of love that follow: "*Come, you blessed children of my Father, and take your kingdom that was ordained for you by my Father from the beginning of the world*" (Matt 25:34).

FOOL

Yes, yes, man, when you have said all of this, it comes to nothing more than "do well and have well."[156] And an owl has as good a soul as a cuckoo, and I believe that for as long as you have lived, you have never seen a soul go blackberrying.[157] By my advice, then, let us be merry and not worry. Among a hundred men, whether seculars or priests, you will scarcely find one who will tell the kinds of tales you do. Whoever does as most men do will be blamed by the fewest men. Now follow my advice, and you will find it is best for you, as it seems to me.

WISE MAN

Brother, remember what Solomon says: "*There is a path that seems* to some men *righteous, but in the end it leads to* the *death* of

257

soul" (Prov 14:12; 16:25). This is very true, as can be proven through the examples of idolaters and misbelievers. Friend, you said before, "Do well and have well." But many things pertain to these two things. For there is no man or woman who may be proven to be a well-doer unless he learns the Ten Commandments of God and keeps them as far as is in his power. For it is written, *"Whoever says that he* loves God *and does not keep his commandments, he is a liar, and truth is not in him"* (1 John 2:4). You should understand well that these ten commandments are enclosed within two, that is, in love for God above all things, and for your neighbor as yourself (Matt 22:37–39; Mark 12:30–31; Luke 10:27). And Christ says that *in these two* loves is enclosed *all the law and the prophets* (Matt 22:40). And according to Paul, whoever loves perfectly has fulfilled the law (Rom 13:8–10; Gal 5:14). For whoever *loves God above all things,* he will not break his commandments. And whoever *loves his neighbor as himself* will not do anything to his neighbor except what he would like his neighbor to do to him. Whoever ends his life in these two loves, he may truly be called a well-doer. And for his well-doing he shall have more wealth than heart may think or tongue tell, of the joy and wealth that God has made ready for all those who love him without feigning. But brother, beware of sinful mirth. Whoever rejoices in the breaking of God's commandments is killing himself. If he ends his life in this state, he will go forth to endless care and sorrow.

You also say that an owl has as good a soul as a cuckoo. It seems from this statement that you are one of the *Sadducees, who say there is no resurrection* (Matt 22:23; Mark 12:18; Luke 20:27; see Acts 23:8). Christ condemns this foul heresy in the gospel when he speaks in this way: "*I am god of Abraham, god of Jacob, and god of Isaac. He is the god of living men, not of the dead*" (Matt 22:32; Mark 12:26–27; cf. Luke 20:37–38). I am sure of one thing: whoever speaks these foolish works you babbled earlier, despising God and his law, if he ends his life without repentance, he will go into everlasting pain, as the Prophet attests: "*Lord, you will* damn *all those who speak* and maintain such false *lies*" (Ps 5:6). By witness of St. John in the Apocalypse, liars of this kind shall dwell in a stinking pool that shall never be quenched (Rev 21:8).

You speak of blackberries. I advise you to leave these scornful words, lest your body and soul be made a black brand in the lasting pains of hell. If you want to know about those pains, what kind they are, I have read of nine very great pains that are there. There is fire most hot and *unquenchable*, as Christ tells (Matt 3:12; Mark 9:42, 44; Luke 3:17). There is water colder than living tongue can tell, as holy Job tells.[158] There, continual *weeping and gnashing of teeth*[. . .][159] These were represented in a figure in Moses' time, when darkness fell on cursed Pharaoh and on his people for their wickedness (Exod 10:21–23). But this darkness did not affect Moses, the blessed servant of God, or his people. Pharaoh and his people, who were in this darkness for three days and three nights, represent the fiend with his retainers, who shall dwell in endless darkness through the righteousness of the Father and the Son and the Holy Spirit. Moses and his people represent Jesus Christ and his chosen ones, who shall be in endless light, without any darkness. In hell there is also a bitter stench, without any sweetness, as John says in the Apocalypse.[160] And there is the gnawing worm of each damned soul's conscience, biting very painfully. It is a horrible place, without any brightness, and within it a very wicked fellowship of foul fiends. There are more glowing tears there than waters in the sea. The knitting together of all these pains is despair of ever coming out; whoever goes there must remain there without end.

You say we should do what most people do, and then we will have little blame. But by this foolish advice, we should not emulate the actions of the holy prophets, or those of John the Baptist, who was more than a prophet, or the works of Jesus Christ, or those of his holy apostles. If they had done what most people do, they would not have suffered the sorts of deaths that they did for their rebukes to sinners. It is better to suffer here from blames, reproofs, slanders, despisings, beatings, and shameful deaths than to appear shameful before God and his holy saints and suffer pains without end at the day of judgment.

Friend, I advise you to abandon your ignorant retorts and only follow God, and ask him forgiveness for your words, which were worse than idle, for they were not only against man but against the maker of all things. Beware, for we read that for this sort of folly Datan and Abiron sank down to hell while still alive, with wife, child, and all that belonged to them (Num 16, esp. 16:31–33). Antiochus for this sin met with a horrible end (1 Macc 6:1–16). And for this sin Christ cursed the cities of Bethsaida and Corozain (Matt 11:21; Luke

10:13), and told his obstinate persecutors that they would die in their sins (John 8, esp. 8:21, 24). Now, he warns us all that *at the day of judgment there will be less pain for Sodom and Gomorrah*, which sank down to hell for sin, *than there will be for the city* or person that will not receive the word of God (Matt 10:15; cf. Luke 10:12).

Further, you say that among a hundred people, whether priests or seculars, scarcely one can be found that will speak wholesomely about the word of God. This should make both of us mournful, and not glad. For Christ says, "*Blessed are those who mourn, for they shall be comforted* in the bliss of heaven" (Matt 5:5). Also, he says "*Woe to you who laugh* in wickedness, *for* your laughter *shall* be turned into weeping and bitterness" (Luke 6:25). Christ and Paul both affirm that there are many who follow the path of wickedness and few who go in the way of goodness. Paul says that many are *enemies to Christ's passion*, for they *make their bellies their God* and *take joy in what will bring their destruction* (Phil 3:18–19). Solomon says that *whoever walks in the right way* is *despised* by those who follow the wrong *way* (Prov 14:2). And Christ says, "*Large and broad is the way that leads to damnation, and many enter by it*, but very *narrow and constricted is the way and the gate that leads to bliss, and very few* enter in by it" (Matt 7:13–14).

Christ decrees that those priests who have *taken the key of the gate of knowing* and will not enter into bliss by it, *or allow those* who badly want to do so, will be rewarded with endless sorrow (Luke 11:52; see also Matt 23:13). Nonetheless, the king of all creation says, "There is much ripe corn, *but* very *few workmen. Pray therefore to the lord* of this ripe corn *that he will send* good *workmen into* his corn" (Matt 9:37-38; Luke 10:2). By the ripe corn is understood those people who would gladly live well if they knew how. By the workmen are understood priests, who should cut away sins from men's souls with good words, and so make them fit to be carried to the high king's barn, that is, the rich bliss of heaven.

FOOL

Oh, now I see in my soul that Christ is *king above kings, lord above lords* (1 Tim 6:15; Rev 17:14; 19:16). And I see that his law is sufficient for salvation, and all laws contrary to it should be despised by true men. But, good friend, what should I do to gain the mercy of this king for my foolish thoughts, my idle words, and my wicked works?

WISE MAN

Brother, we read in the gospel on twelfth day that three kings sought our Lord from a far-off country.[161] When they had found him they offered gold, incense, and myrrh. And when they had slept, they went home by another way. You say that you have had sight now of that same Lord and his law.[162] I advise you to begin by offering gifts to God with these three kings. In place of gold, offer true belief. In place of incense, offer steadfast hope. And in place of myrrh, offer this king lasting love and fear. Make sure that these three virtues dwell in your soul continually. And then wisely turn home again with these three kings, not following the same way by which you came, but another, for fear of Herod.

Our homeland is the bliss of heaven, but mankind was cast out of that bliss for breaking God's commandment. For this sin he was put under the thralldom and bondage of Herod, the fiend, for around fifty-two hundred years. Then Christ, God and man, in meek obedience suffered death in his humanity and redeemed mankind out of thralldom to Lucifer, the prince of pride. So are we now in thralldom, in that we have gone out of any country whatever by breaking God's commandments. Let us turn again, through learning and true keeping of them until the end of our lives. Christ says, *"If you want to enter into* bliss, *then keep the commandments* of God" (Matt 19:17). For there is no other way to heaven. If you have gone from your country by the way of pride, turn again through the virtue of meekness. If you have gone from Christ by the way of wrath, turn again to your country by the way of patience. If you have gone from your country by the way of envy, turn again by the way of love to God and your fellow Christians. If you have gone from Christ by false covetousness, turn again by the way of almsgiving and pity for your needy neighbor. Insofar as you have gone from your heavenly country by the stinking ways of gluttony, sloth, and lechery, turn again by the healthy ways of abstinence, good occupation, and chastity. If you have gone from Christ by misusing your five wits, both bodily and spiritual, turn again by occupying them with the worship of God and the profit of your own soul. If you turn to your country in this way, by forsaking Herod the devil who is the prince of sins of all kinds and by turning to Jesus Christ who is the ground and beginning of all virtues and goodness, then you will not fail to have the mercy that he bought with his own blood. For he says through his prophet that he *does not desire the* everlasting *death of sinners, but that they turn from their* wicked *ways and live* (Ezek 18:23–32; 33:11). In another place he speaks to each sinful soul in this way: "*You have engaged in lechery with many wicked lovers, but nonetheless turn again to me, and I will receive you* in mercy" (Jer 3:1). Again, he says, "*May a mother forget her child, and not have pity on the child of her own body? Though she may forget, I shall not forget you.*[163] *I have written you in my hands*" (Isa 49:15–16). In other places, he says that in whatever hour the sinner may forsake his sin, *he shall live, and not die* (Ezek 18:21; 33:12–15). And as the gospel tells, this is a *great joy* for the Father *in heaven* and for his *angels, in each sinful man who* forsakes his sin (Luke 15:7, 10).

But no man should be bold to do deadly sin while trusting to this mercy. For many through this folly have incurred the pains of hell. Take heed to Peter, Paul, Mark, Matthew, and many others, who when they had forsaken their sins did not willfully turn to them again but continued in virtues, and ended in them. In this way, following their example, let us go home by another way than that by which we ventured out. Then we shall be filled with the seven gifts of the Holy Spirit, and through them we shall be governed both inwardly and outwardly by the four cardinal virtues. What is more, if we are guided by the Holy Spirit in this way, we shall fulfill the seven works of mercy both bodily and spiritual, as far as our power and knowledge allow, ministering to poor blind, to poor feeble, and to poor lame folks, as Christ commands in the gospel (Luke 14:13, 21).[164] And then we will be rewarded with the eight blessings of Christ as named in the gospel of All Saints' Day.

FOOL

Sir, I thank our merciful Lord. Now my desire is to forsake all sin and turn to virtues, remaining in them until my life's end by loving God above all things and my neighbor as myself.

WISE MAN

Brother, keep this clothing of love and charity toward God and your fellow Christians, and then at the day of judgment you shall enter with the king[165] into the country of endless bliss, to which country may he bring us, who lives and reigns without end, merciful God, Amen.

18. A Commendation of Holy Writ[166]

This treatise is also drawn from Cambridge University Library Ii.6.26, where it is the eleventh of the twelve items. It is an interpolation and wholesale adaptation of part of the prologue to Robert of Gretham's *Miroir*, a thirteenth-century collection of sixty sermons in Anglo-Norman presented to a Dame Aline. Neither has been securely identified, but there are six Anglo-Norman manuscripts of the whole cycle, and four more containing fragments or extracts. We know that Gretham's sermon cycle was of great interest to later medieval readers as well, for there is also a Middle English translation of it, also extant in six manuscripts, in addition to the adaptation of part of its prologue presented here.[167] Like *A Dialogue Between a Wise Man and a Fool*, Gretham's Anglo-Norman prologue as a whole argues for the pleasures to be found in the study of scripture and in turning by that means to a good life; these pleasures are greater and more beneficial than those of vain and frivolous diversions like romance reading. This opposition (quite a common topos in vernacular pastoral writings) may have been part of the text's appeal for the Wycliffite redactor, but even if so, he skipped over it in favor of beginning his adaptation at the moment where this first prologue ends and a second prologue begins, in which holy writ is compared to a tree with concealed fruit that may be sought and enjoyed.

For the Wycliffite redactor, what impedes the study of scripture is not only frivolity (as for Robert), not only the failure to focus on living well (as for the Fool, up until his conversion near the end of the "Dialogue"), but the lack of a translated text. Strong words in favor of vernacular biblical translation are certainly not unique to Wycliffite writings, and they do not appear in every Wycliffite text, but they are certainly characteristic of Wycliffism, especially when coupled with complaints about corrupt priests who do not preach and teach as they should, as here. However, in this context remarks about translation are not merely an incidental polemical digression. Rather, they displace Robert's cautions about the intrinsic difficulty of understanding the letter of scripture if it has not been properly explained in favor of an implicit program for reform, and further elaboration of the agricultural metaphor: once the sinful people are properly instructed and turn to living well, they will receive in grace the life-giving rain of a translated text, their bodily and spiritual wits will be moistened, and they will bear fruit by knowing and keeping the commandments.

Holy writ has the likeness of a tree that bears fruit: nut, pear, or apple. When it is thickly leaved, little or nothing is seen of its fruit. But when men shake the tree, the fruit falls down fast and thick. And then sweetness is revealed that was hidden before, and when men eat it, it pleases them well. So it is with holy writ. The letter of the text seems dark and difficult, but if a man sets his heart on seeing the spiritual meaning within, and if he shakes it well—that is to say, through study of it and by living well—by the grace that God will then grant him, he will find much good fruit within. That fruit is wise sayings of many kinds, and its sweetness will turn him to great goodness.

But a man does not understand holy writ until it has been drawn and shaken into his own language. For holy scripture in Latin, Greek, or French is like a dark cloud to an Englishman until he has learned and understands these languages. But when through the words and sounds of his own language it enters into his soul, it moistens all his wits, both bodily and spiritual, and makes them bear fruit by the goodness of God's spirit. This dark cloud also refers to wicked living, which blinds God's lovers, so much so that they lack the light of grace to understand holy scripture truly. For Paul says, "*The letter slays*"—that is, slays those who live by the flesh, breaking the commandments of God—"but *the spirit gives life*"—that is, to all those who live faithfully according to the spiritual meaning of holy writ (2 Cor 3:6). And that is why Paul said, "Be led, or *walk, with the Holy Spirit, and you shall not fulfill the sinful desires of your flesh*" (Gal 5:16). It is as if they are in a dry cloud. They do not understand what they do, or what they are commanded to do, or what they are forbidden to do, whether by holy writings or by their own wits. Then they have no rain, no dew of grace, when no man teaches them or writes to them about holy scripture.

You should understand that the holy Trinity ordained three orders in the church: winners, defenders, and counselors. Winners are common people who labor to sustain knights and priests as well as themselves. Defenders are knights that should maintain God's law and with their power defend its lovers from all the enemies of truth.

As regards those who live contrary to Christ's law in their words and actions: if true priests know about it, and if they will not leave their sins through the preaching of true priests, or through the reproof of knights, then these defenders are bound by God's command to compel them, with loving punishment, to leave their wicked way of life and turn again to Christ's law, whether they are laymen or priests.[168] For St. Paul says, and not without reason, that they *bear the sword* only to defend those who live well and chastise those who openly do wrong (Rom 13:4). Counselors are priests that are given the responsibility by God of teaching both knights and commons how they should live in their social position so as to honor God and benefit their own souls.

These are the three estates that God has established in his church militant here on earth, representing the holy Trinity. Knighthood symbolizes the might and power of the Father, priesthood the wisdom and mercy of the Son, laborers the charity or good will of the Holy Spirit. Each of these three estates should help and support the others, just as each member of a body serves and sustains the others. The feet bear all the other members of a man; just so, the true commons labor to sustain knights, priests, and themselves. A man's arms often defend all his other members from bodily harm; just so, knights should use their power to defend priests, laborers, and themselves from all harm and perils that would hinder their souls. The eyes in a man's head show all his members briars, bushes, valleys, and ditches, to keep them from stumbling and falling into them, and maintain him in the plain, smooth way and so keep him from injury. Just so, priests, devoted to their head, Christ, through their pure living and faithful teaching, should in this way show to all people the plain, high way that leads to bliss and show them how to flee those ways that make many fall into the ditch, by which is understood the perpetual pit of punishment. To keep us out of this muck and maintain us in the steadfast way of grace, our Savior has left us a blessed message, that is, his holy gospel, and has sealed it with water and blood running from his blessed heart. Oh, it shall be very hard for priests and others that will not learn or teach this gospel, or allow those who gladly would do so, to all that are in this state and end in this way.[169] Our Redeemer in the same message, through Matthew, promises them everlasting woe (Matt 23:13).

Ah, Jesus, priests greedily take the penny, the milk, and the wool, but they will not do their duty in feeding their sheep with the bread of life. Of such men Jeremiah the prophet speaks, and says, "*The little children asked for bread, but there was none* who would *break it for them*"—meaning, preaching of God's word, for just as bread sustains and strengthens man's body, so holy writ makes strong the souls of all who love it—that is to say, all those who stand faithfully against all spiritual temptation (Lam 4:4).

Now, dear friends, I pray you were not greatly to blame, those who want to hinder men and women from bestowing bodily works of charity upon those who are about to perish out of need.[170] Yes indeed, he would be greatly to be scorned, and openly opposed to charity, who says these words that follow, "*Give and it will be given to you*," that is, give both bodily and spiritual works of mercy to those who have need, and the bliss of heaven shall be given to you for this action (Luke 6:38).[171] Thus, it is clear that those who hinder the expounding to the people of the blessed bread of God's law are cursed by God and traitors to his church. Paul says that in return for this treachery, "*watch out for those who hinder the law of God, and do not deal with them*."[172] For God says through Solomon, "*His prayer is cursed, who turns away his ears and will not hear the law of God*" (Prov 28:9). Then they must be blamed by God, those who hinder his law from being written, distributed, and preached to the people in their mother tongue. That is why Christ says, "*Whoever loves me will* love and *keep my word*, and *whoever does not love me, does not keep my words*, nor love to hear them" (John 14:23–24). And Paul says, "*He is cursed who does not love our Lord Jesus Christ*" (1 Cor 16:22). And Christ says it is all one thing, to love him and to love his law (John 14:21).

But how should men love it unless they know it in some way? That is why St. Paul teaches a fearful lesson for faint lovers of Christ's law, speaking in this way: "He who *does not know God*'s law, both in words and deeds, shall be unknown and forsaken by God, as an unfaithful servant, at the day of judgment" (2 Thess 1:8–9). Moreover, Christ says, "*Those who believe* in me and love my word *shall cast out fiends* and put away serpents, *they shall speak* sharp words *with new tongues* of truth, contrary to the words and works they were accustomed to before. Also, they *shall put their hands on sick men, who will be freed by this from disease. And if they drink deadly poison, it will not harm* or distress *them*."[173] Look at what powers come to those who wholeheartedly love God and his law.

Friends, if the people were bitten, stung, and envenomed by scorpions, toads, and serpents, who would hinder a man to whom God had given knowledge about how to heal these wounds with salves and ointments, and purge the venom of these venomous worms, if this man wanted to teach the people his knowledge? It seems to me that those who would hate him for this and hinder him in his purpose would be in great peril—especially if they themselves were harmed and defiled by deadly venoms. For if they perished through these worms, those who themselves were in this situation and worthy of God's blame, then those who hinder the true medicines and wholesome salves of our doctor and savior Jesus Christ from being learned and known by the people are in much greater peril, without comparison. Through this knowledge and skill they should purge and destroy all their spiritual sickness, and their sores, with which they are defouled or envenomed by the biting, stinging, or sore wounding of some of their spiritual enemies, that is, their frail flesh, this deceptive world, and the subtle, sly, and false old serpent the fiend, that is the *father of lies* (John 8:44).

Yes, but where shall we find the efficacious herbs with which to make this most wholesome and healthful ointment? Certainly, in the fair meadow and glorious garden of Christ's gospel, which is hedged and fenced about with the writing of his holy prophets, apostles, and other true and faithful disciples of his gracious choosing. Why is the gospel so wholesome and profitable? Because there was never man or woman healed from the biting of these same enemies without the ointment of repentance and mercy written in Christ's testament. And that is why Gregory says, "*For it was neither herb, nor mollifying plaster, that healed them, but your word, O Lord, which heals all things*" (Wis 16:12). That is to say, Lord God, *neither herb nor plaster has healed them, but your word, that is* all-powerful and *able to heal all* spiritual disease (Wis 16:12).[174] For by this word heaven and earth were formed, and all creatures that are in them, both those with reason and those without. He made those without reason for the use, service, and profit of those with reason, and he made those with reason for the service, fear, love, and worship of the maker of all things.

By the might and power of God's word this world shall be ended, as well. Nonetheless, as Christ himself says, his words will remain without end (Mark 13:31; Luke 21:33). At the last, through the strength and power of God's word, all men and women shall arise in body and soul, and appear before the everlasting *word* that St. John calls the *son of God* (John 1:1–34). And then, when they appear in this way before the high justice, the son of God, those who hated this word shall be separated without end from the glorious light of bliss into the horrible darkness of punishment by the power of that same word. The reason why Christ says in his gospel, "*Light came into this world, and* the cursed people *loved darkness more than this light, for their works were evil*," was that those who love the light of God's word and use it as their rule of life, shall enter with Christ into that light where it is always day, and never night (John 3:19). He brings us to this bliss through loving his law and living as it directs. He shall say at the last to the teachers and true lovers of his word these words that follow: "*Come, you blessed children of my Father, and receive the everlasting kingdom made ready for you by my Father from the beginning of the world*" (Matt 25:34).

Now, Christ Jesus, king of bliss, through the intercession of that blessed meek maiden your mother, and by the devout prayers of your holy patriarchs, faithful prophets, true apostles, and steadfast martyrs, with the confessors and pure virgins, inspire our hearts with the gracious beams and burning sparks of the Holy Spirit. Through them we may love you and fear you in keeping your commandments, in order to remain steadfast in charity, in meekness, and in patience with your gracious gospel until our life's end, both in work and word, whatever we may suffer in this *valley of tears*, gracious God (Ps 84:6).[175] Amen.

ECCLESIAL SPIRITUALITY

19. The Lantern of Light (Selections)[176]

We do not know anything about the author of *The Lantern of Light*. We do know that his is an extraordinary book: lyrically written with highly wrought passages in alliterative high style, brilliantly inventive in its exegetical elaborations, ambitious in its scope.[177] We know an unusual amount about one of its early readers; John Claydon, a lollard in London, was burned at the stake as a relapsed heretic in 1415 for having had a copy made and saying that he agreed with its contents. We know, too, that it was one of the lollard writings printed in the early Reformation period, about 1535.[178] There are two extant manuscript copies; neither of them, of course, is Claydon's.

The Lantern of Light is a comprehensive religious manual of a kind that can be found in many late medieval manuscripts, though few of them are as carefully wrought into an integrated whole, and few as polemical, as this one. It incorporates instruction in all the key elements of Christianity as its thirteen chapters labor to elaborate what antichrist is, what the only true church of God is, what the "material church" in which good and bad come together is, how to tell the good from the bad, and what the devil's church is like. As has already been mentioned, *The Lantern of Light* provides commentary on the commandments at great length in its very long twelfth chapter.[179] The two selections here are each complete, shorter chapters. Chapter eight uses the parable of the kingdom of heaven as a net cast into the sea from Matthew 13:47–48 to explain how the good and the evil are mixed together in the material church, in the process elaborating the metaphor of the sea to provide a cursory commentary on the seven deadly sins. Chapter eleven, on joy in tribulation, explains that the evil part of the material church seeks to imprison and slay those who reprove their sins, but that those who are "crucified to the world" by steadfastly opposing them should rejoice that by this means they find their place among the saints.

After this we will speak of two different parts that come together to this church, both of good and evil. First, we take for our ground Christ's holy gospel, where he speaks in a parable to his own disciples. "*Again the kingdom of heaven is like a net cast into the sea, and gathering together of all kind of fishes. Which, when it was filled, they drew out, and sitting by the shore, they chose out the good into vessels, but the bad they cast forth*" (Matt 13:47–48).[180] "*The kingdom of heaven is like a net that is sent into the sea and gathers together* in its confines *every different kind of fish. And when this net was full of fish, the fishermen drew it* to the land, *and sitting beside the shore, they chose the good into* their ships *and sent the evil out*, and *cast them into the sea.*"

This parable means this, according to Jesus Christ's meaning. The second church here on earth is like a net sent into the sea, for as the sea ebbs and flows, so this church now rises and falls in praise and blame, like waves of the sea that often rise and overpower men. Just as the storms at sea are hideous and perilous for the net, so pride that tosses back and forth in this world is very harmful to Christ's church. With beauty of fortune, with goods of grace, all day men swell in highness of heart.

The sea water is all bitter and very sour tasting, and this world is full of envy, which tastes very bitter, and impatience bitter as soot, so much that no one can agree with another.

On the sea come grievous storms, with damaging winds, and in this world wrath arises, with anger of heart that does much damage.

In the sea no grass may grow, as far as the tide may flow, but it lays waste all the ground and makes it naked, without fruit. And in this world is vicious sloth, which destroys virtues in body and soul and makes man foolish in his wits, whatever he attempts.

The sea always gains purchase with its waves over whatever ground it gets near, and is not satisfied with the terms that God has set, if it can escape them. And in this world there is covetousness, of those who wrongly gain their neighbor's ground and possessions with sly tricks of man's law.[181] In this way they gain more and more, and will not wisely spend their own goods, nor thank God in proper form, until they are caught in the fiend's snare.

The sea belches filth, and casts up foul corruption, that is abominable and ugly for man to look upon. And in this world there is lechery, which defiles body and soul and turns the precious temple of God into the lodge of grisly devils. The people that engage in this wretched sin are mad as beasts, without law, and in this bestial condition they fight like beasts, without reason. In this way they waste and dwindle away, repulsive to God and man.

The sea often drowns men, and also ships, and loses them before they come to land, with its great tempests that suddenly rise and cause great harm. And in this world there is gluttony, which drowns the wits of the people until they are unable to reason and do not know whether they do wrong. Indeed, excess of food and drink slays many more than does the sword. For there is no healthfulness in *greedily taking* a variety of *foods* and drinks *at a meal*, says the Wise Man, *but sickness* to both body and soul (cf. Sir 37:32–33).

We must watch out and flee these perils in this grievous sea, and draw this net in the water of wisdom with virtuous living, to the haven of health; with cords of true meekness, with patience and long-suffering, sailing with love and charity, in holy haste and good occupation, extending our hands in works of mercy, that the needy poor may be our almsmen, leading our life in discreet temperance as concerns what we take or leave, clad in purity and chastity. Then Christ will be our comfort, wherever we may be on land or water, as he has granted in his gospel: "*I am with you all days, even to the consummation of the world*" (Matt 28:20). "*I will be with you* in prosperity and woe, *until this world is brought to an end.*"

The fish that swim in this sea are all the people that live in this world, both good and evil, of every rank and estate, temporal and spiritual. Just as the great fishes eat the small, so mighty rich men of this world devour the poor to their bare bones, eating the morsels that please them best, as the Wise Man says: "*The wild ass is the lion's prey in the desert: so also the poor are devoured by the rich*" (Sir 13:23). "*The hunting or the prey of the lion is the field ass in the wilderness; similarly, the food of rich men is poor* and needy *men.*" When the sun shines warm, in mild weather, the great fishes come near to the air and drive down the small ones. But if a hail storm comes, or a cold season, these great fishes go to the depths and put the small above them. Just so, when rich men see an advantage, or any worldly profit, they rise above the clouds in boasting of their riches, and blame the simple common people in every way, and say they may not pay, and confront them and say they are truly nothing but beggars. But when there comes a burden to the country, whether taxes, loans, or any other payment, then the rich men sink down and

271

pretend to be needy, and make their poor neighbors look larger than they are, and claim their neighbors are secretive and are hiding great riches. As almighty God says through the prophet Habakkuk, "*And you will make men as the fishes of the sea, and as the creeping things that have no ruler* (Hab 1:14). *And there is a judgment, but opposition is more powerful. Therefore, the law is torn in pieces, and judgment comes not to the end: because the wicked prevails against the just, therefore wrong judgment goes forth*" (Hab 1:3–4). The prophet sees in his spirit how rich men lay waste the needy poor, and complains in a voice of great lamentation to his God: "Lord, do you allow *men to be made like fishes* that swim in *the sea, and like creeping beasts that have no leader* here in earth. *Judgment is made* more cruel, *and contradiction stronger. As a result the law is all destroyed and judgment comes to no* good *end. For* now *the wicked has might to overcome the righteous, and wayward judgment* that destroys peace *passes forth* among mankind."

But because the fishes are quiver and quick[182] in the water's vastness and do not fear the hideous waves, whether they rise high or fall low, they symbolize in this place true belief in men's hearts. Christ speaks of this meaning in the gospel and urges us to pray: "*Which of you, if he ask his father for a fish, will he for a fish give him a serpent?*" (Luke 11:11).[183] "Truly," Christ says, "*Which of you asks my father for a fish, and will he give him for that fish a snake?*" No, obviously. Chrysostom says about this text that this fish is man's faith, and according to this we should pray to our Father who is in heaven, that he will make us firm in true belief and in the articles that pertain to it.[184] For then we will be well disposed in the water of tribulation to do and suffer whatever pleases God, vigorously rejoicing in this belief. And though there may seem to be peril of death, our conscience will not be abashed, for there is help for all the faithful in the treasure of Christ's passion.

The fishermen who draw up this net are angels sent before the judgment, who will briskly do God's bidding and bring all nations at once before the face of God almighty, into the vale of Jehoshaphat. "*I will gather together all nations, and will bring them down into the valley of Josaphat: and I will plead with them there for my people, and for my inheritance Israel*" (Joel 3:2). The Lord God says that he *will gather together all nations* and he *will lead them into the vale of Jehoshaphat.*

272

And there he will make a righteous reckoning *with them*, upon *his people Israel, his own inheritance.* And then Christ with his saints will separate the evil from the good. Christ chooses the good of his church into the vessel of bliss, but the evil they cast out into the chimney of fire, where there shall be weeping from the bitterness of the smoke and gnashing of teeth from the quaking of the cold.

*   *   *

But because we reprove these sins, this evil part[185] complains and pursues with a strong hand to imprison and slay. Therefore, we must learn the lore of Christ's holy gospel, Matthew 5: "*Blessed are you when they shall revile you, and persecute you, and speak all that is evil against you, untruly, for my sake, etc.*"[186] "*You are blessed when men curse you and have pursued you and said all evil against you, lying, for me. Rejoice and be merry, for your reward is great in heaven.*" And also St. Peter says, "*But if also you suffer any thing for justice's sake, blessed are you*" (1 Pet 3:14). "*When you suffer anything for righteousness, you will be blessed.*" St. Paul affirms this wise saying, that God's true servants shall have pain in this life to keep them in virtue. "*And all that will live godly in Christ Jesus, shall suffer persecution*" (2 Tim 3:12). "*All that* ever *will live* meekly *in Jesus Christ will suffer persecution.*" And St. Luke says of the words of Paul in the Acts of the Apostles, "*Through many tribulations we must enter into the kingdom of God*" (Acts 14:21). "*By many tribulations it is proper that we enter into the kingdom of God.*" And the Prophet says this, "*Many are the afflictions of the just; but out of them all will the Lord deliver them*" (Ps 34:19). "*Many are the tribulations that happen to the righteous, and from them all,* when the time comes, *God will deliver them.*" Christ promised this way of life to his own disciples and gave them as a comfort that they shall have a gracious deliverance, for their bliss shall be much the sweeter when they come to it. "*Amen, amen I say to you, that you shall lament and weep, but the world shall rejoice. And you shall be made sorrowful, but your sorrow shall be turned into joy, and your joy no man shall take from you.*"[187] "*Truly I say to you the truth: you shall mourn and weep, indeed this world shall rejoice and you shall be very sad, and afterward your sadness shall be turned to joy, and your joy* shall be so assured that *no man shall take it from you.*" And so that this joy should be sweet to those who are his lovers, he sends them tribulation, as St. Gregory says: "God makes the journey of this world harsh for his chosen ones, so that none will forget, while taking pleasure along the way, what things are in their home."[188] And again: "The tribulations that oppress us in this world urge us to progress toward God."[189] Again, "Eyes that are closed by sin are opened by punishment."[190] "God shows to his chosen sharpness in this journey lest perhaps if they delighted in this mortal path, they might forget the things that are in the heavenly country." "Tribulations that break us down in this wretched world constrain us to go to God," we who easily might be damned. For "those eyes that sin closes, pain makes them open." Many men who engage in theft, with many other sins, if they were lame, blind, or crooked by God's imposition, they would suddenly stop, and serve their God, and do penance very truly, as Chrysostom says. "The soul is a spirit and fears spiritual punishments. It does not fear those of the flesh. Saints have contempt for punishments in this world, and fear the judgment to come, when the spirit will feel pain. The flesh does not fear spiritual punishments. But it does fear those of the flesh. And so evil men do not stop sinning unless judgments of the flesh and the world force them to. This is why the Lord sends upon his servants temptations of the flesh, so that when their flesh is burned away they do not desire what is evil."[191] "The soul is a spirit and fears spiritual pains. But it will not fear the pains of the flesh. And therefore saints have despised pains of this world and fear the last judgment, where spirits are tormented. Truly the flesh cannot fear spiritual pains to come. But it fears to suffer any pains in this life. And so evil men do not stop sinning unless the judgment of the flesh constrains them to stop. For this reason the Lord will send upon his servants painful punishment of their flesh and other tribulations, so that the desire of the flesh may be burned away from coveting evil things." We must break the nut if we would have the kernel; we must suffer labor if we want rest. So must we suffer pain if we would come to bliss.

He is a false, cowardly knight who flees and hides his head when his master is in the field, beaten among his enemies. But our Lord Jesus Christ was beaten by the Jews and afterward died in the field on the mount of Calvary. To pay our ransom he met his death, for he was in no way guilty, and his body, when it was offered, made a full recompense in redemption of mankind. Therefore, the Wise

Man says, "*Forget not the kindness of thy surety, for he has given his life for you*" (Sir 29:20). "*Do not forget the kindness of your redeemer; truly he has given his life for you.*" This redeemer is our Lord God who without thought of reward came from heaven into this world to redeem his people. In taking flesh and blood of the virgin Mary, he showed us grace and kindness, both in word and action. In giving his life, he laid down his body as a pledge; even unto death he would not hold back because he loved his people so much. If faith is true in us, this may not be forgotten.

Some forsake sins and follow Christ in virtue. This is a great kindness,[192] even if they rise no higher. Some stay awake in abstinence and study holy lessons. This is a greater kindness, provided they also flee from sins. Some are ready when they are called by the Holy Spirit to suffer death for Jesus Christ and be witnesses to his law. Provided they also lead a pure life, this is the greatest kindness, as the gospel shows. "*Greater love than this no man has, that a man lay down his life for his friends*" (John 15:13). "*A greater love* or charity may *no man* have *than to lay down his life* in saving of his *friends' souls.*" We were dear to God when we were baptized. But we are much more dear when we do the works that God has commanded in his law without any complaining. If we maintain this belief, and will not leave it or become apostates despite whatever punishment may befall, but think on Christ's passion that lightens all heaviness, then we are the dearest and most worthy of the highest reward.

That is why St. Paul says to the Galatians, "*But God forbid that I should glory, save in the cross of our Lord Jesus Christ; by whom the world is crucified to me, and I to the world*" (Gal 6:14). "Far be it from me," says St. Paul, "to *glory in anything but the cross*, that is, in the passion of our lord Jesus Christ, *through whom this world is crucified to me and I am crucified to the world.*" For this world despises Paul, and he despises the world. Some are not crucified to the world, but the world is crucified to them, for they despise the world, but this world does not despise them. Some are crucified to the world, but not so the world to them, for though the world despises them, they do not despise it back. Some are neither crucified to the world nor the world to them, for neither do they despise the world, nor the world them. In the first degree were the apostles, and in the second degree, others who live well. But in the third and fourth degree are those that shall be damned. And therefore we understand that some suffer pain to save the people, as did Jesus Christ, when they might not save themselves. He showed his great kindness in this way. Some suffer pain and increase their reward, as did Christ's apostles and many other martyrs. Some suffer pain to purge themselves of their sin that they did previously and cry to God for mercy. Some suffer pain to keep themselves from sin that they might otherwise be encumbered with, if there were no pain. But some suffer pain because they engage frequently in sin. Since they do not stop sinning as a result, their pain will be without end.

Let us join that cross of God to our bare flesh, so that our place may be found among these holy saints that willingly forsake themselves and rejoice in tribulation, as St. James says. "*My brethren, count it all joy, when you shall fall into divers temptations, knowing that the trying of your faith works patience. And patience has a perfect work*" (Jas 1:2–4). "*My brethren*, hope for *all joy, when you are fallen among various temptations, knowing that the proving of your faith is a work of patience. Truly patience has a perfect work, that you may be perfect* in soul *and whole* in body, *and in no way lacking.*"

20. The City of Saints[193]

Like *The Lantern of Light*, *The City of Saints* is lyrically written and thick with metaphor. However, this shorter treatise, the whole of which is included here, focuses squarely throughout its length on the questions of what constitutes Christian community and what obligations its members should fulfill toward one another as well as toward God. God is personified as Charity, mayor of the City of Saints (for "the greatest" [or "major" in Latin] "of these is Charity"; see 1 Cor 13), and Charity rehearses and comments upon his commandments at length by way of a general mandate to all citizens. As in the "Short Rule," what follow next are special instructions for each of the three estates in turn: priests, knights, and commons are respectively the walls, towers, and dwellers within the city. The history of the city's repeated destruction and rebuilding is recounted; there is certainly some continental apocalypticism influencing the writer here. Finally come two briefly sketched architectural allegories of the individual soul, and between them, instructions on how those who dwell in charity should love God and one another. The influences upon this treatise are clearly many, and it is dense with quotation. The single known copy appears in a devotional miscellany, one of six London manuscripts with overlapping contents, some of them Wycliffite, whose affiliations are still in need of further study.[194] Whether or not this treatise should be considered Wycliffite is under dispute.[195] The text's complaints that those who hate sin are called "lollard" place it among texts very aware of the consequences of lollardy's persecution; most, but not all, of these writings have other characteristics suggestive of Wycliffism.[196] The way the text thinks through the relationship between its "little flock" and the larger community by means of architectural allegory is more suggestive of Wycliffite concerns, as is the way it deploys its model of the three estates as it exhorts reform. But most of all, the text's extended engagement with the Ten Commandments aligns it with other extant Wycliffite writings, not only because it treats this topic at inordinate length, but because it does so with characteristic emphases and preoccupations. For example, the discussion of "honor your father and mother" asks readers to engage in spiritual teaching and to be obedient only "in due time," rather than always, while the expansive discussion of bearing false witness censures both "put[ting] away the truth of God's law" and condemning the righteous.[197]

"You are fellow citizens with the saints" (Eph 2:19).[198]

The wise man tells in his book Ecclesiastes that there was at one time *a little city, and few dwellers within. A great king came against this city, and besieged it, and set siege engines against the walls. But there was a poor wise man within the city, and he delivered it through his wisdom* (Eccl 9:14–15).

Spiritually, this city is Christendom, or Christian men's religion, as the prophet David says: *"Jerusalem which is built as a city"* (Ps 122:3). "Christendom *is built as a city* of peace." The few dwellers in this city are the little chosen number that shall come to bliss. And so Christ says, *"Fear not, little flock, for it has pleased your Father to give you, etc."* (Luke 12:32), that is, *"Fear not, my little flock, for it has pleased my Father to give you a kingdom."* Augustine says Christ calls his chosen a little flock in comparison with the great number that are to be damned.[199] And if we behold inwardly the multitude of heathens, of Jews, Saracens, and false Christian men, we shall understand Christ's words and why he calls his chosen number a *little flock*.

This great king is the fiend of hell, both because he is great in malice and because he is great in the number of his members—that is, those he has overcome with falsehood of this world, lusts of their body, and pride of life, as is written in the book of Job: *"He is king over all the children of pride"* (Job 41:25), "The devil *is king over all the sons of pride."* This devil with all his host of false liars besieges this city of Christendom with many painful assaults of temptation, and connives and wishes evil against the dwellers within, with many deceptive siege engines of many kinds of tribulation.

This poor wise man who delivers the city is Jesus Christ, who came from the bosom of his Father into his mother's womb, clad in the poor garment of humanity, to make us rich in his divinity, as the prophet David witnesses, speaking in the person of Christ: *"I am poor, and in labors from my youth"* (Ps 88:15). *"I am poor,"* says Christ through the mouth of his servant, *"and in* hardship *from my youth,"* that is, by the title of man or by civil law.

Augustine bids us read over Christ's life, and read again, and we shall find nothing else but great temptations, trouble, hard work, with many great pains and death at the end.[200] Therefore, Paul says Christ willingly made himself poor to make us rich in virtues (2 Cor 8:9). And the Wise Man speaks of Christ's wisdom, *"All wisdom is from the Lord God, and has been always with him, and is before all time"* (Sir 1:1). That is, *all wisdom* that is needful *is of our Lord*, God and man, and it was with him in his divinity without beginning and shall be without end. For if there is any power on earth that does not come from Jesus Christ, it is no power, but tyranny. If there is any wisdom on earth that does not come of Jesus Christ, it is no wisdom, but heresy. If there is any holiness on earth that does not come of Jesus Christ, it is no holiness, but hypocrisy. Assuredly this poor wise man Jesus Christ, through the example of holy living, faith of true teaching, and painful death of willing suffering, has delivered his city from the fiend of hell and made the dwellers within free to go on the path that leads to heaven.

And therefore Paul says that you are *not strangers and guests, but citizens among the saints, built on the foundation of the apostles and the prophets* (Eph 2:19–20). And *Jesus Christ is the highest corner stone, on which every building that is made rises into a holy temple in the Lord* (Eph 2:20–21). On this stone, too, *you are built into a dwelling place for God in the Holy Ghost* (Eph 2:22). Paul proves faithfully that you are citizens among the saints, not strangers, for four reasons: because you have one God, one baptism, one faith, one kingdom. Nor are you guests, for you are one body in Christ, and one another's members. Instead, you are citizens among the saints.

Here clerks may advance a question: Why does David, speaking in the person of the church, say "*I am a stranger* and *a pilgrim*" (Ps 39:12) when Paul denies this, but says that you are *citizens among the saints*? This question is easily resolved if this reason is known and understood. David is speaking of the bondage and slavery of the old law, and the pain that came of Adam's sin. In this way, you are strangers and pilgrims. But Paul is speaking of the grace of our Lord Jesus Christ, in the freedom of his gospel, and the power of the spiritual bond between Christ and his church, through which you are made Christian men and women. Truly, after this, you are neither strangers nor guests, but citizens.

The mayor that governs these citizens dwelling in this city of Christendom is called Charity, for the apostle says, "*The greatest of these is charity*" (1 Cor 13:13), that is, "*Charity* is mayor over these citizens among the saints."[201] And John the evangelist says, "*God is charity*" (1 John 4:8), that is, "*God* himself *is Charity.*" Thus, it is known as a matter of belief that God himself is mayor over these citizens. And that is why all these citizens must come together in God and take on as a group an obligation that belongs to them all. This obligation is given in the gospel, "*If you will enter into life, keep the commandments*" (Matt 19:17), that is, "*If you want to enter into* bliss, *keep the commandments.*" For without keeping them no man may be saved, and those who despise the commandments will perish.

The first commandment is "you shall worship one God as your God and no more" (Exod 20:3–5; Deut 5:7–9). In this commandment are condemned all witchcraft, enchantments, hanging writings about the head, trusting to dreams, charms, the raising of devils, and the like, in which men busy themselves to know a thing, or do a thing, even though it may be against the will and worship of God. It is true that God has set power in plants, words, and stones, and taught how they shall be used. So, God will smite with vengeance the misuse of these things against his ordinance and his worship, just as he punishes those who misuse food and drink and the like. And if you say that often men are helped by such things, to this true men answer that many suppose themselves to be helped when in fact they are much worse off, as happened under Astaroth in Bartholomew's time.[202] How does it grieve the devil if you have bodily health, but your soul is damned through misbelief? Therefore, worship one God for your God, and worship other created things only inasmuch as God is in them and they are in God, so that this worship stretches forth in accordance with the dignity and status that God has set in his creatures, both higher and lower.

The second commandment is this: *You shall not take the name of your Lord God in vain* (Exod 20:7; Deut 5:11). That is to say, do not be a swearer, or idle talker, or wicked worker. Swearing comes either from pride of life or from anger that is in man's heart or from habit. But certainly, if all these or any of these be combined with swearing, the sin is that much greater. Alas, since there is no hope of bliss but in Jesus Christ, what hope may they have of salvation, those who have grotesquely and horribly dismembered Jesus Christ with their swearing, destroying the morals of this world? Chrysostom says, "Whoever swears by a created thing engages in idolatry."[203] "He who swears by any created thing, either of heaven or earth, he performs idolatry." Indeed, in two ways. First, because in swearing he goes against God's commandment. Second, because he makes what he swears by into his god. Lord, how many idolaters there are then in this world, for now, no man can speak unless with some kind of oath knit to his words, and by this means we perform idolatry at nearly every word. And for this God takes vengeance, as is now seen among us all. Holy writ says *a man who swears excessively is filled with wickedness, and vengeance shall not depart from his house* (Sir 23:12).

In the third decree, or commandment, this mayor Charity, God himself, requires these citizens among the saints to keep their holy day, and says, "*Mind that you* honor your holy day. *On six days do your work, on the seventh* take your rest, with your wife, your children, your servants, your beasts, and the *stranger within your gate. In six days God made heaven and earth and the sea and all that is in them. On the seventh day he took his rest, and blessed this day and made it holy*" (Exod 20:8–11; cf. Deut 5:12–15). If you do not keep this holy day, you are, by God's witness, out of your mind. As a madman you should be bound *and cast into outer darkness, where there is weeping and gnashing of teeth* (Matt 22:13). Therefore, be mindful on this holy day, think on your God, pray to God wholeheartedly and devoutly, and fulfill the works of mercy. Do not chatter in church, or slumber or sleep, or grow weary and faint in God's service. For if you do, you are false to yourself, you hinder your fellow Christians, you defile the holy place, and you *treasure up for yourself* God's *wrath* at the *day of* judgment (Rom 2:5).

In the fourth commandment, the mayor requires you to *honor your father and mother, that God may grant you long life upon earth* (Exod 20:12; Deut 5:16). For if you do not honor your father and mother, you shall have a short life and shameful death. This is what happens to those who are ungrateful to their elders, rebel against their teachers, and are defiant toward their sovereigns. To honor them, on the other hand, for those of you who are citizens, is to minister to them now spiritual teaching, now material support, and in due time, bodily obedience.

The fifth commandment of the mayor is this: *do not kill*, that is to say, wrongfully and against God's law (Exod 20:13; Deut 5:17). Kill neither with your tongue, through backbiting, nor with your hand, through cruel smiting, nor with your actions, through false imprisonment. Consider that it is envious men who backbite, wrathful men who fiercely smite, miserly men who grievously imprison. They must heed this commandment, *do not kill*, or else they will be worthy of Christ's judgment, the fire of hell without end.

The sixth commandment of our mayor is this: *do no lechery* (Exod 20:14; Deut 5:18).[204] By this our mayor teaches maidens to keep the chastity of their maidenhead with Christ, head of maidens; they should bring themselves to the church door and commit themselves to matrimony. And then shall they multiply in grace and in virtue, in themselves and in their children. The prophet David teaches a sweet lesson to all the simple, which is read in the marriage service. He says, "*Rebuke the wild beasts of the reeds, the congregation of bulls with the cattle of the people; who seek to exclude them who are tried with silver*," that is, "You, priest, *blame* those who behave like *wild beasts*, inconstant, wavering in the sin of lechery, who are also like town *bulls*, foolishly defending their sin and going abroad in

281

every pasture, to be killed with the butcher's great axe" (Ps 68:30).[205] So these common lechers, like town bulls, go abroad in their sin on the broad way to hell, to be slain with the great stroke of everlasting damnation. And in this commandment our mayor requires wedded men to keep the chastity of wedlock. Since they may bring forth children and give their bodies free rein by virtue of this sacrament—things that for others, without this sacrament, are deadly sins—those who live in matrimony should treat this sacrament with dread and reverence. For this reason, breaking of this sacrament is a blasphemy against God that requires grievous punishment, here and elsewhere. And our mayor bids widows keep the chastity of their widowhood by fleeing common spectacles, maintaining purity in love, wisely governing their households, discreetly giving alms to the poor and needy, and devoutly attending to prayer.

The seventh commandment of our mayor is this: *do not steal* (Exod 20:15; Deut 5:19). Neither you, priest, by hypocrisy; nor you, lord, by tyranny; nor you, laborer, by robbery. Paul speaks pithily to all these and says, "*He that stole, let him now steal no more, but rather let him labor, working with his hands the thing which is good, etc.*" (Eph 4:28), that is, "*He who stole before, let him now steal no more, much rather he should make with his hands something good that he may give to those who suffer need.*" By this Paul means that no man, whoever he may be, should sinfully hide or waste his own goods, or falsely beg, or take or steal other men's goods, for it is much more blessed to give than to take.

The eighth commandment of our mayor is this: *bear no false witness against your* fellow Christians (Exod 20:16; Deut 5:20).[206] In this God forbids all sorts of lies and lying, for the prophet David says that God shall forsake *all those that speak lies* (Ps 5:6). Much sooner the liar and the lying, also the mouth that lies, slay the soul. And so we should not lie, either in earnest or in jest, even to win all this world. If we want to keep this commandment, we also may not use glossing or flattery to put away the truth of God's law and change it as we please, most of all for pride in our way of life and lusts of our body, so that men believe our gloss as if it were Christ's gospel. Nor may we receive a reward to condemn the truth, or corroborate a falsehood before God or man. God speaks a fearful sentence upon this through his prophet Isaiah: "*Woe to you that justify the wicked for gifts, and take away the justice of the just from him*" (Isa 5:22–23). That is, "*Woe to you that justify the wicked man in return for gifts, and detract from the righteousness of the righteous man.*" For he that condemns the righteous and he that justifies the wicked are both abominable to God.

The ninth commandment of our mayor is this: *do not covet* or desire *your neighbor's wife, servant,* or child. The tenth commandment of our mayor is this: *do not covet* wrongly or by false title *your neighbor's house,* or *land,* or any of his goods, moveable or immoveable (Exod 20:17; Deut 5:21).[207] In the eighth commandment, before, he gave instruction about actions. In these two, he directs toward good and away from evil the desires of man's heart.

This is the general mandate that your mayor Charity, that is, God himself, has enjoined upon you who are citizens among the saints. But now let us see how this mayor calls his estates each in turn and gives them their orders. To priests, God gives this instruction: "*Go you into the whole world, and preach the gospel to every creature*" (Mark 16:15), that is, "You priests, going *into all the world, preach the gospel to every creature.*" Here, Christ orders priests to go and not to stay. Christ bids them to go into all the world and not close themselves in one place like pigs in a paddock. Christ bids them to preach, not to be wild and wanton, full of worldly vanity. Christ bids them preach the gospel, not rhymes and fables and chronicles and poesies or tales of Rome. Christ orders them to preach the gospel to every creature, that is, to each man who is morally pure—as Bede says, every creature—and not to fear to speak truth when they have an opportunity to be heard. [208]

The apostle explains these five statements of Christ's in this way. "*But be vigilant, labor in all things, do the work of an evangelist, fulfill your ministry. Be sober*" (2 Tim 4:5), as if he were saying, "*be vigilant* with continual prayer, *labor* in all your reading of sacred scripture, *do the work of an evangelist* by preaching the gospel, truly *fulfill your ministry* by administering the seven sacraments of the church, *be sober* in word and example."[209] That is to say, "Priest, *awake* in busy prayer, praying for the people devoutly."[210] For *the busy prayer of a righteous man is worth much,* as St. James says, for it pleases God, it opens heaven's gates, it overcomes the devil (Jas 5:16). The second statement is, "Priest, *labor* in the lessons of God's law, studying God's law only." Blessed is that priest that *thinks on the law of the Lord night and day,* for all his deeds shall be worthy (Ps 1:2). The third statement of Paul is this: "*Do the work of* the gospel, preaching the truth of God's word." For that word surpasses all others in its power of awakening man's soul from sin, because it has the power of Christ's blood within it, as Christ witnesses himself: "*The words that I have spoken to you are spirit and life*" (John 6:64), "*the words that I speak to you are* both *spirit and life.*" The fourth statement of Paul is this: "*Fulfill your ministry*, ministering the seven sacraments freely." For Christ says, you priests have received these sacraments freely; freely minister them to the benefit of the people, for they are a remedy against these seven deadly sins, steadying the reasonable creature in the seven gifts of the Holy Spirit. Paul's fifth statement on this topic is this: "*Be sober*, both in word and deed," and persist in both what you do and undergo, for you priests are the *salt of the earth*, as concerns your steadfast living (Matt 5:13). And you priests are the *light of this world*, as concerns your true teaching (Matt 5:14). But if this salt is dissolved, it is worthy of rejection and spurning by men. And if this light is quenched, then there is nothing but blindness, which brings these blind leaders and their followers into the dark dungeon of hell.

Stand forth, knights who are citizens among the saints, and take your orders from your mayor. It is written, "*And he said to them: 'Do violence to no man; neither calumniate any man; and be content with your pay'*" (Luke 3:14). That is, you knights, your obligation is that you do not smite men wrongly, or take away other men's goods through the shameful act called extortion or tyranny, but be satisfied with your stipend. St. Cecilia advises you wisely in this way: "You knights of Christ, cast away from you the works of darkness and clothe you with the arms of light."[211] That is, "Go, knights of Christ, cast away the works of darkness and be clad in the armor of light," that is, the defending of Christ's gospel, the maintaining of righteousness, the excluding of enemies, the punishing of evildoers. For Paul, writing to the gentry in Rome, chiefly counsels them to leave six sins: "*not in rioting and drunkenness*," that is, "Take care that you are not given to eating often, which brings a man to drinking often, nor to long resting on couches, for that draws a man to much lechery, nor to much strife or discord, for that leads a man to enmity or manslaughter. But *be clad in Jesus Christ*," as you are vicars of Christ's divinity (Rom 13:13–14).

Now must commoners come forth and hear their orders. God says to them through the prophet David, "*Blessed are all those that fear the Lord: that walk in his ways. For you shall eat the labors of your hands: blessed are you, and it shall be well with you*" (Ps 128:1–2). That is, "*Blessed are all those that fear the Lord and walk in his ways, you shall eat the labor of your hands. You are blessed and all shall be well with you. Your wife shall be as a vine tree at the sides of your house, and your children shall be as the shoots of an olive tree all about their lord. Lo, thus shall the man be blessed that fears the Lord*" (Ps 128:1–4). The apostle explains these four words, "*Render to all men their dues*" (Rom 13:7). Paul means that you should pay back what you have borrowed. Pay your rent to your lord, pay your servants their wages, give the church its due, the part that God has specified in his law. And if anyone should have extra that he can spare, take heed of those in need, that you may help them as far as you can.

The mayor of this city teaches this lore to you who are citizens among the holy saints. *Christ* is the *corner stone* upon which this city is *built* (Eph 2:20). And well is he called a corner stone, for Christ is king and priest at once, God and man. Matthew, a man, wrote the words of Christ's manhood, the historical understanding. Mark wrote the words of Christ's knighthood, therefore he is symbolized by a calf, the tropological or moral understanding. John wrote the words of Christ's divinity, and he is symbolized by an eagle, that is, the anagogical understanding.[212] The gospel says that he who builds upon stone, though rain and wind may come, his building shall not fall, for its foundation is sure, Jesus Christ, both God and man (Matt 7:24–25). But he who builds beside this stone, his building will sink to hell, for it has no foundation.

The walls of this city are priests, as the prophet David says: "*Deal favorably, O Lord, in your good will with Sion, that the walls of Jerusalem may be built up*" (Ps 51:18), "*Lord, act kindly toward this city, that its walls may be built.*" The towers of this city are knights, as the psalm witnesses: "*Let peace be in your strength: and abundance in your towers*" (Ps 122:7), that is, "*Lord, let peace be made in* accordance with *your virtue, and abundance* or plenty *in your towers.*" The dwellers or laborers in this city are commoners who minister their labor to priests and knights, doing their duty well. Paul says that he *who builds in this city, gold and silver and precious stones, timber, straw or hay, each man's work shall be made known* (1 Cor 3:12–13). Whose work is worthy of thanks, the fire shall prove it. Gold is good living. Silver is true preaching. Precious stones are pure virtues. If the fire passes over these, they become purer as a result. Similarly, if the fire of tribulation passes over good livers or true preachers or virtuous commoners, they become much more constant and so more certain of reward and merit without end. But if that fire should pass over timber, straw, or hay, it burns up into ashes. By timber, understand those who put their trust in this wretched world. By straw, those who lead their life according to pride of life, seeming merry outwardly and hollow within. By hay, those who lead their life according to the body, in lusts and pleasures. The fire that passes over these burns in hell without end.

We should learn, as well, how this city is destroyed. God speaks through his prophet Isaiah of this destruction: "*How is the faithful city, that was full of judgment, become a harlot? Justice dwelt in it, but now murderers. Your silver is turned into dross; your wine is mingled with water*" (Isa 1:21–22). "God, wondering, marvels how his faithful city is made a common whore or strumpet. At one time righteousness dwelt in this city, now murderers dwell within, so much so that there is no righteousness, no peace, no mercy on earth, but only theft, lies, and false oaths. Bloodshed flows out upon earth. The cause of all this is that God's law is mixed with glossing, flattery, and false explaining, through man's pretense and fiendish imagination. Silver is turned to dross; that is to say, the pure speech of Christian men is turned to swearing, cursing, sorrowing, backbiting, villainy, and ribaldry.

O Lord, if a man should come by a city strongly walled, regally towered, and plentifully inhabited, and if he came again another time and saw the walls borne down, the towers destroyed, and the inhabitants fled away, then might this man say, with sorrowful mourning in his spirit, "Here there was once *a glorious city*, how is it now become *a den of* wild *beasts*?" (Zeph 2:15). Similarly, when priests are turned to hypocrisy, lords practice tyranny, and commons engage in robbery, then may men say, "Alas, how is this city turned to sin, and made a den of hell fiends." But because they have forsaken the Lord God almighty and willfully chosen their damnation, Christ wept over this city there destroyed: "*Seeing the city, he wept over it*" (Luke 19:41). "Jesus, *seeing this city* brought to nothing in this way, *wept over it, and said, 'If you knew* about yourself what I know about you, you would weep as I do'" (Luke 19:41–42).

Indeed, if we were so disposed, we might weep with Christ, saying with Jeremiah in his Lamentations: *"How is the gold become dim, the finest color is changed, the stones of the sanctuary are scattered in the top of every street?"* (Lam 4:1). That is, how is *gold* made dust, how is *the best color changed, how are the stones of the sanctuary scattered at the head of all streets? Gold is* not *made dust* except when it is mixed with a less worthy metal, for example, lead or tin, brass, or alchemin.[213] So our Christendom is defiled when it is mixed with error and heresy, with the flesh, the world, or the devil. The *best color is changed* now; virtuous life is despised and sinful life is praised. For he who hates sin is called a lollard, and he who does evil is called a plain liver. The *stones* of the cloister *are scattered* when cloisters are occupied with worldly business. *Into the head of all streets,* when priests depart to lords' houses because of benefices.

Now must we learn to build this city once more, and make a final unity among these citizens. In Christ's time there was a dispute among Christ's disciples, but Christ put them at peace and taught a lesson, how his church should be reconciled for ever. *"And there was also a strife among them, which of them should seem to be the greater"* (Luke 22:24). *"There was a contention among* the disciples of Jesus about *which of them should be seen as greater."* To explain these words speedily, Christ teaches in his gospel two ways of being greater. One belongs to knighthood, and the other pertains to priesthood. Christ said that knighthood is greater in these three ways: worldly lordship and possession, the capacity to imprison or punish, and the giving of worldly goods and benefits to those who do them good service. But priesthood is greater in these three ways: meekness and lowliness of heart, renouncing or forsaking of worldly possession, and the plentiful treasure of God's word. And so that the priest should not be sad about his form of greatness, Christ says that *they have dwelt with* him *in* all their *temptations* and he has *arranged for them, just as* his *Father has arranged for* him, that they may *eat and drink* with him *in his kingdom at* his own *table.* And they may *sit upon* the twelve *thrones, judging the twelve tribes* or kindreds *of Israel* (Luke 22:28–30). In this way this good Lord, by providing discipline to his knights and setting a measure of rule to his clergy, reconciles a final unity in this city.

But the temple of this city that Paul speaks of was first built by Solomon. The second time it was built again by Zorobabel. The third time it was built by Herod. The first time it was defiled by Jeroboam. The second time by Nebuchadnezzar. The third time it was defiled by king Antioch.[214] In Paul's spiritual understanding, Jesus Christ first built the new law. The second time, the apostles, martyrs, confessors, and virgins built this temple of Christ's law again. The third time, the common people will make this temple pure. So, tyrants first destroyed this temple. The second time, heretics laid it waste. Now, in the third time, hypocrites defile this temple. Paul says, *"But if any man violate the temple of God, God shall destroy him. For the temple of God is holy, which you are"* (1 Cor 3:17). That is, *"Whoever defiles the temple of God, the Lord shall destroy him; truly, the temple of the Lord is holy, and that is you."*

Hypocrites defile the temple of the Lord, for they patch their feigned rules onto the pure gospel of our Lord Jesus Christ, and by means of their false and hypocritical signs lead the people to believe lies as if they were the truth of God's word. Bernard speaks sharply to these people in this way: "Hypocrites want to be humble without lowering themselves, poor without lacking for anything, well dressed without effort, delicately fed without labor. Some they flatter, some they envy, some they slander, vicious as dogs, tricky as foxes, proud as lions, outwardly like sheep, inwardly like rapacious wolves. They want to be judges without having authority, witnesses without having seen anything, doctors without receiving training, then in the end, false accusers lacking in every virtue."[215] That is to say, "These pallid hypocrites want to be meek without occupation, well fed without labor, to some flattering, to some envying, to some backbiting, sore biters like hounds, treacherous as foxes, proud as lions, within like ravening wolves, without simple like sheep. They want to be judges without authority, they will bear witness without, finally, having seen, they will be false accusers and lack every kind of good virtue." Thus says Bernard. By these words may all Christian men understand how this temple is destroyed and what are the conditions of those who defile it. And also, how this temple is built and what are the conditions of those that take possession of it.

So far we have heard what is our city, who are the inhabitants, the name of our mayor, the commands our mayor gives, both in general and specifically, how Christ is the stone upon which this city is built, priests the walls, knights the towers, and commoners the laborers; what men shall build in this city, how this city is destroyed, how this city shall be built again, how unity shall be made in this city. We would still like to hear how, according to Paul, each man should build his own dwelling place.

The posts of every man's dwelling place are his two limbs. The walls of his dwelling are his body and back, the right side and the left. The cover of this place is man's head, the windows are his eyes, the gates are his ears. The door of this place is man's mouth. The chief tenant of this place is man's soul. The chief lord over all this is almighty God, Father and Son and Holy Spirit.

We said before that our mayor is called Charity and Love. We want to know, then, what are the conditions of charity, and what the conditions of love. Charity has five conditions. The first condition is this: that every man and woman be a pure, chaste speaker, for the words of the Lord are pure, chaste words. And Gregory says, "What the mind loves very much, it produces very often in speech."[216] That is, "That thing that the mind loves most, it repeats most often in speech." Indeed, it delights all persons to speak much of their love; therefore, those who love their God, that is, their mayor, must speak most of him. The second condition is this, that you be a willing hearer of God's word. For the gospel says, "*He that is of God, hears the words of God*" (John 8:47). "*He that is on God's side,* he *hears God's word.*" And Christ gives pardon to willing hearers of his word in this way: "*Blessed are they who hear the word of God, and keep it*" (Luke 11:28). "*Blessed are those that hear God's word and keep it,*" as true treasure in their heart, to keep them from temptations when they have need. The third condition of those who dwell in charity is this, that you pray devoutly to your God. Bernard says that just as blowing kindles the coal, so devotion quickens man's prayer in the sight of God.[217] The fourth condition of our mayor is this, that you be an almsgiver for God—neither for lordship nor fleshly friendship nor for wine nor for kin—but to him that has need, *what you can spare*, as Christ teaches in his gospel: to him *give alms* (Luke 11:41). The fifth condition of our mayor is this: that you be a patient sufferer under any circumstances, of sickness or loss of goods or slander, if it come, without any complaining. As Paul says, "*And we know that to them that love God, all things work together toward good, for those who, according to his purpose, are called to be saints*" (Rom 8:28).

That is, "*We know well that for those that love God*, our Lord Jesus Christ, *all things are turned to good*, and namely those that are called holy according to their purpose."

But our mayor, in that his name is Love, has four conditions, as the gospel tells: "*You shall love the Lord your God with your whole heart, and with your whole soul, and with all your strength, and with all your mind*" (Luke 10:27).[218] That is, *you shall love the Lord your God with all your heart* without any complaining. The second, you shall love the Lord your God *with all your soul* without forgetting. The third, you shall love the Lord your God *with all your mind* without erring. The fourth, you shall love the Lord your God *with all your strength* without ceasing. For man's heart is called God's chamber, man's soul, God's hall, man's mind, God's chapel, man's strengths are God's houses of office. Then Faith must be steward in the chamber, Hope keeper in the hall, Charity warden in the chapel, Dread porter of the houses of office. For if Dread is porter at the outer gate, no doubt that then no enemy shall come in to menace the Lord God in his dwelling place. But all things shall be ruled in the true order of peace. Thus shall the citizens with mercy and grace be brought to bliss without end. Amen.

To which may Jesus Christ lead us. Amen.

21. A Dialogue between Jon and Richard (Selections)[219]

This antifraternal dialogue draws the names of its interlocutors from the works of Richard FitzRalph, archbishop of Armagh, a vociferous mid-fourteenth-century opponent of the friars. The single extant copy appears in a two-part priest's notebook containing a series of annotations and treatises in English and Latin, many of them strongly linked with Wycliffism, that demonstrate strong interest in marshaling a wide range of authorities against the friars. As is often the case with works in dialogue form, this dialogue stages a debate not only over the legitimacy of the orders of friars, but over the legitimacy of Jon's criticism of them. The issue of whether "sharp speech" is permissible is raised at the opening, in the first selection, and returns at the dialogue's conclusion. The two selections presented here have been chosen because they first elaborate, and then follow out the implications of, an allegory in which the individual soul is represented as the home of a religious community: a cloister for the four cardinal virtues. Friars are the bad example; their false way of life prevents them from cultivating virtue. Instead they should live in Christ's religion, follow Christ's law, and cleave to their abbot Christ in true poverty of spirit, true spiritual chastity, and true obedience to "God's law." The way of life that friars could be enjoying in the true cloister of the soul is lyrically described.

Since Christ tells us to *beware of false prophets*, and teaches us by what signs we may know them, Christian men should be zealous to learn this lore of Christ and publish it for the good of holy church (Matt 7:15–20). And so, two persons speak by turns, Jon and Richard, and discuss this topic.

JON

Since the greatest peril to holy church comes from false friars, we should begin with them and make them better known. Since the description of things explains them more, therefore we should learn what such a friar is. The great clerk Grosseteste describes him in this way: "A false friar who goes out of the cloister of his soul is a dead body crept out of the grave, wrapped in mourning cloths and other false signs, and driven out of the devil to destroy men."[220] The cloister of the soul should be shaped in this way, as is the bodily cloister: to speak spiritually, so that four cardinal virtues are the four walls keeping the soul from the world and worldly things. And so, each vice breaks this cloister.

RICHARD

These words may please virtuous men, but a sophist would be ashamed to speak them, and therefore, I pray you, explain them more.[221]

JON

A man should arrange his speech in sentence and form according to the age of men and the hearers of his words. And I am certain that all the sophists among the friars cannot pinch at these words or disprove their wisdom. Such a friar is a dead body, as these clerks say, for even if he is great and fat in his body, nonetheless, since he lacks the spirit of life, he is a dead body, stinking with sin. He comes out of his cloister—he calls it his grave, for he is buried from the world

291

within four walls there, and only heaven and heavenly things are open to his wits, and the green grass of virtues and birds of heaven teach him to climb toward heaven. But he does not leave his bodily habit, for that hypocrite may better beguile fools of the word by that means. Three colors of the habit symbolize three virtues, that is to say, manual labor and purity and regret for sin. So all friars are clothed in two of these three, two above and two beneath. The shape of his clothes, so deformed, reveals his contempt for his own shape. His girdle symbolizes harsh penance, and every stipulation about these clothes signifies virtue, by their own ordinance at the beginning of their order. But since all these signs deviate from truth, the fiend by his hypocrisy deceives the people. For among all the crafts that the fiend has, none is subtler for him than these new orders. And therefore Christ says in the book of his gospel that a *kindred of whoredom seeks such signs*, and their wedding with them does not advance the service of God, but stirs them to pride and increases their sin (Matt 12:39; 16:4; cf. Mark 8:12, Luke 11:29). Christ, to destroy this wedding with signs, ordained on the Friday that he died that his clothing should be changed three times without sin. Oh, since these blasphemers are the greatest heretics, and all leprous (as St. Bede teaches), how many lords and ladies are smitten with this leprosy![222] Would God they were hermits in the desert with St. John the Baptist, rather than haunting the houses of lords or the chambers of ladies. For the gospel says that lepers should keep their distance (Luke 17:12). Then the breath of their blasphemy should blemish few folk. But antichrist raises them up and puts them in cities. Yet to many men it seems they are high enough, for since it belongs to their craft to tell lies in many ways, it seems that they are worthy to lecture as masters of lies. For not only are their signs bagged with lies, but the mouths of these apostates, perverted as they are, mix lies of mouth with lies of action. Who should be crowned in this craft but such liars? Nor does it disgrace Christ's religion that they are founded in lies contrary to truth, just as the order of honor is in no way made foul if there are kings and bishops among rogues. But since the charity of Christ catches men to counsel, and friars who dwell out of cloister are fishes without water, I would counsel them to come cleave to Christ's religion. Then might they freely wander in the cloister of the soul, and floods of the waters of wisdom would run off their bodies, and then they would not need to be dead to Christ or to gulp after gullets of grace like fish out of water. God save his church from the harm of antichrist's clerks, for of the eight perils, the greatest is in false friars.[223]

RICHARD

I cannot criticize these words, but it seems to me that they are too sharp, like jester's words, and not of the gospel.

JON

Oh, how sharply the gospel teaches us to reprove Pharisees who are contrary to truth, since Christ, who could not sin, himself spoke sharply to the Pharisees. Eight times the gospel teaches that he wished woe upon the Pharisees, and rightly so (Matt 23:13–29; Luke 11:42–52). Christian men should never speak against these sects except when they speak sharply to reprove their vices. And so no man should grant that for them to become masters of arts is founded on the gospel, or else upon reason. For before they commence as masters, they plot in many ways and wastefully spend poor men's goods before they choose one among them to the chair, and so envy is sown and charity exiled. And when they commence as masters, their rule is suspended, for they commence as lords and not as poor beggars. What is more, the money they spend does not come from heaven, for Christ took temporal goods from the earth. And the science of alchemy does not help them, for they are not knowledgeable in it, either the speculative or the practical, for if they were, they would be false: try it if you want. And so poor people must meet their expenses, both for commencing as masters and for other private feasts. Since it is difficult to gather from the poor people as much money as friars spend here, how many lies and flatterings must be sown before all this money is gathered from the people? And since the gospel forbids solicitude about food or clothing (Matt 6:25, 28, 31, 34), and they do the reverse, it is plain that friars go against Christ's gospel. If you want to know what fruit comes of all this, certainly it is only pride and worship of the world, for the friar after he has commenced as a master shall have a chamber and chaplain like a bishop, and be served as richly as a lord. But he is released from rising at midnight, and other works of penance that fall to a friar. If he preaches or reads, as they do lately, he chooses for himself the time when most favor will come his way as a result.

And if he wanders in the world and eats with lords, he expects to be served and seated like a bishop. Such are the fruits of friars commencing as masters. And so all of them in the chapter of Pharisees sit in high chairs, and are first at the food, and are called master by all manner of men. But certainly this is contrary to the gospel's teaching (Matt 23:6–10; see also Luke 11:43). And since friars should strive for meekness and avoid worldly elevation like poison, it seems that they should not plot to attain such degrees.

RICHARD

This sentence seems to be grounded on the gospel. But I have one thing to say to you yourself, that you and many seculars are in the same position. And so you will be reproved by Christ as a hypocrite; he shall say to you, as a traitor to him, "*Wicked servant, I judge you from your own mouth*" (Luke 19:22).

JON

I concede that I have done wrong in many deeds of my life, and if I wanted to justify all I have done, I would be a traitor to God, worthy to be damned. But I meekly acknowledge the sin I have done and hope for God's mercy, for I want to sin no more. And one thing I am certain of: if I had grace to keep me from the hypocrisy of friars and not fall into it again, I should certainly be saved at the day of judgment. I know well I have often sinned in hypocrisy, and especially when I wanted to be placed high in school. But now it seems to me that if my life were all to begin again, I would go another way. For Christ and his apostles did not commence as masters in this way, or martyrs, or the four doctors who are now high in heaven. For this bliss alone should we strive. And I know well that this degree came in through a heathen custom. God has arranged through his grace that some good should come of this, for he will allow no sin unless some good should come of it. But I know well that these words do not excuse our sin. And it seems that friars sin more, here, for they oblige themselves all the more to meekness and poverty, and they are more excessive in expenditure. And likely they gather in an evil way the goods they spend. But one thing I am sure of: I would want no more of this if youth and time came to me as they once did. And would God that these sects were settled in this purpose. Many good things, I know, come of this custom, for example, hard work in school, avoidance of sin, sharpening of wits, knowing of perils, and arrows ready against antichrist's clerks. But none of this excuses us, that we should not better spend our time, as God's law teaches. And so each Christian man should help toward Christ's law, and destroy these pagan customs, and follow Christ's way of life. For in assenting to the contrary Christian men accuse themselves.

* * *

RICHARD

It seems that the friars are the ones who follow Christ the most. For they are the poorest of men, chaste, and obedient, and Christ's religion is based on these three principles.

JON

Our belief teaches us that our rule is better, since it is the gospel that Jesus Christ made, while they must ask for confirmation of their patched-together rule. But if the pope shall be saved, the gospel must confirm him. And as we fall from the gospel, so the friars fall from their patched-together rule. But we may not put the fault in the gospel, as they put the fault in their new rule, and purchase dispensations to have new rules. For God commands that we should not *add to* nor *take away from* his *words* (Rev 22:18–19). Furthermore, our knights are the best men of all, and our abbot is the best, since he is God and man. And so many patches have been added to the friars' rule that if their bodily habit were as varied as their rule, no vagabond in this land should wear a more patched cloak. But since he that gives the greatest part of their rule, and sustains and defends the perfection of their order, should be called the patron of that order, it seems that the patron of all friars is the pope. And so they falsely call themselves friars of Dominic or Francis or Augustine or Jacobins, but they are friars of the pope.

But let us resort to reason. First, we believe that Christ's order is based in poverty of spirit. Forsaking of the world's good is sometimes beneficial, but it is no good without this more fundamental poverty. Next, even if friars have poverty in that they beg, nonetheless their high houses and other goods that they have in common plainly show that they are not poor as Christ was. For the gospel tells that Christ was so poor that he had *no* house *to rest* himself and his convent in, but the friars live contrary to this, in expensive houses (Matt 8:20; Luke 9:58). And so it seems to me that these hypocrites blaspheme against God, for they impute to him such a way of living. Christ damned Judas Iscariot for thirty pence, but many friars have much more than this as their own personal property.[224] So, if each friar that has more were one Iscariot, the orders of friars would be full of Iscariots that never sleep but stay awake night and day through their greed, plotting how to get more and avenge themselves on the members of Christ.

If friars follow Christ, it seems to many men that they follow him in these three points: in their high houses, in their order's excess, and in that they put religion in their bodily habits. And it seems, since Christ knew none of these three things, that they go beyond him—but in an evil way. Since their custom is to have high houses and Christ had none, it seems that in this they go against Christ. Since Christ who was almighty and all-knowing was satisfied with twelve followers and one Iscariot, it seems that friars who go beyond Christ in this blaspheme against God through stupid presumption. If they had no convent or any such prior, it would be good for the church. For neither did the apostles when their abbot Christ went to heaven for them. But just as they abandon Christ's rule as insufficient, so they go beyond Christ's convent. As concerns sin against chastity, I make these friars the judges, whether they surpass secular priests in chastity. But if we speak of spiritual fornication, here in their novelties they diverge from Christ and against nature. As concerns the obedience that friars have feigned, we know by our belief that it is worth nothing unless it teaches them to obey Christ. And so, since they might better obey Christ without such prelates, as the churches did before such warders were brought in by a trick of the fiend, it seems that such obedience serves no purpose. One thing I know: this feigned obedience does much harm to convents and countries. For however foolish a prior there may be in a place, if he should order that they judge no sin, they say that they should do as he says to maintain their obedience. And so, since the Holy Spirit should stir men to good, and the friars leave this guidance and pay attention to their prior, it seems that friars in this way oppose God. And so, the greater part of them seem to be clerks of antichrist.

RICHARD

Since friars keep all the commandments that we do, and beyond this do many things of perfection, it seems that their rule and their life are better and more perfect than ours. For otherwise it would be unlawful to be a friar, or to change men's life from one order to another. But the pope and the people deny this.

JON

Just as friars in many things are contrary to Christ, so they have brought in customs to many that are contrary to God's ways. Christ was a man most patient, and meekest of all, and suffered wrongs without avenging himself. For as a man is more meek, he is more perfect in Christ's religion, and so as Christ is most low, as the middle of the earth, so he is most perfect in the order that God approves. For the love of God, take heed to friars and look whether they are most meek in suffering of wrongs against them. I believe that no men in the world, as is in their power, are more vengeful over nothing. For they feel the malice of the friars, those men who tell the faults of their life and show truly how they deceive the people, as Christ did sharply for the Pharisees. It is known to the world how friars have pursued them, and if help had not come from secular men, they would have burned them or put them to death. And still, they feign falsely that they do this out of charity. But since both merit and sin are in the will, and the will of these friars was to slay Christ's limbs, it is clear that the sin in the will of those friars was as much as if they had killed these priests. And so, by the epistle of John they are manslayers and habitual sinners, all these persons who assented to this, as all of them did.[225]

See how openly they lie in following Christ. And therefore, no doubt, they separate themselves from Christ's children and show themselves to be brats of antichrist's convent. And here, Richard, you may see that you are talking rubbish, for friars do not hold with meekness as seculars do. And further, since God orders men not to add to his words (Rev 22:18), and friars in their rules do the contrary, it is clear how disobedient friars are toward God. But secular priests do not sin in this way. It is lawful to explain the law that God gave and explicate the meaning that the law hides. But friars make new laws, beyond both of these. Where in God's law should any man find these habits of the friars, or else their rites, through which they diverge from the apostles and other good men? Certainly these rules do not explain holy writ. And so it seems that these friars reverse God's commandment and make for themselves a new law, and put God's law behind it.

And so, since the four cardinal virtues should be the four walls to hold these friars in the cloister of their soul, and they break all of these and turn to vices, it is clear that they are false in bodily cloisters. Justice is the first wall that Christ's religion requires. It teaches Christian men to be obedient to the measure of God's law. But this wall they have broken and climbed over. The second virtue is strength, to stand within the limits that God's law has set without sliding away. But this wall is broken, and a new wall made, so they can stand stiffly in their own rites. The third virtue is prudence—and that they have forsaken, since it is no prudence to drink turbid and venomous water and forsake the water of the wisdom of God (Jer 2:13, 18). The fourth virtue of this cloister is called temperance, and that these friars have broken in their way of life. For take heed of their number, and their houses, and their rules, and all that they use, and we may clearly see that their temperance fails. And this error has brought the pope and the people into even deeper errors through the friars' hypocrisy. For they *judge by the face* and not by the works, and they are often deceived through tricks of the fiend (John 7:24). And so friars falsely use the argument of gluttons, that if a thing is good that should be taken by man, ever the more he takes, the better it is. And in this way friars fail in temperance and measure. God gave his law and his order in this measure: so that each might freely and easily hold to it. But friars fail in this measure more than Pharisees under the new law who wanted to keep the rites of the old law, and with them the freedom of the law of Christ. They could not do this, as St. Paul teaches (Acts 15:5–21; Rom 7:4–7; Gal 4, 5).

22. Sermons from Sidney Sussex 74 (Selections)[226]

In the single extant manuscript of the sermon cycle from which these selections are drawn, mutilated as it is, we can see what one Wycliffite preacher did to assemble a comprehensive pastoral program of Sunday preaching on the gospels and epistles that would cover the whole of the liturgical year.[227] For each Sunday, beginning with

Whitsun or Pentecost, he assembles a kind of portmanteau sermon. He quotes from the epistle reading to establish his theme, but then inserts, as a long preamble—the technical term is *protheme*—the whole of the Sunday gospel sermon from the *English Wycliffite Sermons*. Next, he discusses his epistle theme, usually at about the same length. The final third of his sermon addresses the next item on a planned syllabus of pastoral instruction designed to cover the whole year. The first of the selections given here is from sermon 21 and is drawn from the writer's discussion of a theme from the epistle reading for the nineteenth Sunday after Trinity, followed by a discussion of the commandment to love God. (While parts 2 and 3 of some sermons seem quite loosely conjoined, the two topics are thematically integrated quite closely in this sermon.) This sermon's concern with true speech, and that failure to speak the truth is tantamount to consent to (and hence culpability for) a neighbor's sin, is a characteristically Wycliffite development, one that draws on Wyclif's moral theory and his own explanations of consent (see above, pp. 16–18). Yet this example elaborates in unusual detail on the cases where it is better not to speak out.

When the sermon writer turns to discuss love, a topic that he will continue over the course of sermons 22, 23, and 24 (and possibly 25 and 26 too, although most of both of these sermons are now missing), he begins with a similitude: love is like a fire, and there are four directions in which human love in this world should burn, each with its appropriate intensity. Similitudes are a favorite expository technique for this writer and may be found in almost every sermon; while many of his similitudes are from the stock of preaching commonplaces and may be found in other versions elsewhere, his reworking of them generally brings out Wycliffite concerns. Here, in explaining how we should love our enemies, he elaborates on a model of holy church as one body, the one man who shall be saved because he does penance for his sin in Luke 15:7. This author's development of this similitude seems to voice a covert objection to the practice of excommunication; certainly it rejects excluding even enemies from the community of those who might be saved.[228] What is the good of cutting off your hand if it feeds you the wrong food? Instead, you should seek out healthful foods and medicines to heal the body as a whole. Similarly, you should strive to make your enemy well in soul, or else you are killing yourself as well as him.

The second selection, a discussion of meekness, draws only on the section of sermon 44 that addresses pastoral instruction. This sermon appears in the latter half of the sermon cycle, in which the final twenty sermons (beginning with sermon 35) develop an allegory of the soul as a city. Meekness is the ditch around the city, and every Christian should exhibit meekness in his relationships with superiors, equals, and also inferiors. Lords must obey God's law, just as much as any of their subjects must obey them. More, they should humble themselves to equals and to inferiors as well as to their ruler, just as much as any of their subjects. The account of sovereignty as a reciprocal rather than unidirectional affair developed here is, again, characteristically Wycliffite and drawn from Wyclif.[229]

On Truth and Love

"*Speak the truth every man with his neighbor*" (Eph 4:25).[230] *Each of you should speak truth, each one with his* brother." For good and true speech makes love among neighbors, and evil and false speech makes wrath. Most of all man's limbs, the tongue makes love or wrath. And therefore in all that we speak, to good man or to evil, we should be cautious about what we say, and busily guard our tongue. And therefore the Prophet says in the psalter, "*I have set a guard to my mouth, when the sinner stood against me*" (Ps 39:1). "*I put keeping to my mouth when the sinful should withstand me.*"

When a man speaks, he should keep in mind the importance of speaking the truth. Yet men need not always tell the truth. For where it might do harm and profit nobody, or else where it might do more harm than good, there we should be cautious and hold our tongue still. But when you may please God and do good with your speech, then you should not hold still, but speak the truth. For if you hold still and will not speak the truth to help your neighbor when he has need, whether for the sake of a gift or prayer or fear or fleshly love or wrath or hate that you have toward him, then you consent to that wrong that your neighbor does—much more so than someone sins who speaks falsely as a witness or urges his neighbor toward harm with lies or with white lies and other false words. For the law says, "Someone who is silent seems to give consent."[231] And also, Paul says in his epistle, "*they that do such things are worthy of death; and not only they that do them, but they also that consent to those that do them* (Rom 1:32). That is, "he that keeps quiet consents to the deed," and, *"not only those who do such things deserve death, but also those who consent to the ones doing these deeds."*[232]

Therefore, speak the truth when it may profit, and fear God of heaven more than any earthly thing, and always be cautious with your speech, that it may not displease God. *Speak truth, each one with his neighbor,* for David the prophet asks of God almighty, "*Lord, who shall dwell,* etc." (Ps 15:1), *Lord, who shall dwell in your dwelling place,* or Lord, *who shall rest in your holy hill,* that is, in the bliss of heaven. God answers through the same prophet: *He who enters without filth and worships righteousness, he who speaks truth in his heart, and he that neither deceives with his tongue, nor does any wickedness against his neighbor, nor bears a grievance against his neighbor. The wicked spirit is brought to nothing in his sight. Truly God glorifies those who fear him. He who swears to his neighbor and does not deceive him, and he who does not give his goods to usury, and he who does not take a gift against the innocent* (Ps 15:2–5). In these six verses much wisdom is shown, and especially about how a man should act toward his neighbor. The time is too short to explain this now, but I will do so later, if God give me grace. Now I will tell you about the first commandment of the love of God, as I said on Sunday.

Love is compared to fire, with respect to its natural properties and what they do. "There came a divine fire, not burning up but illuminating."[233] Fire usually gives its heat in four directions. A fire usually hurries.[234] The fire burns upward, and after that it burns hot on either side. The least of all its parts is the heat downward. Just so should our love be governed in this world. Our most burning love should be toward God, for he kindles in our souls the coals of his love with the blast of his breath, hanging on the cross, when he cried out for our love, "*It is consummated*" (John 19:30).[235] Next, our love should be hot toward our friends, and we should love them as they do us, as Christ taught his apostles, saying, "*This is my commandment*" (John 15:12), "*This is my commandment, that you love one another.*" Another love should be equally hot, that is, our love for our enemies. You should love them for God's sake, as he asks you to do: "*Love your enemies: do good to those that hate you*" (Matt 5:44). "*I say truly to you, love your enemies and do well toward those that hate you.*" For all men and women who shall be saved are called one man in the gospel, where Christ says, *"There shall be joy in heaven over one sinner that does penance"* (Ps 15:1), *"There will be more joy in heaven about one sinful man doing penance* for his sin while he lives here, *than about ninety-nine righteous men who do not need to do penance."*

And thus all of holy church is called *one body*, and it has many limbs (1 Cor 12:12–13). Christ is the head. Each man naturally loves all his limbs, so that if one limb is sick, the healthy limb helps it. For example, a man's hand, when his eye is hurt, is ready to help and comfort the eye. The eye leads the foot where it should go. And whichever limb is weakest, the stronger limb helps it: the hand feeds the mouth; the mouth chews the food. Just so should each man help another when he has need. So when your brother, even if he is your enemy, has trespassed against you, and so is out of charity, then he is like a sick limb, hurt with deadly sin. Then you have greatest need[236] to help him with your love and bring him into charity and so make him whole. For if your hand has fed your mouth with food and drink that was unwholesome, so that you are sick, and you then wanted to avenge yourself for this by cutting off your hand and making yourself sicker, that would obviously be foolish. Instead, you would work hard to get yourself medicines to make your body well again and save yourself from death. So should you do with your enemy, to make him well in soul, or else you are working to slay yourself as well as him. And that is the greatest folly that a man on earth may commit. Therefore, love your enemy, that he may be your friend. You must do this if you would love your flesh. For it is one of the greatest enemies you have, and yet you do not want to hate it, even if it is always working against you. In this way, your love should burn on both sides. But you should love worldly things less than your enemy, since he is God's image, just as you are yourself. And thus, with love to your enemy, as I said before, each of you should *speak truth with* your *neighbor*.

Least of all other things, you should love this world. And therefore St. John says in his epistle: *"Love not the world, nor the things which are in the world. If any man love the world, the charity of the Father is not in him"* (1 John 2:15). *Do not love the world, nor those things that are in it, for whoever loves the world, the charity of the Father is not in him.* Afterward he explains the reason why, and also what he means by "the world." *"All that is in the world, is the concu-*

piscence of the flesh, etc." (1 John 2:16). *Everything that is in the world is desire of the flesh and of the eyes and pride of life, which are not of the Father, but of the world. "And the world passes away, and its desires"* (1 John 2:17). *And the world shall pass away, with all its desires.* That is why you should love the world least of all. For whoever sets his love most on this wretched world, sets the charity of the Father that he should love most as the least, beside the love of the world. For you should love God above all things, as he himself commands, and if you look, you will see that there are but few who do. Turn, therefore, from false love, and love God as you ought to, and let your love for this false world take the lowest place. But to tell you how you should love your Lord God almighty, we must wait until next Sunday, for the time is too short, and the matter long. But keep well these four degrees that I have spoken of today, and *speak*, as I said, *each one truth with* other, and may Christ that is true truth grant all of us grace for that purpose, and heaven's bliss as our reward when we go from here. Amen.

On Meekness

Men should have three degrees of meekness, if each man wants to keep his soul in peace against the king of pride, which is the beginning of all other vices and shuts the door of the soul against God almighty. And therefore St. Gregory speaks in this way in his homily: "Whoever elevates his mind in pride, whoever gasps with the heat of avarice, whoever fouls himself with the iniquities of lust, that man closes the door of his heart against truth, and so that the Lord does not come to him, he damns the cloister of his soul with the bolts of vices."[237] "Whoever lifts his heart to pride, whoever busily desires in the heat of avarice, whoever defouls himself with the filths of lechery, he shuts the door of his heart against truth, that is, Christ, and damns the cloister of his soul, so that God does not come to him." Therefore, be followers of God, as his dearest children, and keep these three degrees of meekness, as I said.

Each man should humble himself to his sovereign, his neighbor, and his subject. For Christ the king's son of heaven taught us this himself, and St. Paul commands it where he says, "Be obedient to those set above you, *not only to the good and gentle, but also to the cruel*" (1 Pet 2:18).[238] All of us must do this by the rule of God. First, our sovereigns, by ruling themselves after God's law—or else they begin to break this decree, as for example those who follow Lucifer, who would have no sovereign. How should they rule others well that have no rule themselves? Popes, emperors, and kings should rule themselves according to Christ, each one in the social position into which he has been called. And each lower person should be meek to his sovereign. If all were ruled in this way, this would make peace between kings and kings, lords and commons, husbands and wives, and so all the people would live in love and peace. This is what Christ taught when he suffered for us and said, "*Father . . . not as I will, but as you will*" (Matt 26:39).[239]

The next kind of meekness should be between equals, that is, each man and his neighbor. Each, without any envy, should put up with the other without vengeance, and the wisest should be most meek and most ready to serve. Christ gave us an example of this in his own person when he washed his disciples' feet, saying, "*I have given you an example, that as I have done to you, so you do also*" (John 13:15). "*I have given you an example now, that as I have done, so should you.*" Whoever is the greatest among you, I want him to humble himself in this way, for the disciple should not be greater than the master. And in this way we are all brothers, whether rich or poor, who live as Christ's children and rule ourselves in meekness. Whoever makes himself most humble, shall be greatest in heaven.

The third degree of meekness is for a man to humble himself to someone lower than him—not to despise poor men, not to be cruel to servants, or to his household, or to those who have done him wrong—and to pray for those who are your enemies, as God teaches. Christ commands this himself in the gospel, "*Pray for them that persecute and calumniate you*" (Matt 5:44).[240] Here lords and rich men should take heed to themselves, to be meek and merciful to bond men and their tenants, even if these people are lower in this life than they are. For Christ redeemed us all and made us all free. Christ gave an example of how to humble ourselves in this way when he allowed the cursed Jews to buffet him and scourge him and spit in his face and crown him with thorns, and afterward nail him on the cross between two thieves. But he with a word of his mouth might have destroyed them all. He prayed for them to his Father, saying, "*Father, forgive them for they know not what they do*" (Luke 23:34), "*Father, forgive them for they do not know what they are doing.*"

And so, be followers of Christ in this way, as his dearest children. For meekness is like a tree. The lower the roots go, the higher the tree grows, and the stronger it stands, and the more fruit it bears. If we, the roots, do not go low but lie above the earth, then they are dried with the heat or slain by cold, and so the tree dries up. It *brings forth no fruit*, and is worthy of nothing when it is dry and rotten except to be *chopped down and thrown in the fire* (cf. Luke 3:9). Thus, the meeker you are and the more you humble yourself, the higher your soul rises in love to God, making you full of fruit that is pleasing to God, and the more strongly it withstands the blasts of the devil when he stirs you to sin with wind of temptation. But if you are not meek, you will soon be blown over, or become dry from the grace of God almighty, or be slain with cold for lack of charity. And so you bear no fruit, but you are like a dead tree that shall be felled by death and thrown into hell fire. Therefore, let meekness and patience spring up in your heart, and your fruit shall be fair and will never rot. Make the ditch around the city of your soul in this way, so that with grace you may be sure to withstand your enemies and be followers of God, as his dearest children. So that you may dwell with him in heaven evermore, may he grant you grace to follow and hold to the way that leads to him, where he is *king of* all *kings* (1 Tim 6:15; Rev 17:14; 19:16). Amen.

23. The Sermon of Dead Men (Selections)[241]

This text presents another lens through which to view the ecclesial dimension of Wycliffite spirituality. Unique among the dissenters' vernacular writings, it is a long funeral sermon that forms part of a larger collection of sermons for holy days and festivals.[242] The sermon is systematic in its presentation of the three reasons why Christians may celebrate funerals (to comfort their fellow Christians, to contemplate their own death, and to pray for those who have died); the four last things that should always be borne in mind (bodily death, the day of judgment, the pains of hell, and the joys of heaven); the reasons people should fear death (that it is uncertain, that it is painful, and that it is dreadful); the reasons death is dreadful; and the arguments that the devil will make to catch a soul at the point of dying. The excerpt we have printed here includes the introduction to the sermon and the preacher's discussion of the pains, opportunities, and temptations that accompany death.

Once again, readers coming to this text with the expectation that Wycliffites held proto-protestant views on key theological topics may be surprised; the preacher allows that those who have died may be experiencing "pains, which they have deserved for their sins" and suggests that the prayers of the living may release them from this purgation. The doctrine of purgatory is not named explicitly, yet it is clear that this preacher by no means denies the existence of purgatory. The sermon is conventional in many other ways, as well, invoking the medieval traditions of *memento mori* (indeed, its scriptural theme is "remember your last end," from the book of Sirach) and *ars moriendi*. Perhaps most striking about a sermon that envisions a communal audience is that much of the preacher's discussion is individualistic; he does not mention the church, or even the community of believers, in narrating the process of dying. Death is a matter for the individual to face alone, with the devil on one side and the prospect of salvation on the other.

Remember thy last end (Sir 7:36).

Christian brothers, it seems to me that men may rightfully come together at the funerals, burials, or memorials of dead men for three reasons grounded in holy scripture.

One is in order to comfort their brothers who have been made sorrowful or mournful by the death of their friends who have recently passed away from them out of this world. In this way our Lord Jesus Christ comforted both in word and in deed the two devout women, Mary and Martha, about their dead brother, Lazarus, as we read in the gospel of John (the eleventh chapter), when they made their complaint to him that their brother had died in his absence. He comforted them in word when he said to Martha, "*Your brother will rise,*" like those who say, "Do not be disheartened at your brother's death, for he will rise and live!" And he comforted them also in deed, when he called Lazarus out of his grave and restored him fully to life again (John 11:21–24, 43–44). Also, as Luke reminds us, when Christ saw a widow weeping for the death of her only son, who was being borne out of the gate of the city toward his grave, he gently comforted her with mild words, saying, *Do not weep*. And immediately afterward he comforted her with his deed, when he raised her son from death to life and took him back to his mother (Luke 7:12–15).

So every Christian man, who is a living member of holy church and who sees his brother in sorrow or distress over the death of his friends or for any other reason, should take the example of our Lord Jesus Christ and comfort him at least with gentle words, and also, if it lies in his power, with charitable deeds, bearing in mind the words of the Wise Man: *Be not wanting in comforting them that weep*, which is to say, *Do not fail to comfort those who are crying* or grieving (Sir 7:34).

The second reason for which men may rightfully come to the funerals of dead men is to look in the mirror and to see an illustration: just as the dead have passed hence, so also will they. This mirror or example should be to a man a great bridle or restraint, to keep him from sin. Therefore, St. Bernard says, "I look into the graves of dead men and see nothing there other than worms, stench, and ashes. Such as I am, such were they; and such as they are, such will I be."[243] Also Solomon says in his proverbs, speaking in the person of one who is dead to one who is living, "Remember my sentence of death, which God has given me, for it will also be yours. Mine was yesterday; yours perhaps will be tomorrow."[244]

The third reason why men may rightfully be gathered together at the funerals of dead men is to pray for those who have died, that God out of his endless mercy might deign sooner to release them from their pains, which they have deserved for their sins, and bring them to his bliss, for which he has redeemed them.[245] For the Philosopher says, "Stronger is virtue united and knitted together than disunited," for many men may better bear or withstand a thing together than each of them by himself.[246] Indeed, when many men are gathered together to pray and are joined in one will and one heart in love and charity, the more they will be heard by God for the thing that they are praying for.

Thus were the holy apostles gathered together in prayer after the ascension of our Lord Jesus Christ, as Luke reminds us in the Acts of the Apostles: *All these were persevering with one mind in prayer*, which is to say, *They were all together persevering in prayer with one will*, and therefore their prayer was heard by God, whatever they were praying for (Acts 1:14).

In this way, also, St. Peter encourages us to pray, saying *Be ye all of one mind*, which is, *Be together in prayer, all in one will* (1 Pet 3:8). And therefore, since prayer is a good reason to come together, holy scripture says, *It is therefore a holy and wholesome thought to pray for the dead, that they may be loosed from sins*, which is, *It is a holy and healthy thought to pray for those who are dead, that they may be delivered from their sins*, that is, of the punishments that they have deserved for their sins (2 Macc 12:46). And this is the third rightful and good reason, as I have shown you.

Therefore, for the three reasons I have touched upon, or for some of them, and especially for the last, I hope that you are gathered here together this day, that is, to pray devoutly for the soul of our dead friend for whom you are gathered, who has recently passed away from us. And not only for the dead, but also for the living, that is, for all holy church, both resting in purgatory and fighting on earth.

So lift up your hearts, with one heart and one soul knitted together so tightly with the bonds of charity that all the fiends of hell will never be able to dissolve them, saying with the holy apostle Paul, *Who then shall separate us from the love of Christ?* That is, if we are thus knitted together, *who will separate us from the love of Christ?* (Rom 8:35). That is, no man! The prayer of such men is always able to be heard, for Christ says to such men in the gospel of Mark: *Therefore, I say unto you, all things, whatsoever you ask when ye pray, believe that you shall receive; and they shall come unto you*; that is, *Whatever you ask for when you pray, believe that you will receive it, and it will be done unto you* (Mark 11:24). If you are knitted together with this blessed bond, then I pray you at the beginning, as you customarily do, to pray for all the estates of holy church.

First, for those who are in grace and live virtuously, that God increase them and sustain them out of his endless goodness, for *he who perseveres to the end, he will be saved* (Matt 10:22). And for those who are in mortal sin and live in vice, that God out of his endless mercy may give them the grace of true contrition and space to make satisfaction and to live and end their lives in perfect charity and the right faith of holy church.

Pray also, I beseech you, for me, unworthy servant though I am, that God of his great courtesy may at this time send me grace in order to open or declare to you his word, and that you may devoutly hear it, bear it in your mind, and perfectly enact it in deed, so that it may first give him honor and pleasure, and after, save us both. Let us have in mind the counsel of St. Paul, where he says this: *Be instant in prayer; watching in it with thanksgiving, praying withal for us also, that God may open unto us a door of speech to speak the mystery of Christ (for which also I am bound), that I may make it manifest as I ought to speak.* That is, *Make yourself busy at prayer, watching by giving thanks, and praying for me, that God may open to me the door of his word,* that is, true understanding, *to speak the mystery of Christ, that I may make it open, as it behooves me that I should* (Col 4:2–4). That is, neither for flattery, nor for covetousness, nor for vainglory, but only for the love of God and the benefit of his people.

St. Paul teaches that a true preacher should do this, speaking about himself as an example for all true preachers: *For neither have we used, at any time, the speech of flattery, as you know; nor taken an occasion of covetousness, God is witness; nor sought we glory of men, neither of you, nor of others,* which is, *We did not at any time offer flattering words, as you know; neither on any occasion were we covetous, as God is witness; nor did we seek vainglory* or the worship of men, *neither of you, nor of others* (1 Thess 2:5–6).

I pray you to pray for me out of charity, that I may perform this worshipful office in the way that St. Paul teaches us in this text. And not only for me, but for all those whom God wishes to be prayed for, both living and dead: *Pater noster, et Ave, etc. Memorare novissima tua, etc.*[247] May the help and the grace and that we have asked for be with us now and forever. Amen.

* * *

Christian brothers and friends, God almighty, the Father of heaven, is a plowman. Consider the example of his own son in the gospel of John, working always and tilling the faith of the gospel in Christian men's souls. In his team all Christian men should pull as oxen, under the soft and light yoke of love, and those who have taken the office of priesthood should be the drivers of this team, crying unceasingly with their mouths the true preaching of the word of God, as Isaiah the prophet says, *Cry, cease not*, and also biting with sharp sentences, as with a prick in a goad, to stir the people to pull correctly without blunders of sin in this blessed tilling (Isa 58:1). Of these drivers I alone, although I am unworthy, am set here at this time to drive this worthy team, and of all the sayings that I can find in scripture which will prick you the most sharply to move you to draw speedily and evenly, I have put this one in my goad at this time, saying the words that I have taken for my theme: *Remember thy last end*, which is, *Be mindful of your last things*, and so forth (Sir 7:36).

Holy scripture speaks diffusely in many places of the many things that men should bear in their mind, but because we cannot now in this short time speak of them all, I intend, with God's leave, to speak of what is most pertinent and appropriate for this time, that is, "to remember the last things," as our theme says.

Brothers, you should understand that there are four last things that should always principally be held in man's mind: the first last thing is man's bodily death; the second is the day of judgment; the third is the pains of hell; and the fourth is the joys of heaven.

The first last thing is man's bodily death, for that is the last end of his temporal life. Holy scripture speaks about it in this way: *We all die, and like waters that return no more, we fall down into the earth*, that is, *We all die, and like water, which does not flow uphill, we will slide into the earth*; and if we do not turn back, then that will be our last end here (2 Sam 14:14). We should always bear in mind this last thing, that is, our death, for three reasons in particular. The first reason is that it is uncertain; the second is that it is painful; the third is that it is dreadful.

First, it is uncertain, as St. Bernard says: "Nothing is more certain than death, and nothing is more uncertain than the hour of death," that is, "No thing is more certain than death, and no thing is more uncertain than the hour of death."[248]

If a man had a precious jewel by which, if it were well kept, he might prosper forever, and if it were stolen, he might be lost forever; and if such a man had no other house to keep it in but a weak one with plastered walls; and if a thief had espied it and had sent a message to the man, saying that he would steal it, but giving no certain day or hour, that man would be a great fool unless he were always awake, never slumbering or sleeping but always lying in wait for the coming of the thief. In just the same way every Christian man should act, for every man has a soul that is a very precious jewel. Its preciousness may be known from the price that was given for it, for the wisest merchant there ever was gave for it his precious life, which was worth more than all heaven and earth. But man keeps this jewel in a very brittle house or vessel, his earthly body, as St. Paul says, *We have this treasure in earthen vessels*, that is, *We have treasure in earthen vessels* (2 Cor 4:7). By this jewel, if it is kept well, may a man be advanced into the bliss of heaven; if it is lost, he will be ruined and abandoned to the perpetual pain of hell.

Death, which comes as suddenly as a thief, has sent word to every man that he will come, for every man is certain of it. But he has not set the day or the hour in which he will steal this precious jewel out of this feeble house. Therefore, it seems to me that there is a great need to follow the wise counsel of our Lord Jesus Christ, where he advises this: *Watch ye therefore...Know this ye, that if the goodman of the house knew at what hour the thief would come, he would certainly watch, and would not suffer his house to be broken open.* That is, *Keep wakeful*, says Christ, that is, live always a virtuous life, out of mortal sin, *for this*, he says, *know well: if the owner of the house knew what hour the thief would come, truly he would wake and not permit his house to be undermined* (Matt 24:43). No man readily knows when this thief, that is, death, will come, for the Wise Man says, *Man knoweth not his own end, No man knows his end*, whether it be in youth, middle age, or old age. So I think it would be great wisdom always to lie in wait for the sudden coming of this thief, that is, to eschew sin and live virtuously and always have death in mind (Eccl 9:12).

But alas, it seems by their deeds that there are many men in this world who are totally reckless and pay little heed to keeping this jewel and watching for this thief. Instead, they sleep and slumber in sin until the thief comes and robs them of this jewel and all their other goods. These are the kind of men who continually live in arrogant and horrible cursed pride, following their father Lucifer. They indulge in extravagant apparel (both for themselves and for their households), like the rich man who was buried in hell; they do cursed extortions and wrongs to their neighbors, with usury, simony, and false purchases in order to maintain their lusts and likings in sloth, gluttony, and lechery. They will not stop doing this as long as they can live this way.

These men are like fishes that have, as clerks who study nature say, a natural desire to sleep much, and when they sleep they hover in the water as still as though they were dead, nothing moving except the tail. And crafty fishermen see this and come upon them at that time and capture them with their nets. So it goes with men who take delight in the lusts and desires of this life, as a man who is asleep, with only his tail moving in virtue. That is, if men speak to him and counsel him to leave his sin, he says that he hopes to repent at the end and he will be saved. But often it happens to these men as the Wise Man says, *As fishes are taken with the hook, and as birds are caught with the snare, so men are taken in the evil time.* That is, *Just as fish are taken by the hook and birds with the snare, so such men will be taken in an evil time,* that is, in time of mortal sin, for which they will be damned (Eccl 9:12).[249] Of these men the holy man Job also speaks, saying, *They spend their days in wealth, and in a moment they go down to hell.* That is, *they lead their days in* lusts and desires, *and in a moment they fall down into hell* (Job 21:13). For often such men imagine that they will have a long life, and when they desire most to live, in the middle of their days or before, suddenly they are taken by death before they are aware of it. Of such men David speaks in the psalter, saying, *Bloody and deceitful men shall not live out half their days,* that is, *Men of blood,* that is, sinful men, *and treacherous men,* that is, men who commit treasons against God and their brothers and their own soul, *will hardly live half the days* that they should if they had pleased God with virtuous lives (Ps 55:23). It seems to me that these words of Isaiah the prophet apply to these men: *Thou hast not laid these things to thy heart, neither hast thou remembered thy latter end,* that is to say, *You have not put these things upon your heart, or borne in mind your last things* (Isa 47:7).

Thus, as I have shown, the uncertainty of death is the first reason, as I said, why men should bear their death very much in mind.

The second reason, as I said, is that death is so painful. That seems true and may be proved by Christ's example, by authority, and by reason. Our Lord Jesus Christ, who was both God and man, who knew all things by his divinity before they were done, said to his Father or his disciples these words a little before he went to his passion: *My soul is sorrowful even unto death*, that is, *Sorrowful* or heavy *is my* life *to the death*, seeing through his divinity how painful was the death that he would in a short while suffer in his body (Matt 26:38; Mark 14:34). Since the life of our Lord Jesus, who died so willingly and only out of love, was so painful, how painful will our death be, when we die against our will and on account of sin.

That death is painful is also proved by the authority of St. Augustine, where he says this: "Death is so evil and so grievous that the pain may not be told or avoided by any reason."[250] For this reason the Wise Man, seeing death so painful, said this: *O death, how bitter is the remembrance of thee*, that is, *O death, how bitter is your memory* (Sir 41:1). It is bitter to him who hears it and more bitter to him who sees it, but most bitter to him who feels it. For though a healthy man may be in a house and a man beginning to die beside him in another, with a wall between them, nevertheless if the healthy man hears the noise of the sighing, grunting, and groaning of him who is drawing near to death, it is very painful to hear. But it is much more painful to him if he goes into the house where the sick man is lying and sees the wanness and paleness of his countenance, the staring of his eyes, the contortions of his face and the frothing of his mouth, the swelling of his breast, the beating of his arms, and the many other signs that he makes before his death. But yet it is most painful to him who feels it, and this can be shown well by an analogy.

If a tree that has many roots were planted through your mouth into your body, and its principal root were set in your heart, and one of the roots were set in every limb of your body, and then if this tree were to be pulled out through your mouth all at once and with great force, reason teaches that this should cause severe pain. Just so it happens at man's death: the life is suddenly pulled all at once out of his body, which life is principally rooted in his heart and also in all his other parts. And this must be a surpassingly great pain. Thus by this argument it seems that death causes a very great pain indeed, which, as I said, is the second reason why we should keep death much in mind.

The third reason, as I said, is that death is so dreadful. This is the case for three principal reasons: the first is the dreadful sight of fiends, which every man will see in that hour; the second is the great battle that will take place between man and the fiend in that hour; and the third is that no man knows for certain where he will be after that hour.

The first is, as I said, the dreadful sight of fiends that will appear to a man in that hour. That they should appear seems well, for in the life of St. Martin it is written how the fiend appeared at his death to that holy saint, whom holy church calls gem of priests, which is to say the precious stone of all priests.[251] If the fiend appeared to so holy a man, how much more to lesser men! Also, as some doctors say, he appeared at the passion of Christ upon the cross, to see if he might be able to catch hold of him for some sin. This rings true in the words of our Lord Jesus Christ, where he says, *The prince of this world cometh, and in me he hath not any thing. Truly, the prince of the world has come, and in me he has no thing*, that is, no thing of sin (John 14:30).

The appearance of the fiend at that time will be very dreadful to the dying man, for there is a doctor who says, "only the sight of demons surpasses every kind of torments." That is, "only the sight of fiends surpasses all kinds of torments."[252] Therefore, David the prophet, seeing spiritually the great fear that he should have in that sight, prayed to the Father of heaven and said these words, *Deliver my soul from the fear of the enemy*. That is, not only from the power, but *from the fear of the enemy, Lord, deliver my soul* (Ps 64:1). Thus the dreadful sight of fiends that man will have in the hour of his death is the first reason why death is so dreadful.

The second reason is, as I said, the great battle that will take place between man and the fiend in that hour.

If there were set between the lists a tournament between you and a great champion who was mighty, cunning, wily, and who had overcome many men in that same tournament; and if the day of the tournament were unknown to all men except the king, yet the king would not tell it to you; and if the tournament were set upon the condition that if you were overcome, you would be cast perpetually into prison without any remedy, but that if you overcame him, you would be crowned king of a glorious realm, you would be a great fool unless you always feared that day, when it would come; and unless you were to make yourself ready for the battle, come when it may, with armor

314

and with all things appropriate to the fight; and unless you were to learn the tricks of your enemy, by which he would try to deceive you. Thus it is with every man who lives here in the world: the day of our death is set, known only to God, when we will fight with the crafty fiend, and we may not escape it. Of this battle this is written in the third chapter of the book of Genesis, where God said to the serpent, *You will lay in wait for his heel* (Gen 3:15). By the heel, that is, the last part of a man, is meant the end of his life, when the fiend lays most in ambush, and at that time he fights most sharply, for he knows well that if he loses the man then, he will never again regain him. And in that battle he has overcome many a man until now, and whoever has grace to overcome him, that man will be crowned in heaven with the crown of life; but if he is overcome by the fiend, he will be thrown into hell, there to remain forever.

Since this battle is so perilous and the day unknown, it would be good for us always to keep it in mind, regardless of when it may come, and fully arm ourselves against this mighty enemy, and seek out and learn the tricks he uses most often. The most reliable armor that we may have is the armor of a knight who has fought with and overcome him in this battle, armor that was so solid that he could not hurt him anywhere.[253] This worshipful knight is our Lord Jesus Christ, who was both God and man and of whose armor the apostle Paul speaks, when he says, *Put you on the armor of God*, that is, *Clothe yourselves with the armor of God* (Eph 6:11).

The first part of this armor is to gird the loins with truth, that is, to restrain all the limbs of the body with abstinence, as with a girdle, and to restrain all the powers of the soul from all kinds of vice. The second part is the mail-coat of justice, that is, to give to every creature what belongs to it. First, to God, worship, love, and fear; to your lords, both spiritual and temporal, subjection and obedience; to your own soul, holiness and the keeping of God's commandments; to your brothers, both friends and enemies, love and charity; to your subjects, teaching and correction; to your poor brothers, relieving them with your goods. The third part of this armor is that all the affections of your soul, that is, your spiritual feet, be directed principally toward preaching truly the gospel of Christ, if you are a priest, and if you are not, that your love be directed principally toward living your life in accordance with the holy gospel. The fourth part is that you should

315

take the shield of true belief, of which three corners should be painted with the Father and the Son and the Holy Spirit and the middle with all the other articles of faith, engraved with scenes of charity. The fifth is the helmet of hope, that is, that a man, through the mercy of God and through his own merits, may have trustworthy hope of his salvation. The sixth is the sword of the word of God, of which the fiend is very much afraid, for by that sword he was overcome in all three of the battles he undertook against our Lord Jesus Christ. Therefore, take it in your hand and never permit him to come within its point, for all his desire will be to come within the point of this sword, that is, to deceive the simple soul with his subtle and sly arguments into misunderstanding the word of God and hence to bring him into despair, and then he will have the victory.

The first argument that he will make is this: "You have committed many great and horrible sins without number, from the time that you first could sin up until this day, and now you have no time left to make satisfaction for them all. For this is the last hour, and God is just and will not let any sin go punished. Accordingly by God's justice you must be damned!"

But here beware of this cunning fiend and do not permit him to come within the point of your sword by this sleight of hand. Stretch out your sword in this way and point it boldly at his face: "Cursed fiend! I fully believe that God is just, as you say. But his mercy is surpassing, and he says by his prophet that he *desires not the death of a sinful man, but rather that he be converted and live* (Ezek 18:23). And also he says, in another place, that in whatever hour a sinful man repents and is sorry for his sin, he will be saved (Ezek 18:21). The merciful Lord demonstrated this, to the comfort of all sinful men, when, hanging on the cross, he granted to the thief hanging beside him (who in the last hour of his death the Lord saw was in great sorrow, humbly accepting his punishment) not only that which he had asked him but also that *he would be with him that day in paradise*, without any further suffering (Luke 23:39–43). And I know well that the Lord is generous even to this day and will always be so, without end, and I hope in his mercy for all my sins, so long as I have sorrow." Thus keep the fiend at the point of your sword, and he will never do you harm.

The second argument that he will make is this: "I was damned, as you know well, for one sin alone, and you have committed innumerable sins just as grievous or more grievous than that one ever was. Then if God would condemn me, who committed only one sin, and save you, who have committed so many, he must be unjust, which he cannot be. Therefore, by God's justice you must be condemned!"

Yet keep him at the point of your sword and answer him in this way: "Cursed fiend! The sin that you committed, you committed out of your own malice, and the sin that I committed, I committed at your encouragement—you envious fiend who have lain in wait for me night and day out of the great envy that you have that I might return to the place you fell from—and at the encouragement of my flesh, from which I cannot escape; and at the encouragement of the world, which is always before my eyes. For this reason, the blessed and merciful Lord, against whom I have offended, took on my nature in order to save me yet never took on your nature to save you. Thus I hope to be saved by his mercy from all my sins, whereas you, cursed fiend, will be damned for that one."

The third argument that he will make is this: "I was the highest angel in heaven and knew there the mysteries of God. And there I knew ahead of time who will be damned and who will be saved, and among other things I knew that you will be damned, and since a thing which has already been ordained by God cannot be changed, then you must be damned!"

Yet take God as your help and stand steadfastly in this battle, and keep him at the sword's point, and you will not fail to have the better part of it. Reply to him in this way: "False fiend! This has always been your custom, to beguile men with lies, for as Christ witnessed of you, you are a liar and the father of lies. For with your lies you deceived our ancestors in paradise, and with your lies you wished to deceive our Lord Jesus Christ. Therefore, I am not surprised that with lies you wish to deceive me. False fiend! You are lying when you say that you knew in heaven who will be damned and who will be saved, for you did not know of your own damnation, and if you did not know your own damnation, then even less did you know mine. And so, despite all your cursed lies, I hope that you will never bring me to despair, as you wish to do." If you overcome him in these three arguments, through the virtue of the Trinity, he will

317

turn his back and flee and never again tempt you, and thus you will have a glorious victory in this dreadful battle.

This perilous battle that man will have at his death is the second reason, as I said, why death is dreadful. The third reason why death is dreadful is that no man knows for certain where he will be after he is dead.

If, after a certain day, you were to be exiled out of the kingdom in which you were born and fed, and this day were known to no man but only to the king's will; and if you did not know into what land you should go after you had been exiled, or whether you would be loved or hated there, in such a case you would remain in great fear and, unless you were a true fool, always would be planning for your departure. Every man in this world is in the same situation. All of us will be exiled out of this world, where we have been born and fed, after the day of our death, which is known only to God, and that day is set in stone, so that we may in no way escape from it. Whether we will go to heaven or hell, where we will be loved or hated, is not known to any man here but is reserved until afterward. The Wise Man witnesses well to this in his book, where he says, *There are just men and wise men, and their works are in the hand of God: and yet man knoweth not whether he be worthy of love, or hatred.* That is, *There are just and wise men, and their works are in the hands of God; nevertheless a man does not know whether he is worthy of love or hate, for all things are kept uncertain until a time to come* (Eccl 9:1–2). And since it stands so perilously for us, I think that we have good cause to fear our death.

Thus then, for these three reasons that I have shown to you— that death is so uncertain, so painful, and so dreadful—I counsel you, as I said in our theme at the beginning, to reflect on this last thing, that is, on your death, which is the first of the last things that I spoke of.

PART III

Heresy Trials

24. Heresy Trials in Norwich Diocese, 1428–31[1]

The following selections come from John Exeter's court-book of heresy trials in late medieval Norwich; they record the trials of John Godesell, a parchment-maker who in 1428 resided in the town of Ditchingham in Suffolk; Margery Baxter, who lived in the town of Martham in Norfolk; and John Kynget, who lived in Nelond in Norfolk. There is nothing in the records to suggest that Godesell and Baxter, who were tried approximately six months apart, knew one another, yet they both pointed to the same man, William White, as their spiritual guide. White, a former priest of the diocese of Canterbury and a prolific evangelist for Wycliffite Christianity in East Anglia, had earlier been arrested and burned by the ecclesiastical authorities. His itinerant preaching had clearly brought him to Godesell's village, where Godesell had "knowingly received into his house on many occasions heretics and lollards," as well as to Martham, where Baxter "received him in her house as a place of refuge and for five consecutive days protected and concealed and sheltered him" (pp. 323, 327). Baxter's reverence for White is reported in the court-book to have taken on theological terms: one of the witnesses against her reported that Baxter had said that White "is a great saint in heaven and a most holy teacher ordained and sent by God," a saint to whom Baxter prayed every day "in order that he might deign to intercede for her before the God of heaven" (p. 332).

Perhaps on account of the shared origin of their beliefs, perhaps on account of the presuppositions of their inquisitors (many of whom participated in both trials), the propositions that Godesell and Baxter abjured resembled one another. Both renounced heterodox beliefs about confirmation (knowledge of the word of God is sufficient confirmation), confession (it need not be made orally to a priest, but only to God), the Eucharist (it remains material bread), marriage (it requires no solemnization by the church), and the clergy and church hierarchy (the pope is antichrist; any faithful man or woman is a priest). They also forswore their former beliefs about church traditions, for instance, that it is not unlawful to eat on fasting days, to show no honor to images, to abstain from pilgrimages, to withdraw tithes from the church, and for priests and nuns to marry. Both also received penances: Godesell was remanded to prison for seven years, and Baxter was ordered to be flogged around her parish church and the public square of the nearby town of Acle, and to appear before the bishop in the cathedral of Norwich the following Ash Wednesday and Corpus Christi day.

Readers will note that the record of Baxter's trial is by far the more detailed, not least because it includes the testimony of three witnesses against her. Since they are dated some months after the conclusion of her trial, it is unlikely that these depositions were the source of the original accusation of heresy made against Baxter; they do, however, suggest that Baxter remained a prominent figure in her community and a spokesperson for dissent against the church. Unlike the stiff, formal language of Godesell's and Baxter's trials, the depositions convey something of Baxter's vernacular; they include several extensive quotations in Middle English, which may reflect Baxter's actual comments about oaths, images, and pilgrimage. The longest of the three depositions, that of Joan Clifland of Norwich, also suggests that Baxter was not above extortion to preserve her good *fama*. According to Clifland, Baxter had threatened to embarrass her if she reported on Baxter's heretical views, just as she had previously made a false accusation of sexual impropriety against a friar who threatened to denounce her for her beliefs.

I. The trial of John Godesell, March 18–21, 1428

In the year of our Lord 1428; in the seventh indiction; in the twelfth year of the pontificate of our most holy father and lord in Christ, Martin, by divine providence pope, the fifth of that name; on the eighteenth day of March; in the chapel of the palace of Norwich; in the presence of me, John Exeter, clerk and notary public, and in the presence of the witnesses subscribed below; in the presence of the reverend father and lord in Christ William, by the grace of God bishop of Norwich, seated judicially, assisted by master William Worstede, prior of the cathedral church of Norwich and professor of the sacred page, and also Richard Caudray, archdeacon of Norwich, and Thomas Hunter, master of arts, and other ecclesiastical men,

John Godesell, parchment-maker of Ditchingham in Norwich diocese, was brought in for judgment.

To him the aforesaid reverend father said and proposed that he was vehemently suspected of heresy and was commonly held and believed to be a heretic in the city and diocese of Norwich, and in particular he said that John Godesell often received notorious and famous heretics into his house and sustained them, supported them, concealed them, and maintained them; that he provided them counsel, help, and favor; that he knowingly permitted the heretics to hold schools and read books in his house; and that he was a disciple of them.[2] John Godesell responded and legally, publicly, and explicitly confessed, saying that he had knowingly received into his house on many occasions heretics and lollards—namely, William White, priest; Hugh Pye, priest; and Bartholomew Cornemonger, John Waddon, John Fowlyn, Thomas Everdon, and others—and that, knowing that they were notorious heretics, he had supported, concealed, and maintained these men as he was able; and that he knowingly had permitted them to read and teach their heresies and errors. And the same John Godesell learned from these heretics all the heresies and errors written below, which John had asserted, maintained, and affirmed:

In the first place, John said legally and confessed that he had held, believed, and affirmed that the sacrament of baptism, done in water according to the form customarily used in the church, should be counted for little or nothing if the parents of the child are faithful people.

And also he confessed that he had held, believed, and asserted that the sacrament of confirmation, done by the bishop in the form commonly used in the church, is not required, nor is it meritorious, because however quickly an infant comes to the age of discretion to receive and understand the word of God, that is sufficient confirmation.

And also he confessed that oral confession need not be made to any priest, but only to God, because no priest has the power to absolve anyone from sin.

And also he confessed that he had held and affirmed that no priest has the power to consecrate the body of Christ in the sacrament of the altar, and that after the sacramental words have been duly said by the priest, there remains on the altar pure material bread.

And also he confessed that the mutual consent of love between a man and a woman alone suffices for the sacrament of marriage, without any expression of words or solemnization in the church.

And also he confessed that he had held and affirmed that the pope is antichrist and the head of the dragon of whom mention is made in sacred scripture, and that the bishops and prelates of the churches are the body of the dragon, and that mendicant friars are the tail of the dragon.[3]

And also he confessed that he had held and believed that any faithful man and any faithful woman is a priest and has full power to consecrate the body of Christ to the same degree that any other priest can.

And also John Godesell confessed that he had held and affirmed that it is right for any one of the faithful to cultivate lands and do any sort of servile work, excepting works of sin, on Sundays and feast days of the church, provided that he does these works privately in order to avoid scandal.

And also that the catholic church is the congregation of only those who will be saved.

And also that all material churches are only synagogues and should be held in only a little reverence, or in none at all, because God hears prayers said in the plains just as well as God hears prayers said in these synagogues.

And also that no one is bound to fast on the fasting days proclaimed by the church, but instead it is permitted for the whole population to eat meat indifferently in Lent, on the six weekdays, on the Ember Days, and on the vigils of the saints.[4]

And also that no honor is to be shown to any images.

And also that pilgrimages are in no way necessary to be made.

And also that it is permitted for priests to take wives, and nuns to take husbands, and for them to live as if they were married.

And also that it is permitted to take tithes and oblations away from churches and curates and to give them to the poor.

And also that censures and excommunications handed down by the bishops or other ecclesiastical ordinaries are in no way to be feared.

And also that in no way is it right to fight for the king or for hereditary right, or plead for any cause.

And also that the ringing of bells serves no one inwardly, except to amass money in the purses of men.

When these foregoing articles had all and individually been legally confessed by John Godesell in the presence of the said father, the father declared to John that the said articles contained many heresies and errors against the catholic faith and the determination of the Roman church. And John Godesell wished, as he stated judicially, and desired with a pure heart, to put away forever the said heresies and all other heresies whatsoever, and to repudiate them in word and in deed, and to abjure and return to the unity of the church. For this purpose the father set Monday, the twenty-first of March, in the same place, as the day for the abjuration of the heresies and errors written here.

There were also present master John Bury (in decretals), John Sutton and Ada Cokelot (bachelors of law), John Wylly (notary), Thomas Rodeland (chaplain), and many others.

On the Monday, which is to say the twenty-first day of the month of March, before the said reverend father seated judicially in the chapel of the palace already mentioned, being assisted by master William Worstede, prior of the cathedral church of Norwich and professor of the sacred page, and also masters William Bernham and John Bury, bachelors in decretals, and other legal experts, and also in the presence of me, John Exeter, and of the witnesses subscribed below, the said John Godesell was brought in for personal judgment, asserting that he had heard in full and understood the tenor of his abjuration, which had been written in handwriting and been indented, in which form he said he freely wished to abjure.[5] And because he asserted that he was a lay man and did not know how to read an abjuration of this sort, John committed his voice to master Robert Aylmer, a notary public and a proctor of the consistory court of Norwich, who was also present, in order that Robert might read for him and in his name his abjuration. And the said Robert Aylmer, taking up the duty of reading the abjuration on behalf of and in the name of John Godesell, publicly read out the abjuration in a high and intelligible voice, with the said John Godesell putting his right hand on the book of the gospels and swearing that he wished firmly and inviolably to observe the oath in the said written indenture, just as if it had been in his own handwriting. And in testimony of this thing John Godesell made a cross on the parchment with his own hand on each part of the indenture. And then, having taken a second oath, touching the sacred gospels, to be obedient to the commands of the church and to carry out the penance that would be enjoined upon him for his crimes, the said reverend father absolved him from the sentence of excommunication that existed on account of the foresaid things, by using the form contained in a certain paper schedule, which the said father at that very moment judicially took up and read from. And the substance of this schedule, which is the same as the said handwritten indenture, is contained below.

There were also present there John Sutton, bachelor of laws; Ada Cokelot, bachelor in decretals; John Benet, John Blitheburgh, Thomas Rodelond, chaplains; and Robert Aylmer, notary public; along with many other witnesses specially called or sent for.

In the name of God, amen. Because we, William, by divine permission bishop of Norwich, proceeding by our own legitimate office against you, John Godesell, parchment-maker of Ditchingham in our diocese, our subject, have discovered through your confession made legally before us that you often received many notorious and famous heretics into your house in our diocese; and that you supported them with your counsel and provided them with your help; and that you supported and concealed them; and that you held, believed, and affirmed many heresies and errors repugnant to the orthodox faith and the determination of the holy and universal church, concerning which much fuller mention has been made in your handwritten indentured abjuration, of which one part will remain in our archives—and by this decree we desire that it be inserted there—you have incurred by all this the sentence of excommunication. Now, however, taking wiser counsel, you ask for mercy and of your own will return to the unity of the church; on that account, therefore, a sworn oath to abjure all heresy and to obey the commands of the church having been made by you and received by us according to the rite of the church, we absolve you of all the bonds of excommunication by which you were bound. And because through the foregoing things you have rashly failed to hold to and believe in God and holy mother church, we now enjoin upon you as a penance seven years of prison in a way to be assigned by us. And because you have held, believed, and affirmed that it was permitted for any member of the faith to eat meats and any kind of food indifferently on the six feasts and the days of Lent....[6]

[*The record of the proceedings ends abruptly at this point.*]

II. The trial of Margery Baxter, October 7, 1428

In the name of God, amen. Through the present document may it appear openly to all that in the year of our Lord 1428; in the seventh indiction; in the eleventh year of the pontificate of our most holy father in Christ and lord Martin, by divine providence pope, the fifth of that name; on the seventh day of the month of October; in the chapel of the episcopal palace of Norwich; in the presence of me, John Exeter, a cleric, by apostolic authority notary public; and in the presence of those witnesses whose names are subscribed, there appeared in person Margery Baxter, wife of William Baxter, a wright, of Martham in Norwich diocese, suspected of lollardy and heresy. She appeared before the reverend father in Christ and lord, the lord William, by the grace of God bishop of Norwich, sitting on a tribunal, assisted by the masters John Thorp, OCarm., and Robert Colman and John Elys, OFM, and John Gaysle, OP, professors of the sacred page; and Jacob Walsyngham, licentiate in laws; and also William Bernham, bachelor of decretals. At the command of the said reverend father Margery touched physically the holy gospels of God and swore an oath that she would tell the truth concerning the questions that would be put to her concerning the matter of the faith.

Then, the said Margery having been sworn, interrogated, and examined by the said reverend father, she admitted judicially and recollected that she had known sir William White, the condemned heretic; and that though the said sir William was and is known by the people as a heretic and a lollard and was being diligently and frequently sought for, she received him in her house as a place of refuge and for five consecutive days protected and concealed and sheltered him; and that she gave and supplied to the same William counsel, help, and favor to the degree that she was able; and that she secretly

327

transported the books of the said William White from the village of Yarmouth to the village of Martham and hid them.[7]

Afterward, the said Margery confessed and acknowledged judicially before the said father that, from the doctrine and teaching that she received from the said William White, she held, believed, and affirmed the following articles or opinions, namely:

1. That there is no Christian on earth except he who keeps the commandments of God.
2. That oral confession is in no way to be made to priests, for the reason that very many inconsistencies and sins are committed under the outward show of confession, because anyone who proposes to be confessed sins venially before confession, which he would not do if he did not confess.
3. That pilgrimages should not be made in any way, except to poor people; nor should images be adored in any way, because Lucifer after his fall has obtained daily on earth that thing which he could not obtain in heaven, namely, the adoration of stocks and stones and dead men's bones.[8]
4. That in no way is it lawful to kill anyone, or by a legal process to condemn a defendant.
5. That any good person is a priest, and that no person will finally come to heaven unless he or she is a priest.
6. That oaths are commanded only to preserve one's reputation before a judge.

These foregoing articles having legally been declared errors and heresies by the said father before the said Margery, it pleased the said Margery (as she asserted) to abjure the foregoing heresies and all other heresies and errors. And then, with the said Margery physically touching the holy gospels, and (as it appeared) of her own will, she publicly swore upon them that from that hour she would never knowingly maintain or affirm or teach errors or heresies or any opinions contrary to the determination of the holy Roman church and its sound doctrine; nor would she sustain, maintain, or receive heretics or other persons suspected of heresy or persons holding, teaching, or affirming opinions against the sound doctrine of the holy Roman church; nor would she provide counsel, help, or favor to such persons, publicly or secretly, under the penalty of law. Indeed, the foresaid reverend father declared to Margery in the vulgar tongue that this penalty was the penalty of death.

Then, she having sworn a corporal oath to carry out the penance that would be enjoined upon her for her crimes, the said father enjoined upon Margery this penance for her crimes in this matter: four floggings around the parish church of Martham before the solemn procession on four Sundays, holding a waxen offering candle weighing one pound in her hands, with her neck, head, and feet uncovered, and her body covered only by a short garment; and two floggings around the market or public square in Acle in similar fashion; and in addition that she would present herself before the said reverend father or his successors, with other penitents, in the cathedral church of Norwich on Ash Wednesday next and on the feast of the Lord's Supper next following, to do solemn penance for her crimes.

These proceedings were just as has been written and recited above: that is to say, in the same year of our Lord, indiction, pontificate, month, day, and place as above. Present were the wise masters Nicholas Derman, bachelor in decretals; William Ascogh, bachelor in sacred theology; Hugh Acton, notary public; William Bamburgh and Thomas Rodelond, chaplains; and Thomas Walsham, clerk; and many other witnesses.

Depositions against Margery, the wife of William Baxter, wright[9]

On the first day of April, in the year of our Lord 1429, Joan Clifland, the wife of William Clifland, dwelling in the parish of St. Mary the Lesser in Norwich, having been cited, appeared personally before the reverend father and lord in Christ, the lord William, by the grace of God bishop of Norwich, seated judicially in the chapel of his palace. And at the command of the said father she swore on the holy gospels of God, which she touched physically, to speak truthfully in response to all and every question put to her concerning the matter of the faith.

Having sworn this oath, the said Joan Clifland said that on the Friday before the most recent feast of the purification of the blessed Mary, Margery Baxter, the wife of William Baxter, wright, recently abiding in Martham, in Norwich diocese, sitting and sewing with this witness in her chamber next to the chimney, in the presence of this witness and Joan Grymell and Agnes Bethom, servants of this witness, said and informed this witness and her said servants that in no way should oaths be sworn, saying in her mother tongue: "Dame, beware of the bee, for every bee will sting, and therefore look that you swear neither by God nor by our Lady nor by any other saint, and if you do the contrary, the bee will sting your tongue and poison your soul."[10]

Then the witness said that the said Margery asked her what she did every day in the church. And she responded, saying that first after entering the church, she was accustomed to genuflect before the crucifix, saying in honor of the crucifix five Our Fathers and the same number of Hail Marys in honor of the blessed Mary, the mother of Christ. And then the said Margery, rebuking her, said to this witness, "You do an evil thing by genuflecting and praying before images in churches, because God was never in any church, nor did God nor will God ever go out from heaven. God makes available or concedes no greater merit to you for these genuflections, adorations, or prayers made in churches than a light completely concealed by the wide cover of the baptismal font can create light in the church at nighttime. It is not a greater honor to display images or images of the crucifix in church than to display the yokes from which your brother had been suspended," saying in her mother tongue, "ignorant wrights of stocks carve and form such crosses and images, and after that ignorant painters glorify them with colors, and if you desire to see the true cross of Christ, I will show it to you here in your own house."[11] And this witness asserted that she would gladly see the true cross of Christ. And the said Margery said, "See," and then she extended her arms to their full length, saying to this witness, "this is the true cross of Christ, and you should and can see and adore this cross every day in your own house, and to the same degree that you in vain labors go to churches to adore or pray to whatever images or dead crosses."

And then this witness said that the said Margery asked of her how she believed concerning the sacrament of the altar. And this witness, as she asserted, responded to her, saying that she believed that the sacrament of the altar after the consecration is the true body of Christ in the species of bread. And then the said Margery said to this witness, "You believe wrongly, because if this sacrament is God and the true body of Christ, then there are an infinity of gods, because a thousand priests and many more consecrate a thousand gods every day and afterward eat those gods and then emit them from their rear with a repulsive stink, where if you wish to look carefully you can find sufficient gods; and for this same reason you may know firmly that that thing you call the sacrament of the altar was never my God, through the grace of God, because the sacrament was falsely and deceitfully ordained by the priests in the church in order to induce the simple people to idolatry, for this sacrament is only material bread."

And then Margery, asked by this witness, said to this witness, as she asserted, that the Thomas of Canterbury whom the people call St. Thomas of Canterbury was a false traitor and is damned in hell, for he endowed the churches with wrongful possessions, and he stirred up and supported many heresies in the church that seduce the simple people, and for this reason if God was blessed, then Thomas was and is cursed, and if Thomas was and is blessed, then God was and is cursed, and these false priests who say that Thomas patiently sustained his death before the altar are liars, because that false, mad traitor was slain in the door of the church as he was fleeing.

Then this witness said that the said Margery, asked by this witness, said to her that the cursed pope, cardinals, archbishops, bishops, and particularly the bishop of Norwich, and others who support and sustain the heresies and idolatries reigning generally in the people had in a short while incurred the same or a lesser vengeance than had that cursed Thomas of Canterbury, for they falsely and cursedly deceive the people with their false idols and laws[12] in order to extort money from the simple people in order to sustain their pride, luxury, and leisure. [And she said that Margery had said:] you may know without doubt that the vengeance of God will quickly come to those who most crudely kill the most holy sons and teachers of God—namely, the holy father Abraham; William White, the most holy and learned teacher of divine law; John Waddon; and others of the sect of the law of Christ—indeed, that vengeance would have come before this time to the said Caiaphas, the bishop of Norwich, and his ministers, who are members of the devil, except that the pope had sent to these parts those false indulgences that these Caiaphases had falsely obtained to induce the people to make processions according to their status and the church, which indulgences lead the simple people into cursed idolatry.

And then this witness said that the said Margery said to her that no little boy or infant born of Christian parents needs to be baptized in water according to common practice, because it is sufficient that an infant be baptized in the uterus of his mother, and for that reason that idolatry which these false and cursed priests commit who dip infants in fonts in churches, they do only to extort money from the people in order to maintain themselves and their concubines.

And the said Margery then said to this witness that only the consent of mutual love between a man and a woman suffices for the sacrament of matrimony, apart from any expression of other words or any solemnization in churches.

And the said Margery said to this witness that no faithful man or woman is beholden to fast in Lent, on the Ember Days, the six weekdays, the vigils of the saints, and other days appointed by the church; and that anyone who wishes may licitly on these days and times eat meat and all kinds of food; and that it was better on fasting days to eat the meat left over from Thursday in pieces than to go to the market and to spend money to buy fish; and that Pope Sylvester invented Lent.

And the said Margery said to this witness that William White, who was condemned as a false heretic, is a great saint in heaven and a most holy teacher ordained and sent by God; and that she prayed every day to the said saint William White, and that she would pray to him every day of her life in order that he might deign to intercede for her before the God of heaven; and that the said William White said to Margery, as she asserted to this witness, that Margery herself would come after him to the place of his punishment because she would then see that he would do many miracles because he wished to convert the people through his preaching and make the people rise up against and kill all traitors who stand against him and his doctrine, which was the law of Christ. Indeed, Margery said these things to this witness: that Margery herself was at the place of the death of the said William White and saw what was done by William White; and Margery saw that when the said William White, in the place where he was burned, wished to preach the word of God to the people, then a devil, the disciple of Caiaphas the bishop, struck William on his lips and stopped up the mouth of the said teacher with his hand, so that he could in no way proclaim the will of God.

And then this witness said that the said Margery taught and informed her that she would never make a pilgrimage to Mary of "Falsyngham" or to any other saint or any other place.[13]

And Margery said that the wife of Thomas Mone is most secretly and most wisely a woman of the doctrine of William White, and that the son of the brother of Richard Belward was a good doctor and first formed her in her doctrine and opinions.

And this witness said that the said Margery invited this witness and the said Joan, her servant, to come secretly into the room of the said Margery at night and in that place to hear her husband read to them from the law of Christ, which law was written in a book that her said husband was accustomed to read to Margery at night, and she said that her husband was the best teacher of the Christian religion.

And the said Margery said that she had communicated with Joan West, a woman abiding in the cemetery of St. Mary of the March, concerning the law of Christ, and that this Joan is in the good way of salvation.

In addition, the said Margery said to this witness: "Joan, it appears from your face that you intend and propose to reveal this information which I have said to you to the bishop." And this witness swore that she never wished to reveal this information in that way unless Margery herself gave her an occasion to do so. And then the said Margery said to this witness, "And if you accuse me to the said bishop, I will make of you as I made of the Carmelite friar of Yarmouth, who was the most learned brother of the whole country." The witness responded to her, saying and asking of her what she had done to the said brother. And Margery responded that she had communicated with the said friar, rebuking him because he had lied and that tithes neither done nor given would be good for him unless he wished to set aside his habit and go to the plow and thus please God more than by following the life of other friars. And then this friar asked of Margery if she knew anything else that she could say or teach to him. And Margery, as this witness asserted, expounded for the said friar the gospels in the English language. And then the said friar withdrew from Margery, as this witness asserted. And afterward the same friar accused Margery of heresy. And the said Margery, hearing that the said friar had thus accused her, accused the friar that he had wished to know her carnally and that the friar accused her of heresy because she did not wish to consent to him. And therefore the said Margery said that her husband wished to kill the friar, and thus on account of fear the friar became silent and left those parts in shame.

And the said Margery said to this witness that she often went falsely to confession to the dean of St. Mary in the Fields, so that the dean might think that she had a good life. And therefore he often gave Margery money. And then this witness said to her, surely she confessed all her sins to the priest? And Margery said to her that she never did wrong to any priest, and for that reason she never wished to confess to a priest or submit herself to a priest, because no priest had the power of absolving anyone from sins, and priests sinned every day more gravely than other men. And indeed Margery said that every man and every woman who was of her opinion were good priests, and that holy church is only in the place where those of her sect lived. And for this reason Margery said that confession is to be made only to God and not to priests.

And the said Margery said to this witness that the people honor devils who fell from heaven with Lucifer, and that these devils in falling to earth entered into the images standing in churches and continue to live there and remain in hiding there still, so that by adoring them, the people commit idolatry.

And the said Margery said and informed this witness that blessed water and blessed bread are only deceits and are of no virtue, and that all bells are to be pulled down from churches and destroyed, and that all those who ordain bells to be rung in churches are excommunicates.

And then Margery said to this witness that Margery should not be burned, even if she were to be convicted of lollardies, because she, as this witness asserted, had and has a charter of salvation in her womb.

And Margery said that she was conquering in judgment the lord bishop of Norwich and Henry English and the lord abbots who opposed her.

And this witness said that Agnes Bethom, a servant of this witness, having been sent to the house of the said Margery on Sabbath immediately following the Ash Wednesday last passed, with the said

Margery not being in her house, discovered a copper pot standing on the fire, in which pot was boiling a piece of salted meat of a hog with oatmeal, just as the said Agnes reported to this witness.

* * *

Joan Grymell, servant of William Clifland, of the age of sixteen years and more, sworn to tell the truth in this matter, interrogated and examined about all of the things that the said Joan Clifland had deposed, one by one, said by virtue of her oath that she was present with the said Joan Clifland and Agnes Bethom in the chamber of the said co-witness examined above, next to the fireplace, where this witness heard the foresaid Margery Baxter say all and each of the things contained in the deposition of her co-witness examined above. And in addition, this witness added that the foresaid Margery said to her that her husband often went out at night through the enclosed precincts of the said priory, through the great doors, and came to his own house by means of the lane of the Friars Minor of Norwich, and no monk ever knew. And this witness said that she heard the said Agnes Bethom say that she saw on the said Sabbath day the boiling copper pot with the salted pig meat and oatmeal in Margery's house. And in other matters this witness said that she heard the whole conversation between the said Margery and the previous witness, just as it was contained in her deposition, and she concurred with her co-witness.

Agnes Bethom, servant of William Clifland of Norwich, of the age of fourteen years, sworn to tell the truth regarding all and every one of those things on which she was interrogated concerning the matter of the faith, having been summoned and examined concerning all and every one of the things which the aforesaid Joan Clifland had deposed, said and concurred in all those things with the said Joan Clifland, with these additions or changes: that the said Margery said around the feast of the purification of the blessed Mary last passed, in the presence of this witness and Joan Clifland and Joan Grymell in the house of the said Joan Clifland, that "the sacrament that the priests after the consecration elevate above their heads and show to the people is not the body of Christ, which these false priests affirm in order to deceive the people, but if it is not a loaf of bread trodden underfoot by a pastor, then it is a loaf of bread consecrated so that priests will eat and expel it from their posteriors, and for this reason the sacrament will never be my God, but the great ancient God who never went out or will go out from heaven will be my God, and not this God whom the people worship in these days."[14] And this witness added that on the Sabbath day after Ash Wednesday last passed, having been sent to the house of the said Margery to have a footstool made for her mistress, she saw a copper pot standing on the fire in the house of the said Margery, boiling and covered and, the said Margery not being in her house, the said witness uncovered the pot and saw in it a piece of bacon[15] being boiled in water with oatmeal.

III. The trial of John Kynget, August 20, 1429

On the twentieth day of the month of August in the year of our Lord 1429, John Kynget of Nelond personally appeared before the reverend father and lord in Christ, the lord William, by the grace of God bishop of Norwich, who was seated judicially in the chapel of his manor at Thorpe. Accused by the said reverend father of the crime of heretical depravity, he judicially confessed that he had been noted and defamed of receiving, supporting, and maintaining heretics—William White and Hugo Pye, priests; Bartholomew Thaccher, Thomas James, and other notable heretics. Having been instructed and formed in their doctrines and teachings, as he asserted, this John Kynget held, believed, and asserted the heresies and errors written, contained, spelled out, and specified in his indentured abjuration. All and each of these errors and heresies John said he wished to lay aside and abjure perpetually, with a pure heart, in word and in deed, in the form written out and indentured for him in the English language. The tenor of which abjuration was ordered by the said reverend father to be read out publicly to the said John Kynget by master William Ascogh, bachelor of the sacred page. The tenor of the said indenture having been read out by the said master William Ascogh to the same John Kynget, the same John Kynget, in full knowledge, confessed and acknowledged that he was and is guilty and culpable concerning the said errors and heresies written in the said indenture, and that he wished to abjure those errors and heresies in the form that had previously been read to him, as it had

336

been sent ahead. But because he was, as he asserted, disabled in the vision of his eyes, he could not read the abjuration in any way. For this reason the said John Kynget appointed the said master William Ascogh as the organ of his voice for the purpose of reading his abjuration in his name and for him. And indeed master William Ascogh, taking on himself the duty of reading, read out publicly in court the tenor of the said indentured abjuration of the said John Kynget, containing in itself the whole of his words, with the said John Kynget in the meantime listening and continuing to hold his right hand on the book of the gospels. And thus the said John abjured all errors and heresies of any sort. And in testimony of this abjuration the same John Kynget made the sign of the cross with his own hand on each part of the said indenture. And on the one part of the indenture remaining in the register of the said father he set his signet. And afterward, John Kynget having made his oath, physically touching the book of the gospels, to remain within the commandments of the church and to carry out the penance for his crimes enjoined upon him by the said father, the said father absolved John Kynget from the sentence of excommunication which he had previously incurred. And for his crimes in this matter the said father enjoined upon John Kynget three floggings around the cemetery chapel of Nelond, before the solemn procession, on each of the three Sundays following the next feast of St. Bartholomew, with his neck, head, and feet uncovered, and wearing only a linen shirt to the length of his thighs, carrying in his hands a waxen candle weighing one pound; and on the last Sunday after he had carried out this penance to offer to the high altar another candle during the time of offering at High Mass; and to walk in similar fashion around the market of Nedham, carrying the same or a similar candle, on three market days in the next time of harvest, which was then approaching; and to genuflect at four points during the said procession on the Sundays and market days and to humbly and devoutly receive from the vicar of Stoke Nelond, who will be following him clothed in skins, a flogging with a rod.

Present for the proceedings of this day and assisting the said reverend father in these things were masters Thomas Ryngstead and Thomas Ludham, bachelors in decretals; William Ascogh, bachelor in the sacred page; and John Sutton, bachelor in laws; and also friars Richard Barton and Richard Norton, of the order of Friars Minor;

and John Wylly, notary public; and me, John Exeter, notary public, as scribe of the proceedings.

[Kynget's abjuration follows in Middle English.]

In the name of God, before you, the worshipful father in Christ, William, by the grace of God bishop of Norwich, I, John Kynget of Nelond of your diocese, your subject defamed and noted hugely of having received, supported, and maintained heretics, that is to say, sir William White, sir Hugh Pye, Bartholomew Thatcher, Thomas James, and other famous heretics, aware and understanding that by their doctrine I was informed of these errors and heresies, which I held and believed:

That is to say, that the sacrament of baptism, which the heretics call the "shacklement" of baptism, done in water in the form customary in the church is of no avail, nor is it to be thought about.

Also, that oral confession made to a priest is of no avail, nor pleasing to God, for confession ought to be made only to God and to no other priest.

Also, that no priest has the power to make God's body in the sacrament of the altar, but God made all priests, and no priest has the power to make God, for God was made a long time before the priests were made.

Also, that no matrimony should be solemnized in the church, but consent of heart between a man and a woman alone should suffice for matrimony.

Also, that no man is bound to fast on Fridays, vigils of saints, or on any days or times bidden by the church for fasting.

Also, that prayer should be made only to God, and to no other saint.

Also, that no prayer should be said other than the Pater Noster.

Also, that no pilgrimage ought to be made, but only to poor people.

Also, that the ringing of bells is antichrist's horns.

Because of these errors and heresies I am called before you, worshipful father, who have the cure of my soul. And having been fully informed by you that the articles that I have confessed are open errors and heresies, contrary to the determination of the church of Rome, I

338

willingly follow and adopt the doctrine of holy church, and depart from all manner of error and heresy, and return with good will and heart to the unity of the church. Considering that holy church does not refuse her bosom to him who will return, and that God does not will the death of a sinner but rather that he should be converted and live, with a pure heart I confess, detest, and despise my said errors and heresies. And I confess that the said opinions are heretical and erroneous and repugnant to the faith of the church of Rome and all holy church universal. And just as much as by the things that I so wickedly held and believed I showed myself corrupt and unfaithful, so I promise, from henceforth, to show myself uncorrupt and faithful, to keep truly the faith and doctrine of holy church. And I abjure and foreswear all manner of error and heresy, doctrine, and opinion against the faith of holy church and the determination of the church of Rome, especially the opinions I have rehearsed above, and I swear by these holy gospels that I am physically touching that from henceforth I shall never hold any error or errors, any heresy or heresies, or any false doctrine against the faith of the church and the determination of the church. Nor shall I obstinately defend any such things, nor shall I defend any man or woman holding or teaching such manner of things to me or any other person, publicly or privately. I shall never after this time be the receiver, favorer, counselor, or defender of heretics or of any men or women suspected of heresy. Nor shall I place my confidence in them, nor shall I knowingly keep fellowship with them, nor be familiar with them. I shall never give counsel, favor, gifts, or comfort to them. If I know any heretic, or any man or woman suspect of heresy, or any favorers, comforters, counselors, or defenders of heretics, or any men or women making private conventicles or assemblies or holding any diverse or singular opinions divergent from the common doctrine of the church, I shall inform you, worshipful father, or your vicar general in your absence, or the diocesan bishops of such men, immediately and readily. So help me God at my judgment and these holy gospels.

In witness of this, I subscribe here with my own hand a cross: + . And to this part indented to remain in your register I set my signet, and that other part indented I will receive under your seal to abide with me until my life's end. Given in the chapel of your manor of Thorpe the twentieth day of the month of August in the year of our Lord 1429.

[*The record of the proceedings concludes with a letter from Bishop Alnwick to the curate of Stoke Neylond, repeating the penances enjoined upon Kynget and requiring him to certify that they had been performed.*]

25. Heresy Trials in Winchester Diocese, 1511–13[16]

The second and longer set of the records published in this volume comes from the episcopal register of Richard Fox, the early sixteenth-century bishop of Winchester, patron of humanist scholarship, and confidant of Henry VII. In 1512, Fox and his vicar general, John Dowman, commenced proceedings against two groups of dissenters in his diocese, one community located in the London borough of Kingston-upon-Thames and another centered some thirty miles to the southwest around the towns of Farnham, Dogmersfield, Mattingley, and Crondall.[17] The dozen or so suspects whose names appear in these records acknowledged that they were members of a number of overlapping networks of dissenting belief; they indicated who taught them, what books they had read, and how they had met to share their beliefs, to make new converts, and to shore up the faith of those flagging in the face of persecution. Unlike in the Norwich court-book, where the scribe John Exeter included some of the defendants' vernacular explanations of their beliefs as well as the testimony of witnesses against them, the records in Bishop Fox's register are much more straightforward; for each defendant, the scribe presents a list of charges against him or her, along with his or her responses, a formal abjuration, and the sentence of the court. In only one of these trials (and indeed only one of all the trials presented in this volume) was the defendant remanded to the secular arm for execution. Dowman condemned the Kingston defendant Thomas Denys to death on March 5, 1512; he was burned the following day.

Since many of these defendants knew each other well and had some common intellectual and theological forebears, it should not be surprising that the beliefs they admitted to holding are consistent from one trial to the text. Just as in Norwich, however, this is also the effect of the formulaic schedules of beliefs prepared for each defendant; the records explicitly refer to these schedules, which the defendants produced at the time of their abjuration, in the case of the trials held at Farnham. In the main, the points at issue resembled those in the Norwich trials: the Eucharist, confession, images, the priesthood and the papacy, pilgrimage, and the reading of unauthorized vernacular scriptures. In contrast to many defendants tried in fourteenth-, fifteenth-, and sixteenth-century England, however, the defendants in Winchester did not merely deny the doctrine of transubstantiation; they rejected the notion of Christ's presence in the sacrament altogether, saying, in the words of Thomas Wattes's abjuration, that the Eucharist "is only a piece of bread and a thing done only in the memory of the passion of Christ, and nothing else" (p. 355). This commemorative doctrine of the Eucharist may owe much to these defendants' familiarity with the vernacular text *Wycklyffes Wycket*, which offers a similar explication of the sacrament.

1. Heresy trials in Southwark and Kingston, *February–March 1512/13*

On the nineteenth day of the month of February and in the year of our Lord (according to the computation of the English church) 1512, in the conventual priory church of St. Mary Overy in Southwark, in Winchester diocese, before the venerable man, master John Dowman, doctor of laws and vicar-general in spirituals and commissioner of the reverend father and lord in Christ, the lord Richard, by divine permission bishop of Winchester, appeared personally Thomas Denys, of the parish of Maldon in the same diocese, to whom the said commissioner administered and publicly objected, read, and declared certain articles or questions in our English vernacular. The articles and the responses that the said Thomas made to them follow in these words:

In the name of God, amen. We, John Dowman, doctor of civil laws, vicar-general and chancellor of the right reverend father in God and lord, the lord Richard, by the grace of God bishop of Winchester, lay, propose, and object these following articles, and every part of them, to and against you, Thomas Denys of the parish of Maldon, in the diocese and jurisdiction of Winchester; and to these articles we demand, ask, and require of you to give a true and plain answer:

First, we lay and object to you that you are of the parish of Maldon and of the diocese and jurisdiction of Winchester.

Also we lay, propose, and object to you and against you that you are baptized and christened and expressly professed to the holy faith of Christ, and to the determinations of our mother, holy church, and by reason thereof you have utterly renounced all manner of errors, heresies, erroneous doctrines, and opinions contrary to and against the determinations of our mother, holy church.

Also, we lay and object against you that it is not lawful for you or any other, and most especially any lay person to make doubts or to reason or dispute openly or secretly about anything concerning the faith of Christ or the determinations of our mother, holy church, or of the absolute power of our holy father, the pope, or to advance or hold any erroneous opinions, disputations, or questions against the determination of holy church.

Also, we lay and object against you that every christened person, man or woman, who holds, preaches, teaches, instructs, upholds, defends, or believes concerning the articles of the faith or the determinations of our mother, holy church, otherwise than our said mother, holy church, holds, preaches, teaches, instructs, upholds, defends, or believes; or who makes any new erroneous expositions, determinations, or opinions of perverse learning obstinately contrary to the said articles and determinations of holy church, is a heretic and should be held, taken, and reputed as a heretic.

Also, we lay and object to you and against you that every heretic so forwardly, erroneously, and obstinately believing, preaching, teaching, defending, and damnably departing from the true determinations of our mother, holy church, is by that same deed excommunicated and accursed by the law.

Also, we lay and object to you and against you that it is the responsibility of the said reverend father in God, my lord bishop of Winchester, and his officers, in this regard your ordinary, to examine, correct, and reform such matters and to punish those who are guilty and culpable of such crimes and all others done or committed within the city and diocese of Winchester.

Also, we lay and object to you and against you that you know or believe that in the aforesaid parish of Maldon, and various other places in the diocese of Winchester, you are sorely detected, suspected, and defamed upon certain errors and false opinions of heresy, as hereafter follow.

Also, we lay and object to you and against you that about twenty years ago, then living in the town of Waltham Abbey, in the diocese of London, you were detected and taken by the officers of the bishop of London, who was then your ordinary, upon certain various points and articles of heresy and erroneous opinions contrary to the determination of holy church, and that you abjured the same and did public penance at Paul's Cross and at Waltham, bearing a faggot at both places according to the manner and form customarily used in such matters.

Also, we object and lay to you and against you that various and many times since your said abjuration and the penance you did, and in the presence of and to various and many persons and especially to one John Jenyn, *alias* Broderer, recently detected of heresy within the said parish of Maldon and also within the parish of Kingston, and many others of the diocese and jurisdiction of Winchester, you have spoken, published, recited, rehearsed, declared, and taught many and various points and articles of heresy and erroneous and damnable opinions contrary to the determinations of our mother, holy church, and contrary to your abjuration, especially these articles and points which follow:

First, against the blessed sacrament of the altar, saying and affirming that the sacrament of the altar in form of bread was not the true body of Christ but a commemoration of Christ's passion and Christ's body in a figure and not the true body.

Also, that the offerings given by men or women to images in the church are but idolatry and worth nothing, for the images are but stocks and stones made by men's hands.

Also, that priests might not absolve one man for offenses done to another man, but that one man should ask another for forgiveness for the said trespass and not be absolved thereof by a priest.

Also, we lay and object to you and against you that many times since your abjuration and penance, you have persuaded many people and also had communication and made private conventicles and been in company, especially with the aforesaid John Jenyn, *alias* Broderer, of Kingston, who was recently accused and detected of heresy but is now deceased; and Philip Braban, also accused, detected, and defamed of heresy; and Lewis John, recently abjured of various and many points of heresy and erroneous opinions. And that you and the said Philip Braban brought to the said John Jenyn, *alias* Broderer, various books of heresy and especially a book of heresy called "Wiclif," exhorting him to look upon it and follow and believe its contents, and to copy the same, which John so did, according to your false and erroneous mind and exhortation.[18]

Also, we lay and object to and against you that after you had taught to the said John Jenyn the aforesaid articles and points of heresy, you, thinking and perceiving that the said John Jenyn, *alias* Broderer, had but little delight in the same, did with Philip Braban bring back to him the said book called "Wiclif," which book the said John Jenyn and you oftentimes read together and in which the said Jenyn believed through your counsel.

[*Denys's responses to the articles follow.*]

To the first and second articles the said Thomas responded and admitted that they, and each of them, were true. To the third, fourth, and fifth articles, he confessed that he believed that each of them was true in content. To the sixth article or question he confessed that the said article contained truth. To the seventh article or question he responded and confessed that he believed that it was true in content. To the eighth, ninth, tenth, eleventh, twelfth, thirteenth, and four-teenth articles or questions he responded and confessed that all of those articles, and each of them, were and are true in their content.

[*John Dowman, the vicar-general, proceeded to establish that Denys was a relapsed heretic, having previously learned his heresies from one Richard Hortop, whom Denys knew in Waltham Abbey but who had since died in Turnmill Street, London. On March 5, Dowman gave sentence: that though the excommunication against him should be lifted as a result of his confession, as a relapsed heretic Denys should be "relaxed to the secular arm" for punishment. A letter of Bishop Richard Fox, dated March 6, absolved Denys of his excommunication and confirmed Dowman's sentence; he was burned "before a great multitude of men and women" in the public market of Kingston-upon-Thames that day. The next trial in the register is that of Philip Braban of Kingston.*]

On the nineteenth day of the month of February, in the year of our Lord and in the conventual church written above, before the aforesaid vicar-general in spirituals and commissioner sitting judicially as on a tribunal, appeared personally Philip Braban, of the parish of Kingston, of the said diocese of Winchester, to whom the reverend father objected and administered and had read publicly in judgment and declared in the vernacular the articles written and contained here:

In the name of God, amen. We, John Dowman, doctor of civil laws, chancellor, and vicar general to the right reverend father in God and lord Richard, by the grace of God bishop of Winchester, lay and object these following articles, and every part of them, to and against you, Philip Braban, of the diocese and jurisdiction of Winchester, for the health and salvation of your soul, and to these articles we demand of you to have a true and plain answer:

First, we lay, propose, and object to you and against you, Philip Braban, that you are of the diocese and jurisdiction of Winchester.

Also we lay, propose, and object to you and against you that you are christened and expressly professed to the holy faith of Christ, and to the determinations of our mother, holy church, and by reason of the holy sacrament of baptism and your profession to the said holy faith and religion of Christ you have utterly renounced all manner of false errors, erroneous doctrines, and opinions contrary to and against the determinations of our mother, holy church.

Also, we lay and object against you that it is not lawful for you or any other, and most especially any lay person, to make doubts or to reason or dispute secretly or openly about anything concerning the faith of Christ or the determinations of our mother, holy church, or of the absolute power of our holy father, the pope, or to advance or hold any erroneous opinions, disputations, or questions against the determinations of holy church.

Also, we lay and object against you that every christened person, man or woman, who holds, teaches, preaches, instructs, upholds, defends, or believes concerning the articles of the faith or the determinations of our mother, holy church, otherwise than our said mother, holy church, holds, teaches, preaches, instructs, upholds, defends, or believes; or who makes any new erroneous expositions, determinations, or opinions of perverse learning obstinately contrary to the said articles and determinations of holy church, is a heretic and should be held, taken, and reputed as a heretic.

Also, we lay and object to you and against you that every heretic so forwardly, erroneously, and obstinately believing, preaching, teaching, defending, and damnably departing from the true determinations of our mother, holy church, is by virtue of that same deed excommunicated and accursed by the law.

Also, we lay and object to you and against you that it is the responsibility of the said reverend father, the bishop of Winchester, who in this behalf is your ordinary, and his officers, to examine, correct, and reform such matters and to punish those who are guilty and culpable of such crimes and all others done or committed within the city and diocese of Winchester.

Also, we lay and object to you and against you that you know or believe that in the parish of Kingston, and various other parishes of the diocese of Winchester, you are sorely detected, suspected, and defamed upon certain errors and false opinions of heresy, as hereafter follow:

First, we lay and object against you that about seven years ago, when you were dwelling in the parish of Amwell beside Ware in the diocese of London with one Stephan Carder, who was then your master, whose father was burned for heresy, you were taught by the said Stephan and did believe; and also many times since you have made public and rehearsed these following words to various people, namely, that the holy sacrament of the altar in form of bread was not the true body of our Lord Jesus Christ, but a figure of the body and not the body.

Also, we lay and object against you that you were taught by the said Stephan and have also made public, held, and believed that an offering given by a man or a woman to an image in the church is but idolatry and worth nothing, for images are but stocks and stones made by men's hands; and that it was through the covetousness of priests that it became customary to make offerings to images.

Also, we lay and object against you that you were also taught by the said Stephan and have also made public, taught, rehearsed, and believed that our holy father the pope and his power and indulgences were worth nothing nor were of any strength; and that priests could not absolve one man for an offense done to another man, but that one man should ask another forgiveness for the said trespass and not be absolved thereof by a priest; and that an ill priest[19] might not administer the sacrament of the altar until the time that he was reconciled.

Also, we object and lay against you that ever since the time that you learned the aforesaid erroneous and false points and articles from the said Stephan, you believed in them and in every one of them inasmuch that since that time you have taught them to various persons and had communication with them on the same and various other erroneous points and articles of heresy, especially with one Robert Cosyn of Harrow on the Hill, of the diocese of London; and with Thomas Denys of the parish of Maldon, of the diocese of Winchester, which Thomas (as you did know and now know) before that time, his ordinary then being at London, abjured the same and similar points of heresy and did public penance at Paul's Cross and at Waltham, bearing a faggot for his crime; and also with one aforesaid John Broderer of Kingston.

Also, we lay and object against you that you have at various and many times made private conventicles, accompanied by the said Thomas Denys and John Broderer and others, in the house of the said John in the said parish of Kingston, and various other places, and there you have read diverse books and especially a book called "Wiclif," which is clearly contrary to the determination of holy church, and many others.

Also, we lay and object to you and against you that you and the said Thomas Denys went together to the said John Broderer and delivered to him a book of heresy called "Wiclif," which book the said Broderer through your motion and exhortation read many times and believed in the same.

These are the responses made by the said Philip Braban:

To the first, second, third, fourth, and fifth articles he responded and confessed that they, and each of them, were true in content. To the sixth and seventh he responded and believed that they contained the truth. To the eighth, ninth, tenth, eleventh, twelfth, and thirteenth articles he responded and confessed that all, and each of them, were and are true in content.

[*Having heard Braban's responses, Dowman, the vicar-general, set March 6 as the date for his formal abjuration and the assignment of penance. On that day Dowman acknowledged that Braban wished to abjure the heresies and errors that he had confessed and assigned him the penance of going that day to the public market of Kingston to watch the execution of Thomas Denys, with an uncovered head and carrying a bundle of wood on his shoulders, and at the four corners of the marketplace to receive "discipline" from his curate. Dowman also ordered him, for the rest of his life, to wear a badge of wood on the exterior layer of clothes covering his chest and back, and not to leave the town of Kingston without ecclesiastical permission. The text of Braban's written abjuration follows in the register.]*

In the name of God, amen. Before you, worshipful sir and master doctor Dowman, doctor of civil laws and vicar-general and chancellor of the right reverend father in God, my lord Richard, by the grace of God bishop of Winchester, my ordinary, I, Philip Braban, of the diocese and jurisdiction of Winchester, detected and denounced to and before you, having been greatly suspected of heresy, errors, and other evil-sounding articles, and being in judgment before you, and understanding, knowing, and perceiving well that before this hour, I, the said Philip, have held, showed, declared, published, affirmed, and expressed various articles and opinions that are truly erroneous and against the faith of all holy church, and contrary to the determination of the same, and especially evil sounding in the ears of well-disposed Christian men:

First, that the holy sacrament of the altar in form of bread was not the true body of our Lord Jesus Christ but a figure of the body and not the body. And that an offering made by a man or a woman to images in the church was but idolatry and worth nothing, for the images were only stocks and stones made by men's hands. And also that our holy father the pope and his power and indulgences were worth nothing nor were of any strength; and that priests could not absolve one man for offenses done to another man, but that one man should ask another forgiveness for the said trespass and not be absolved thereof by a priest; and that an ill priest might hear no confessions nor administer the sacrament of the altar until the time that he is reconciled.

And also I have had with me certain books of heresy and especially "Wiclif," which I have brought to certain men for them to read, with the intent that they should learn from the same. And after I heard the contents thereof, I have believed the same, concealing the said books and their readers until the time of my arrest.

Wherefore I, the said Philip Braban, before you, right worshipful sir, and the others here present, having been truly and faithfully informed, acknowledge and know well that the articles rehearsed above are erroneous and against the true belief, faith, and determination of holy church, and truly evil sounding in the ears of well-disposed Christian people; and am willing with a pure heart and free will to forsake the said errors, books, and articles, especially the book of "Wiclif," and all other kinds of errors, heresies, and erroneous opinions against the true faith and determination of holy church, along with the books of the same erroneous opinions, and to return to the unity and the determinations of the said holy church and to believe henceforth the teachings and determinations of holy church. Furthermore, I forsake, renounce, and abjure the said errors, erroneous opinions, and evil-sounding articles and books, as are listed above, along with all other kinds of heresies, errors, articles, opinions, and doctrines against the true faith and determination of holy church.

And I swear upon this book that after this hour I shall never openly or secretly believe, hold, declare, or teach heresy, errors, or any manner of doctrine against the faith and determination of holy church; or keep or have any books of heresies; or shall I receive, favor, counsel, defend, succor, or support by myself or by any other means those who secretly or openly hold, teach, or maintain any such manner of false doctrine; or knowingly keep fellowship with them; or comfort them or receive them into my house; or give them food or drink, clothing or money; or succor them in any other way.

Furthermore, I swear that if I know any persons, men or women, suspect of errors and heresies; or who are protectors, counselors, comforters, defenders, receivers of heretics; or who make private conventicles against the common doctrine of holy church, I shall denounce them to the said right reverend father or to his officers or to their ordinaries as soon as I reasonably can, so help me God and holy judgment and this holy writing. In witness and record of this I subscribe my name.

[*The register continues the narrative of the proceedings against Braban. The defendant having signed his abjuration with a cross, Dowman added an additional penance: on the following day, a Sunday, Braban should be at the front of the procession at his parish church, carrying a bundle of wood. Dowman commanded Braban not to enter the parish church that day, or indeed any day until he had received formal absolution. Braban completed his penance and received absolution from Dowman the following day, March 7. There follows in the register a short note, dated June 8, 1513, indicating that Braban was from that day no longer required to wear the badge of wood that had signified his status as someone who had abjured heresy. The next trial recorded in the register is that of John Langborowe and Margery Jopson of Kingston.]*

Here follow the articles administered to John Langborowe and Margery Jopson of the parish of Kingston, in the Diocese of Winchester, on the fifth day of March, in the year of our Lord and the parish church aforementioned, them having appeared before the said reverend vicar general and commissioner; and also the responses they made to them:

In the name of God, amen. We, John Dowman, doctor of civil law and vicar-general of the right reverend father in God and lord Richard, by the grace of God bishop of Winchester, lay, propose, and object these following articles, and every part of them, to and against you, John Langborowe and Margery Jopson, of the parish of Kingston, in the diocese and jurisdiction of Winchester, for your souls' health, and to these articles we demand and ask of you, and of each of you, to give a plain and true response:

First, we lay and object to you and to each of you that you are and each of you is of the parish of Kingston and of the diocese and jurisdiction of Winchester aforesaid.

Also we lay and object to you and to each of you that you are and each of you is baptized and christened and expressly professed to the holy faith of Christ, and to the determinations of our mother, holy church, and by reason thereof you have utterly renounced all manner of errors, heresies, erroneous doctrines, and opinions contrary to and against the determinations of holy church.

Also, that it is not lawful for you or any other, especially lay person, to make doubts or to reason or dispute openly or secretly about anything concerning the faith of Christ or the determinations of our mother, holy church, or to hold any erroneous opinions, disputations, or questions against the determination of holy church.

Also, that every christened man or woman that holds, preaches, teaches, defends, or believes concerning the articles of the faith or the determinations of holy church otherwise than our said mother, holy church, holds, preaches, teaches, defends, or believes, or who makes any new erroneous expositions, determinations, or opinions obstinately contrary to the determinations of our said mother, holy church, is a heretic and should be held, taken, and reputed as a heretic.

Also, that not only every heretic so forwardly, erroneously, and obstinately departing from the determination of holy church, but also all those who believe, receive, defend, hide, aid, or succor heretics is by doing so excommunicated and accursed by the law.

Also, that it is the responsibility of the said reverend father in God, my lord bishop of Winchester, and his officers, to examine, correct, and reform such matters and to punish those who are culpable and guilty of this crime and all others done or committed within the diocese and jurisdiction of Winchester.

Also, we lay and object to and against you that you, the said Margery, have been at various times in the company of one Thomas Denys of Maldon, at the time an abjured heretic, and that you, the said John Langborowe, have been at various times in the company of John Jenyn, *alias* Broderer, of Kingston and of one Lewis John, also abjured, within the aforesaid parish of Kingston, and with them have read various books of heresy. And each of you received them into your houses and kept their counsel and favored them.

Also, that you, Margery Jopson, when a gentlewoman came to your house and was thirsty and would have drunk, but said that she would not until she had made an offering to the Rood, said, "Why will you drink so sparingly; why should you offer your money to the Rood? Give it to a poor body, for priests have enough money!"

Also, we lay and object to you, John Langborowe, that you have been at various times in company within the house of John Broderer, in Kingston, with the said John and Lewis John, when they have read various books of heresies, and that you had and kept with you a book of such matters, which you received from the said Lewis John. And as soon as you heard tell that the said John Broderer had been taken

351

on suspicion of heresy, you burned the same book secretly in the night because nobody should know thereof or see you doing it.

Also, we lay and object to and against you, Margery Jopson, that you heard the said Thomas Denys say in your house in Kingston that when a poor woman came to you to ask for alms, it was greater alms to give to her, who is the image of God, than to offer to images in the church, which are only stocks and stones made by men's hands, for our Lady is in heaven, and it is but idolatry to offer to images in the church. But notwithstanding that Thomas spoke so erroneously and damnably, you did not detect him but kept his counsel and favored him in that regard.

Also, we lay and object to you and to each of you that for these reasons you were called to appear before my said lord of Winchester, and that you know or believe that in the aforesaid parish of Kingston and in various other places in the diocese of Winchester you are, and each of you is, suspected, detected, and defamed upon these premises.

[*Langborowe and Jopson confessed each of these points, and Dowman accordingly rendered judgment that they were guilty of heresy and had incurred major excommunication. They submitted themselves to the correction of the church, and Dowman assigned them the following penance: John (wearing nothing on his shins, feet, or head, and wearing only a shirt) and Margery (wearing nothing on her shins or feet) should go to the public market that day and receive "discipline" from their curate at each of the four corners of the market. They should then go to the place of Thomas Denys's execution, remain there during the execution, and at its end throw their books of heresy into the fire. On the next Sunday, John, dressed as before, should be at the head of the procession around the cemetery of the church but not enter the church until he had been absolved. Dowman ordered both to appear again before him on the following Monday, March 7, to receive absolution. The register then records the decree of their absolution.*]

2. Heresy trials at Farnham, September 1512

On the last day of the month of September, in the year of our Lord 1512, in the parish church of Farnham, in Winchester diocese, before the reverend father and lord in Christ, the lord Richard, by divine permission bishop of Winchester, judicially seated as on a tribunal, personally appeared Thomas Wattes of Dogmersfield; Anne Wattes, his wife; Laurence Swaffer of Mattingley; Elisabeth, his wife; as well as William Wickham, *alias* Bruar; Alice, his wife; and Robert Winter of Crondall. They produced, and each of them produced, their abjurations contained in individual paper schedules; and they recognized and were confessed, and each of them recognized and was confessed, and they renounced all of the errors and heretical opinions contained in the schedules, and each of them confessed that he or she renounced all and each of the heresies and errors....Which things having been done, the said Thomas Wattes publicly abjured the said errors and heretical opinions contained in the schedule of his abjuration, touching the holy gospels; and the others did the same with the errors and heresies contained in their abjurations. Thomas then signed his name on the said abjuration with his own hand, and then the said reverend father absolved the same Thomas Wattes from his excommunication with the form of absolution, which he read. Afterward, the said Anne Wattes; Laurence Swaffer; Elisabeth, his wife; William Wickham, *alias* Bruar; Alice, his wife; and Robert Winter abjured all the errors and heretical opinions contained in their abjurations, and others that had been confessed by them, and by each of them, and each of them abjured all and each of the things contained in his or her individual schedule, each of them touching the holy gospels of God, and they desired, and each of them desired, just as was contained in their abjurations. To these schedules of abjuration, each of them put his or her sign, and so the said reverend father assigned the following penance to the said Thomas Wattes; Anne, his wife; Laurence Swaffer; Elisabeth, his wife; William Wickham, *alias* Bruar; Alice, his wife; and Robert Winter, that is, that on the following day, which is to say the first of the month of October, in the said church of Farnham, each of the men with naked shins and feet, and with uncovered heads, would carry a tied bundle of wood on his back; and each of the women, with heads covered and wearing boots and shoes, would carry a book on her head; and they would kneel on a footstool in the middle of the nave of the church until the time of the going out of the procession, and then, at around the time of the procession, they would rise and precede the said procession around the cemetery, and when the procession returned they would go to their place, where they would genuflect until the end of the sermon to the people and the mass. These things having finished, each of the said men and women would proceed to a certain fire and into it the men would throw their bundles of faggots and the women would throw their books, and these things having been done, each would return to his or her own house and dwelling place. During their life they would not venture from the place in which they dwelled to any other place more than five miles away from the place where they dwelled, nor outside the diocese of Winchester. And during their life they would present themselves once each year to the bishop of Winchester in his castle at Farnham, if it happened that the bishop were at that castle, and that for five full days they would carry out the same penance that each of them had previously carried out, in the aforesaid parish church of Farnham, and one of them in the parish church of Crondall....

The reverend father reserved to himself the power of enjoining a further penance on these foresaid individuals, Anne Wattes; Laurence Swaffer; Elisabeth, his wife; William Wickham, *alias* Bruar; Alice, his wife; and Robert Winter, and each of them, and reading their written sentence of absolution, he absolved them and relaxed the excommunication. There were present there the masters John Dowman, John Batmanson, doctors of laws, and Edward, a reader in arts, and Aylone Hay, notary public, along with not a few others.

On the fourth day of the month of October, in the said year, in the interior of a certain room in the said castle personally appeared before the said reverend father Thomas Wattes; Laurence Swaffer; William Wickham, *alias* Bruar; and Robert Winter. The reverend father, on account of certain causes and considerations in this matter, commuted the penance he had assigned to them and to their wives, that is, on the fifteenth day of the month of October, in the parish church of Crondall, they would do penance as follows: each of the men on the said day and in the said place, with naked shins and feet and uncovered heads, would kneel on a footstool in the middle of the nave of the church up to the time of the procession, and then about the time the procession goes out, each carrying a candle weighing a quarter of a pound in his hands, would proceed the said procession, and at the time of the procession returning each would kneel in his place until the end of the sermon; and at the offertory of the mass, at the time of the offering, each would offer his candle into the hands of the priest celebrating the mass, and then return to his place, and remain there until the end of the mass, at which time each would say in honor of the Eucharist five Our Fathers and the same number of Hail Marys and the same number of Apostles' Creeds. And also, the women would go on the same day to the said place and kneel on the footstool in the middle of the nave during the whole time of the sermon, and do no other penance that day.

[The defendants' abjurations then follow; the first is that of Thomas Wattes.]

In the name of God, amen. In the presence of you, the reverend father in God Richard, by the grace of God bishop of Winchester, my ordinary, I, Thomas Wattes of Dogmersfield, in your diocese of Winchester, having been detected, accused, and put up as a misbelieving man, because I have learned from one Gardener the Younger, who is now dead, and John Hacker, in the company of others heretics and lollards, and because I taught others, confess myself to have read, taught, held, spoken, and believed all these erroneous opinions that follow, that is to say:

First, that the host consecrated by the priest is not the body of Christ in the form of bread, but it is only a piece of bread and a thing done only in the memory of the passion of Christ, and nothing else; and that the priest cannot make God, for God made the priest.

Second, that the images in the church are nothing but stocks indeed, for which reason men should not go on pilgrimage or give offerings to them, but give their offerings to poor people, who are the image of God.

Third, I confess myself to have erred in making a false interpretation of the clause of the Creed that says, "God ascended into heaven, and from thence he is to come to judge both the living and the dead." On this article I erroneously declared and believed thus: "If you, good Lord, are in heaven and will come to judge both the living and the dead, then you are not here on earth in flesh and blood in the form of bread on the altar, for you do not wish to be eaten by the chewing of teeth but by the hearing of ears."

Fourth, I have erred in misbelieving that there is no purgatory, except in this world, because after a man is dead he will go straight to heaven or to hell.

Fifth, I acknowledge myself to have erred in misconstruing and mis-declaring this clause contained in the Ten Commandments, "You shall not worship foreign gods" (Exod 20:3), for I expounded upon this article by saying that images of saints made by men's hands and set up in the church to be honored are foreign gods; therefore, men should set up no candles before them or go on pilgrimage to worship them.

Sixth, I confess that I have secretly and openly kept and read books prohibited by the church to be kept or read, such as books of the New Testament translated into English, and those I read not only secretly in my house to myself but also oftentimes in the presence and hearing of my wife; my children; William Bruar (otherwise called Wickham) and Alice, his wife; Laurence Swaffer and Elisabeth, his wife; and Robert Winter.

Seventh, I, the said Thomas Wattes, have erroneously believed and declared to others that there are no holidays but Sunday, which God made himself, for on all other days a man may do what work he will.

Eighth, I erroneously believed that there are no fasting days but the Ember Days and Lent, which God himself made, for on all other days men may eat fish or flesh, so long as they abstain from sin; but on those days I ate no flesh for fear of being slandered and detected, though I did eat bread and cheese on many fasting days and on the vigils of the apostles.

Ninth, I erroneously believed that a priest cannot cause a man's soul to come to heaven, be he in or out of sin, for he has no power from almighty God to absolve a man from his sins.

Tenth, that the said priest has no power over or cure or charge of another man's soul, for he has enough to do with his own soul.

Eleventh, that the said priest is given no power when he is consecrated other than to preach and teach and give good counsel, which power all other men have, for all men should know the scripture of God, which should be preached to all men.

Twelfth, I heard one Stilman, who was in my house at All Hallows' Eve, at the beginning of May, and at Whitsuntide last passed, read various English books prohibited by the church, for which I deserve to be punished as a heretic; I heard also from the same Stilman many of the heresies and opinions above rehearsed, declared, and expounded.

Of all these foresaid errors and heresies judicially objected to me here in your presence and confessed by me, I hold myself guilty and culpable, and the same erroneous damnable opinions, errors, and heresies, and all other teachings and doctrines repugnant and contrary to the determination of the church and hurtful to my soul, which can deceive other Christian people of simple understanding, I, the said Thomas Wattes, being sorry, contrite, and truly repentant of the same, solemnly abjure, forswear, forsake, and expressly renounce the said erroneous opinions and heresies, and every one of them, and also [I renounce, etc.] the keeping and concealing of English books forbidden by the laws of the church, submitting myself openly and expressly to the pain, rigor, and harshness of the penalty that a relapsed person ought to suffer by the law if at any time hereafter I do or attempt anything contrary to my present abjuration and renunciation, or if I knowingly favor, counsel, or assist secretly or openly any heretics or persons misbelieving in the faith of the church; or persons who are held as suspect, defamed, or polluted with the leprosy or infection of heresy; or any persons who hold, read, teach, or obstinately defend any opinion or matter contrary to and against the determination of holy church; or any who are keepers, receivers, or counselors of the said heretics and misbelieving people or of such forbidden English books as I have before rehearsed—ceasing in all these matters all kind of fraud, deception, deceits, and dissimulations, so help me God and these holy gospels. And in witness hereof I put my sign to this abjuration: + . And for all my foresaid offenses I beseech you, my said ordinary, to assign me a solemn penance and give me your absolution according to the customary form of the church used in such cases.

[*Bishop Fox, having heard Wattes's abjuration, absolved Wattes of his excommunication, with the condition that he perform the penance that the bishop had assigned him.*]

In the name of God, amen. The merits and circumstances of this case of heretical depravity, having been heard, seen, understood, and fully investigated by us, Richard, by divine permission bishop of Winchester, which case we have brought against you, Thomas Wattes, of the parish of Dogmersfield in our diocese and jurisdiction, for the correction of your soul and the souls of all others, out of our pure legal office and your public reputation in our diocese. Because we have found through these proceedings and through your confession and abjuration that you have maintained, held, spoken of, said, taught, and believed not a few errors, heresies, and heretical opinions, not only against the sacrament of the altar but also against the determinations of holy church; and that you kept with you various books of sacred scripture translated into the English language, the reading of which is prohibited by the constitutions of the church, and also read them publicly and privately; and that you abjured these errors and heretical opinions and the keeping and reading of the said books with a penitent heart and as a penitent man, therefore, we, Richard, the said bishop, having first invoked the name of Christ, and with God alone before our eyes, with the counsel of our theologians and judicial advisers, absolve you by these writings from major excommunication, since it so appears and since we believe that you are truly and not falsely penitent and that you have abjured the said errors and heretical opinions, and others, if you perform a penance for these crimes in the way that we will assign to you and fully observe the commands.

[*The other abjurations follow; this is Anne Wattes's.*]

In the name of God, amen. In the presence of you, the reverend father in God Richard, by the grace of God bishop of Winchester, my ordinary, I, Anne Wattes of Dogmersfield, in your diocese of Winchester, having been detected, accused, and put up for a misbelieving woman, because I have learned from and been taught by Thomas Wattes, my husband, and others in the company of heretics and lollards, confess myself to have held, spoken, and believed all these erroneous opinions that follow, that is to say:

First, that the host held up in the priest's hands at the elevation is not the body of Christ in form of bread, but it is only a piece of bread and a thing done only in the memory of the passion of Christ, and nothing else; and that the priest cannot make God, for God made the priest.

Second, that the images in the church are nothing but stocks indeed, for which reason men should not go on pilgrimage or give offerings to them, but give their offerings to poor people, who are the images of God.

Third, I confess myself to have erred in hearing and believing in the false interpretation of the clause of the Creed that says "God ascended into heaven, and from thence he is to come to judge both the living and the dead." On this article I erroneously believed thus: "If you, good Lord, are in heaven and will come to judge the living and the dead, then you are not here on earth in flesh and blood in the form of bread on the altar, for you do not wish to be eaten by the chewing of teeth but by the hearing of ears."

Fourth, I have erred in misbelieving that there is no purgatory, except in this world, for after a man dies he will go immediately to heaven or to hell.

Fifth, I acknowledge myself to have erred in misconstruing and mis-declaring this clause contained in the Ten Commandments, "You shall not worship foreign gods," for I expounded upon this article by saying that images of saints made by men's hands and set up in the church to be honored are foreign gods; therefore men should set up no candles before them or go on pilgrimage to worship them.

Sixth, I have damnably and erroneously said, held, and believed that I might as well confess to a stock as to a priest.

Seventh, I had an English book of my husband's, with a roll containing heresy, which after the arrest of my said husband I burned, and I had two other books, one of the epistles, gospels, and the apocalypse, and the other of the Pater Noster, the Ave Maria, the Creed, and the Ten Commandments, along with a treatise on the sacrament of baptism, all translated into English, which I hid in a ditch.

Of all these foresaid errors and heresies, and all other teachings and doctrines repugnant and contrary to the determination of the church and hurtful to my soul, which can deceive other Christian people of simple understanding, I, the said Anne Wattes, being sorry, contrite, and truly repentant of the same, solemnly abjure, forswear, forsake, and expressly renounce the said erroneous opinions and heresies, and every one of them, and also [I renounce, etc.] the keeping and concealing of English books forbidden by the laws of the church, submitting myself openly and expressly to the pain, rigor, and harshness of the penalty that a relapsed person ought to suffer by the law if at any time hereafter I do or attempt anything contrary to my present abjuration and renunciation, or if I wittingly favor, counsel, or assist secretly or openly any heretics or persons misbelieving in the faith of the church; or persons who are held as suspect, defamed, or polluted with the leprosy or infection of heresy; or any persons who believe, read, teach, or obstinately defend any opinion or matter contrary to and against the determination of holy church; or any who are keepers, receivers, or counselors of the said heretics and misbelieving people or of such forbidden English books as I have before rehearsed—ceasing in all these matters all kind of fraud, deception, deceits, and dissimulations, so help me God and these holy gospels. And in witness hereof I put my sign to this abjuration: + . And for all my foresaid offenses I beseech you, my said ordinary, to assign me a solemn penance and give me your absolution according to the customary form of the church used in such cases.

[This is the abjuration of Laurence Swaffer.]

In the name of God, amen. In the presence of you, the reverend father in God Richard, by the grace of God bishop of Winchester, my ordinary, I, Laurence Swaffer of Mattingley, in your diocese of Winchester, having been detected, accused, and put up for a misbelieving man, because I have been taught by Hacker Weston and Thomas Wattes in the company of other heretics and lollards, confess myself to have held, taught, spoken, and believed all these erroneous opinions that follow, that is to say:

First, that the host consecrated by the priest is not the body of Christ in form of bread, but it is only a piece of bread and a thing done only in the memory of the passion of Christ, and nothing else; and that the priest cannot make God, for God made the priest.

Second, that the images in the church are nothing but stocks indeed, for which reason men should not go on pilgrimage or give offerings to them, but give their offerings to poor men, who are the images of God.

Third, I confess myself to have erred in hearing, saying, and believing a false interpretation of this clause of the Creed, "God ascended into heaven, and from thence is to come to judge both the living and the dead." On this article I erroneously declared and believed thus: "If you, good Lord, are in heaven and will come to judge the living and the dead, then you are not here on earth in flesh and blood in the form of bread on the altar, for you do not wish to be eaten by the chewing of teeth but by the hearing of ears."

Fourth, I have erred in misbelieving that there is no purgatory, except in this world, for after a man is dead he will go straight to heaven or to hell.

Fifth, I acknowledge myself to have erred in misconstruing and mis-declaring this clause of the first of the Ten Commandments, "You shall not worship foreign gods," for I expounded upon this article by saying that the images of saints made by men's hands and set up in the church to be honored are foreign gods; therefore, men should set up no candles before them or go on pilgrimage to them or worship them.

Sixth, I have erred in keeping an English book of Luke and John translated out of Latin into English and in delighting to hear this and other English books to be read, contrary to the prohibition and commandment of the church, and in hiding the same before being detected.

Seventh, I, the said Laurence Swaffer, have erroneously believed and declared to others that there is no holiday but Sunday, which God himself made, for on all the other days a man may do what work he will.

Eighth, I erroneously believed that there are no fasting days but the Ember Days and Lent, which God himself made, for on all other days men may eat fish or flesh, so long as they abstain from sin; but on those days I ate no flesh for fear of being slandered and detected, though I did eat bread and cheese on many fasting days and on the vigils of the apostles.

Ninth, I erroneously believed that a priest cannot cause a man's soul to come to heaven, whether he be in or out of sin, for the priest has no power from almighty God to absolve a man of his sins.

Tenth, that the said priest has no power over or cure or charge of another man's soul, for he has enough to do with his own soul.

Eleventh, that the said priest, when he is consecrated, has no power given to him except the power to preach and teach and give good counsel, as all other men have, for all men should know the scripture of God, which should be preached to all men.

Twelfth, that I heard one Stilman, who was in my house at All Hallows' Eve and the beginning of May, read various English books prohibited by the church; and also he came to my house last Whitsuntide, but at that time he read in no book for which I deserve to be punished as a heretic. I also heard from the same Stilman many of the heresies and erroneous opinions I have above rehearsed, declared, and expounded.

Of all these errors and heresies...[20] so help me God and these holy gospels. And in witness of this my present abjuration I put my sign: + . And for all my foresaid offenses I beseech you, my said ordinary, to assign me a solemn penance and give me your absolution according to the customary form of the church used in such cases.

[This is the abjuration of Elisabeth Swaffer.]

In the name of God, amen. In the presence of you, the reverend father in God Richard, by the grace of God bishop of Winchester, my ordinary, I, Elisabeth Swaffer of Mattingley, in your diocese of Winchester, having been detected, accused, and put up for a misbelieving woman, because I have learned from and been taught by one Hacker Weston and my husband, Laurence Swaffer, in the company of other heretics and lollards, confess myself to have held, spoken, and believed all these erroneous opinions which follow, that is to say:

First, that there is no purgatory, except in this world, because when a man dies he goes straight to hell or to heaven.

Second, I have damnably and erroneously believed that the body of almighty God in heaven cannot be in flesh and blood in the form of bread on the altar, for that thing that is done there by the priest is done in signification of the passion of Christ, and it is no other thing.

Third, that a priest cannot cause a man's soul to come to heaven, whether he is in or out of sin, for the priest has no power from almighty God to absolve a man of his sins; and that the said priest has neither power over nor cure nor charge of another man's soul, for he has enough to do with his own soul.

Fourth, that a priest, when he is consecrated, has no power given to him except the power to preach and teach and give counsel, as all other men have, for all men should know the scripture of God and the gospel of Christ, which should be preached to all men.

Fifth, that prayers, matins, masses, and almsgiving after a man is dead cannot profit him, for he goes straight either to heaven or to hell.

Sixth, that the images in the church are nothing but stocks indeed, and for this reason men should not go on pilgrimage or give offerings to them, but give the said offerings to poor people, who are the image of God, for it is better to give alms to the image or picture of God that is a poor man than to the pictures or images made by man's hand that men call saints, such as Our Lady of Walsingham, St. Thomas of Canterbury, and such others.

Of all these errors and heresies…so help me God and these holy gospels. And in witness of this my present abjuration I put my sign: + . And for all my foresaid offenses I beseech you, my said ordinary, to assign me a solemn penance and give me your absolution according to the customary form of the church used in such cases.

[*This is the abjuration of William Wickham,* alias *Bruar.*]

In the name of God, amen. In the presence of you, the reverend father in God Richard, by the grace of God bishop of Winchester, my ordinary, I, William Wickham, otherwise called William Bruar, of Crondall, in your diocese of Winchester, having been detected, accused, and put up for a misbelieving man, because I have learned from and been taught by one Newman, recently of London, and Thomas Wattes of Dogmersfield, in the said diocese of Winchester, in the company of other heretics and lollards, confess myself to have held, spoken, and believed all these erroneous opinions that follow, that is to say:

First, that the host consecrated by the priest is not the body of Christ in form of bread, but it is only a cake and a piece of bread and a thing done only in the memory of the passion of Christ, and nothing else; and that the priest cannot make God, for God made the priest.

Second, that the images in the church are nothing but stocks indeed, for which reason men should not go on pilgrimage or give offerings to them, but give their offerings to the poor people, who are the image of God.

363

Third, I confess myself to have erred in the misconstruing and mis-declaring of the Pater Noster and the Creed and in the wrong exposition of the holy scriptures in sermons and preachings of my erroneous opinions. And also I erred in misinterpreting this clause of the Creed, "God ascended into heaven and from thence is to come to redeem both the living and the dead," by making the false declaration, "if you, good Lord, are in heaven and will come to judge the living and the dead, then you are not here on earth in flesh and blood in the form of bread on the altar, for you do not wish to be eaten by the chewing of teeth but by the hearing of ears."

Of all these errors and heresies...so help me God and these holy gospels. And in witness of this my present abjuration I put my sign: + . And for all my foresaid offenses I beseech you, my said ordinary, to assign me a solemn penance and give me your absolution according to the customary form of the church used in such cases.

[*This is the abjuration of Alice Wickham*, alias *Bruar*.]

In the name of God, amen. In the presence of you, the reverend father in God Richard, by the grace of God bishop of Winchester, my ordinary, I, Alice Wickham, otherwise called Alice Bruar, of Crondall, in your diocese of Winchester, having been detected, accused, and put up for a misbelieving woman, because I have falsely learned from and been mistaught by one Robert Weston, recently of Mattingley, in the said diocese of Winchester, in the company of other heretics and lollards, confess myself to have held, spoken, and believed all these erroneous opinions that follow, that is to say:

First, that the body of Christ was not on the altar in the form of bread, but it is only a cake and a piece of bread and a thing done only in memory of the passion of Christ and nothing else; and that the priest cannot make God, for God made the priest.

Second, that the images in the church are nothing but stocks indeed, for which reason men should not go on pilgrimage or give offerings to them, but give offerings to poor people, who are the images of God.

Of all these errors and heresies...so help me God and these holy gospels. And in witness of this my present abjuration I put my sign: + . And for all my foresaid offenses I beseech you, my said ordinary, to assign me a solemn penance and give me your absolution according to the customary form of the church used in such cases.

[*This is the abjuration of Robert Winter.*]

In the name of God, amen. In the presence of you, the reverend father in God Richard, by the grace of God bishop of Winchester, my ordinary, I, Robert Winter, of Crondall, in your diocese of Winchester, having been detected, accused, and put up for a misbelieving man, because I have been taught by Thomas Wattes, of the parish of Dogmersfield, in the company of other heretics and lollards, confess myself to have held, taught, spoken, and believed all these erroneous opinions that follow, that is to say:

First, that the host consecrated by the priest on the altar is not the body of Christ in form of bread, but it is only a cake and a piece of bread and a thing done only in the memory of the passion of Christ, and nothing else.

Second, that notwithstanding that I should have received the blessed sacrament last Easter Day, I refrained from doing so for twelve months, yet reputing it but a cake of bread and drink, I received it contrary to my spiritual father's injunction.[21]

Third, that the images in the church are nothing but stocks indeed, for which reason men should not go on pilgrimage or give offerings to them, but give their offerings to poor people, who are the images of God.

Fourth, that God made no holy days except Sunday, for on all the other "holidays" a man may do whatever work he will, for they are not holy days.

Of all these errors and heresies...so help me God and these holy gospels. And in witness of this my present abjuration I put my sign: + . And for all my foresaid offenses I beseech you, my said ordinary, to assign me a solemn penance and give me your absolution according to the customary form of the church used in such cases.

[*Having heard all these abjurations, Bishop Fox absolved the other defendants, Anne Wattes, Laurence and Elisabeth Swaffer, William and Alice Wickham, alias Bruar, and Robert Winter, from excommunication, on the condition that they perform the penance he had assigned them.*]

In the name of God, amen. The merits and circumstances of this case of heretical depravity, having been heard, seen, understood, and fully investigated by us, Richard, by divine permission bishop of Winchester, which case we have brought against you, Anne Wattes; Laurence Swaffer; Elisabeth Swaffer; William Wickham, *alias* Bruar; Alice Wickham, *alias* Bruar; and Robert Winter, and each of you, in our diocese and jurisdiction, for the correction of your souls and the souls of all others, out of our pure legal office and your public reputation in our diocese. Because we have found through these proceedings and through your confessions that you, and each of you, have maintained, held, spoken of, said, taught, and believed not a few errors, heresies, and heretical opinions, and that you acquired not a little understanding of heretical depravities; and that you abjured these errors and heretical opinions and all other knowledge of the said heresies with penitent hearts and as penitent people, therefore, we, Richard, the said bishop, having first invoked the name of Christ, and with God alone before our eyes, with the counsel of our theologians and judicial advisers, absolve you, and each of you, by these writings from the major excommunication that you had incurred through your erring disposition, since it so appears and since we believe that you are truly and not falsely penitent and that you have abjured the said errors and heretical opinions, and others, if you perform a penance for your crimes in the way that we will assign to you and fully observe the commands.

NOTES

INTRODUCTION

1. See A. S. McGrade, "The Medieval Idea of Heresy: What Are We to Make of It?" in *The Medieval Church: Universities, Heresy, and the Religious Life: Essays in Honour of Gordon Leff*, ed. Peter Biller and Barrie Dobson, Studies in Church History, Subsidia 11 (Woodbridge: Boydell and Brewer, 1999), pp. 111–39.

2. See Alister McGrath, *Heresy: A History of Defending the Truth* (New York: HarperCollins, 2009); and Ben Quash and Michael Ward, eds., *Heresies and How to Avoid Them: Why It Matters What Christians Believe* (London: SPCK and Hendrickson, 2007).

3. Ian Forrest, *The Detection of Heresy in Late Medieval England* (Oxford: Clarendon Press, 2005), pp. 14–15. See also John H. Arnold, *Belief and Unbelief in Medieval Europe* (London: Hodder Arnold, 2005), p. 197.

4. On the early history of heresy, see Rowan Williams, "Defining Heresy," in *The Origins of Christendom in the West*, ed. Alan Kreider (Edinburgh: T & T Clark, 2001), pp. 313–35; and J. Rebecca Lyman, "Heresiology: The Invention of 'Heresy' and 'Schism,'" in *The Cambridge History of Christianity*, vol. 2, ed. Augustine Casiday and Frederick W. Norris (Cambridge: Cambridge University Press, 2008), pp. 296–313. The best general history of later medieval popular heresies is still Malcolm Lambert, *Medieval Heresy: Popular Movements from the Gregorian Reform to the Reformation*, 3 ed. (Oxford: Blackwell, 2002).

5. *Knighton's Chronicle 1337–1396*, ed. and trans. Geoffrey Martin (Oxford: Clarendon Press, 1995), pp. 243–325.

6. While Knighton says that Wyclif himself translated the Bible, most modern scholars agree that the scope of the project and some independent evidence of collaborative work suggest that a team of translators was involved. Some argue that Wyclif was involved, even a major contributor, but most agree that he encouraged or perhaps simply inspired the project. See below, pp. 3–4 and note 9.

7. How well this list of views describes the views of Wyclif and his followers will be considered in greater detail below.

8. For helpful summaries of the debates over Wycliffism's persistence and influence, see Geoffrey Martin, "Wyclif, Lollards, and Historians,

1384–1984," in *Lollards and Their Influence in Late Medieval England*, ed. Fiona Somerset, Jill C. Havens, and Derrick G. Pitard (Woodbridge: Boydell and Brewer, 2003), pp. 237–50; and Peter Marshall, "Lollards and Protestants Revisited," in *Wycliffite Controversies*, ed. Mishtooni Bose and J. Patrick Hornbeck II (Turnhout: Brepols, 2011), pp. 295–318.

9. See most recently Mary Dove, *The First English Bible: The Text and Context of the Wycliffite Versions* (Cambridge: Cambridge University Press, 2007).

10. For a persuasive statement of this position that has remained unchallenged, see Anne Hudson, *The Premature Reformation: Wycliffite Texts and Lollard History* (Oxford: Clarendon Press, 1988), pp. 9–10.

11. See Marshall, "Lollards and Protestants Revisited."

12. John Bale was the first to call Wyclif the Morning Star, in *Image of Both Churches* (London: John Daye, 1547).

13. See below, pp. 24–29, and J. Patrick Hornbeck II, "*Wycklyffes Wycket* and Eucharistic Theology: Two Series of Cases from Sixteenth-Century Winchester," in Bose and Hornbeck, *Wycliffite Controversies*, 279–94.

14. On Wyclif's views, see most recently Stephen E. Lahey, *John Wyclif* (Oxford: Oxford University Press, 2009), pp. 102–34. See also Ian Christopher Levy, *John Wyclif: Scriptural Logic, Real Presence, and the Parameters of Orthodoxy* (Milwaukee: Marquette University Press, 2003), pp. 217–319; and Stephen Penn, "Wyclif and the Sacraments," in *A Companion to John Wyclif: Late Medieval Theologian*, ed. Ian Christopher Levy (Leiden and Boston: Brill, 2006), pp. 241–91, esp. pp. 249–72. For some early Wycliffite views and their circulation, see Fiona Somerset, "Here, There, and Everywhere? Wycliffite Conceptions of the Eucharist and Chaucer's 'Other' Lollard Joke," in Somerset, Havens, and Pitard, *Lollards and Their Influence in Late Medieval England*, pp. 127–38; and David Aers, *Sanctifying Signs: Making Christian Tradition in Late Medieval England* (Notre Dame, IN.: University of Notre Dame Press, 2004), pp. 67–98; and J. Patrick Hornbeck II, *What Is a Lollard? Dissent and Belief in Late Medieval England* (Oxford: Oxford University Press, 2010), chap. 3.

15. See Ian C. Levy, "Grace and Freedom in the Soteriology of John Wyclif," *Traditio* 60 (2005): 279–337; Lahey, *John Wyclif*, pp. 169–98; and below, pp. 18–20. See also Hornbeck, *What Is a Lollard?* chap. 2.

16. On Wyclif's views, see Penn, "Wyclif and the Sacraments," pp. 283–89. Fiona Somerset's assessment of Wycliffite views on the sacrament of confession is forthcoming in chapter 1 of *Feeling like Saints*.

17. For more thoughtful assessments of Wycliffite engagement with

Christian tradition, see, for example, pp. 7–24 below; and Dove, *The First English Bible*, pp. 95–102.

18. For this label, see Eamon Duffy, *The Stripping of the Altars*, 2nd ed. (New Haven, CT: Yale University Press, 2005), p. xxvii. For the wondering, see pp. xxv–xxviii.

19. See especially Shannon McSheffrey, "Heresy, Orthodoxy, and English Vernacular Religion 1480–1525," *Past and Present* 186 (2005): 47–80. The foundational study of the trials is J. A. F. Thomson, *The Later Lollards, 1414–1520* (Oxford: Oxford University Press, 1965).

20. See "The Testimony of William Thorpe," in *Two Wycliffite Texts*, ed. Anne Hudson, Early English Text Society 301 (Oxford: Oxford University Press, 1993); "The Trial of Richard Wyche," ed. F. D. Matthew, *English Historical Review* 5 (1890): 530–44; "The Sermon of William Taylor," in Hudson, *Two Wycliffite Texts; The Works of a Lollard Preacher*, ed. Anne Hudson, Early English Text Society 317 (Oxford: Oxford University Press, 2001); *Four Wycliffite Dialogues*, ed. Fiona Somerset, Early English Text Society 333 (Oxford: Oxford University Press, 2009); and *Pierce Plowman's Crede*, in *The Piers Plowman Tradition*, ed. Helen Barr (London: Dent, 1993), pp. 63–97.

21. For general brief surveys of Wycliffite writings, see Fiona Somerset, "Wycliffite Prose," in *A Companion to Middle English Prose*, ed. A. S. G. Edwards (Woodbridge: Boydell and Brewer, 2004), pp. 195–214; Anne Hudson, "Wycliffite Prose," in *Middle English Prose: A Critical Guide to Major Authors and Genres*, ed. A. S. G. Edwards (New Brunswick, NJ: Rutgers University Press, 1984), pp. 249–70; E. W. Talbert and S. H. Thomson, "Wyclif and His Followers," in *A Manual of the Writings in Middle English 1050–1500*, ed. J. Burke Severs (Hamden, CT: Archon, 1970), pp. 354–80, 521–35, with crucial additions and corrections in Anne Hudson, *Lollards and Their Books* (London: Hambledon Press, 1985), pp. 1–12 and 249–52. On early lollard book production, see Anne Hudson, "Compilations for Preaching and Lollard Literature, II: Lollard Literature," in *The Cambridge History of the Book in Britain, vol. 2: 1100–1400*, ed. Nigel Morgan and Rodney M. Thomson (Cambridge: Cambridge University Press, 2008), pp. 329–39.

22. John Bossy, "Moral Arithmetic: Seven Sins into Ten Commandments," in *Conscience and Casuistry in Early Modern Europe*, ed. Edmund Leites (Cambridge: Cambridge University Press, 1988), pp. 214–34.

23. On concern for moral and spiritual improvement through cultivation of the virtues in the Devotio Moderna, see John Van Engen, *Sisters and Brothers of the Common Life: The Devotio Moderna and the World of*

the Later Middle Ages (Philadelphia: University of Pennsylvania Press, 2008), pp. 266–304.

24. See Robert R. Raymo, "Works of Religious and Philosophical Instruction," in *A Manual of the Writings in Middle English 1050-1500*, ed. J. B. Severs and A. E. Hartung (Hamden, CT: Archon, 1986), vol. 7, especially pp. 2284–90; and the comprehensive introduction and detailed commentary on versions in Judith Anne Jefferson, "An Edition of the Ten Commandments Commentary in BL Harley 2398 and the Related Version in Trinity College Dublin 245, York Minster XVI.L.12, and Harvard English 738, Together with Discussion of Related Commentaries," 2 vols. (Ph.D. diss., University of Bristol, 1995), vol. 1, pp. lxxxi–cxciii.

25. For more examples of this phenomenon, see items 8 and 19. For more on the *Lantern of Light,* see below.

26. The commandments are reordered in the sequence 1, 4, 3, 2, 7, 5, 8, 6, 9 and 10 together. The numbering of the decalogue used here is the Catholic numbering. See Bossy, "Moral Arithmetic," pp. 216–17.

27. On the collective or communal voice of many Wycliffite texts, see further Christina Von Nolcken, "A 'Certain Sameness' and Our Response to It in English Wycliffite Texts," in *Literature and Religion in the Later Middle Ages: Philological Studies in Honor of Siegfried Wenzel*, ed. R. Newhauser and John Alford (Binghamton, NY: Medieval and Renaissance Texts and Studies, 1995), pp. 191–208; cf. Matti Peikola, "Individual Voice in Lollard Discourse," in *Approaches to Style and Discourse in English*, ed. Risto Hiltunen and Shinichiro Watanabe (Osaka: Osaka University Press, 2004), pp. 51–77.

28. Throughout the volume, quotations from the Bible are presented in italics so that readers may easily distinguish explanations of the meaning interpolated into the quotation from the biblical text itself. For further explanation of this and other editorial practices, see *Notes on the Translations.*

29. See, for example, *The Two Ways,* p. 167; *The Ten Commandments,* p. 202; *A Dialogue between a Wise Man and a Fool,* p. 261; *The City of Saints,* p. 279.

30. Hudson quotes the version in York XVI.L.12 in *The Premature Reformation,* p. 4. Jefferson has edited the whole of this commentary in parallel-text with the related version excerpted here as *The Ten Commandments* in item 12; for her edition of this passage and notes, see "Edition of Ten Commandments Commentaries," vol. 2, pp. 123–28, 209–10.

31. As Jefferson explains; see "Edition of Ten Commandments Commentaries," vol. 2, pp. 177–83.

32. For a broad-ranging survey of iconoclasm in England, see Margaret Aston, *England's Iconoclasts* (Oxford: Clarendon Press, 1988).

33. Two commentaries are printed in Thomas Arnold, *Select English*

Works of John Wyclif (Oxford: Clarendon Press, 1871), vol. 3, pp. 93–97 and pp. 98–110, while the one included here as item 11 appears in Matthew. The polemical works are *On Holy Prayers*, item 9, and "Seven Heresies," in Arnold, *Select English Works of John Wyclif*, vol. 3, pp. 441–46. See Anna Lewis, "Textual Borrowings, Theological Mobility, and the Lollard Pater Noster Commentary," *Philological Quarterly* 88 (2009): 1–23; Vincent Gillespie, "Thy Will Be Done: *Piers Plowman* and the Pater Noster," in *Late Medieval Religious Texts and Their Transmission: Essays in Honour of A. I. Doyle*, ed. A. J. Minnis (Woodbridge: D. S. Brewer, 1994), pp. 95–119.

34. See, for example, *Commentary on Psalm 87*, verse 1, p. 230.

35. For a compelling evocation of this agony and wavering in response to persecution, see Matthew, "The Trial of Richard Wyche."

36. For an unusually lengthy treatment, see "The Seven Deadly Sins," in Arnold, *Select English Works of John Wyclif*, vol. 3, pp. 119–67.

37. See Kate Crassons, *The Claims of Poverty: Literature, Culture, and Ideology in Late Medieval England* (Notre Dame, IN: University of Notre Dame Press, 2010), pp. 89–176. On Franciscan poverty and the controversies it inspired, see Malcolm Lambert, *Franciscan Poverty: The Doctrine of the Absolute Poverty of Christ and the Apostles in the Franciscan Order, 1210–1323* (St. Bonaventure, NY: Franciscan Institute, 1998); and David Burr, *The Spiritual Franciscans: From Protest to Persecution in the Century after St. Francis* (University Park: Pennsylvania State University Press, 2001).

38. These associations predated lollardy and the controversy over "lollard" specifically: see Wendy Scase, *'Piers Plowman' and the New Anti-clericalism* (Cambridge: Cambridge University Press, 1989), pp. 150–1; and Michael Wilks, "Wyclif and the Great Persecution," in *Wyclif: Political Ideas and Practice*, ed. Anne Hudson, pp. 179–203 (Oxford: Oxbow, 2000), pp. 186–87.

39. For a different reading of this passage as well as other examples and different conclusions about the word *lollard*, see Andrew Cole, *Literature and Heresy in the Age of Chaucer* (Cambridge: Cambridge University Press, 2008), pp. 46–74.

40. For architectural metaphors, see, for example, *Commentary on Psalm 87*, p. 230–31; *The City of Saints*, pp. 285–90; and *A Dialogue Between Jon and Richard*, pp. 291, 298. For corporate metaphors, see *The City of Saints*, p. 279; and *Sermons from Sidney Sussex 74*, p. 302.

41. Wyclif, *Sermones*, ed. Iohann Loserth (London: Trübner, 1887–90), vol. 1, pp. 321/10–324/14, esp. 321/17–18. See also Edwin Craun, "Discarding Traditional Pastoral Ethics: Wycliffism and Slander," in Bose and Hornbeck, *Wycliffite Controversies*, pp. 228–42.

42. For the twelfth- and thirteenth-century background in this para-

graph we draw on the work of Peter D. Clarke, *The Interdict in the Thirteenth Century: A Question of Collective Guilt* (Oxford: Oxford University Press, 2007), pp. 14–58, esp. 29–50; and idem, "Peter the Chanter, Innocent III, and Theological Views on Collective Guilt and Punishment," *The Journal of Ecclesiastical History* 52 (2001): 1–20.

43. *The Ten Commandments*, pp. 219–20; *A Dialogue between a Wise Man and a Fool*, p. 255.

44. "Consentit cooperans, defendens, consilium dans, / Ac autorisans, non iuvans nec reprehendens." For a long list of citations in Wyclif's and Wycliffite works, see *Four Wycliffite Dialogues*, pp. 85–86. A more detailed discussion of Wyclif's and Wycliffite theories of consent appears in Somerset, *Feeling like Saints* (forthcoming).

45. See *Sermons from Sidney Sussex 74*, pp. 300–301 and note 232.

46. Those who argued for this position in the twelfth century, even if only that subjects should correct their rulers' sins rather than preventing them, would have been surprised that the seventeenth of the first list of forty-five articles against Christian faith attributed to Wyclif and condemned at the Council of Constance was that the "people can correct sinful lords at their discretion" (*Decrees of the Ecumenical Councils*, trans. and ed. Norman Tanner [Washington, D.C.: Georgetown University Press, 1990), vol. 1, p. 412]).

47. Modernized from the edition based on Bodley 789 in Arnold, *Select English Works of John Wyclif*, vol. 3, p. 87.

48. For the term *true men* see Anne Hudson, "A Lollard Sect Vocabulary?" in *So Meny People Longages, and Tonges: Essays Presented to Angus McIntosh*, ed. Michael Benskin and M. L. Samuels (Edinburgh, self-published, 1981), pp. 15–30, repr. in Hudson, *Lollards and Their Books*; and Matti Peikola, *Congregation of the Elect: Patterns of Self-Fashioning in English Lollard Writings* (Turku, Finland: University of Turku, 2000), pp. 81–229. For the "church of those that shall be saved," see Hudson, *Premature Reformation*, pp. 314–27.

49. For recent assessments see Rob Lutton, "Lollardy, Orthodoxy, and Cognitive Psychology," and Maureen Jurkowski, "Lollard Networks," both in Bose and Hornbeck, *Wycliffite Controversies*, pp. 97–119, 261–78.

50. For discussion of this point, see, among other studies, James L. Halverson, *Peter Aureol on Predestination: A Challenge to Late Medieval Thought* (Leiden: Brill, 1998). Stephen E. Lahey distinguishes helpfully between the doctrines of predestination current in Wyclif's day in *John Wyclif* (Oxford: Oxford University Press, 2009), chap. 6.

51. For a historical survey of discussions of the three estates (also called the three orders) across the Middle Ages, see Giles Constable, "The

Orders of Society," in *Three Studies in Medieval Religious and Social Thought* (Cambridge: Cambridge University Press, 1995), pp. 249–360.

52. For a thoughtful exploration of the concept's semantic range and uses, see Howard Kaminsky, "Estate, Nobility, and the Exhibition of Estate in the Later Middle Ages," *Speculum* 68 (1993): 684–709.

53. For a detailed study of the ways that literary and other writings divide society into different sorts of estates in medieval England, see Jill Mann, *Chaucer and Medieval Estates Satire* (Cambridge: Cambridge University Press, 1973).

54. See Alexandra Walsham, "Inventing the Lollard Past: The Afterlife of a Medieval Sermon in Early Modern England," *Journal of Ecclesiastical History* 58 (2007): 628–55.

55. See Andrew W. Cole, "Trifunctionality and the Tree of Charity: Literary and Social Practice in *Piers Plowman*," *English Literary History* 62 (1995): 1–27.

56. Earlier studies of lollardy based on the evidence of extant trial records agreed that most lollards were villagers, many of them artisans; see, for example, J. A. F. Thomson, *The Later Lollards*. Newer studies based on other sorts of legal records such as wills and proceedings in other courts are finding evidence of lollard activity among the middle classes; see, for example, Robert Lutton, *Lollardy and Orthodox Religion* (Rochester, NY: Boydell and Brewer, 2006); and Maureen Jurkowski, "Lollardy and Social Status in East Anglia," *Speculum* 82 (2007): 120–52.

57. For the claim that reform will begin with the commons, see *The City of Saints*, item 20, p. 288. For the claim that subjects should obey heathen lords in such a way as to convert them, see *A Short Rule of Life*, item 6, p. 162. For claims that subjects should disobey sinful lords, see Hudson, *Premature Reformation*, p. 362.

58. See, for example, Nicholas Watson, "Vernacular Apocalyptic: On the *Lanterne of Liȝt*," *Revista canaria de estudios ingleses* 47 (2003): 115–27; Kantik Ghosh, "Wycliffite Affiliations: Some Intellectual-Historical Perspectives," in Bose and Hornbeck, *Wycliffite Controversies*, pp. 13–32. Contrast Fiona Somerset, "Wycliffite Spirituality," in *Text and Controversy: Essays in Honor of Anne Hudson* (Turnhout: Brepols, 2005), pp. 375–86.

59. For an innovative reading of biblical catenae in a Huntington manuscript, see Michael P. Kuczynski, "An Unpublished Lollard Psalms *Catena* in Huntington Library MS HM 501," *Journal of the Early Book Society* 13 (2010), pp. 95–138. In this volume, see item 17, *A Dialogue between a Wise Man and Fool*, and item 20, *The City of Saints*. For another example, see *The Holi Prophete Dauid*, in *The Earliest Advocates of the*

English Bible: The Texts of the Medieval Debate, ed. Mary Dove (Exeter: University of Exeter Press, 2010), pp. 150–59.

60. Kantik Ghosh, *The Wycliffite Heresy: Authority and the Interpretation of Texts* (Cambridge: Cambridge University Press, 2002), pp. 112–46. See also Anna Lewis, "Exegesis of the End: Limitations of Lollard Apocalypticism as Revealed in a Commentary on Matthew 24," *Literature and Theology: An International Journal of Religion, Theory, and Culture* 23 (2009): 375–87.

61. See p. 334, below.

62. See p. 333, below.

63. See p. 330, below.

64. See p. 332, below.

65. See p. 351, below.

66. See p. 328, below; see also J. H. Dahmus, *The Metropolitan Visitations of William Courtenay* (Urbana: University of Illinois Press, 1950); *Fasciculi Zizaniorum* (Rolls Series, 1858), p. 387. On the meaning of *predestined* in a Wycliffite context, see our comments below under "Ecclesial Spirituality," as well as Ian C. Levy's excellent study "Grace and Freedom in the Soteriology of John Wyclif."

67. Norman P. Tanner, ed., *Heresy Trials in the Diocese of Norwich, 1428–1431* (London: Royal Historical Society, 1977), p. 81.

68. Both quotations are from Shannon McSheffrey and Norman Tanner, eds. and trans., *Lollards of Coventry, 1486–1522* (Camden Fifth Series 23, 2003), p. 96. The emphasis on the moral state of the person praying echoes concerns of Wyclif's as well as of Wycliffite texts.

69. See p. 334, below.

70. For biographical details, see G. R. Evans, *John Wyclif: Myth and Reality* (Downer's Grove, IL: IVP Academic, 2006). See also Levy, *A Companion to John Wyclif*; Lahey, *John Wyclif*.

71. For recent scholarship on Wyclif's Oxford years, see Alessandro Conti, "Wyclif's Logic and Metaphysics" in Levy, *A Companion to John Wyclif*, pp. 67–126; see also Conti, "John Wyclif," in *The Stanford Encyclopedia of Philosophy*, available online.

72. See Vaclav Mudroch, *The Wyclyf Tradition*, ed. A. Compton Reeves (Athens: Ohio University Press, 1979).

73. Literature on Wyclif's controversies is extensive. What follows is a selection of the most recent treatments of those described above. Ian Christopher Levy, "John Wyclif and the Primitive Papacy," *Viator* 38, no. 2 (2007): 159–90; Levy, *John Wyclif*; Dove, *The First English Bible*.

74. Howard Kaminsky, "Wycliffism as Ideology for Revolution" *Church History* 32 (1963): 52–64.

75. Stephen Lahey, *Philosophy and Politics in the Thought of John Wyclif* (Cambridge: Cambridge University Press, 2003); Takashi Shogimen, "Wyclif's Ecclesiology and Political Thought," in Levy, *A Companion to John Wyclif*, pp. 199–240.

76. For a full account of Wyclif's trials and conflicts with the church, see Joseph Dahmus, *The Prosecution of John Wyclyf* (New Haven, CT: Yale University Press, 1952). See also Mishtooni Bose, "The Opponents of John Wyclif," in Levy, *A Companion to John Wyclif*, pp. 407–57.

77. See Hudson, *Premature Reformation*, pp. 62–63. A fuller bibliography on lollardy can be found in the notes to the introductions of Wycliffite writings provided elsewhere in this book.

78. See Howard Kaminsky, *A History of the Hussite Revolution* (Berkeley and Los Angeles: University of California Press, 1967; repr. Eugene, OR: Wipf and Stock, 2004).

79. See John Wyclif, *On the Truth of Holy Scripture*, trans. I. C. Levy (Kalamazoo, MI: Medieval Institute, 2001).

80. For a catalogue of Wyclif's extant works, see Williel R. Thomson, *The Latin Writings of John Wyclyf* (Toronto: Pontifical Institute of Mediaeval Studies, 1983). Modern scholars are in agreement that, while there are likely to be vernacular works by Wyclif in existence, none can be established with certainty. Hence, collections like Matthew's *The English Works of Wyclif* are now understood to contain Wycliffite material, but not Wyclif's own works.

81. *Trialogus* was the first of Wyclif's works to see print, in an edition by Froben in Basel, 1525. It was edited from a different, now likely nonexistent manuscript, by L. P. Wirth in 1753, and finally by Gotthard Lechler (from four complete manuscripts) in 1869. Stephen Lahey hopes to finish his translation of this treatise in 2012; please see http://theology.unl.edu/ for a searchable version of the 1753 edition (planned to include the 1869 version as well), and http://daten.digitale-sammlungen.de/~db/0002/ bsb00029051/images/ for a digitized version of the 1525 edition.

82. Translations of Wyclif's works include versions of *De Eucharistia, De Officio Pastoralis, De Civili Dominio I, De Officio Regis, De Veritate Sacrae Scripturae, De Simonia,* and *De Universalibus*.

83. Johann Loserth, "Johann von Wyclif und Guilelmus Peraldus: Studien zur Geschichte der Entstehung von Wyclif's *Summa Theologiae*," *Sitzungsberichte der Kaiserliche Akademie der Wissenschaften zu Wien*, philosophische-historische Klasse 180, 1917.

84. See Jean-Pierre Torrell, *Saint Thomas Aquinas, Spiritual Master*, trans. Robert Royal (Washington, DC: Catholic University of America, 2003), pp. 322–23.

85. For Wyclif's sermon on the Creed, see Sermon 44 in Loserth, *Sermones*, vol. 1.

86. Robert Grosseteste, *De Decem Mandatis*, ed. Richard C. Dales, Auctores Britannici Medii Aevi 10, British Academy (Oxford: Oxford University Press, 1987).

87. Wyclif's thought on *ius* and politics is the focus of Stephen Lahey's "Wyclif on Rights," *Journal of the History of Ideas* 58 (Jan. 1997): 1–21.

88. Again, the idea is not new with Wyclif; see *Summa theologiae IaIIae* Q.100, a.10.

89. See Sermon 29, in Loserth, *Sermones*, vol. 1, pp. 197–99.

90. For a selection of fourteenth-century English preaching, see Siegfried Wenzel, *Preaching in the Age of Chaucer: Selected Sermons in Translation* (Washington, D.C.: Catholic University of America, 2008); see also Beryl Smalley, *English Friars and Antiquity in the Early Fourteenth Century* (Oxford: Blackwell, 1960).

91. See, for example, the doubts of J. A. F. Thomson about "The Two Ways" in "Orthodox Religion and the Origins of Lollardy," *History* 74 (1989): 39–55, on pp. 44–45. Wycliffites do, on occasion, treat the Eucharist in detail; see, for example, the lengthy *Tractatus de oblacione iugis sacrificii*, in Hudson, *The Works of a Lollard Preacher*, pp. 157–256.

92. For rethinking of this assumption in scholarship on Wycliffism, see Hudson, "Who Is My Neighbour?" in Bose and Hornbeck, *Wycliffite Controversies*, pp. 79–96; and McSheffrey, "Heresy, Orthodoxy, and English Vernacular Religion 1480–1525." For a comparative perspective, see Marina Rustow, *Heresy and the Politics of Community: The Jews of the Fatimid Caliphate* (Ithaca, NY: Cornell University Press, 2008); and Hornbeck, *What Is a Lollard?* chap. 1.

93. For a list of these core writings, and further references, see above, pp. 7–8.

94. Alan Fletcher has suggested the first phenomenon in "A Hive of Industry or a Hornet's Nest? MS Sidney Sussex 74 and Its Scribes," in Minnis, *Late Medieval Religious Texts and Their Transmission*, pp. 131–55. For the second, see Margaret Aston, "Lollardy and Literacy," in *Lollards and Reformers: Images and Literacy in Late Medieval Religion*, (London: Hambledon Press, 1984), pp. 193–217 at p. 211; and Dove, *The First English Bible*, p. 52.

95. For more detailed accounts of late medieval courts and inquisitorial practice, see Richard M. Wunderli, *London Church Courts and Society on the Eve of the Reformation* (Cambridge, MA: Medieval Academy of

America, 1981); and Forrest, *The Detection of Heresy in Late Medieval England.*

96. There were, of course, exceptions. Individuals caught up in rebellions against royal authority who also were suspected of heresy were often tried and sentenced by civil courts.

97. Forrest, *The Detection of Heresy in Late Medieval England*, p. 58.

98. Quoted in Malcolm Lambert, *Medieval Heresy*, 3rd ed. (Oxford: Blackwell, 2002), p. 5; the current canon law of the Roman Catholic Church preserves key elements of Grosseteste's view by defining heresy as "the obstinate denial or obstinate doubt" of a theological truth (canon 751).

99. On the legal and social ramifications of the concept of *fama*, see Forrest, *The Detection of Heresy in Late Medieval England*, p. 198.

100. The penances assigned to heresy suspects have been the focus of too little scholarship, but see Norman P. Tanner, "Penances Imposed on Kentish Lollards by Archbishop Warham, 1511–12," in *Lollardy and the Gentry in the Later Middle Ages*, ed. Margaret Aston and Colin Richmond (Sutton: Stroud, 1997), pp. 229–49.

101. See, for instance, the Coventry and Lichfield diocese case of Joan Warde *alias* Wasshingburn in McSheffrey and Tanner, *Lollards of Coventry, 1486–1522*, p. 239.

102. For critiques of this sort, see, among other sources, Derek J. Plumb, "John Foxe and the Later Lollards of the Thames Valley" (Ph.D. thesis, University of Cambridge, 1987), pp. 12–13; Charles Kightly, "The Early Lollards: A Survey of Popular Lollard Activity in England, 1382–1428" (Ph.D. thesis, York University, 1975), p. 576; Paul Strohm, "Counterfeiters, Lollards, and Lancastrian Unease," in *New Medieval Literatures*, vol. 1, ed. Wendy Scase, Rita Copeland, and David Lawton (Oxford: Oxford University Press, 1997), pp. 31–58; R. N. Swanson, *Church and Society in Late Medieval England* (Oxford: Blackwell, 1989), p. 335.

103. J. A. F. Thomson, "John Foxe and Some Sources for Lollard History: Notes for a Critical Reappraisal," in *Studies in Church History 2*, ed. G. J. Cuming (London: Nelson, 1965), pp. 251–57.

104. Anne Hudson, "The Examination of Lollards," repr. in *Lollards and Their Books*, pp. 124–40.

105. On this point, see Leonard E. Boyle, "*Montaillou* Revisited: Mentalité and Methodology," in *Pathways to Medieval Peasants*, ed. J. Raftis, pp. 119–40 (Toronto: Pontifical Institute of Mediaeval Studies, 1981); and Peter Biller, "'Deep Is the Heart of Man, and Inscrutable': Signs of Heresy in Medieval Languedoc," in *Text and Controversy from Wyclif to Bale: Essays in Honour of Anne Hudson*, ed. Helen Barr and Ann M. Hutchinson, pp. 267–80 (Turnhout: Brepols, 2005).

106. Williams, "Defining Heresy," p. 95.

107. The next several paragraphs contain a condensed version of the argument in favor of using trial records in whatever way feasible presented in the preface to Hornbeck, *What Is a Lollard?*

108. London, Westminster Diocesan Archives MS B.2, p. 250.

109. London, Westminster Diocesan Archives MS B.2, p. 234; see also the printed edition in Tanner, *Heresy Trials in the Diocese of Norwich, 1428–1431*, p. 74.

110. McSheffrey and Tanner, *Lollards of Coventry*, pp. 182–83, 117.

PART I

Sermon 29

1. This sermon, for the fifth Sunday after Easter, is translated from *Iohannis Wyclif Sermones*, ed. J. Loserth (London: Wyclif Society, 1888), vol. 1, pp. 192–99.

2. Wyclif argued that while Christ's sacrifice benefited both elect and damned, his life was intended only for the elect. See *Sermones* I.34, I.52, II.24, IV.9, IV.10, IV.11. This is associated with his complex position on God's foreknowledge and human sin. See Ian Levy, "Grace and Freedom in the Soteriology of John Wyclif," *Traditio* 60 (2005): 279–337.

3. This is a reference to the Muslim philosopher Averroes (ca. 1126–98), who in his *Long Commentary on the De Anima of Aristotle* argued in favor of a single, eternal material intellect for the whole of the human species, existing apart from individual human beings, and against the immortality of the soul. When Scholastic philosophers incorporated Aristotle's philosophy into Christian theology, Muslim interpreters of Aristotle like Averroes were very influential; this teaching of the unity of the intellect was a matter of considerable dispute in the thirteenth century.

4. The reference is to John 18:4, which in the Vulgate is simply "Whom do you seek?" The implication of betrayal by a friend comes from Psalm 41:9 and 55:12, which were usually understood as prefiguring Judas's betrayal of Jesus.

5. See Aristotle, *Nicomachean Ethics* Bk.8, c.5 1157b35.

The Six Yokes

6. This composite text has been translated from the following passages in Wyclif's sermons: sermon 27 (Matt 5:1), pp. 202–3; sermon 28 (Matt 4:18), pp. 206–10; sermon 31 (Matt 10:16), pp. 232–34; sermon 32

(Luke 10:1), pp. 237–40; and sermon 33 (John 12:24), pp. 244–47, all in *Iohannis Wyclif Sermones,* ed. J. Loserth (London: Wyclif Society, 1888), vol. 2.

7. In Sermon 27, those who "may have material for preaching" are "the ignorant (*idiote*) and the simple." Lechler presents the variant that I am using.

8. Wyclif uses the term *caesarian* throughout his writings to refer to the hierarchical system of ecclesiastical government resulting from the Donation of Constantine, one of the hallmarks of the church's fall from its early purity.

9. The reference is to Aristotle, *On the Generation of Animals* II.3, widely quoted in Scholastic thought.

10. See 1 Corinthians 7.

11. The published sermon has "why momentary wonders and matters without foundation in this matter," but the alternative reading has "civil momentaries," which I translate as "trivialities."

12. It is important to bear in mind that Wyclif was active at the time of the Peasants' Revolt in August 1381; in fact, this is when he left Oxford for Lutterworth. The chronicler Thomas Walsingham accused him of having inflamed the sensibilities of John Ball, the priest who, along with Wat Tyler, led the rebellion. It is easy to imagine Wyclif writing this section after the events of the revolt, and given the likelihood that he divided *De Sex Iugiis* and inserted it into sermons at Lutterworth, suggests that Wyclif was still actively revising earlier works at this late date.

13. Wyclif has *timentibus,* those who fear, while Romans has *diligentibus,* those who love.

On Love

14. Translated from *Iohannis Wyclif Opera Minora,* ed. J. Loserth (London: Wyclif Society, 1913), pp. 8–10.

15. See Williel Thomson, *Latin Writings of John Wyclyf: An Annotated Catalog* (Toronto: Pontifical Institute of Medieval Studies, 1983), item 393 and more generally pp. 234–44. One copy in a Prague manuscript is ascribed to Wyclif. The attribution of this and the other occasional pieces to Wyclif seems fairly certain, though it is not impossible that one or more followers may have taken a hand in editing or even producing some of these short digests of Wyclif's pastoral and polemical positions.

16. For an introduction to the genre, see Giles Constable, *Letters and Letter Collections,* Typologie des sources du Moyen Age occidental, 17 (Turnhout: Brepols, 1976). See also John Taylor, "Letters and Letter

Collections in England, 1300–1420," *Nottingham Medieval Studies* 24 (1980): 57–70.

17. See Ralph Hanna, "Dr. Peter Partridge and MS Digby 98," in *Text and Controversy: Essays in Honor of Anne Hudson,* ed. Ann Hutchison and Helen Barr (Turnhout: Brepols, 2005), pp. 41–65, esp. p. 51.

18. The resemblance was first noted by Hope Emily Allen. See *English Writings of Richard Rolle, Hermit of Hampole,* ed. Hope Emily Allen (Oxford: Clarendon Press, 1931), p. 161. For a detailed comparison of the three texts, see Fiona Somerset, "Wycliffite Spirituality," in Hutchison and Barr, *Text and Controversy,* pp. 375–86.

On the Divine Commandments (Selections)

19. What follows is an abridgement of chapters 11, 12, 13, 15, 16, 19, and 20. The repetition in which Wyclif frequently indulged has been reduced, and some digressions excised. All translation is from *Johannis Wyclif Tractatus de Mandatis Divinis,* ed. J. Loserth, Wyclif Society (London, 1922), which makes use of fourteen of the seventeen extant manuscripts.

20. This is the basic principle of Wyclif's theory of lordship. The inherent reciprocity in the relation between lord and subject requires that while the subject owes the lord obedience, the lord is in fact a steward, or servant, to his subjects, putting their own needs before his own. See A. S. McGrade, "Somersaulting Sovereignty: A Note on Reciprocal Lordship and Servitude in Wyclif," in *The Church and Sovereignty c. 590–1918: Essays in Honor of Michael Wilks (Studies in Church History: Subsidia 9),* ed. Diana Wood (Oxford: Basil Blackwell, 1991), pp. 261–78.

21. Wyclif departs from the Thomist tradition on a few points, and this is one. Thomas had famously argued that human reason could use five arguments to arrive at the evident truth of God's existence in *Summa Theologiae Ia* Q.2, a.3. Wyclif rejects this approach and any philosophical reasoning that does not have scripture as its basis. The means for human beings to recognize truths about God's nature in addition to what is revealed in scripture is through reasoning about the divine ideas and universals. This makes Wyclif an heir to the Neoplatonic tradition of the Scholastics of the twelfth century, which explains why Anselm, the great twelfth-century archbishop of Canterbury and theologian, is given pride of place in what follows.

22. The term *intuition* refers to what philosophers today call direct perception, perceiving the object itself rather than perceiving its appearance and inferring the nature of the object.

23. This is Anselm's definition of God in his famous "ontological"

demonstration of the necessity of God's existence in *Proslogion* Chap.2. The reference in Aristotle's *Metaphysics* is to VII.17, 1041b5–10.

24. "Existence in kinds" means creatures as they exist in creation and refers to Wyclif's theory of universals. A universal like *horse* has a primary reality in creation through which all individual horses have their being. The universal is the "kind" and the individual creatures exist in them.

25. Wyclif's opponents are those who, following William Ockham, argue that universals are only concepts in our minds without correspondent reality in creation. Ockhamists argued that while our ideas may naturally represent individual creatures, like horses, it does not follow that there is such a thing as a universal "horse." Because of this metaphysical disagreement, Wyclif argued, the intellectual heirs of Ockham (later to be called *Moderni*) could not understand the relation of scripture to morality and the spiritual life.

26. Ockham and his followers argued that God's power was so great as to admit that God could conceivably command that a man sin mortally; some followers may have gone so far as to say that God could will that someone sin mortally, even if Ockham never quite put it this way.

27. Wyclif discusses mental acts, which include acts of willing, in *De Actibus Anime*.

28. This is a part of Wyclif's realism. The "more common" is more "useful" because it has a higher degree of being. The universal "horse" is more common than individual horses and so is more useful because it provides the form for an entire set of creatures. "Animal" is even more common, because there are more animals than horses, and "substance" is even more common, and so on up to "Being" which, in God in its purest form, is "most useful."

29. Augustine, *Epistle* 167.

30. Throughout the later Middle Ages there was considerable argument regarding the possibility of the salvation of "virtuous pagans." Wyclif's position is formulated against those of Ockham and Holcot; see Janet Coleman, *Piers Plowman and the Moderni* (Rome: Storia e Letteratura, 1981), pp. 108–47.

31. Wyclif did not compose a treatise on virtues and vices, but he regularly argued that it is simplistic to correspond a given virtue to a given vice, as was the habit of many friars in their sermons. Further, he argued vigorously against the possibility that one might excel in one virtue while lacking others, which had been suggested by Ockham and Holcot. See *Trialogus*, book III, chap. 9. See also Siegfried Wenzel, "Preaching the Seven Deadly Sins," and Bonnie Kent, "On the Track of Lust: *Luxuria*, Ockham, and the Scientists," both in Richard Newhauser, *In the Garden of*

Evil: The Vices and Culture in the Middle Ages (Toronto: Pontifical Institute of Medieval Studies, 2005), pp. 145–69; 349–70.

32. This apparently puzzling statement reflects Wyclif's conviction that one individual's sin harms not only himself but the created order, and so all else in creation, past, present, and future.

33. Memory and reason are the first two parts.

34. This chapter is important because some lollards would pursue idolatry as one of their main points of criticism of the church.

35. Haymo of Halberstadt, *PL* 117, pp. 374–75.

36. Jerome, Ep.51.

37. The normal use of *hyperdulia* is reserved for the Blessed Virgin. See Aquinas, ST IIaIIae, Q.103, a.1. In IIIa Q.25 a.2 Aquinas recognizes the legitimacy of *dulia* rendered to Christ because of perfect humanity. This he draws from Peter Lombard, *Sententia* III, Dist.9, c.1, in which there is a distinction between *dulia* due to Christ's humanity and that due other creatures. Wyclif appears to be conflating this species of *dulia* with *hyperdulia*.

38. Wyclif switches from third to first person in this sentence. This paragraph is important because it shows Wyclif's subordination of virtue ethics to preaching the law of God as given in scripture.

39. Lincolniensis is Robert Grosseteste, bishop of Lincoln (1175–1253), a figure of great importance in Scholasticism in England, and a figure who would become a "patron saint" for lollards.

40. See Robert Grosseteste, *De Decem Mandatis, Auctores Britannici Medii Aevi* X, ed. Richard Dales and Edward King (Oxford: Oxford University Press, 1987), p. 7.

41. These are the four cardinal virtues.

42. Augustine, sermon 283.

43. What follows is citation of Hugh of St. Victor, *De Modo Orandi* (*On the Way of Praying*), chaps. 2 and 3; see *PL* 176, pp. 979C–981C.

44. Robert Grosseteste, *Dictum* 82, available on the grosseteste.com website.

45. Peter Comestor, *Historia scholastica* PL 180, 1070–71, ca.1170.

46. Innocent refers to Satan's speech in Isaiah 14, "I will ascend to heaven; I will exalt my throne above the stars of God; I will sit in the mountain of the covenant, in the sides of the north."

47. "The poet" is Horace, in *Ars Poetica*, and the second citation has been attributed to Hugh of St. Victor and Bernard of Clairvaux.

48. Incorrect citation of Sirach 41:1; Gregory, *Magna Moralia in Iob* Bk.16, c.69.

49. Innocent III's *De Miseria Condicionis Humane* was well known and widely cited throughout the later Middle Ages, thanks to the notoriety

of the author and the scope of its contempt for worldly goods. Innocent's dour eye surveys every stage of human life, the breadth and depth of vice, and the grim subjects of death, decay, and the suffering of the damned. Its recent editors count 672 manuscript copies of the work, and 52 printed editions by the middle of the seventeenth century. It seems apparent that Wyclif uses either an incomplete edition or an abridged version in this extended citation in *De Mandatis*. See Lotario dei Segni (Innocent III), *De Miseria Condiciones Humane*, ed. Robert E. Lewis (Athens: University of Georgia, 1978). All direct citations from this edition and translation rely heavily on Lewis's translation.

50. See Thomas Aquinas, *Summa Theologiae* Ia, Q.24, a.2, a.4.

51. Wyclif's theory of election and damnation is complex. It is developed in *De Sciencia Dei, De Intellectione Dei,* and *De Volucione Dei*. For a brief summary, see Stephen Lahey, *John Wyclif* (Oxford: Oxford University Press, 2008).

52. This citation of Matthew 6:6 is certainly from memory. This section is significant because of latter accusations of Wyclif having discounted the need for churches.

53. This sort of comment illustrates the attitude that led contemporary chroniclers to associate Wyclif with the Peasants' Revolt of 1381. Wyclif had no sympathy with the violence of that summer, but his condemnation of the uprising as a whole is anything but vigorous.

54. This also appears in *Sermones*, IV.39, p. 255.

55. This is a reference to Augustine's Letter 130 "To Proba," chap. 10.

56. This is odd, given that the passage begins "And when it was now noon, Elias jested with them." Perhaps this indicates Wyclif's desire to equate heresy with the Gentile enemies of Israel. By the late fourteenth century there was an increased tendency to equate demonic incantation with heresy. See Norman Cohn, *Europe's Inner Demons* (Chicago: University of Chicago Press, 1977).

57. John Chrysostom, *Opus Imperfectum*, Homily 23.

58. This is a technical philosophical term fundamental to Wyclif's understanding of the relation of God's eternal foreknowledge to created free action; for an articulation of this, see Lahey, *John Wyclif*, pp. 169–99.

59. *oracio = oris racio.*

60. Reference is to Aristotle, *On the Soul*, II.8, 420b5–21a6.

61. It was a medieval commonplace to refer to the Lord's Prayer as *exemplum* for human prayer, a model one ought to choose to follow but not necessarily a reality in which one's prayer participates. Wyclif's metaphysics intensifies the prayer's authority. Wyclif introduces the argument that something has a more powerful reality insofar as its being is more general

and more capable of being instantiated. This is a departure from the more ordinary understanding of the Lord's Prayer as a model prayer. See Corey Barnes, "Thomas Aquinas on Christ's Prayer," in *A History of Prayer: The First to the Fifteenth Century*, ed. Roy Hammerling (Leiden: Brill, 2008), pp. 319–36.

On the Lord's Prayer

62. From *De Oracione Dominica*, in *Opera Minora*, ed. J. Loserth (London: Wyclif Society, 1913), pp. 383–92. The sermon is on John 16:23, for the fifth Sunday after Easter, and is in *Sermones*, ed. J. Loserth (London: Trübner, 1887–90), vol. 1, pp. 192–99; the commentary in *Opus Evangelicum* II, chaps. 5–17, was edited for the Wyclif Society by Loserth. The *Postilla* has yet to be fully edited; brief selections appear as an Appendix to Gustav Benrath, *Wyclifs Bibelkommentar* (Berlin: De Gruyter, 1966).

63. This is not as contradictory as it appears. Wyclif's understanding of the relation of God's knowledge of the Elect is grounded in a nuanced description of necessity, allowing him to say that while God wills that all people be saved, God does not will that the foreknown, or those known to be going to be damned, be saved. See Ian C. Levy, "Grace and Freedom in the Soteriology of John Wyclif," *Traditio* 60 (2005), pp. 279–337.

64. The Earthquake Council was a council convened by Bishop William Courtenay of London in May 1382 to condemn specific positions taught by Wyclif; on May 21, the day the council convened to discuss the positions in question, an earthquake shook London.

65. *Theosebia* was commonly used to mean "worship due God alone" (from Augustine, *City of God*, Bk.10, c.1).

PART II

A Short Rule of Life

1. From Appendix B of Mary Raschko, "Common Ground for Contrasting Ideologies: The Texts and Contexts of A Schort Reule of Lif," *Viator* 40:1 (2009): 387–410, 407–10.

2. See Nicholas Watson, "Middle English Versions and Audiences of Edmund of Abingdon's *Speculum Religiosorum*," in *Texts and Traditions of Pastoral Care: Essays in Honour of Bella Millett*, ed. Cate Gunn and Catherine Innes-Parker (Woodbridge, UK: Boydell and Brewer/York Medieval Press, 2009), pp. 115–31. Fiona Somerset thanks Jennifer Arch

for generously sharing her unpublished work on the *Speculum Ecclesie* and for much useful discussion.

3. That is, in the three social statuses of priests, lords, and laborers. See Introduction, p. 21.

Five Questions on Love

4. From Thomas Arnold, *Select English Works of John Wyclif* (Oxford: Clarendon Press, 1871), vol. 3, pp. 183–85, compared with the single manuscript copy in Oxford, New College MS 95, fols. 123r–24r.

5. The single manuscript of this text is missing something here: there is a garbled phrase that does not make sense. This translation makes sense of what remains with minimal addition, in a way that is consistent with the source being translated (see item 3) and with statements about love elsewhere in Wycliffite writings.

6. See Introduction, pp. 21–22.

The Two Ways

7. Printed in V. J. Scattergood, "The Two Ways—An Unpublished Religious Treatise by Sir John Clanvowe," *English Philological Studies* 10 (1967): 33–56.

8. The epithet "the Prophet" was usually used by medieval writers to refer to the prophet David, but some of the texts we have translated here use the same term to refer to other prophetic writers.

9. The word *babel*, in Middle English, means in this context "a scourge with spiked balls on thongs," though it can also refer to a trinket. Here the author may be creating a play on words between the weapon and the trinket, suggesting that one is worth no more than the other.

10. The epithet "Wise Man" was used by medieval writers to refer to the author of the sapiential books of the Old Testament.

11. See Introduction, p. 15.

12. The original has "the *charity* of God."

13. The use of the word *bishop* in this context, to refer to the Jewish high priest, may raise some eyebrows; it was, however, not entirely idiosyncratic in late medieval England. For instance, in the N-Town cycle play of the marriage of Mary and Joseph, another Jewish priest is named *Episcopus*. See Stephen Spector, ed., *The N-Town Play: Cotton MS Vespasian D.8*, 2 vols. (EETS s.s. 11–12, 1991).

On Holy Prayers

14. From *Select English Works of John Wycliffe*, ed. Thomas Arnold (Oxford: Oxford University Press, 1869–71), vol. 3, pp. 219–29.

15. For further discussion, see the survey of Wycliffite views of the priesthood in J. Patrick Hornbeck II, *What Is a Lollard?* (Oxford: Oxford University Press, 2010), chap. 5.

16. Augustine, *Letter* 130 "To Proba" (see especially chap. 3).

17. For a similar account of the superiority of the Pater Noster over all other prayers, see the text *The Our Father* elsewhere in this volume.

18. None of the manuscripts of *On Holy Prayers* indicates which saint is being referred to in this passage, but Fiona Somerset has located its source in St. Edmund of Abingdon's *Speculum ecclesiae*. See Oxford, Bodleian Library MS 416, fol. 128v.

19. This sentiment, though not these exact words, may be found in Chrysostom's *Homily* 73 on the gospel of Matthew, quoting the same passage from Matthew as earlier in this paragraph.

20. Augustine, *Exposition on the Book of Psalms*, Psalm 147, 2.

21. We have been unable to locate the source of this citation from Gregory.

22. The author is using the phrase "pope's law" to refer to canon law, the law of the church.

23. Gratian, *Decretum*, part I, dist. 32, c. 6, "Non est audienda missa presbiteri, qui concubinam habet" (the mass of a priest who has a concubine is not to be heard).

24. *Decretum*, part I, dist. 81, c. 15, "Non ingrediantur ecclesias presbiteri, diaconi, subdiaconi, qui in fornicationis crimine iacent" (priests, deacons, and subdeacons who have fallen into the crime of fornication are not to enter churches).

25. See, for instance, 2 Samuel 15:23.

26. *Decretum*, part I, dist. 81, c. 16, "Offitio et beneficio privetur episcopus, presbiter, diaconus uxorem suscipiens, vel susceptam retinens" (a bishop, priest, or deacon who shall take a wife, or who, having taken one, keeps her, shall be deprived of office and benefice).

27. *Decretum*, part I, dist. 83, c. 1, "Suspendatur ab offitio, clericorum suorum fornicationi consentiens episcopus" (a bishop shall be suspended from his office if he consents to the fornication of his clerics). The Middle English text has *parische* for the word we have translated as "diocese," but since it is the bishop's sphere of authority being discussed, "diocese" seems the better rendering.

28. Quoted in Gratian, *Concordia discordantium canonum*, dist. LXXXIII, c. 2. We are grateful to Jennifer Illig for locating this reference.

29. Grosseteste compares sinful priests to the people of Sodom in *The Testament of the Twelve Patriarchs*, ed. Anthony Gilby (London: R. Feeny, 1837), p. 45.

30. What the author means by the phrase "by prayer or service" is not entirely clear. It is certain that he is condemning the sale of ecclesiastical offices, and it seems likely that he is also rejecting the practice of giving benefices as rewards to civil servants, but how it would be simony to obtain office by means of prayer is uncertain.

31. The binding and loosing of the beast in the biblical book of Revelation was a common eschatological trope for medieval authors, some of whom equated the thousand years the beast was bound with the peaceful millennium before Armageddon and the Last Judgment. See, for instance, Marjorie Reeves, *The Influence of Prophecy in the Later Middle Ages* (Oxford: Oxford University Press, 1969), p. 295.

32. Contrary to some earlier accounts, this passage suggests that it was not the existence of the clerical estate in and of itself to which this author, like many other Wycliffite writers, objected, but rather the failure of some clergymen to perform their duties well. For a more extensive discussion of Wycliffite views on the clergy, see Hornbeck, *What Is a Lollard?* chap. 5.

33. In this passage the author may be appealing to Paul's logic in 1 Corinthians 11:27–29, where the Apostle argues that those who receive the eucharist without "discerning the body of Christ" do so to their damnation.

34. Augustine, *Confessions*, X.33.

35. While not a direct quotation, this is the theme of Augustine's work *De opere monachorum* (*On the Work of Monks*).

36. Gregory, *Pastoral Rule*, I.5.

Of Wedded Men and Wives

37. From *Select English Works of John Wycliffe*, ed. Thomas Arnold (Oxford: Oxford University Press, 1869–71), vol. 3, pp. 183–85.

38. For doubts, see Anne Hudson, *The Premature Reformation: Wycliffite Texts and Lollard History* (Oxford: Clarendon Press, 1988), p. 425.

39. Shannon McSheffrey, *Gender and Heresy: Women and Men in Lollard Communities 1420–1530* (Philadelphia: University of Pennsylvania Press, 1995); and J. Patrick Hornbeck II, "Theologies of Sexuality in English 'Lollardy,'" *Journal of Ecclesiastical History* 60 (2009): 19–44.

40. This last sentence carries a different meaning in one manuscript of the tract, which has instead: "Paul also commands that bishops and priests teach wives to teach [*lerne*] their husbands to be prudent, chaste,

and sober; to take responsibility for the house; and to be gentle and submissive, or subject, to their husbands, so that the word of God is not blasphemed against."

41. This long paragraph is a close paraphrase of Ephesians 5:22—6:4.

The Our Father

42. From *The English Works of Wyclif Hitherto Unprinted*, ed. F. D. Matthew, rev. ed. (Early English Text Society 74, 1902), pp. 172–75.

43. For a useful introduction, see E. A. Jones, "Literature of Religious Instruction," in *A Companion to Medieval English Literature and Culture*, ed. Peter Brown (Malden, MA: Blackwell, 2007), pp. 1–5.

44. For a survey of works treating the Lord's Prayer in all three languages, see Vincent Gillespie, "Thy Will Be Done: *Piers Plowman* and the Pater Noster," in *Late Medieval Religious Texts and Their Transmission: Essays in Honour of A. I. Doyle*, ed. A. J. Minnis (Woodbridge: D. S. Brewer, 1994).

45. Morton W. Bloomfield, et al., *Incipits of Latin Works on the Virtues and Vices, 1100–1500 AD, Including a Section of Incipits of Works on the Pater Noster* (Cambridge, MA: Medieval Academy, 1979), pp. 567–686.

46. Anna Lewis, "Textual Borrowings, Theological Mobility, and the Lollard Pater Noster Commentary," *Philological Quarterly* 88 (2009): 1–23, traces many; for more, see Fiona Somerset, "Lollard Prayer," in *Feeling Like Saints* (forthcoming).

47. See, for example, Lewis, "Textual Borrowings, Theological Mobility, and the Lollard Pater Noster Commentary," p. 2.

48. For the quotation, see p. 198. On the Wycliffite understanding of prayer without ceasing, see above, p. 12.

49. Subsequent quotations from the Pater Noster also follow the text given in Matthew's gospel, with some emendations by the Wycliffite commentator.

50. In at least one manuscript of this tract, the words "and purgatory" are crossed out. While it is impossible to say with certainty, it is likely that the erasure occurred in or after the Reformation period, when the Church of England declared purgatory "a fond thing vainly invented."

51. The idea that even married people should regulate their sexual appetites appears in other Wycliffite texts, including some passages of the tract *Of Wedded Men and Wives* that do not appear in the excerpt printed here. For detailed discussion of Wycliffite theologies of marriage and sexuality, see Hornbeck, "Theologies of Sexuality in English 'Lollardy,'" pp. 1–26.

The Ten Commandments

52. From the single copy of this version of the text in London, British Library, Harley 2398, fols. 73r–106r, excerpting the prologue and the commentary on the first two commandments only, from fols. 73r–89v. Judith Jefferson's excellent thesis edition of the commentary in Harley 2398 and of a closely related version in three other manuscripts has been heavily consulted, as have its very thorough notes. Where we have learned from Jefferson's notes, ours are marked with JJ. We gratefully acknowledge Jefferson's permission to use her work and eagerly await her published edition of the whole.

53. For details see Jefferson, "Edition of Ten Commandments Commentaries," pp. xxxiii–xxxiv, cxli–clxxv.

54. Augustine, *Sermones de Scripturis*, Sermo 39 (*PL* 38.241); JJ.

55. Augustine, *De Civitate Dei* xx, c. 20 (*PL* 41.687ff); JJ.

56. Pseudo-Bernard, *Meditationes Piissimae de Cognitione Humanae Conditionis*, c.iii (*PL* 184.491.C); JJ.

57. For example, see Augustine, *De Civitate Dei* xiii, c. 10 (*PL* 41.383); Bernard, *Sermones de Tempore*, Sermo xvii (*PL* 183.250); JJ.

58. Not traced.

59. Augustine, Homily 9 on the first epistle of John, chap. 4.

60. Augustine, *Exposition on the Book of Psalms*, Psalm 62, chap. 13.

61. Augustine, source not traced.

62. Pseudo-Chrysostom, *Opus Imperfectum in Matthaeum*, sermon 37 PG 56:835.

63. All but the comparison with a fish in a trap here also comes from Pseudo-Chrysostom's sermon 37, PG 56:835.

64. Bernard, *Dominica VI Post Pentecosten*, sermo 3, part 5, abridged. *PL* 183.343B; JJ, corrected.

65. Probably not Gregory; see *De conflictu vitiorum et virtutum* chap. 2, *PL* 40.1093. The authorship of this work is unknown.

66. For the whole of this paragraph and the two paragraphs that follow, see Gratian, *Decretum* 2 C. 26 q 7 c 15–16; JJ. The attributions to Augustine also appear in the *Decretum* but appear to be spurious.

67. Not traced.

68. Cf. Wycliffite Bible Ps 95:5 for the translation "fiends."

69. Bede, *On the Temple of Solomon*, chap. 19, *PL* 91.790C–91C. This passage draws its quotation of Bede from the abridged version in Wyclif, *De Mandatis*, pp. 159–60; see the translation of this passage in this volume, pp. 109–10.

70. The "great clerk" here is Wyclif, and this whole paragraph draws on and paraphrases *De Mandatis*, p. 156; see the translation in this volume, p. 108.

71. Gregory, Letter 13, in *Epistolarum Libri Quatuordecim* 11, *PL* 77.1128; JJ.
72. Actually, from the same letter; JJ.
73. Robert Holkot, *Commentary on Wisdom*, chap. 12 lection 157B; JJ.
74. Augustine, *Exposition on the Book of Psalms,* Psalm 96 [modern number 97], chap. 12 *PL* 37.1245; JJ.
75. Pseudo-Bernard, *Tractatus de Interiori Domu*, chaps. 38–9, sections 79–80 *PL* 184.546D–47D; JJ.
76. Pseudo-Bernard, *Tractatus de Interiori Domu*, chaps. 38–9, sections 79–80 *PL* 184.546D–47D; JJ.
77. Pseudo-Chrysostom, *Opus Imperfectum in Matthaeum*, homily 35, final sentence, *PG* 56.832; JJ.
78. Pseudo-Clement, *Recognitiones*, book 5 chap. 23, *PG* 1.1341B; JJ.
79. Pseudo-Clement, *Recognitiones*, book 5 chap. 23, *PG* 1.1341B; JJ.
80. Pseudo-Clement, *Recognitiones*, book 5 chap. 23, *PG* 1.1341B; JJ. Similar comparisons between images in churches and living human beings are made in the records of the trials of Margery Baxter (item 24) and Margery Jopson (item 25) below.
81. See, for example, Ps 115:4–7; 135:15–18; Isa 44:9; 46:5–7; Hab 2:18.
82. See, for example, Wyclif, *De Mandatis*, p. 168.
83. Wyclif, *De Mandatis* p. 168.
84. See, for example, Jer 3:6–10, Ezek 16:17, Hos 4:12.
85. Grosseteste, *De Decem Mandatis*, p. 18, quoted in Wyclif, *De Mandatis*, p. 168.
86. Pseudo-Chrysostom, *Opus Imperfectum*, homily 42 *PG* 56.873, quoted and truncated in the same way in Wyclif, *De Mandatis*, p. 169.
87. Wyclif, *De Mandatis*, p. 184. Wyclif is probably the author's source, but Wyclif here draws on an extensive tradition and is probably citing Stephen Langton (see Peter D. Clarke, "Peter the Chanter, Innocent III, and Theological Views on Collective Guilt and Punishment," *The Journal of Ecclesiastical History* 52 [2001]: pp. 4–6).
88. Cf. Wyclif, *De Mandatis*, p. 96; JJ.
89. Wyclif, *De Mandatis*, p. 96.
90. Wyclif, *De Mandatis*, pp. 82, 98–99; JJ.
91. Cf. Wyclif, *De Mandatis*, p. 200; JJ.
92. Wyclif, *De Mandatis*, p. 187, quoting Grosseteste.
93. Augustine, Homily 9 on the first epistle of John, chap. 4.
94. See, for example, Genesis 22:16, Isaiah 45:23, Jeremiah 49:13, Amos 6:8, John 3:3, Galatians 1:20, 2 Corinthians 11:31, Romans 1:9. See also Wyclif, *De Mandatis,* pp. 194–96.

95. The argument laid out in this paragraph resembles Wyclif, *De Mandatis*, pp. 187–88.

96. Augustine, *De Trinitate* book 11 chap. 10 part 18, *PL* 42:983–84. The Bernard reference is probably to the previously quoted Pseudo-Bernard, *Tractatus de Interiori Domu*, chaps. 38–9, sections 79–80 *PL* 184.546D–47D.

97. See Introduction, pp. 21–22.

Sermon 57

98. Sermon 57, or Sermon 3 for the day of an apostle, Commune Sanctorum cycle, English Wycliffite Sermons. From Anne Hudson and Pamela Gradon, eds., *English Wycliffite Sermons*, 5 vols. (Oxford: Oxford University Press, 1983–96), vol. 2, pp. 11–15.

99. Augustine *PL* 35 col 1853.

100. On Wycliffite ideas about predestination, see Introduction, pp. 19–20.

Commentary on Psalm 87

101. Commentary on Psalm 87, excerpted from the longest of the three versions of Rolle's commentary on the psalter interpolated by Wycliffites (known as RV3). Drawn, with grateful acknowledgment, from Anne Hudson's transcription of the text at it appears in the single copy in London, Lambeth Palace Library MS 34, ff. 183v–87, and compared with the manuscript.

102. Fiona Somerset thanks Michael Kuczynski for supplying an excerpt including the text and glosses for Psalm 87 from the edition of Bodley 554 he is preparing.

103. Like some other selections in this volume, this text's method of providing biblical evidence is somewhat unusual among lollard writings. It quotes the whole of the biblical passage it is citing in Latin, and then translates it into Middle English and interprets it. Often, as is commonly the case in lollard writings, the translations are interpolated and the interpretations are tendentious. In this volume we supply a translation of the Vulgate derived from Douai-Rheims in place of the author's Latin quotation, and then a translation into modern English of the lollard writer's translation.

104. Traditionally, the "reproofs of the cross" are Christ's admonitions that the observers should not be afraid.

105. For measured reassessments of Wycliffite views of the papacy, which have sometimes been characterized as more extreme than what is presented here, see Ian Christopher Levy, "John Wyclif and the Primitive

Papacy," *Viator* 38 (2007), 159–89; and J. Patrick Hornbeck II, "Of Captains and Antichrists: The Papacy in Wycliffite Thought," *Revue d'histoire ecclésiastique* 103 (2008), 806–38.

106. In interpreting the psalm verse under discussion, the author has inverted its two phrases, simplified the new first verse, and substituted "holy church" for "you" within it.

The Seven Works of Mercy

107. From Dublin, Trinity College MS 245 fols. 218r–v. Collation with the copies in Cambridge University Library MS Nn.4.12 fols. 37v–39r, and Leeds, Brotherton MS 501 fols. 81r–v, and that in *Book to a Mother*, ed. A. J. McCarthy, Salzburg Studies in English Literature 92, Studies in English Mystics 1 (Salzburg: Institut für Anglistik und Amerikanistik, 1981), pp. 5–7, reveals that the CUL copy and *Book to a Mother* agree against BC 501 and TCD 245 seventeen times. BC contains five unique readings, *Book to a Mother* twenty-two, and TCD 245 forty-seven. These data suggest that the CUL copy and *Book to a Mother* either derive from a common source or are adapted one from the other, while BC 501 adapts the content of a similar text, and TCD 245 makes many systematic changes to a version more similar to BC 501's than CUL's. Variation will not be traced in detail here, for this is not a critical edition.

108. McCarthy, *Book to a Mother*.

109. Here the copy in TCD 245 breaks off. The final section is supplied from BC 501.

A Form of Confession

110. From Bodley 789, fols. 105r–108v, collated with the other extant copy in Oxford, Bodleian Library MS Rawlinson C 699, fols. 88v–92r. Assistance from Michael Cornett, who brought this text to our attention and generously allowed us access to his images and transcriptions, is gratefully acknowledged.

111. Fiona Somerset thanks Michael Cornett for highly informative discussion of the characteristics of the genre.

112. Augustine's painstaking elaboration of how the trinity of understanding, will, and memory creates an image of God in man, pointing the way to how man is to love God, is frequently cited in medieval writings, often imprecisely. For a very full version see *On the Trinity* Bk.10, c.11 and 12; Bk.14, c.14, and Bk.15, c.21–24.

113. This highly condensed commentary on the commandments in many ways echoes the themes of item 12, *The Ten Commandments*. For its

biblical bases, see Romans 13:8–10; Matthew 22:37–40; Exodus 20:1–17; Deuteronomy 5:6–21.

114. Psalm 11:5, but compare with the Wycliffite Bible Psalm 10:6 for this version.

115. The distinction here is between the corporeal wits of the body and the spiritual wits of the soul.

116. While the following passage begins with references to seeing and hearing Christ, what follows is derived from item 18 or a text very much like it, and similarly relies on Matthew 25:34–36.

117. Yet this does not seem to be Augustine's final position. See *Letter* 167 to Jerome. For explanation, see Aquinas, ST Ia IIae Q. 73, a. 1.

118. Augustine, *Confessions*, VIII.5.10.

119. Cf. Wycliffite Bible Psalm 24:17.

120. The Rawlinson copy here reads "spiritual wits." While in general the Rawlinson copy seems inferior and derivative, here "spiritual wits" refers to the "five wits that live on with the soul after the death of the body" mentioned earlier and fits better with the reference to Christ's words that follows. If the discussion of the seven works was derived from a text something like item 15 in order to be incorporated into a form of confession drawn from some other model, then the Bodley 789 copy's "spiritual works" were quite likely substituted for a reference to "spiritual wits" in an earlier form of the text.

121. Matt 11:15, 13:9, 13:43; Mark 4:9, 4:23; Luke 8:8, 14:35. See also Rev 2:7, 2:11, 3:6, 3:13, and 13:9.

A Dialogue between a Wise Man and a Fool

122. From the unique copy in Cambridge University Library MS Ii 6 26, fols. 58v–65r. Mary Dove includes this dialogue, along with item 18, in her *Earliest Advocates* volume; we were unable to consult with her on this item, as we did on item 18, owing to her untimely death. However, her finished edition was consulted during final revisions of the present volume, and one of her emendations has been incorporated, as noted. The annotations of this version and Dove's version were composed independently and differ on several points.

123. Not traced, but see the Catena Aurea on Luke 6:25; this may be a paraphrase of the statement there attributed to Bede. In comparison with other Wycliffite writings, an unusually large number of quotations in this text are difficult to trace because they are paraphrased or misattributed.

124. Not traced, but see the Catena Aurea on Matthew 12:36.

125. Not traced, but similar to *Moralia in Job: PL* 76, col. 0042C.

126. Any of Augustine's writings against heresy might be intended, but the author may be thinking especially of "To Consentius: Against Lying."

127. That is, hanged.

128. See Esther 3–7 for this episode.

129. Matt 26:14–16, 47–50; Mark 14:10, 43–45; Luke 22:3–6, 47–48; John 13:22–30, 18:2–5.

130. For the blaspheming thief, see Luke 23:39.

131. These three injunctions are an interpretative paraphrase of Matthew 11:29; "take my example" may also recall 1 Corinthians 1:11.

132. The word *hate* is drawn from the first phrase of Matthew 5:44 and substituted here for *slander*.

133. The Wise Man moves from anticipating the Fool's objections indirectly, as on p. XXX, to rehearsing them at length in direct discourse, as here. The Fool will finally speak up for himself on pp. 248, 253.

134. Luke 14:26–27; and see Luke 14:33; Mark 8:34, 29:30; and Matt 19:29, 16:24, 10:38.

135. Matt 19:29; Mark 10:29–30; Luke 18:29–30; see also Luke 9:24.

136. Cf. Wycliffite Bible, Psalm 115:4.

137. Not traced.

138. Lebeus is very probably Libeaus Desconus, the "Fair Unknown," later in his romance named as Gingalain, a son of king Arthur's knight Gawain. (Thanks to Nicola McDonald for her expert opinion here.) Each of the heroes named features in romances (or in the case of Robin Hood, ballads) set in England and extant in Middle English versions. All have older roots: the first three have Anglo-Norman sources, while the name "Robin Hood" is found in thirteenth-century English legal records.

139. In the Vulgate numbering of the psalms, this is Psalm 5:7.

140. Not traced.

141. Wisdom 16:20 seems the closest quotation, yet this author typically attributes Wisdom to Solomon; see also Psalm 78:24.

142. Sir 15:3.

143. Not traced.

144. Here again the Wise Man anticipates and reports the Fool's reply rather than allowing him to speak for himself.

145. Cf. Matt 7:20.

146. Through a copying error, some text has evidently been omitted at this point. Where we would expect "the teeth of children to be set on edge," the sentence is unfinished. The following complete sentence is preceded by the word "sin"; this has been omitted here, since the sense cannot be reconstructed.

147. "Enclose his mind in" is an unusual rendering of "meditate."

148. Not traced.

149. Not traced.

150. Not traced.

151. This quotation is drawn from the *Office of the Dead*, resp. 7. Cf. Job 26:6.

152. This statement might be viewed as a loose summary of the earlier chapters of Philippians.

153. Not traced.

154. For a similarly literal translation of the Vulgate's "mors peccatorum pessima" (Ps 33:22 in the Vulgate's numbering), see the Wycliffite Bible.

155. For this translation, see the Wycliffite Bible.

156. This proverbial phrase also appears in the priest's dismissive translation of the pardon Piers receives from Truth in *Piers Plowman* B 7.112/C 9.290.

157. Use of "go blackberrying" to mean "go to hell" occurs elsewhere in written sources only in the prologue to Chaucer's *Pardoner's Tale*, but it may have been a common expression.

158. Perhaps Job 24:19.

159. Matt 8:12; 13:42; 50, 22:13; 24:51; 25:30; Luke 13:28. Some text has been omitted here by the copyist. I omit the fragmentary "bi...witke and palpable" from my modernization; it evidently refers to the kind of darkness that fell on the Pharaoh, but unless another copy of this text is found, it adds nothing to our understanding.

160. Perhaps Rev 18.

161. Twelfth day is the feast of Epiphany.

162. The emphasis on sight as a metaphor for faith here may recall Luke 2:29–32, Simeon's greeting to Christ, and the second line of the *Nunc Dimittis*, the canticle that in the liturgy forms part of Compline or Evensong.

163. I adopt Mary Dove's emendation here; the text is clearly corrupt, and "forget you" makes more sense than an oddly spelled "follow you."

164. The decision in exposition of Luke 14:13 to treat "poor" as an adjective attached to the blind, feeble, and lame alike, rather than as a separate category preceding them, was highly controversial among controversies over mendicant poverty. Many Wycliffite writings give this reading, and in doing so they draw on Richard Fitzralph's battle with the friars in the mid-fourteenth century. For details see Margaret Aston, "Caim's Castles," in *Faith and Fire: Popular and Unpopular Religion, 1350–1600* (London: Hambledon Press, 1993), pp. 103 and 125.

165. The next phrase in the manuscript is garbled through incomplete

copying: "and yueþ... lyuereþ" is omitted here since the sense cannot be reconstructed.

A Commendation of Holy Writ

166. From the unique copy in Cambridge University Library Ii 6 26. Mary Dove's kindness in sending a draft copy of her edition of this text is gratefully acknowledged.

167. For these details, see *The Middle English* Mirror: *Sermons from Advent to Sexagesima*, ed. Thomas G. Duncan and Margaret Connolly, Middle English Texts vol. 34 (Heidelberg: Universitätsverlag, 2003), pp. x–xxviii. See also Nicholas Watson, "Lollardy: The Anglo-Norman Heresy?" in *Language and Culture in Medieval Britain: The French of England, c. 1100–c. 1500*, ed. Jocelyn Wogan-Browne (Woodbridge: Boydell and Brewer/York Medieval Press, 2009), pp. 334–46.

168. The syntax here deliberately blurs lay and clerical status and so has been retained even though it is confusing. The key assertion is that knights as well as priests might legitimately correct both laymen and priests.

169. That is, to those who are in the muck.

170. The bodily works of mercy were those enjoined in Matthew 25:31–46, with the addition of burial of the dead; cf. item 15, *The Seven Works of Mercy*.

171. Quoted in Latin only.

172. This seems to be a conflation of 1 Corinthians 16:13 and 22.

173. Mark 16:17–18, reordered.

174. Why this quotation is attributed to Gregory rather than Solomon, the usual attribution for the sapiential books, is unclear.

175. For this translation see Psalm 83:7 in the Douai-Rheims version.

The Lantern of Light

176. From *The Lanterne of Liȝt*, ed. L. M. Swinburn (Early English Text Society 151, 1917) (excerpting pp. 43–47, 76–80).

177. An attentive, sympathetic reading of the text appears in Nicholas Watson, "Vernacular Apocalyptic: On the *Lanterne of Liȝt*," *Revista canaria de estudios ingleses* 47 (2003).

178. *The Lanterne of Lyght* is STC 15225. On this printed book and the early print history of lollard writings more generally, see Anne Hudson, "No Newe Thyng," in *Lollards and Their Books* (London: Hambledon Press, 1985), pp. 227–48; and Anne Hudson, *The Premature Reformation:*

Wycliffite Texts and Lollard History (Oxford: Clarendon Press, 1988), pp. 483–94.

179. See above, p. 9.

180. Like the *Commentary on Psalm 87* (item 14), the *Lantern of Light* quotes the whole of the biblical passage it is citing in Latin, then translates it into Middle English and interprets it. See above, pp. 52–53, 55, for an explanation of our editorial practices.

181. "Man's law" for Wycliffites contrasts with God's law or Christ's law; it refers to any law instituted by humankind and implies that this law is not congruent with God's law but a superfluous addition.

182. That is, vibrant and lively.

183. The first example given in the verse, asking for bread, is elided.

184. Not in the published works of Chrysostom, but this comparison is attributed to Augustine in the *Catena Aurea*, and to Bede in the *Glossa Ordinaria*.

185. That is, the evil part of the church on earth, its cursed members who, as the previous paragraph explained, are intent on poisoning the people in misbelief.

186. Matthew 5:11, continuing into verse 12 in the English translation that follows.

187. John 16:20, with the last phrase coming from the end of John 16:22.

188. Gregory the Great, *Moralia in Job*, PL 76, cols. 279–80. The Latin quotation in the text is substantially modified, perhaps because it is being reconstructed through memory. My translation, here and in the following two notes.

189. Again, this is substantially modified; the reference is perhaps to book 26 section 64, PL 76, col. 387B.

190. Again, modified: book 15 section 58, PL 75, col. 1111B.

191. Chrysostom, homily 3, in Opera, ed. Sigismund Gelenius (Basel, 1547), vol. 2, col. 763.

192. The Middle English adjective *kindness* has a wider range of meaning than ours. It implies behavior in accordance with our best nature, and that our actions may be prompted by or rewarded with gratitude or recompense in turn, as well as the modern sense of generous, friendly conduct.

The City of Saints

193. From the unique copy in Oxford, Bodleian Library MS Laud Misc 23, fols. 61r–70r.

194. See Margaret Connolly, "Books for the 'helpe of euery persoone

þat þenkiþ to be saued': Six Devotional Anthologies from Fifteenth-Century London," *Yearbook of English Studies* 33 (2003): 170–81.

195. See Stephen Kelly and Ryan Perry, "Devotional Cosmopolitanism in Fifteenth Century England," in *After Arundel*, ed. Vincent Gillespie (Turnhout: Brepols, 2012), pp. 363–80.

196. Exceptions would be Chaucer's "Epilogue" to the "Man of Law's Tale" and John Audelay's "Marcol and Solomon," in Poems and Carolcs (Oxford, Bodleian Library MS Douce 302), ed. Susanna Fein (Kalamazoo, MI: Medieval Institute Publications, 2009), each of which presents the complaint in a voice clearly not the author's own. Examples in this volume include *The Two Ways* and *A Dialogue between a Wise Man and a Fool*.

197. See also above, pp. 74, 77, 86, 89, 112, 183.

198. As is the case in the *Lantern of Light*, this text reproduces most quotations in Latin, in most cases following with an English translation. This verse is quoted only in Latin.

199. Augustine discusses the numbers of the saved and the damned in his *Homilies on the Gospels*, 61. However he does not discuss Luke's "little flock." Typically the statement given here is attributed to Bede; see, for example, his *Exposition on the Gospel of Luke*, PL 92, col. 494. But it also appears in the *Catena Aurea*.

200. Not traced.

201. The Latin version given in the manuscript is "Maior horum est caritas," and in translating this verse the author translates "maior" as "mayor" (this is, after all, the etymology of "mayor") and personifies Charity. See above, pp. 39, 54, for a discussion of the relationship of *caritas* and *amor* in Wyclif's and Wycliffite writing.

202. Pseudo-Abdias, *Historia apostolica*, in J. A. Giles, ed., *Codex Apocryphus Novi Testamenti* (London, 1852), pp. 410–21.

203. Pseudo-Chrysostom, *Opus Imperfectum*, homily 12, PG 56, col. 698.

204. Middle English "lechery" includes adultery alongside any form of what was considered lascivious sexual behavior, and even, by extension, any form of self-indulgence more generally.

205. Translation modified from Douai-Rheims.

206. "Against your neighbor" is here understood as "against your fellow Christians."

207. The author subdivides what is given in both biblical books as a single list and interprets and summarizes its contents slightly.

208. Not traced.

209. This exposition is quoted in Latin; the source is not yet found. My translation.

210. The verb *vigilare*, used in the biblical verse, was often taken to imply staying awake at night and keeping watch. Hence the translation "awake" here.

211. Jacobus de Voragine, *The Golden Legend (Aurea Legenda)*, vol. 6, legend of St. Cecilia. Cf. Rom 13:12. This translation is taken from Caxton's *Golden Legend* in the *Medieval Sourcebook*, available on the Fordham.edu website.

212. Luke is missing from what was probably originally a list of the four evangelists and their standard iconography. Assigning one of the four senses of scripture to each evangelist is more unusual, though.

213. The last is apparently an obsolete term for a yellow alloy, or fake gold (*Middle English Dictionary*, s.v. "alkamie," n. 3).

214. The chronology here is rather obscure, and obscure to the scribe copying it as well, for the temple's third building has had to be reinstated after it had been eliminated, presumably because the scribe inadvertently skipped ahead to a later repetition of the same word in copying the text ("eyeskip").

215. *Ypocrite volunt esse humiles sine despectu, pauperes sine defectu, bene vestiti sine solicitudine, delicate pasci sine labore, aliis adulantes, alii inuidentes, aliis detrahentes, mordaces ut canes, dolosi ut wulpes, superbi ut leones.* See also *The Middle English Translation of the Rosarium*, ed. Christina von Nolcken, Middle English Texts 10 (Heidelberg, 1979), p. 103, lines 12–19 and n., for other quotations in lollard works of this untraced passage.

216. Gregory the Great, *Moralia in Job*, *PL* 75, col. 676D.

217. Not traced.

218. Cf. Matt 22:37; Mark 12:33; Deut 6:5.

A Dialogue between Jon and Richard

219. From *Four Wycliffite Dialogues*, ed. Fiona Somerset, Early English Text Society 333 (Oxford: Oxford University Press, 2009), pp. 1–6, 12–15.

220. Robert Grosseteste, *Dicta*, 135, available on the grosseteste.com website.

221. Like the word *sophomore*, the word *sophist* in late medieval English both describes an academic rank (a university student who has finished the first stage of his study in arts) and has pejorative connotations; especially in vernacular writing, a sophist is preoccupied with pointless technicalities and ignores common sense.

222. Bede, *Commentary on the Pentateuch*, compares lepers and heretics: *PL* 91, cols. 346–48.

223. The eight perils are the source of Christ's eight condemnations, or eight woes: see Matt 23:13–23.

224. Judas forms the plan of betraying Christ for thirty pieces of silver in Matthew 26:14–16, and in Matthew 26:24 Christ comments on Judas's woeful fate, though he does not curse or condemn him. See also Mark 14:10–11, 21; Luke 22:3–6, 22.

225. 1 John 3:10–15 argues that ill will toward another is tantamount to manslaughter.

Sermons from Sidney Sussex 74

226. Two excerpts from the unique copy of a sermon cycle in Cambridge, Sidney Sussex 74 fols. 54v–56r and 118v–119r.

227. Fiona Somerset, *Feeling Like Saints* (forthcoming), chap. 1.

228. On Wycliffite attitudes to excommunication and their relationship to contemporary practice, see Ian Forrest, "William Swinderby and the Wycliffite Attitude to Excommunication," *Journal of Ecclesiastical History* 60 (2009): 246–69.

229. See A. S. McGrade, "Somersaulting Sovereignty: A Note on Reciprocal Lordship and Servitude in Wyclif," in *The Church and Sovereignty 590–1918: Essays in Honour of Michael Wilks*, ed. Diana Wood, *Studies in Church History, Subsidia* 9 (Oxford: Blackwell, 1999), pp. 261–68; see also p. 22 above.

230. As is the case with the *Lantern of Light* (item 19) and *The City of Saints* (item 20), these sermons commonly quote in Latin before translating into Middle English.

231. This legal maxim may be traced to the *Liber sextus*, VI 5.12.43, but is cited frequently without attribution. It is used in argument in the polemical Wycliffite "The Church and Her Members" in *Select English Works of John Wycliffe*, ed. Thomas Arnold (Oxford: Oxford University Press, 1869–71), vol. 3, p. 349; and cited in *Mum and the Sothsegger*, in *The Piers Plowman Tradition*, ed. Helen Barr (London: J. M. Dent, 1993), line 745.

232. What the author adds to Paul, by means of the quotation from the *Liber sextus*, is a tacit expansion of the definition of consent to include not only verbal acquiescence but any failure to speak out against wrongdoers. He heightens the impression that the two quotations are part of the same idea by quoting both, then translating them together. This was not a new association: Ambrose had glossed Romans 1:32 by explaining that either silence or praise is a form of consent, and he was cited by Peter Lombard, in the *Glossa ordinaria*, and by a whole string of canonists. (Peter D. Clarke, *The Interdict in the Thirteenth Century: A Question of Collective Guilt* [Oxford: Oxford University Press, 2007], p. 29.)

233. This is an antiphon from the Matins of Pentecost. Also quoted in *Piers Plowman* (see B.12.286 and C.14.208).

234. "Lyer" in this sentence is very probably an error for "fyer."

235. No translation of the Latin is provided.

236. The text says "mede," or "reward," giving the sense "then you would have the greatest reward, to help . . . " Since the argument is based on need, not reward, and since the syntax with "mede" is awkward, this is likely a scribal error—though a revealing one.

237. Gregory the Great, *Forty Gospel Homilies*, homily 7, *PL* 76, col. 1100C. My translation.

238. The first half of the verse is quoted in what appears to be an alternative Latin version, but the sense is similar. While the quotation is actually from 1 Peter, Paul does discuss obedience to rulers, though not in the same terms (see Rom 13:1–7). Note that this quotation is not translated in the text but quoted only in Latin.

239. Cf. Mark 14:36; John 5:30. No translation of the Latin is provided in the text.

240. No translation of the Latin quotation is provided.

The Sermon of Dead Men

241. From "The Sermon of Dead Men," in *Lollard Sermons*, ed. Gloria Cigman, Early English Text Society 294 (Oxford: Oxford University Press, 1989), lines 11–84, 157–486; checked against Oxford, Bodleian Library MS Rawlinson c.751.

242. Cigman, *Lollard Sermons*.

243. Bernard of Clairvaux, *Meditationes de cognitione humanae conditionis*, II, *PL* 184, col. 487D.

244. This quotation is not to be found in Proverbs; it does, however, have some affinities with Sirach 41:5.

245. Like the text "The Pater Noster" printed above, this sermon appears here and in the next two paragraphs to endorse a version of the doctrine of purgatory: those who die without having done penance for their sins will deserve and experience "pains" and "punishments." It is worth noting that many early accounts of Wycliffite theologies of salvation suggest that most Wycliffites were predestinarians who would have denied the doctrine of purgatory. On this point generally, see J. Patrick Hornbeck II, *What Is a Lollard? Dissent and Belief in Late Medieval England* (Oxford: Oxford University Press, 2010), chap. 2; and on the collection of sermons from which this excerpt has been taken, see idem, "*Lollard* Sermons? Soteriology and Late-Medieval Dissent," *Notes and Queries* 53 (2006): 26–30.

246. Aristotle, *Physica*, vii.5; this text was likely mediated through one of two Latin florilegia identified by this sermon's first editor (see Cigman, *Lollard Sermons*, p. 265).

247. The text *Memorare novissima tua* (literally, "Remember your last things") the preacher has taken from Sirach 7:40, but its appearance here in a list of commonly used prayers is unusual. In its original context it is not a prayer but rather an imperative.

248. Bernard of Clairvaux, *Letter* 162, *PL* 182, col. 621A.

249. This citation of Ecclesiastes serves as a bookend to the section of the sermon that began with the author's first citation of Ecclesiastes two paragraphs earlier.

250. Neither we nor the previous editor of this sermon have been able to locate the source of this quotation.

251. St. Martin of Tours is referred to as *gemma sacerdotum*, "the jewel of priests," in the third nocturn of Matins on his feast day, November 11 (see the breviary.net website).

252. This unknown doctor is the author of the *Speculum peccatoris*, a text attributed without certainty to Augustine of Hippo in *PL* 40, col 990.

253. The phrase "and overcome him" is missing from the printed edition but present in Rawlinson c.751, fol. 8v. We are grateful to Jennifer Illig for noticing this omission in the printed edition.

PART III

Heresy Trials in Norwich Diocese, 1428–31

1. From the records of the anti-heresy prosecutions of Bishop William Alnwick of Norwich, 1428–31, in *Heresy Trials in the Diocese of Norwich, 1428–1431*, ed. Norman P. Tanner (London: Royal Historical Society, 1977).

2. Though the examining official here was William Alnwick, bishop of Norwich, the text refers to him as "reverend father" (*reverendus pater*) or even simply "father."

3. This article is strikingly reminiscent of another use of apocalyptic metaphor by an English heresy suspect, that which can be found in the case of Thomas Bikenore, who during his trial before Bishop William Aiscough of Salisbury abjured the claim that the pope is antichrist, like the head of a dragon whose body is the episcopate and whose tail is the monastic and fraternal orders (Salisbury, Diocesan Registry, Register of William Aiscough, fol. 53r). Bishop Aiscough may have been the same "William

Ascogh" present for many of the heresy trials in Norwich, including those of Margery Baxter and John Kynget printed here.

4. Literally, "on the days of the four times." The Ember Days were kept four times each year, in the first week of Lent, in the week following Pentecost, in September preceding Michaelmas, and in December. A contemporary explanation of the Ember Days is found in *The Golden Legend*, available on the Fordham.edu website.

5. An "indented" or "indentured" document was a medieval form of carbon-copy paper; a document was copied several times, in this case twice, so that one copy could remain with the bishop and his officials, and the other be given to the defendant.

6. Though the record is fragmentary, it seems likely from this sentence that Bishop Alnwick assigned Godesell a penance related to at least one of the propositions he abjured. Some other medieval English bishops did likewise; see (among only a few scholarly treatments of penances in English heresy trials) Norman Tanner, "Penances Imposed on Kentish Lollards by Archbishop Warham, 1511–12," in *Lollardy and Gentry in the Later Middle Ages*, ed. Margaret Aston and Colin Richmond (New York: St. Martin's Press, 1997), 229–49.

7. Even though William White is here being referred to as "sir," he was not a knight; the honorific *dominus* was commonly used in the Middle Ages for ecclesiastics as well as knights. Our choice to use a smaller-case *s* in sir reflects this usage.

8. In several places in these records, the scribe notes the defendants' words in Middle English; where this happens, as in this sentence, the original text will appear in the notes: *of stokes and stones and ded mennes bones*. Future instances of this phenomenon will be introduced by the abbreviation "MidE."

9. There is quite a substantial gap in time between the proceedings against Margery in October 1428 and these depositions, dated April 1429. Whether these depositions arose in the course of other investigations, whether the witnesses had denounced Margery to the bishop and his officials, or whether the bishop procured them in order to charge Margery with relapse into heresy cannot be divined from the records.

10. MidE: *dame, bewar of the bee, for every bee wil styngge, and therfor loke that ʒe swer nother be Godd ne be Our Ladi ne be non other seynt, and if ʒe do the contrarie the be will styngge your tunge and veneme your sowle.*

11. MidE: *lewed wrightes of stokes hewe and fourme such crosses and ymages, and after that lewed peyntours glorye thaym with colours.*

12. MidE: *that cursed Thomma of Canterbury, for thay falsly and cursedly desseyve the puple with thair false mawmentryes and lawes.*

13. The pun here is on the shrine of Our Lady of Walsingham, a major medieval English pilgrimage site.

14. The word we have translated here as *pastor* could also mean "shepherd," in the ordinary sense of one who tends sheep, but is more likely that Agnes Bethom reported this statement, as in her testimony as a whole, as an anticlerical remark of Baxter's.

15. MidE: *bakon.*

Heresy Trials in Winchester Diocese, 1511–13

16. Newly edited and translated from Winchester, Hampshire Record Office MS 21M65/A1-19, fos. 69r–76v.

17. For detailed discussion of these trials, see J. Patrick Hornbeck II, "*Wycklyffes Wycket* and Eucharistic Theology: Two Series of Cases from Sixteenth-Century Winchester," in *Wycliffite Controversies,* ed. Mishtooni Bose and J. Patrick Hornbeck II (Turnhout: Brepols, 2011), 279–94.

18. For one suggestion as to the identity of this "book called Wiclif," as well as more detailed discussion of these trials, see Hornbeck, "*Wycklyffes Wycket* and Eucharistic Theology."

19. Spiritually ill, i.e., in a state of mortal sin.

20. The long formulaic apology and request for absolution that appears above in the trial of Anne Wattes recurs almost verbatim in each of the subsequent trials; due to the demands of space, we have abbreviated it in the record of this and each of the trials that follow.

21. This article contains something of a tension in meaning. It seems, on the surface, that there is a contradiction between Winter's not receiving the sacrament and yet receiving it "contrary to my spiritual father's injunction." This may best be explained by hypothesizing that Winter's spiritual director had urged him not to receive the Eucharist while he had doubts about transubstantiation, yet he received it anyway after a period of abstaining from the sacrament.

INDEX

Abell, Thomas, 52
Agápe, 39
Aiscough, William (bishop), 49
Alexander (pope), 187
Alnwick, William (bishop),
    50–51, 322, 323, 326–27,
    329
Anselm, Saint, 94, 106
Antichrist, 71, 72, 152, 153,
    161–62, 190, 252, 269; pope
    as, 321, 324
Aquinas, Thomas. *See* Thomas
    Aquinas, Saint
Aristotle, 94, 142; friendship,
    69–70; happiness, 97; heart,
    117, 120–21; virtues, 103
Arundel, Thomas (archbishop),
    29
Ascogh, William, 336–38
Augustine, Saint, 36, 37, 88, 91,
    102, 143, 147, 212, 224, 249,
    254, 256, 278; Christ's
    choice to become man, 67;
    commandments, 205–6;
    contemplation, 191; death,
    132, 200–203, 257, 313;
    "Egyptians," 212; fear and
    love, 206–7, 222; gluttony,
    186; idolatry, 216; Lord's
    Prayer, 152; moral virtues,
    103; necessity of ideas, 93;
    prayer, 122, 138–39, 152,
    183, 190; predestination, 32;

scripture, 23; sin, 152, 188,
    246
Augustinians, 35
Avarice, 154
Averroes, 68
Aylmer, Robert, 325

"Bad luck days," 212
Baptism, 208, 323, 332; as
    idolatry, 25
Baxter, Margery, 18–19, 24–29,
    321, 322, 327–36
Bede, Venerable, 109–10, 213,
    214, 292
Bekynton, Thomas (bishop), 49
Bernard, Saint, 216, 224, 288,
    289; on death, 203, 310;
    desire of the flesh, 209–10;
    prayer, 125
Bethom, Agnes, 330, 334–36
Bible. *See* Scripture
Book to a Mother, 242
Bossy, John, 8–9
Braban, Philip, 343–50
Bradwardine, Thomas, 32
Broderer, John. *See* Jenyn, John
Bruar, Alice. *See* Wickham, Alice
Bruar, William. *See* Wickham,
    William
Burell, John, 51–52

Carder, Stephan, 346
Caritas. See Charity
Carmelites, 35

405

Other Volumes in This Series

Other Volumes in This Series

Other Volumes in This Series

Other Volumes in This Series

Other Volumes in This Series

The Classics of Western Spirituality is a ground-breaking collection of the original writings of more than 100 universally acknowledged teachers within the Catholic, Protestant, Eastern Orthodox, Jewish, Islamic, and Native American Indian traditions.

To order any title, or to request a complete catalog, contact Paulist Press at 800-218-1903 or visit us on the Web at www.paulistpress.com.